Contemporary German
Cultural Studies

Contemporary German Cultural Studies

Edited by

ALISON PHIPPS

Senior Lecturer in German
Glasgow University

A member of the Hodder Headline Group
LONDON
Distributed in the United States of America by
Oxford University Press Inc., New York

First published in Great Britain in 2002 by
Arnold, a member of the Hodder Headline Group,
338 Euston Road, London NW1 3BH

http://www.arnoldpublishers.com

Distributed in the United States of America by
Oxford University Press Inc.,
198 Madison Avenue, New York, NY10016

British Library Cataloguing in Publication Data
A catalogue record for this book is available from the British Library

Library of Congress Cataloging-in-Publication Data
A catalog record for this book is available from the Library of Congress

ISBN 0 340 76401 5 (hb)
ISBN 0 340 76402 3 (pb)

1 2 3 4 5 6 7 8 9 10

Production Editor: Rada Radojicic
Production Controller: Bryan Eccleshall
Cover Design: Terry Griffiths

Typeset in 10/12pt Sabon by Phoenix Photosetting, Chatham, Kent
Printed and bound in Great Britain by MPG Books Ltd, Bodmin, Cornwall

What do you think about this book? Or any other Arnold title?
Please send your comments to feedback.arnold@hodder.co.uk

Contents

Contributors

Holger Briel is Lecturer in German literature, media studies and cultural studies at the University of Surrey, UK. He is the author of *Adorno und Derrida, oder wo liegt das Ende der Moderne?* (1993) and the co-editor of *Adorno in Practice* (2001). He has published widely on the Frankfurt School, and contemporary German and European literature and media. He is currently working on Public Access Media and the Internet.

Dickon Copsey is a final year PhD student studying at the University of Glasgow in the Department of German. His MA degree was also completed at Glasgow University. Drawing on Cultural Studies approaches to the notion of identity, his doctoral research has focused primarily on the German cinema of the 1990s. This research has included separate investigations into the representation of gender within the mainstream romantic comedies of the early 1990s, a survey of the post-*Wende* filmic treatment of the GDR and *neue Bundesländer* and its implication in the articulation of neo-nationalist identities, and the representation of ethnic minority voices in the context of an increasingly visible and popularly and critically acclaimed Turkish–German cinema.

Osman Durrani taught German at the University of Durham for 23 years before his appointment to a professorship in 1995 at the University of Kent at Canterbury. He is the author of *Faust and the Bible* (1977), *German Poetry of the Romantic Era* (1986), *Fictions of Germany. Images of the German Nation in the Modern Novel* (1994), and is co-editor (with Colin Good and Kevin Hilliard) of *The New Germany: Literature and Society after Unification* (1995). An edited volume on the historical novel appeared in 2001. Having written extensively on modern drama and prose, he is currently working on popular music and cabaret in Germany and Austria.

Gavin Jack is a member of the Department of Management, Keele University, UK and a Visiting Lecturer at the University of Linz, Austria. His research interests include critical management studies, contemporary consumer cultures, intercultural communication and contemporary social and cultural theory (especially Foucauldian post-structuralism, postcolonialism and queer theory). He is a member of the Editorial Board of *Language and Intercultural Communication* and the Executive Board of the Standing Conference on Organizational Symbolism.

Helen Kelly-Holmes is Lecturer in German and European Studies at Aston University, Birmingham, UK. Her main research interests include language and intercultural communication; media language and identities; intercultural aspects of the language of advertising and marketing. She is one of the editors of *Current Issues in Language and Society*.

Sharon Macdonald is Senior Lecturer in the Department of Sociological Studies at the University of Sheffield. Her main interests lie in local, regional, national, transnational and supernational identities in Europe, and this has led her to look particularly at museums. Recent publications include *Theorizing Museums* (ed. with G. Fyfe, 1996), *Reimagining Culture* (1997), *The Politics of Display* (ed. 1998), *European Historical Consciousness* (2000) and *Behind the Scenes at the Science Museum* (2002). In 2000 she was an Alexander von Humboldt fellow at the Friedrich-Alexander University of Erlangen-Nürnberg and began research on the post-war representation of Nazi sites.

Meg Mumford is Lecturer in the Department of Theatre, Film and Television Studies at the University of Glasgow. She has published widely on the subject of Brecht's theatre and contemporary appropriations of his theory and practice. Her current research and teaching interests include: western acting methods, nineteenth- and twentieth-century German theatre, European Tanztheater – the work of Pina Bausch in particular, and the issue of translation and dramatic performance as cultural transfer.

Alison Phipps is Senior Lecturer in German at the University of Glasgow. She is author of *Acting Identities* (2000) on open-air German theatre. Her publications are in the area of anthropology, ethnography, theatre and performance studies and in the field of Languages and Intercultural Communication. She is Chair of the International Association for Languages and Intercultural Communication. Her current research with Gavin Jack focuses on German tourism and cultural exchange. She was a visiting scholar in the Department of German, Johns Hopkins University, USA for the Fall semester 2000.

Gillian Pye is Lecturer in German at University College Dublin, Ireland. Her research and teaching interests include contemporary drama and comedy theory, nineteenth- and twentieth-century architecture, and literature post-1945. Recent publications include *Comic Resistance: Approaching Comedy in Contemporary German Dramas* (forthcoming).

Simon Richter is Associate Professor of German at the University of Pennsylvania. He is the author of *Laocoon's Body and the Aesthetics of Pain* (1992) and numerous articles on the history of the body, gender and sexuality, literature, art, and music. With Susanne Kord and Burkhard Henke, he co-edited *Unwrapping Goethe's Weimar* (2000). Since 2000, he has been the editor of the *Goethe Yearbook*. He is presently writing a book on fantasies of the breast in eighteenth-century Germany.

Colin Riordan is Professor of German at the University of Newcastle upon Tyne. He has published widely on post-war German literature, and is the editor of a volume entitled *Green Thought in German Culture: Historical and Contemporary Perspectives* (1997). Since 1997 he has been working on environmental discourse in German literature, and has published an entry on Goethe in the volume *Fifty Key Thinkers on the Environment*, edited by Joy A. Palmer (2001), as well as articles on ecological implications in works by Martin Walser, Patrick Süskind and Uwe Timm.

Susan Tebbutt is Senior Lecturer at the University of Bradford and a member of the Comenius European Intercultural Education Project: She has taught in secondary, further, adult and higher education and produced teaching materials for the BBC and OU. Publications include *Klaro!*, a practical German grammar (2001), an edited volume on the Sinti and Roma (1998), a monograph on Gudrun Pausewang (1994), co-edited volumes on European Romanies (2002), *Ab initio German* (1999) and *Wirtschaftsdeutsch* (1998), and numerous articles on Sinti and Roma, *Jugendliteratur* and German culture and society. She is working on a monograph on autobiography and the Romany Holocaust and has a Fellowship at the US Holocaust Memorial Museum in 2001.

Lois R. Weinthal is an Assistant Professor in the School of Architecture at the University of Texas at Austin. She received her Bachelor of Architecture and Bachelor of Fine Arts from the Rhode Island School of Design and her Master of Architecture from Cranbrook Academy of Art. She has practised architecture in New York City, with a specific focus on housing. She teaches architecture and interiors. Her current research on the relationship between politics and domestic spaces led to a series of domestic objects that have been exhibited at galleries in Texas and Michigan.

Jane Wilkinson is a postgraduate student in the Department of German at the University of Glasgow, UK. She is currently funded by the Student Awards Agency for Scotland, under the 'Major Scottish Studentship' scheme. Her PhD topic is the contemporary theatre landscape of Lake Constance and her related research interests are popular German theatre, literature from Lake Constance, theatre and tourism, and border theory.

Acknowledgements

I would like to take this opportunity to thank numerous friends and colleagues. Moray McGowan initially worked alongside me in developing a structure and conception of this book and has continued to offer support and advice throughout the project. His quiet, critical advice and humour have always been invaluable and illuminating. I am grateful to Robert Holub, Regina Bendix and Mary Beth Stein for their suggestions which have helped me in my attempts to open this book beyond the European context and to embrace some North American perspectives. In this respect I also benefited from a visiting scholarship to Johns Hopkins University, Baltimore during the Fall 2000. I have gained much from working with my students of German Cultural Studies at the University of Glasgow, and especially from the insights of my research students Dickon Copsey, Philippe Pourhashemi Katja Riek, Jane Wilkinson. Gavin Jack has provided sustained, energizing critical friendship throughout. Robert Swinfen read the final manuscript and his supportive comments and duty of care to this project have been invaluable.

I wish to record my thanks to Lesley Riddle for her original approach with the idea for this book, and to Eva Martinez and Elena Seymenliyska as commissioning editors for their dedicated, understanding and above all professional approach. I am grateful to my initial three reviewers for their warm endorsement and practical, critical suggestions. In addition, I wish to thank Meta Jamison for her cool and patient dedication to detail in the final stages of preparation of the manuscript. All errors which have escaped undetected in the final process, are, however, my own responsibility.

Every effort has been made to trace copyright holders of material reproduced in this book. Any rights not acknowledged here will be acknowledged in subsequent printings if notice is given to the publisher.

The Editor

Introduction

BY ALISON PHIPPS

A common culture is not, at any level, an equal culture.

(Raymond Williams, *Culture and Society*)

Encountering contemporary German Culture

encounter – both a noun and a verb. 1. Meet as adversary; meet especially by chance or unexpectedly 2. Psychological benefit through close contact with one another (*OED*) [from Old French *encontre*]

encounter – 1 *vt* enemy, opposition *treffen* or *stoßen auf* + acc; difficulties – *stoßen auf* + acc; danger *geraten in* + acc; person *begegnen* (+dat); *treffen*. 2 *n Begegnung* (f), *Treffen* (nt); (in battle) *Zusammenstoß* (m) (*Collins German-English Dictionary*)

Introduction

This book works rather like a travel guide for the student of German Cultural Studies. It is structured around the idea of an encounter with contemporary German culture. As the definitions of 'encounter' demonstrate, to meet with German culture is not simple or clear-cut. Encounters are often fraught with contradictions and difficulties. It is possible to smooth over complexity with simplistic explanations and stereotypical statements, such as those that often pervade the media and some popular understandings. However, to do so is neither interesting nor productive.

How, then, can we encounter contemporary German culture productively? How can we 'study' culture when culture is slippery and imprecise

and in constant process? What 'tools' may be useful in aiding an understanding of what we encounter? What sense can we begin to make from the
fragments of our experience? How can we move beyond simple assumptions
and adversarial positions that understand culture as being about 'us' and
'them'? This book seeks to provide illustrative answers to some of these
questions through contemporary Cultural Studies.

Just as travel guides to Germany are divided into useful sections such as
'facts for the traveller', 'attractions', 'things to do and see', 'off the beaten
track', 'money', 'getting there and away', 'history', 'culture', 'further reading', so this guide works with a similar structure. Travel provides the
metaphors for the overall architecture of the book. And just as travel guides
are of little use if they are out of date, so this guide is interested in contemporary German culture and in contemporary Cultural Studies. Cultural
Studies provides a way of analysing and understanding something of the
complexity of our encounters with contemporary German culture. The next
section examines how Cultural Studies may aid our journey and our
encounters with aspects of contemporary German culture.

Getting there: using Cultural Studies

There are many different ways of travelling: expensive holidays, backpack-
ing, study periods abroad, flying business trips, asylum seeking. Equally
there are many different ways and methods of encountering contemporary
German culture. The ways chosen by the authors of the chapters in this
book may be loosely termed Cultural Studies. The range of their interests
and concerns, the issues they highlight and the examples they select to illuminate their arguments demonstrate an interest in the production of everyday cultural practices such as eating and drinking and cultural forms such as
architecture. However, what makes these analyses recognizable as aspects of
contemporary Cultural Studies is the concern that is shown throughout for
questions of power, inequality, social justice, for marked patterns of difference and division between rich and poor, male and female, black and white.

Cultural Studies has a particular history, a characteristic style, and a dis-
tinctively political way of questioning given facts. In questioning facts,
Cultural Studies invites us to engage in a process of learning and relearning,
of deconstruction and reconstruction, a process which is similar to the experience of travel and residence abroad, as described by the anthropologist
James Clifford: 'Sojourning somewhere else, learning a language, putting
oneself in odd situations and trying to figure them out can be a good way to
learn something new, simultaneously about oneself and about the people
and places one visits' (1997, 91).

Learning, unlearning and relearning all occur and are demonstrated in the
reflections on everyday cultural practices and everyday objects throughout
this book. This journey allows a structuring of experience which focuses on

lived events, as well as concrete practices. The people, practices, spaces and processes encountered along the routes are surveyed, exemplified, examined critically and interpreted – for the multiple and contested meanings they contain. Each encounter is interrogated for the way it may bear the imprint of the past.

There are already several very good books that deal with Germany's history and with its so-called 'high' culture, especially with literature and thought. This book does not attempt to replicate these books or these approaches to German culture, which are almost invariably histories or analyses of 'the great' and 'the good'. The aims of this guide to German culture concern everyday encounters with the materials and practices of culture. Literature and history take their respective places in these analyses as facets of the cultural practices occurring within Germany rather than as the prime framing paradigms. So, getting there, using Cultural Studies involves a readiness to engage in learning, unlearning and relearning habits of mind.

Off the beaten track

The encounters selected are based on examples of what a 'non-native' reader could discover or be required to confront as part of her/his encounter with German cultures. Contemporary German culture forms the context for study although some of the aspects described may also have their equivalents or be similar to those in other countries, especially German-speaking countries such as Austria and Switzerland. This is not a reference work but rather a series of critical, cultural essays which seek to communicate the processes which have led certain forms, structures, practices, and peoples to inhabit contemporary German culture. The examples chosen are precisely that, *examples* and therefore this is not an exhaustive description of everything in a 'big box' labelled Germany. Instead, the encounters are part of an epistemological project densely describing and articulating processes, which occur along porous cultural boundaries, but by which we may know we are in Germany or encountering German culture.

It is worth remembering that we encounter German culture in many different ways and forms. In order for an encounter to occur we do not necessarily need to leave home, nor will our encounter always be characterized by the same emotions and affect. We do not encounter other cultures as empty vessels, but already shaped by a whole history of experiences and of other encounters. They may be chance encounters, some brief, some lingering, some deepening over a lifetime, some meaning little upon first meeting but perhaps growing in significance as the encounters are repeated. They may be encounters with our roots, full of fascination because of family history and linguistic heritage, or they may be encounters required by educational and economic necessity such as those of business travellers or asylum seekers. They may be encounters with great art, music, literature or film that sparks an interest. Or they may be quirky and unpredictable encounters, like Helen and Roger who befriended the German couple they met on holiday after they pulled their car out of sinking sand.

Encountering early twenty-first-century German culture is also a different collective experience for those from the USA or most other European countries, than encountering German culture during much of the twentieth century. During that difficult phase in history, encounters were with a cultural and political adversary rather than a respected economic power, and the legacy of such difficult encounters can still be felt. Travelling off the beaten track implies a willingness to see different things, meet different people, to have experiences that will make an impact and to do so with a critical awareness of history, your own and that of others.

Using the travel guide

Just as a guidebook is never a book that is read from cover to cover, so this book is one to dip in and out of in order to illuminate encounters with German culture. There are many different ways of using this book, depending on interests and intentions. This book will supply certain overviews of topics and suggestions for further research, on the factual level. It also analyses and interprets many different examples of contemporary German culture. Questions are raised about the assumptions behind certain forms and practices, about what they are, how they work, how they have come to exist. It is important not just to be able to source knowledge and facts about German culture, as we shall see later, but to find ways of handling this knowledge, of comparing and contrasting the many metaphors used, the concepts applied, the theories that are exemplified. It is important to raise questions about the attitudes encountered towards different cultural forms and practices and to trace their roots and development. The chapters in this book and the examples presented provide sites for learning to understand and for learning to engage with a different culture. In short, contemporary German Cultural Studies is potentially an intercultural learning ground.

Cultural encounters are particularly marked by the presence of borders or boundaries. In recent years borders have been central concerns in cultural and intercultural studies, because of the inevitable role they play in questions of national and cultural identity. Just as travel guides give visa requirements and border regulations in factual detail, our book begins with a discussion of the passport and German border crossings. And just as travel guides then divide up a country's space into areas and 'things to see and do', so the kinds of things that are 'first seen and then done' in encounters with German culture are explored, beginning with spatial cultural practices – the landscape and environment, public and private architecture, and the museums that tell cultural stories. These spatial practices are followed by a look at the routine events that make up everyday life, such as schooling, eating and drinking, business, celebration and protest and then by the creative practices of film, theatre, music and media.

In each of the chapters we begin with a cultural trace, a chance encounter, a problem, seeking to unpack assumptions and find ways of understanding the phenomenon. And in all of these encounters, whatever reading route is taken, the same problems occur again and again. Germany is not a thing, it is not a single place, it cannot be found and isolated like a gene. Nor is Germany contained within its borders and when German culture is encountered it is in an array of mobile forms, figures and relationships, many of which leak out of its borders down trade routes and travel lines through history. German culture is not something that people or forms *have* in any intrinsic, stable fashion.

Encountering German culture means encountering division and inequality, both within and outwith Germany's physical borders. Encounters with German culture do not leave us unchanged but make us agents of cultural process, actors in the collective work of living together and make us uncertain as to who we are or where Germany may actually be located. Such questions are not easily resolved and are part of the troubling, culture-shocking but beneficial nature of critical intercultural encounters. We may see this if we begin by encountering some 'facts for the traveller'.

Facts for the traveller

Germany wears its riches well: elegant big-city charm, pagan-inspired harvest festivals, a wealth of art and culture and the perennial pleasures of huge tracts of forest are all there for the enjoying. But Germany's history, both recent and still in the making, weighs heavily. No visitor will remain untouched by this country's complex past and the way it affects the nation today.

Full country name: Federal Republic of Germany

Area: 357,000 sq km

Population: 82 million

Capital city: Berlin (pop: 3.4 million)

People: Predominantly white European, with significant Turkish minority. Germany has absorbed most of the refugees from the former Yugoslavia.

Language: German

Religion: 90 per cent Christian. There are a couple of million Muslims and about 82,000 Jews (the pre-Holocaust figure was over half a million).

Government: Federal republic

Source: Lonely Planet Guide to Germany

Facts, in Cultural Studies, are always a little suspect. Facts and the ways in which they are presented can be chosen and modified to present certain types of perspective. They are no more objective than any other forms of cultural representation and their presentation as 'facts' will often raise as many questions as it answers. This is not to say that 'facts' do not have important and valuable uses. For certain purposes it is important to have data available for social and economic planning. It is, however, always worth questioning who may be served by the facts as they stand.

For instance, who is best served by highlighting the drop in the Jewish population of Germany and why is the drop in this particular population singled out, as opposed to say other populations that were devastated during the period but are not 'statistically significant', such as the Romanies? Or what about facts such as 'language: German'? German is indeed the official language, but walk down the *Ku-damm* in Berlin and it's not the only language you will hear. Work in an accountancy department in a German firm and you will find an ever-increasing number of technical terms are English. And what of statistics? Who do they serve and why might they be presented? Does a traveller need to know the area of the country in square kilometres or the total population? This information assumes that all that is German is contained within 357,000-sq. km., and yet some of that total population will not be 'at home'. Such facts impose a rigidity onto German culture seeking to control it so that it is all there for the traveller to consume and for the powerful to control. And it is not, as captured in the following:

> The currency of culture and identity as performative acts can be traced to their articulation of homelands, safe spaces where the traffic across borders can be controlled. Such acts of control, maintaining coherent insides and outsides, are always tactical. Cultural action, the making and remaking of identities, takes place in the contact zones, along the policed and transgressive intercultural frontiers of nations, peoples, locales. Stasis and Purity are asserted – creatively and violently – against historical forces of movement and contamination.
>
> (Clifford 1997, 7)

German culture today is not what it was yesterday. Were I writing this a couple of years ago the capital city would still have been Bonn. In Cultural

Studies nothing stays still for long and trying to nail culture down into hard facts is highly problematic. This understanding of culture, within Cultural Studies and anthropology has led some to even go so far as to speculate, radically, whether Germany exists, or whether there is such a thing as 'German-ness'. Such questioning sits alongside the questions of race, gender and class, the three dominant identity-based concerns of Cultural Studies.

These concerns assume that nothing is simply 'there', 'given', 'fixed' and that race, gender and class are constructed through cultural processes, and as Stuart Hall (1996) maintains, identities 'relate to the invention of tradition as much as to tradition itself – not the so-called return to roots as the coming-to-terms with "routes"'. Equally, Benedict Anderson (1991) argues that nation–states are not 'given' but came into being through the development of printing and the creation of empires and as such they are 'imagined communities' which could, therefore, be unimagined, just as constructed identities can be de- and re-constructed.

In the context of German history and German identity such theoretical questioning and impulses have been particularly significant as the country has remade itself several times in the last century, each time sifting through the debris of the past and forming new representations of its identity, celebrating different aspects of its literature and arts and reflecting its new visions for the future in different cultural practices. In contemporary German Cultural Studies, then, facts for the traveller are productive places to begin raising questions of basic assumptions and for demonstrating that nothing is simply 'given'.

Highlights: cultural identity

Questions of cultural identity have dominated debates in Cultural Studies over the last two decades and have led Lawrence Grossberg to ask 'Identity and Cultural Studies – Is that all there is?' (Grossberg, 1996). However productive, questions of cultural identity are also limited and problematic. However 'imagined' the German community, it also takes on and expresses itself in 'real', material forms because the people who live in that geographical locale and who travel from their homes within it engage in the human activity of making culture, of living. The insight that identities can be made and remade is helpful but what this book focuses on is the spaces, places and relationships in which and through which this making and remaking occur. We may accept the theoretical point that 'German culture' is constructed, through history, but for our purposes this is really only helpful as a starting point. The question whether or not German culture 'exists' or is 'real' is now rather unhelpful and no longer so much to the fore as a concern in contemporary Cultural Studies. Equally, it is possible to give working, adequate definitions of what we understand by the concept 'culture', but only if we bear in mind that the definitions of culture have themselves been made and remade many times over – the current cultural fashion being to understand culture as a verb – in order to stress the process of culture, making it so intangible and complex a concept as to be of rather questionable use.

To talk of culture and of German culture, as we do out of necessity and in the absence of suitable terms, begs the question 'Which culture?' Are we talking here of 'high culture' – the one amply documented and discussed in the many works on literature, art, music, etc., and the things that make one a 'cultured' distinguished person? Or are we talking of other so-called cultures, those of everyday life such as the popular, the hybrid, the 'working-class'? And what happens when we reify culture – treating something abstract as if it were a simple object, easily spoken of therefore easily understood, as discussed in Gavin Jack's chapter on German business or Holger Briel's on German mediascapes. What happens when we as 'other culturals' study the big box labelled 'German culture'?:

> In this opposition lies the connection between the two contradictory usages: we are cultured and they are not *because* they live in a culture and we do not. Like works of art, their ways of life become objects of contemplation for us, but not *vice versa*, since we are the spectators in the gallery of human variety, whereas they are the figures in the pictures. In effect, the concept of culture operates as a distancing device, setting up a radical disjunction between *ourselves*, rational observers of the human condition, and those *other people*, enmeshed in their traditional patterns of belief and practice, whom we profess to observe and study.
>
> (Ingold 1993, 212)

To move away from the problems of thinking of culture as a noun, or even as a verb, I would suggest thinking of culture as adjectival, as descriptive. In contemporary German Cultural Studies the emphasis is on how we study what may be described, in the first instance, as German and as cultural. The questions we ask, the descriptions, surveys and examples we provide and the concerns we express with intercultural relations, and with interconnections, point to the workings of power in a given place at a given moment. The enterprise here is not to exert control. It is quite the opposite, for Cultural Studies is a messy business, constantly spilling over and defying categories such as 'high and popular culture'. Indeed, Raymond Williams describes 'culture' as 'one of the two or three most complicated words in the English language' (1983, 87) and Tim Ingold (1993, 230) sees it as such a divisive and categorizing term as to be no longer of use. To proceed at all, without creating divisive categories, or cultural panoptica it is important to understand what is the history and the purpose of *cultural* study.

Getting around: understanding Cultural Studies

Cultural Studies, as characterized by its concerns, has shifted its focus throughout its history. It has travelled as a movement – it is hard to term it a discipline – and changed in the process. There are several excellent guides to Cultural Studies (see bibliography) and I do not intend to duplicate their work here. It is, however, useful to point out that, from its emergence in the Birmingham School and Hoggart's *The Uses of Literacy* (1957) and works by Williams, perhaps most notably *Marxism and Literature* (1977) and *Keywords: A Vocabulary of Culture and Society* (1983), the ideas and perspectives of Cultural Studies have not stayed 'at home'. Initially 'made in England' – though never of purely 'English' parts (Williams, of course, was Welsh) – Cultural Studies has been remade repeatedly through the action of thought in other places over time. Always struggling with the influence of Marxism, in particular, Cultural Studies found other inequalities to concern its reflections and other theoretical tools beyond Marxism with which to address them.

In America, for example, these focused, largely, though not exclusively, on race, in India, on postcolonial issues, questioning assumptions that the colonial era had been civilising. In France, influenced by psychoanalysis and by structuralism – the study of relations in language – theoretical interest turned to questions of subjectivity. Subjectivity focuses on the idea that individuals are not unified, stable entities, but rather split, 'subject' to different and competing powers and creating themselves through language and through other discursive practices. The break with the idea of a unified subject and with it the turn to focus on language as a site of power and resistance, also marked an important intellectual departure from the tendency, within modernism, to see, for instance, 'women', or 'the working classes' as unproblematic wholes, in other words, to essentialize. It saw a break with so-called *grand narratives*, the universal ideas of progress or of rationalism which were no longer seen as satisfactory explanatory devices for the workings of culture. Much of the work of post-structuralism, influenced largely though not exclusively by the French theorists Jacques Derrida and Michael Foucault, has helped the theoretical work of Cultural Studies to problematize all that is 'given' but has hindered its practical, empirical focus on the materials and practices of everyday life.

It is here that the value of newer anthropological perspectives are particularly helpful and have largely influenced the conception of this book. Culture has often been described as anthropology's great gift to humanity. It is its founding concept, rooted in the discovery of new worlds, the colonial era and the development of science. There is much that is problematic in anthropology's history and it does not share either the youth or the concerns with power and politics of Cultural Studies. It does, however, have a strong concern with empirical work, with ethnography – the meticulous observation of and participation in the lives of other people in other places. It assumes encounter with both the general and the specific for within anthropology culture is both general and specific. Culture becomes adjectival. Culture is both understood as a phenomenon that is part of all human experience but also, as is the case with this book, it is associated with a specific culture. It allows us to view specific cultures, not so much as big boxes to be described or solely as constructs of the mind, but as fluid, contested and shaped by a variety of agents.

In Germany Cultural Studies has not been the powerful and influential force it has been in America, France and the UK, or in post-colonial cultures. This is perhaps largely due to the highly influential home-grown social theories of the Frankfurt School's Institute of Social Research, of Adorno, Horkheimer, Marcuse, and the influence of other founding fathers of sociology such as Georg Simmel, Max Weber and cultural critics like Walter Benjamin, in the 1930s, 1940s and 1950s through to the present day influence of Jürgen Habermas. Their perspectives on the rise of capitalism and the role of culture in late capitalist society have certainly leaked over Germany's borders and over its language thresholds influencing Cultural Studies from its inception. During the Second World War the Frankfurt School went into exile in the USA where its influence has been strongly felt. The flow, however, has not been equal, with relatively little influence felt by the Birmingham School, for instance, or until recently, by post-colonial thought. It may therefore be suggested that the considerable contribution of the Frankfurt School's critical theory and the work of German sociologists and cultural critics have provided a certain focus and tradition for the study of social and cultural issues within Germany. German critical theory and the writings of German social and cultural theorists certainly possess a distinctive style which has been described as meditative and contrasted with Anglo-Saxon empirical approaches. This said, however, there are also many common concerns and common objects of study and the German discipline of *Volkskunde* (ethnology and folklore studies) in particular has drawn upon and contributed significantly to Cultural Studies.

What this section demonstrates is that Cultural Studies, like German culture, continues to take many different forms and is influenced by many sources. Understanding the contribution of Cultural Studies comes through engagement with its history, through critical reflection on its theories and concepts, and through working with its concerns.

Getting away: *Gute Reise*

Encountering German culture through Cultural Studies means encountering difference; difference in other ways of doing things, in other ways of seeing and understanding the world, in other material objects. These differences may appear to be all about 'German-ness' but may often be equally affected, as the chapters in this book demonstrate, by the presence of different ethnic minorities, by gender and sexuality, by class, by the differences of education and the environment. Encountering German culture also involves encounters with yourself, your own expectations, false assumptions, likes and dislikes, and often deeply rooted unexamined opinions. To really engage with German Cultural Studies involves what Raymond Williams describes as 'a long and difficult remaking ... a struggle at the roots of the mind ... confronting ... the hard practical substance of effective and continuing relationships' (1977, 212).

Throughout this book and in the final conclusion intercultural aspects of German culture are highlighted and reviewed repeatedly. What these examples demonstrate is the transformative power of the process of critically engaged cultural encounter:

> For real people, dwelling in a real world, that world is revealed to them through their active engagement with it. It is an historical world, which is forever coming into being in the process of engagement, just as they themselves come into being in the process of their dwelling.

> (Ingold 1993, 223)

The common assumption is that travel broadens the mind. Some recent research has suggested that this is only the case if travellers are prepared to engage and to allow themselves to be broadened, deepened and transformed by the experiences of encounter (Coleman 2001). To use this guide well, to derive the psychological benefit from the encounters represented here will mean reflecting on the questions raised, grappling with new concepts, overcoming prejudices towards certain styles or ways of 'travelling' and becoming interculturally competent, able to stand among others and understand, appreciate, critique, situate and learn.

Gute Reise!

References

ANDERSON, B. 1991: *Imagined communities: reflections on the origin and spread of nationalism*. London and New York: Verso.

BYRAM, M. 1997: *Teaching and assessing intercultural communicative competence*. Clevedon: Multilingual Matters.

CLIFFORD, J. 1997: *Routes: travel and translation in the late twentieth century*. Cambridge, MA: Harvard University Press.

COLEMAN, J. 2001: What is residence abroad for? Intercultural competence and the linguistic, cultural academic, personal and professional objectives of student residence abroad, in DI NAPOLI, R., POLEZZI, L. and KING, A. *Fuzzy boundaries? Reflections on modern languages and the humanities*. London: CILT, 121–40.

GROSSBERG, L. 1996: Identity and cultural studies: Is that all there is? In HALL, S. and DU GAY, P. *Questions of cultural identity*. London: Sage, 87–108.

HALL, S. 1996: Who needs 'identity'?, in HALL, S. and DU GAY, P. *Questions of cultural identity*. London: Sage, 1–18.
HOGGART, R. 1957: *The uses of literacy*. Harmondsworth: Penguin.
INGOLD, T. 1993: The art of translation in a continuous world, in PÁLSSON, G. *Beyond boundaries: understanding, translation and anthropological discourse.* Oxford: Berg, 210–30.
LONELY PLANET GUIDE http://www.lonelyplanet.com/destinations/europe/ germany
WILLIAMS, R. 1977: *Marxism and literature*. Oxford: Oxford University Press.
WILLIAMS, R. 1983: *Keywords: a vocabulary of culture and society*. 2nd edn. London: Collins.
WILLIAMS, R. 1993: *Culture and society*. London: The Hogarth Press.

Further reading

Contemporary German culture

BAUSINGER, H. 1990: *Folk culture in a world of technology*. Bloomington and Indianapolis: Indiana University Press.
BURNS, R. 1995: *German cultural studies: an introduction*. Oxford: Oxford University Press.
DENHAM, S., KACANDES, I. and PETROPOULOS, J. 1997: *A user's guide to German cultural studies*. Ann Arbor, MI: University of Michigan Press.
DURRANI, O., GOOD, C. and HILLIARD, K. 1995: *The new Germany: literature and society after unification*. Sheffield: Sheffield Academic Press.
LEWIS, D. and McKENZIE, J.R.P. 1995: *New Germany: social, political and cultural challenges of unification*. Exeter: Exeter University Press.
MILICH, K. and PECK, J.M. 1998: *Multiculturalism in transit: a German-American exchange*. New York: Berghahn.
ROCHE, J. and SALUMETS, T. 1996: *Germanics under construction: intercultural and interdisciplinary prospects*. Munich: Iudicium.
SANDFORD, J. 1999: *Encyclopedia of contemporary German culture*. London and New York: Routledge.

On Cultural Studies

BROOKER, P. 1999: *A concise glossary of cultural theory*. London: Arnold.
DURING, S. (ed.) 1993: *The cultural studies reader*. London and New York: Routledge.
EAGLETON, T. 2000: The idea of Culture. Oxford: Blackwell.
EASTHOPE, A. and McGOWAN, K. 1992: *A critical and cultural theory reader*. Buckingham: Open University Press.
FISKE, J. 1989a: *Reading the popular*. London: Routledge.
FISKE, J. 1989b: *Understanding popular culture*. London: Routledge.
JENKS, C. 1993: *Culture*. London: Routledge.
STRINATI, D. 1995: *An introduction to theories of popular culture*. London and New York: Routledge.

Cultural theory

APPADURAI, A. 1986: *The social life of things: commodities in cultural perspective.* Cambridge: Cambridge University Press.

BAUMAN, Z. 2000: *Liquid modernity.* Oxford: Polity.

BHABHA, H. 1994: *The location of culture.* London: Routledge.

BOURDIEU, P. 1984: *Distinction: a social critique of the judgement of taste.* London: Routledge.

CALLINCOS, A. 1989: *Against postmodernism: a Marxist critique.* Cambridge: Polity Press.

FOUCAULT, M. 1980: *Power/knowledge.* New York: Pantheon Books.

HARVEY, D. 1990: *The condition of postmodernity: an enquiry into the origins of cultural change.* Oxford: Blackwell.

LYOTARD, J.F. 1984: *The postmodern condition: a report on knowledge.* Manchester: Manchester University Press.

Anthropological and intercultural approaches to Cultural Studies

AGAR, M. 1994: *Language shock: understanding the culture of conversation.* New York: William Morrow.

AGAR, M. 2000: *The professional stranger: an informal introduction to ethnography.* London: Academic Press.

BYRAM, M., ZARATE, G. and NEUNER, G. 1997: *Sociocultural competence in language learning and teaching.* Strasbourg: Council of Europe Publishing.

CLIFFORD, J. and MARCUS, G.E. 1986: *Writing culture: the poetics and politics of ethnography.* Berkeley and Los Angeles: University of California Press.

DE CERTEAU, M. 1984: *The practice of everyday life.* Los Angeles and London: University of California Press.

GEERTZ, C. 1973: *The interpretation of cultures.* London: Collins.

HANNERZ, U. 1996: *Transnational connections.* London and New York: Routledge.

INGOLD, T. (ed.) 1994: *Companion encyclopedia of anthropology: humanity, culture, social life.* London and New York: Routledge.

PART

I

PASSPORTS

Part I of this book looks at two different kinds of passports – the passports that are shown in order to cross the state borders of Germany and the passport to German culture in all its diversity, that of language. Other passports are also present, however, such as those of education – of questioning, understanding, knowledge and engagement. Passports are keys to the door, ways of entering into new relationships and new spaces just as the German language in all its varieties is a collective cultural practice that helps represent German life and also lives German life through its speakers.

In Chapter 1 Jane Wilkinson sets out to ask questions of the familiar activity of 'crossing borders' and holding a passport. Germany's borders have been highly contested throughout history. Wilkinson poses questions of these borders and their changes, giving a survey of the history of Germany's borders, providing a detailed focus on the famous, metonymical former border 'The Berlin Wall' and presenting some empirical interview data to demonstrate the experiential dimension of crossing into Germany. The first step onto Germany soil is not seen as an obstacle but as an intrinsic rite of passage in the change to foreign or alien status. Wilkinson then draws on theories of borders and boundaries, notably those of the anthropologists Van Gennep, Turner and Cohen to illuminate the cultural processes at work when we cross over the border and into German space. This in turn raises questions of outsider status; who may or may not hold a passport, the power of the German state to define its own and say who may cross the border and who holds the key to the door.

In Chapter 2 we encounter the German language and are taken through a discussion of the link between language, culture and identity. Helen Kelly-Holmes provides us with several different ways of encountering the language, but, interestingly, focuses initially on the classroom, perhaps the most intensive form of language encounter for non-German speakers engaging with German culture. Academic work outside of educational research often tries to airbrush the fact that we are in part products, in late modernity, of systems of mass education and our lives lived in classrooms learning German are not insignificant in determining how we relate to German culture. In this chapter we also explore facts and figures and questions of linguistic hegemony before looking at the cultural studies concerns of race, gender, and social identity through the prism of German language.

1

Passports and the German border: who holds the key to the door?

BY JANE WILKINSON

Questions of borders

The crossing of the German border constitutes the visitor's first encounter with German culture. Before the visitor may pursue his/her cultural journey through Germany he/she must hold the key that opens the door to Germany. In other words, the traveller must be able to complete the rituals of border crossing, which include the checking of passports, the searching of belongings and bodies and the possible questioning by border functionaries.[1] In an age of international travel, most people undertake such rituals without question or further reflection. The crossing of the border and the need for a passport are seen merely as necessary, and sometimes inconvenient, requirements of the state, as obstacles to free travel. However, on closer inspection, borders themselves make interesting sites for study.

Let us begin by considering what we are actually crossing when we cross the boundary line[2] that separates Germany from its neighbouring states, and what it is that makes this border 'German'. Clearly we are crossing territory, land that is divided between different political entities, or states. The boundary lines drawn on the political map of the world arbitrarily demarcate the natural landscape into political territories, often with little regard for natural features such as rivers, seas and mountain ranges (Anderson 1991; Ingold 1993). Throughout history, Germany's official political borders have fluctuated backwards and forwards across the natural borders of the Rhine in the west and the Oder in the east and across the Alps in the south. The Alps now cross a number of national boundaries, including those of the member-states of the German-speaking world, Germany, Austria and Switzerland. These political boundaries are, nevertheless, accepted to the extent that the map, a symbol or 'logo' for the world (Anderson 1991, 175), has become 'one of the most common cultural metaphors in our conception of the world' (Richard 1996, 71). Consequently the everyday traveller does not question the location of the lines that he/she is required to cross in order to enter German territory. The reasons behind their existence and the consequences of their positioning are, however, very interesting. These lines are the cause and the result of wars, they divide and differentiate between peoples, they include and they exclude, they are controlled by the state and can, on the whole, only be crossed with official permission, with a passport. Boundary lines can, therefore, explain a great deal about Germans' opinions of themselves and attitudes towards others.

Germany's outer borders are politically defined, which means that they are not fixed but rather historically determined. Our concept of 'Germany' has changed through the course of European history, a history dominated by territorial wars and the shifting of political boundaries. Germany's arguably unsettled history of contested and shifting borders has been, in part, the result of its geographical location at the centre of Europe (Demandt 1991, 12; Kitchen 1996, 9). Germany currently borders nine other states[3] and its eastern borders constitute the border between Western Europe and the former Soviet Bloc countries of Eastern Europe. The eastern border in particular has moved backwards and forwards as Germany has expanded and then been re-contained. During the Cold War this border divided Germany in half. To cross the German border is, therefore, also to cross history, to cross historically determined space.

To cross the German border is not only to cross from one politically and historically defined territory to another, but also to cross from one cultural space to another. Since the French Revolution, the 'nation–state' has been the political ideal in Europe (Anderson 1991). The ideal state is one which encompasses within its boundaries only one nation, i.e. a homogeneous community of citizens united by a common language and a common culture. If this ideal were realized, the traveller could expect to observe distinct cultural differences in terms of language, customs and traditions when he/she crossed the border into or out of Germany. In reality, however, culture transcends politically determined boundaries. The German language, for example, is spoken in Austria and in northern Switzerland, as well as in parts of French Alsace (Demandt 1991, 13–14) (see Chapter 2). Evidently, cultural and political boundaries do not always correspond. The traveller to Germany may therefore cross several borders during his/her journey.

The fact that the political and the cultural borders of Germany may not coincide leads us to question where the traveller might encounter the cultural German border. The official crossing into Germany occurs either at a land border between Germany and one of its neighbouring states, or at the passport and customs controls in a German airport. This border may constitute a cultural border of Germany, but Germany's cultural borders can also be found within the German territory at the regional borders between *Länder* or even at the borders between towns and villages within regions, i.e. at Germany's many *Binnengrenzen* (inner borders) (Demandt 1991, 26). Moreover, cultural borders are encountered wherever people of different cultures meet. It is therefore possible to encounter a German 'border' in Britain or in the United States, when meeting and interacting with a German citizen. As Clifford (1997) illustrates, intercultural encounters can take place in any space. Borders mark difference (Donnan and Wilson 1999, 107) and difference need not be territorially or politically defined.

Many questions surrounding the German border have been raised here. This chapter will provide possible answers to these questions in its examination of the German border as a site of cultural experience, as the place of encounter with German culture on a traveller's cultural journey. Theories on borders and boundaries from a variety of disciplines, such as Geography, History, Politics and Anthropology, will be used to reflect on individual experiences of crossing the German border, in an attempt to gain an idea of what this border stands for and what it means to those who cross it. The characteristics of the passport, as a symbol of citizenship and nationality and as a cultural and historical symbol, will be used to structure this analysis of the German border.

What is Germany?

At this stage, it is helpful to consider what the name 'Germany' actually refers to. We all have a basic concept of what 'Germany' is. Germany is the territory demarcated by the German boundaries on the political map of the world. Germany is also where the German people live and where the German language is spoken. Our two basic concepts immediately present us with the problem of whether to define Germany politically or ethnically. They present us with the problem of the state versus the nation. Demandt (1991, 12) identifies this problem when he asks 'Was bedeutet „Deutschland"?' He concludes: 'Für die Abgrenzung dessen, was wir „Deutschland" nennen, bieten sich einerseits politische, andererseits ethnische Kriterien an', (ibid., 13). (What does 'Germany' mean? The delimitation of the entity we call 'Germany' is determined according to political criteria on the one hand, and ethnic criteria on the other.)[4]

The term 'state' refers to a political entity, to a group of people living within a territory controlled by one authority (Breuilly 1998, 44). The state of Germany is, therefore, the people and territory ruled by the German Chancellor and his/her government. The nation of Germany is more difficult to determine. The term 'nation' is generally used to refer to a group or a community of people of common ethnic descent who share in a common culture, i.e. a common language, history and traditions. According to Benedict Anderson (1991, 19), the population of Europe was formally divided into nations during the seventeenth and eighteenth centuries, when Latin ceased to be the dominant language in cultural and intellectual life (see

Chapter 2). The vernacular languages, formerly used only in everyday conversation, became the languages of politics, education and literature. Political boundaries were tightened around these different language communities or 'nations' and Europe became the home of the 'nation–state', of the political territory inhabited by only one nation.

The problem with this model of the nation–state is that languages often spill over boundaries. Throughout history many Germans have believed Germany to be 'soweit die deutsche Zunge reicht' (as far as the German tongue reaches) (poet Ernst Moritz Arndt, cited in Demandt 1991, 15 and Kitchen 1996, 11). However, although German is spoken in Germany, Austria and Switzerland, the Austrians and the Swiss would no longer call themselves Germans. The German nation must be united by more than a common language: Germany is, to quote Demandt (1991, 13), 'eine ethnische Einheit, verbunden durch Sprache, Geschichte, Siedlung und Brauchtum' (an ethnic unity, bound by language, history, territory and customs). Moreover, official German citizenship is largely based on blood-ties and German ethnicity, not language (Ardagh 1995, 16; Breuilly 1998, 52).

There are clearly many conflicting definitions of Germany, which should be borne in mind throughout this chapter. Although a perfect match between state and nation has thus far proved impossible, the German nation does, today, 'have its own territorial state' (Breuilly 1998, 44). Germany will thus be treated as both a state and a nation for the purposes of this chapter. The borders of Germany are national and state borders.

The key to the door of Germany: the rituals of border crossing

Boundaries are porous. The German border encloses the territory and, to a certain extent, the culture that is Germany, but it can be crossed. In most cases, states neither want to imprison their citizens within their boundaries nor to make it impossible for others to enter the territory.[5] Nevertheless, state security is seen to require that such movements across the boundaries be regulated and it is for this reason that border controls exist at most crossing points. These controls aim to ensure that nobody and nothing of risk to the state crosses the boundary into, and that nothing of value crosses the boundary out of, the state. In this capacity the border is analogous to Simmel's (1997) understanding of the door. The door constitutes a boundary between the person who closes it and the rest of the world, but the fact that it can be opened again at any time means that, according to Simmel, 'its closure provides the feeling of a stronger isolation against everything outside this space than the mere unstructured wall' (ibid., 172). Open borders, which citizens of both sides are free to cross, can be read as a sign of a state that is more secure in its identity than closed, strictly policed borders, which are better compared to walls than doors or gateways (and are often physically reinforced by walls, such as the border between the former East and West Germany). In order to be granted entry to or exit from Germany, in whatever capacity, the traveller must, therefore, pass through border controls and complete the rituals of border crossing. The traveller must be able to open the door. In this section I will focus on the rituals necessary for entering Germany.

The significance of these rituals and of the whole experience of border crossing can be better understood when compared to the three-stage rites of passage analysed by Arnold Van Gennep (1960) and later by Victor Turner (1969; 1982).[6] Like these rites of passage, which allow members to gain new social status and new identities within their tribes, border crossing can also be seen as 'un véritable rite magique et religieux' (a truly magical and religious rite) (Van Gennep 1922, 152), which allows travellers to enter new worlds and to gain new identities. In 'semi-civilized'[7] societies each stage in a person's life is marked by a rite of passage, in other words, certain rituals must be completed before a person is permitted to proceed to the next stage, for example from puberty to adulthood. These rites of passage are structured into three phases: 'rites of separation', 'transition rites' and 'rites of incorporation'. The ritual of border crossing fits neatly into this structure. Indeed, Van Gennep (1960, 15) bases his analysis of all social rituals on the structure of territorial or 'threshold' rites. The traveller as ritual participant must first 'separate' from his/her normal space, in this instance his/her home country. He/she then enters the second phase of 'transition rites', which Van Gennep terms the 'liminal' phase. This expression is taken from the Latin word 'limen', meaning 'threshold'. The liminal phase of travel is the phase during which the traveller is between the point of exit from his/her home country and the point of entry into the destination country, Germany. The traveller is at the border or 'threshold' of Germany. 'Rites of transition' or liminal rituals, Van Gennep believes, prepare the participant for the third and final phase of 'rites of incorporation', during which the traveller is granted entry to and thus 'incorporated' into Germany. At this point the traveller gains a new identity, such as that of tourist, 'foreign' businessperson, migrant worker or exchange student.

Let us now examine more closely the rituals completed at Germany's border crossing points, which correspond to the liminal 'rites of transition'. The checking of passports or identity cards, searches of baggage and bodies, the completion of immigration forms and the answering of questions are common rituals which constitute the vital 'in between' or transitional phase on the journey to Germany. The particular rituals that a traveller is required to undertake depend upon the traveller's country of origin and its political relationship with Germany and on the traveller's reasons for crossing the border. Tourists or business-people from Europe or North America, for example, will generally have to participate in fewer formal rituals than migrant workers from Asia or Africa.

The liminal phase of social rituals is often associated with feelings of fear and excitement, because it is a phase of uncertainty and change. These feelings are evident in students' descriptions of travelling to Germany for the first time. One student displayed contradictory, but typically liminal emotions when describing her experiences of crossing the German border:

> I'm quite childish, I always get excited when I see 'Willkommen in Deutschland' ['welcome to Germany'] on the road signs or in the airport, but I always feel a bit paranoid. Even when I know that I've got my passport, and that it's valid, I feel paranoid. And I always think they're going to find something on me, like drugs. Even though I don't take drugs and I don't have them on me, I always think that there's going to be something. When somebody asks for my passport and I've given it to them, I always feel a bit sort of like 'phew'. I feel quite … sort of … relieved![8]

This student experiences both the positive emotion of excitement and the negative feelings of paranoia and anxiety when crossing the German border. It is exciting to be going somewhere new and to see the signs which welcome the traveller to Germany, but the rituals that it is necessary to perform at the border controls in order to be granted permission to cross that border, can produce feelings of fear and uncertainty. The traveller's passage across the border is at the sole discretion of the German officials. The ritual participant is temporarily powerless (Donnan and Wilson 1999, 108). The uncertainty is not resolved until the rituals have been completed and the traveller has been incorporated into Germany on the other side of the border.

As in Van Gennep's rites of passage, the traveller is between identities at the point of crossing the border. He/she is no longer a 'native' at home, but is yet to be granted his/her status as a visitor to Germany. The result is a feeling of liminal anonymity at border crossing points. This sense of anonymity is heightened by the lack of communication between border functionaries and travellers. Many students noted that the only words uttered by German border officials were the necessary and functional *Ausweis* (identity card) or *Reisepaß* (passport). To be granted entry to Germany the traveller requires above all a passport or equivalent identity card. The appearance of the passport varies between nation–states, as will be examined later, but most passports contain the bearer's name, nationality and/or citizenship, date and place of birth, photograph and an individual passport number. The bearer's identity is thus encapsulated in the passport information. In a sense, at the moment of border crossing, the unique individual is reduced to the information contained in his/her passport. If that information is in order, entry is granted to Germany; the border officials require no further information about the traveller. If the information in the passport is not in order, or if the traveller is not in possession of a valid passport, any other information, positive or negative, about that traveller is irrelevant and entry is prohibited. It is therefore unsurprising that the traveller should feel like 'an anonymous entity' (Martínez 1986, 1) when crossing the border.

The ritual of searching travellers and their belongings at the border also contributes to this sense of fear and anonymity. Donnan and Wilson (1999, 131) note that in the liminal spaces of borders where 'state power is absolute and can be imposed upon even that most intimate element of our being, our body', 'the usual western conventions of bodily contact cease to apply' (see Chapter 8). People are reduced to objects with no individual identity. However, not everyone is searched and the choice of people to search appears to be based on random selection or on the intuition of the border guards. It seems that at the German border, as at most international borders, families, elderly people and people in uniform are rarely stopped and searched, while young people travelling in large groups or alone are often stopped. One girl noticed this when travelling back from Germany with her parents:

> It's completely random. Like, when my parents drove over to take all my stuff home, we didn't get stopped. I guess maybe if you're with older, 'responsible-type' people they don't stop you, and if you're like five young people in a car, then they stop you.

A woman who has spent a lot of time in North America and Canada noticed that she was frequently stopped and searched in the airport when flying back to Europe. She told me: 'I think they always stop girls who are travelling alone. It is almost as if they expect you to have some kind of dangerous, drug-smuggling boyfriend waiting for you across the border.' This treatment of lone female passengers is illustrative of the old-fashioned but still surprisingly prevalent view that women do not and should not travel alone. This view is underlined by the fact that, until fairly recently, married women in most European countries travelled on their husbands' passports. Border crossing can, therefore, make people more aware of their gender.

Border crossing also heightens the traveller's awareness of his/her national identity. Not only is he/she carrying a passport that asserts that national identity, but he/she is crossing a border which, as mentioned above, is a marker of identity and difference. Borders divide nations, demarcate national territory and are therefore powerful symbols of national identity. According to Kavanagh (1994, 75): 'It is precisely at these "marked boundaries", at the "periphery" and not at the centre or "core", that the cultural identity of a community is frequently most emphasized.'

One of the ways in which social identity is constructed is with reference to an 'other', or to all who are different. As Banchoff (1999: 268) explains: 'For states, like other social groups, identity has both an internal and an external dimension, it is what binds the group together and what situates it with respect to others.' The sharing of a common citizenship and the carrying of the same passport are aspects of the 'internal dimension' of identity construction, while the crossing of international borders and the encounter with other people constitute 'external dimensions'. When we travel and cross international borders, we are directly confronted by the foreign 'other' and are reminded of our own national identities.

If border crossing is the liminal phase in the rite of passage of international travel, the border constitutes a liminal space. It is the space on the edge of the politically and culturally defined territory of Germany, it is the space that lies in between Germany and its neighbours. It is the space where the state has absolute power (Donnan and Wilson 1999, 131) and citizens are reduced to anonymous entities, for a short time. The airport is a particularly anonymous international space with little cultural differentiation between countries. In airports everyone is in transit, all travellers are 'in between' point of departure and point of destination. Advances in air travel have changed the traditional image of borders and border crossing, as passengers can now cross several international borders unawares and entry to a new country does not appear to involve the physical displacement of the person across the actual territorial border. Just as land is divided by state boundaries, so too is 'horizontal airspace' (Prescott 1987, 26), yet the speed with which an aeroplane crosses the borders between state 'airspaces' makes it impossible to perform border controls in the air, at the actual moment of border crossing. For this reason, border controls are carried out in airports, both on departure from the country of origin and on arrival in the destination country. Travellers therefore cross a symbolic state boundary on arrival in a German airport, a boundary which may be located many miles from the actual territorial border of Germany. Passengers must go through customs and passport control before being allowed to leave the 'international arrivals' section of the airport, and enter the main part of the building, at which point they enter and are 'incorporated into' Germany.

Citizenship and national identity

We have seen that the passport is the vital key to the crossing of the German border. It is the key that allows the traveller to proceed from the liminal phase of border crossing to the phase of incorporation into Germany. It is also the key to the door for Germans who wish to cross the border and to travel abroad. What are the characteristics of the passport that make it such a significant tool in the crossing of the German border? According to O'Byrne (2001, 400), 'the passport carries a significant political meaning and a subtle cultural or symbolic one'. In its political role, the passport functions as certification of the bearer's citizenship, i.e. of his/her official belonging to a certain state (*Staatsangehörigkeit*). In this capacity the passport is both an official travel permit and an official identification card, equivalent to the German *Personalausweis* (identity card). This dual function leads O'Byrne to conclude that the state issues passports to its citizens both in order to protect them during travel and in order to control them (ibid., 405).

The passport acts as a request from one state to another to allow its citizens safe passage across the border, but it also provides a means by which the state can identify and control its citizens both at home and abroad. The latter function also ensures that the travelling citizen will return home. In addition, the passport allows the state to monitor the movements of foreign citizens across and within its boundaries, as seen in the analysis of border crossing rituals.

If we understand Germany to be both a state and a nation, the German passport serves as official documentation of both citizenship and nationality. To be eligible for a German passport or *Personalausweis,* one must be a German citizen. The distribution of passports by the German state is, therefore, indicative of who is officially included or excluded by the state. To be automatically eligible for German citizenship one usually has to be born to at least one parent who is a German citizen. Until very recently it was almost impossible to become a German citizen, and thus to hold a German passport, unless one was descended from native Germans. It was, however, not necessary to speak the German language or to live within German territory (Parkes 1997, 102). These criteria contradict both Anderson's theory that 'from the start the nation was conceived in language not in blood' (1991, 145) and historical views of the German nation being 'soweit die deutsche Zunge reicht' (Arndt, cited in Demandt 1991, 15 and Kitchen 1996, 11).[9]

German citizenship and the official definition of German nationality introduced in 1913 were, and to a certain extent still are, based principally on blood ties. Under these criteria, foreign immigrants or *Gastarbeiter* (guest workers), who had lived, worked and paid taxes in Germany for many years, were rarely granted German citizenship. Many foreign workers living in Germany thus remained 'aliens', with German residency permits but foreign passports (see Chapter 9). Their children, even if born in Germany, were similarly considered aliens, despite the fact that they went to German schools, spoke fluent German and identified with German culture and values (Kolinsky 1998, 117). Germany opened its doors to the *Gastarbeiter,* but was not prepared to incorporate foreign nationals fully into German society. These laws and the problems they cause illustrate again the impossibility of maintaining a pure nation–state.

In January 2000, Gerhard Schröder's SPD coalition government changed the naturalization laws. Legal immigrants can now apply for citizenship after living in Germany for eight years, although they must still renounce their original citizenship. Children born to foreign parents in Germany are now automatically granted citizenship at birth, as long as one of their parents has lived legally in Germany for eight years. These children are allowed to hold dual citizenship until they are 23 years old, at which point they must choose between their German and their other citizenship (www.germany-info.org). Rights of blood are gradually being replaced by rights of soil. Becoming officially 'German', if one is not so born, does, however, remain a lengthy and complicated procedure. The German state is not keen to let just anybody become identifiably German and, thus, to travel with a German passport under the protection of the German state. There are still many legal aliens living and working in Germany.

Let us return now to the specific role of the passport as travel permit. The passport acts as an agreement between states to grant travellers safe passage. The study of the treatment of different passports at the German border can, therefore, contribute to our understanding of Germany's relationship with other states and can help to explain the characteristics of Germany's various political borders. In his geographical study of borders, Martínez (1994) provides a useful, if somewhat simplistic, typology of borderlands, in which he identifies the areas surrounding and determined by state borders as 'alienated', 'co-existent', 'interdependent' or 'integrated'. Borders, according to Martínez, range from the closed and rigidly controlled in alienated borderlands, through various stages of openness to the obsolete or redundant border in integrated borderlands. We can use these characteristics as a model for understanding Germany's borders, both the physical territorial borders with the nine neighbouring states, and the symbolic political borders encountered in international travel further afield.

Germany's current borders with fellow member states of the European Union fit neatly into the category of integrated borderlands. Over the past decade the borders between the EU member states have become increasingly open, to the extent that when crossing many borders, for example the borders between Austria and Germany or France and Germany, it is no longer necessary even to show a passport. As a result, the familiar roadside buildings which previously housed passport controls and customs, have now been destroyed or converted into houses, shops or cafés. These open borders are, however, still marked by the familiar welcome signs and often by national flags. They may not be used as instruments of political control, but they are still used as sites for nation-building, for a display of friendly pride in a nation's history and traditions.

Together with the opening of borders within the European Union, a European passport is being introduced. Passports of member states are already identified as passports of the European Community, but it is intended that eventually all citizens of the member-states of the Union will become European citizens and will hold a European rather than a national passport. Because borders within the Union are disappearing, they will only need this passport for travelling outwith the European Union, for crossing the *EU-Aussengrenze* (the outer border of the EU).

Although in principle it should now be possible to travel as freely within the European Union as it is to travel within one country, in reality some border controls do still exist and the stringency of these controls varies between borders. It seems that some Europeans are reluctant to let go of their national borders and the rituals of border crossing, despite a general shift towards a united Europe. Sue Best (1996, 67) observes that:

We may all publicly declare that boundaries have, or should, come down, or have, or should, be blurred. We may think they are violent and divisive but when it comes down to it, we are all profoundly invested in their continuation.

Attitudes to borders depend on the state's attitude towards European integration and EU policy in general. Britain, a nation, it seems, of Euro-sceptics, is still relatively strict about passport controls, even for EU travel. When travelling to Germany from Britain it is normal for travellers to have their passports checked before leaving British territory, whether the point of departure be an airport, a ferry port or a rail or bus station, but passports will only sometimes be checked again before entering German territory. The British-German border (a symbolic border, as Britain and Germany are not neighbouring states) remains more closed and controlled than, for example, the French-German or Austrian-German borders. This discrepancy is illustrated in one student's surprise at the stringency of British border officials:

> I've taken the bus from London, Victoria Station, to Germany quite often, and I've noticed that they're much more uptight about checking your passport on the English side. In France and Germany it's much more laid back. In Berlin they did have it that you checked in, but in France and any other places I've been in, you didn't have to check in at all, you just go up to the bus driver and show him the passport and that's it!

Germany's more relaxed attitude towards passport controls stems from the nation's active role in European integration. Banchoff (1999) attributes the growth of a supranational European identity in Germany to Germany's unsettled history of nationalism. Ardagh (1995) and Breuilly (1998) similarly maintain that for German leaders of the post-war years, 'the priority was to integrate the Federal Republic into the supranational institutions of the west' (Breuilly 1998, 62), in order to help 'Germany to find a new identity within a new kind of European framework' (Ardagh 1995, 25).

Some people believe that the opening of borders between member states of the European Union has been accompanied by the strengthening and closing of the *EU-Aussengrenze*, i.e. the border separating the member states from the rest of the world. As national barriers are removed, new 'supranational' barriers are imposed, writes Malcolm Chapman (1994, 230), to the effect of creating what Ruth Mandel (1994) calls a 'fortress Europe'. This means that while travel within the European Union is generally without barriers and restrictions for members of the Union, non-members continue to face complications at the border. The *EU-Aussengrenze* of Germany constitutes the border with Switzerland in the south and the borders with Poland and the Czech Republic in the east. Ease of travel into and out of Germany depends on the status of both the border and the traveller.

The contrast can be clearly observed in the region around Lake Constance, a region intersected by the borders of Austria, Germany and Switzerland. Austria and Germany are member states of the EU but Switzerland is not. Travel across the Swiss border is, therefore, comparatively more complicated than travel between Austria and Germany. As previously mentioned, it is no longer necessary to show passports when crossing the Austro-German border, but a valid passport is still required to enter or leave Switzerland. The Swiss town of Kreuzlingen has spread over the years to join with the larger town of Konstanz in Germany, to the extent that it now bears the appearance of a suburb of the German town. Most inhabitants of Kreuzlingen work and shop in Konstanz, and therefore take the local train or bus daily across the Swiss-German interstate border. Despite the impression that he/she is travelling within the same town, the worker or shopper is required to pass through a customs point and passport control in the station before entering or leaving Konstanz, where the station buildings and platforms are divided into *Schweizer Bahnhof* and *Deutscher Bahnhof*. Similarly, when travelling by train between St Gallen in Switzerland and Bregenz in Austria (a 50-minute journey) all passengers are required to present their passports to border guards on the train.

Similar restrictions are evident along Germany's eastern Border with the Czech Republic. A student described to me her experience of the Czech border. Used to the relaxed border policies of the EU, she forgot to take her passport and had only her *Aufenthaltserlaubnis* (residence permit) with her. She had been issued with this identification card on arrival in Germany, having completed all the relevant forms and having shown all the necessary identification, including a British passport. However, this card alone was insufficient to grant her entry into the Czech Republic, as it had not been issued in her home country. She was not equipped with her official certification of citizenship or the request from the British state to grant her safe passage across the border. She could not unlock the door and was turned away.

Another Scottish student travelled from Germany to the Czech Republic with a friend from the Caribbean. The Czech border guards were confused by the appearance of the Caribbean girl's passport:

> She had this really strange passport and the guards on the Czech side stopped us, well, they didn't stop us but they came onto the train and checked our passports and they saw her passport and they asked me in German if she'd made it herself … ha ha ha … because it was such an unusual passport.

Because the Caribbean student's passport was unfamiliar to the border guards, who are used to seeing German and other European passports, they reacted warily and suspiciously to her. This particular key, at first glance, did not fit the lock. It is also possible that an underlying racism influenced this particular incident. Not only was the Caribbean student's passport different, but so too was her appearance. The combination aroused suspicion and animosity. Despite their hesitations, however, the international agreement embodied in the passport meant that they allowed the girl to cross the border. In both instances at the Czech border the border functionaries, as official representatives of the Czech and German states, were in complete control, they had complete power over the travellers, both of whom wished to cross the border.

The image of a 'fortress Europe' has most resonance with immigrants from outside the EU, who are seen to represent a potential threat to the economic, political and cultural stability of the Union. Visitors from other countries of the wealthy western world, such as the USA, Canada, Australia and New Zealand generally have fewer difficulties crossing the *EU-Aussengrenze* than do immigrants from poorer countries of the developing world or from Eastern Europe. Having said this, Germany is more generous than most other European countries in granting political asylum to genuine asylum seekers who cross the German border. Asylum is granted to all genuine cases, i.e. to all people who travel to Germany directly from a country where they live under the threat of political persecution (Parkes 1997, 105). The problem with the amended law is that asylum seekers who have passed through a 'safe' land *en route* can legally be turned away at the German border, and sent back to the first safe land that they entered. Those who are allowed into Germany are, nonetheless, required to present official identity documents to the German authorities. They still need a passport to open the door to 'fortress Europe' (Mandel 1994).

History

In order to understand the status of the passport and the border as they stand today, it is necessary to look back at the passport and the border in history. History plays a large part in the construction of a nation's identity. National identity, as mentioned earlier, is based on a community's identification with a shared culture, shared values, shared traditions and a shared history. It is, therefore, unsurprising that passports, as symbols of national identity, often contain illustrations or emblems from a nation's history. O'Byrne (2001) uses the examples of the Dutch and the US passports to illustrate this symbolic 'nation-building' function of the passport. The former contains 'a page-by-page history of the Dutch nation' (ibid., 404) while the latter 'is decorated with individual state emblems' (ibid., 405). Similarly, the German passport is decorated with the historic state emblem of the *Reichsadler* (imperial eagle) and the British passport with the coat of arms of the United Kingdom.

The history of the passport is illustrative of the history of international travel and of international relations. Borders have always existed between territories, but passports have not always been necessary to cross borders.

O'Byrne (ibid., 400) traces the origins of the modern passport back to the eleventh century and the *guidaticum*, or request for safe travel, issued by the Spanish authorities to their citizens. Thereafter, he maintains, 'passport letters' were issued by states 'to grant safe passage of travellers during wartime' (ibid., 400). It was not until the nineteenth century that European countries began to issue passports or equivalent travel documents to 'any citizens at any time' (ibid., 400). At this time travellers could still cross borders without a passport, but they were not guaranteed the protection of their state. Passports were thus 'luxuries enjoyed by the rich' (ibid., 401). It was not until the twentieth century that all citizens were able to apply for and be granted with a passport. Therefore, it was not until the twentieth century that passport controls were established at almost all borders world-wide. International relations, which had previously been of concern princi-pally to politicians and those in power, became the concern of every normal citizen who wished to travel outwith the boundaries of his/her home state.

How have Germany's borders changed within the historical framework of international relations and international travel? The borders of Germany, and consequently what we understand to *be* 'Germany', have changed many times since the formation of the kingdom of Germany in AD 911. The fact that the political entity of Germany has been unable to contain all ethnic Germans and all German speakers supports Demandt's (1991, 14) con-tention that throughout history the German nation and the German *Reich* or state have been incompatible. The desire to overcome this incompatibil-ity has led to several attempts by German rulers to push the German borders outwards in order to expand the German state, or *Reich*, and to fulfil the ideal of the nation–state. At the same time, other European states, such as France, Britain and Russia, have endeavoured throughout history to contain Germany's power by dividing the nation into more manageable pieces and destroying the *Reich*. Germany's *Binnengrenzen* (inner borders) have thus changed together with its *Aussengrenzen* (outer borders).

At the end of the eighteenth century, for example, Napoleon succeeded in fragmenting the German empire into a confederation of sixteen states (Kitchen 1996, 11). In 1848 the German *Reich* was reformed to create the first German 'national state' (Breuilly 1998, 44). However, Germany remained a federalist state, in which the individual German states or *Länder* of the *Reich* maintained a considerable degree of independence under their own governments. Breuilly (ibid., 50) observes that former restrictions on crossing borders between German states were removed at this time, in an attempt to foster a stronger sense of German unity and of German national identity:

> Cross-border migration pushed governments towards bilateral agree-ments, reducing the tendency to treat each other's subjects as foreign-ers. Large numbers of Germans could now move from one German state to another more easily. Arguably such mobility did more to

stimulate a national sense of identity amongst Germans than any amount of nationalist propaganda.

Previously, the relevant border rituals were performed at both the *Aussengrenzen* and the *Binnengrenzen* of Germany, which led to the isolation of the individual states and to a fragmented sense of national identity. The Treaty of Versailles in 1918 again reduced the extent of the territory to be included within German boundaries. The limitations imposed by this treaty were later undone by the expansionist policies of Hitler's Third Reich. The Third Reich, claims Breuilly (1998, 61), 'made national boundaries irrelevant' as Hitler extended German rule first over Austria and the Sudetenland and later over much of Europe. After the Second World War Germany was contained and divided once more. The eastern border was moved westwards as parts of German territory were returned to Poland and Hungary. The southern border moved northwards as Austria regained independence. What was left of Germany was divided between the western allied and the Soviet victors.

The Cold War led to the creation of the internal German border, which is undoubtedly the most famous German border, and perhaps *the* most famous border, in recent history (see Chapter 5). The heavily policed border between the two states, and between two ideologies, created the archetypal 'alienated borderland' (Martínez 1994). Martínez's 'alienated borderlands' are found in areas of intense international and ideological conflict, where the border is rigidly controlled and generally remains closed to the populations on either side. On the whole, the populations of alienated borderlands are likely to be constantly reminded of the existence of the border by its physical presence within the landscape. This presence may take the form of walls, barbed wire fences, watchtowers and the human form of border guards, often armed with guns (ibid., 2). The internal German border was marked by such fortifications, both along the infamous Berlin Wall and along the 870-mile border between the *Bundesrepublik Deutschland* (BRD), or Federal Republic of Germany (FRG), in the West and the *Deutsche Demokratische Republik* (DDR), or German Democratic Republic (GDR), in the East.

The presence of the border led to the reintroduction of internal German travel restrictions, little more than a century after they had been removed. In 1961 the Soviet powers in the East closed the border with the FRG (Federal Republic of Germany) and built a wall around West Berlin. The Communist regime was determined to halt the out-migration of its able workers to the West. East Germans thus became essentially imprisoned by the border. Only certain citizens were allowed to cross the border to the West, and they needed special travel permits from the state. The passport alone was ineffective as the key to the door of West Germany. The GDR's (German Democratic Republic's) borders to the east, i.e. to other Soviet Bloc countries such as the former Czechoslovakia and Poland, remained open. Because living standards in East Germany were higher than in any other Soviet state, the regime had no fears about permanent migration eastwards. The Western powers did not want to set up any border controls on their side of the border. The FRG believed that the GDR was still a part of the Federal Republic of Germany and thus considered international travel restrictions to be inappropriate. However, Westerners, or *Wessis*, travelling to the East were closely monitored by the Soviet powers, for fear that they might pose a threat to the Communist regime. As insecurities and anxieties grew within the Eastern government, it was decided in 1961 to restrict Western allied forces' and West Berliners' access to East Berlin to one crossing point along the recently built wall. The West responded with the opening of the world-famous border control, Checkpoint Charlie. This control constituted a liminal and highly symbolic space between territories and ideologies and represented a refusal to allow the door to East Germany to be locked.

Checkpoint Charlie became an iconic site along the wall and it remains an iconic site today. In a divided Germany it stood both for the separateness of the two German states and for the eternal hope of reunification and restored freedom of movement (www.checkpoint-charlie.de). In 1962 a museum was opened in the last building before the wall, called 'Haus am Checkpoint Charlie' (see Chapter 6). The various exhibitions housed in the museum are related to the subject of the Berlin Wall and to the theme of freedom. In 1973, for example, there was an exhibition entitled 'Maler interpretieren die Mauer' (Artists interpret the Wall) and in 1984 the museum housed 'Von Gandhi bis Walesa – Gewaltfreier Kampf für Menschenrechte' (From Ghandi to Walesa – The non-violent fight for human rights). One exhibition contained examples of actual vehicles used for escaping across the border. Hot air balloons, homemade cars and even a mini-submarine were included in the display entitled 'Flucht macht erfinderisch' (Inventive escapees) (www.mauer-musem.com). Today the museum remains a store of memories of the divided Germany. It is a site where stories can be kept and retold, where memories of the border and elements of GDR culture can be stored and displayed (Clifford, 1997: 8–9). The crossing of the internal German border from East to West, whether legally or illegally, was often an emotionally charged experience. The liminal phase of border crossing held even greater excitement and uncertainty. Legal border-crossers feared being turned back at the border and escapees feared being caught or even shot by the armed border guards. All experienced the excitement of anticipating what lay beyond the border. These experiences are an important feature of contemporary German collective memory.

All borders can be sites for storytelling and memory collection, as has been shown in students' recollections of crossing the German border. Similarly, the passport has become a form of souvenir. Like the souvenirs that people buy on their travels, the photos they bring back and store in albums and the scrapbooks that they make, the passport acts as a reminder and a proof of where they have been. Travellers collect customs stamps as souvenirs and feel a great sense of pride and fulfilment if their passport becomes filled. Many people who travel within Europe today feel slightly disappointed by the fact that they no longer have their passport stamped when crossing borders within the EU, as this means that they can no longer collect stamps as souvenirs. One student described her experience of crossing the Austro-German border in 1995, when controls still existed but had been relaxed:

> They just glanced at my passport, they didn't even look at me. I was quite insulted. I thought they would be like, 'ooh, foreigner', but they just glanced at it. I thought I would get a nice little stamp on my passport, but I didn't.

Just as some EU countries seem to have a certain attachment to their borders (Best 1996), some travellers feel a sense of nostalgia for the rituals of border crossing.

Culture

As has been stated in the previous sections, to cross borders is to cross between cultures, and the passport is a symbol of different cultures. Nations contain, to a certain extent, national cultures, but we have seen that aspects of German culture, such as the German language, spread across the boundaries of the nation–state. The boundaries of the *deutschsprachiger Raum* (German-speaking area) are not the same as the boundaries of Germany, but include the Austrian and Swiss boundaries. In addition, the boundaries of Germany do not enclose a pure German culture. Germany is a land of regional differences. On a large scale, distinct, if somewhat stereotypical, differences are noted between the jovial, relaxed Germans in the south and the quieter, hard-working, more sensible Germans in the north (see Chapter 8). On a smaller scale, differences are evident when one crosses the borders between neighbouring *Länder*. Many Germans feel an affinity with their *Land* and view Germans from other *Länder* as almost foreign. A German acquaintance from Bavaria felt it necessary to inform me every time we crossed the unmarked border into Baden Württemburg, only 5 kilometres from his home village, that 'hier sind die Leute etwas anders' (the people are somewhat different here). The different *Länder* have different festivals and holidays, as well as different styles of music and different tastes in food and drink (see Chapter 9 and also Chapter 5). There are also language differences within Germany. People from different regions speak different dialects, which are often incomprehensible to Germans from outwith the region (see Chapter 2). The German *Binnengrenzen* (Demandt 1991), therefore differentiate between different 'Germanic' cultures. The traveller can cross borders without ever leaving Germany.

German cultural borders can also be encountered far away from Germany. To hold a national passport is to hold a symbol of one's nationhood (O'Byrne, 2001). In this way the passport is similar to markers of national identity such as the national flag and the national anthem. Germans abroad have their passport or *Personalausweis* with them and this identifies them to others as German, as being from another culture. But what other cultural baggage is carried across the German border, both by Germans travelling abroad and by visitors entering Germany? The most obvious cultural baggage is that of language differences. Whenever people travel to countries where other languages are spoken, they encounter a language barrier between themselves and the speakers of the native language.[10] In this way the German border can be encountered anywhere in the world where Germans meet people who speak different languages. Other cultural baggage will include different histories, as discussed above, different habits, manners and customs and also different knowledge and interests. Part of the home country is taken across the German border with the traveller.

In his study of the construction of communities, Cohen (1985) explains that all communities surround themselves by both physical and symbolic boundaries. Physical boundaries are temporally and spatially fixed, they are territorially defined, but symbolic boundaries based on community identity will travel with members of that community. Even when physically displaced from the territory of Germany, Germans still identify with and practise the habits of Germany. Because cultures travel and take their cultural borders with them (Clifford 1997), it is possible to encounter a German border and German culture without ever going to Germany.

To discover a 'displaced' German border should not be at all difficult if we are to believe Ardagh's contention (1995, 218) that 'the Germans are the world's greatest tourists', who ' travel to foreign countries in greater numbers than any other nation'. The Germans, like most other Western nations today, have become world travellers, who venture to all corners of the globe. However, many German holidaymakers venture south. They travel either into Austria, where German is spoken and the food is similar, or venture further south to the Mediterranean, where the climate is warmer and the beaches are better (ibid., 218–19). The South has romantic connotations in German culture. Greek and Roman mythology and culture impress and inspire the Germans, while the supposedly sensitive, romantic people of the Mediterranean are thought to pose an appealing alternative to the more sensible intellect of the Germans in the North (Bohnen 1993).

However, while this *Drang nach Süden* (drive towards the South, or yearning for the South) is arguably prevalent in German society, it is counteracted by the equivalent *Mythos vom Norden* (myth of the North) in German culture (Bohnen, 1993). Bohnen believes that Germans are naturally more attached to the North than they are to the South. This attachment led, during the nineteenth and early twentieth centuries, to a revival of German intellectual interest in Nordic mythology (ibid., 473). This intellectual interest in and emotional attachment to the North is reflected in the literary works of Thomas Mann, who as a native of Lübeck on the Baltic coast, claimed to be 'nordisch gestimmt' (to feel 'northern') (ibid., 471). His novel *Der Tod in Venedig* describes the moral and physical destruction of the protagonist, Aschenbach, which arises from his fateful decision to leave the 'safety' of Germany and travel South to Venice. The North was thought to be in German blood, while the south was an unattainable romantic myth. Bohnen (1993: 473) cites the Prussian minister for culture, Carl Becker, who in 1929 said:

> Der Süden ist etwas anders, das wir nicht haben, aber nach dem wir verlangen. Den Norden fühlen wir irgendwo in der Tiefe unsres persönlichsten Lebens gegenwärtig, wir können ihm nicht entrinnen, er lebt in unserem Blut, in der geheimnisvollen Tiefe unserer Persönlichkeit als Volk wie als Individuum.

> (The South is something different, something that we do not have, but that we desire. We feel the presence of the North somewhere in the depths of our most intimate being, we cannot escape it, it lives in our blood, in the secret depths of our personality, both on a collective and on an individual level.)

The magic of the North and its portrayal in art and literature has created in many Germans a *Drang nach Norden*. Scandinavia and Scotland inspire images of dark, misty mountains, deep lakes and haunted castles. According to Bohnen (1993), there is an urge in Germans to travel to the North, to the lands with which they feel such an affinity. Locked into the centre of Europe, Germans seem to want to escape across the border to the coasts and mountains of the South and the lakes and mountains of the North.

To cross cultural borders within and beyond Germany, it is not even necessary to complete the border rituals discussed above, and it is not necessary to hold a valid passport. Other border rituals, however, may be encountered. As mentioned earlier, Van Gennep (1960) draws an analogy between the threshold rites practised in 'semi-civilized' societies when entering a place of worship or another person's place of dwelling and the territorial rites of passage practised in international travel (ibid., 20). When entering a German person's home, the visitor might perform a variety of silently agreed rituals demonstrating politeness, gratitude and respect (see also Chapter 5). These could include taking his/her shoes off at the door, to show respect for the peace and cleanliness of the home, shaking the host's hand as a means of greeting and/or introduction and the offering of gifts as a display of friendliness and gratitude. The performance of these rituals at the threshold allows the visitor to be temporarily integrated into a German home. When meeting Germans in public places, such as hotels, restaurants and airports, there may be no physical border to be crossed, but similar rituals of politeness, such as introductions and handshakes, may be practised as a way of bridging the cultural gap. Different borders require different types of passports. Different keys fit different doors.

Conclusions

The internal German border, which constituted part of the Iron Curtain, has made Germany famous, or infamous, for its borders. This chapter has attempted to demonstrate the complexities of the German border. It has questioned the positioning, the functions and the characteristics of the German border in order to reach an understanding of how this border shapes Germany. It has also examined the requirements for crossing this border, in order to enter or leave Germany, which illustrate the nature of Germany's international relations.

It is evident that the German border is very difficult to define. Only multiple definitions can be reached. First and foremost, it is the territorial border that surrounds Germany, but it is also the regional German borders, the German language border and the travelling cultural borders between Germans and people of other nationalities. The German border in history is not the German border now, but it has shaped the contemporary German border. In addition, the anonymous international characteristics of liminal border spaces make it difficult to differentiate the German border from any other border when travelling. Border crossing points, both on land and in airports, are never 'particularly German'. The rituals that it is necessary to undertake at the border are also 'the same everywhere'. So is the German border really 'German'?

Although they change and they share characteristics with borders worldwide, although they correspond only to lines drawn arbitrarily on the map of the world (Anderson 1991), although they are gradually becoming open and effectively disappearing from the European landscape, Germany's borders give definition to the cultural space that we identify as Germany at any give time. They are, therefore, physical and real, at least temporarily. Without borders we would not be able to identify the territory, people and culture that make up Germany, the world would simply be 'an unbounded and continuous landscape' (Ingold 1993, 226) without national and cultural definition. We need borders, claims Beatriz Colomina (1996, 52), because without the orientation that they provide, we become disturbed and even sick. The German border, although problematic, is therefore necessary in our understanding of Germany and of the world. As Demandt (1991: 21) emphasizes: 'Im weitesten Sinne ist die Grenze eine metaphysische Notwendigkeit, denn ohne sie ließen sich die Dinge weder unterscheiden noch benennen'. (In the broadest sense the border is a metaphysical necessity, because without it we could neither differentiate between nor name things.)

The German border is also worthy of study because it constitutes the door through which all travellers must pass in order to encounter German culture. This door, or threshold, constitutes the visitor's first encounter with the new culture of Germany. Just as the airport lounge and the hotel lobby (Clifford 1997, 17–18) constitute important sites of intercultural encounter, spaces where people of many different nationalities and cultures come together, so too does the border crossing point. Travellers who want to learn about German culture would therefore be advised to start their investigations at the German border, with the German functionaries and the Germans in transit. After all, it was suggested earlier that people are most aware of their national identities when travelling, when 'abroad', and that the international border is a most powerful symbol of national identity. The meeting of peoples in transit at national borders, could therefore be an ideal site for learning about other nationalities and new cultures. In brief, the border is what makes Germany 'German' and it provides a point of entry and exit for visitors. The traveller need only know how to unlock the door.

Notes

1. In the first part of this chapter, the crossing of the German border will be treated very generally. Varying passport requirements will be discussed later in the citizenship and history sections.
2. The German border will be referred to both as a border and as a boundary or boundary line. In literature on borders and boundaries the differentiation is usually made between the boundary as the line drawn on maps, which demarcates one territory from another and the border as the narrow zone which incorporates the boundary line but also the 'adjacent areas which fringe the boundary' (Prescott 1987, 12).
3. Germany borders Denmark, The Netherlands, Belgium, Luxembourg, France, Switzerland, Austria, the Czech Republic and Poland.
4. All English translations of German quotations are my own.
5. This holds true for all borders in Western Europe today, but is not a universal characteristic of borders.
6. See also Donnan and Wilson (1999, 110).
7. 'Semi-civilised' is the term used by Van Gennep to refer to non-industrialized societies, societies which differed markedly from those of Europe and the Western World at the beginning of the twentieth century (1960, 2).
8. Student quotations are taken from interviews conducted with students studying German at the University of Glasgow, March 2001.
9. It should be noted that neither Demandt nor Kitchen agree with Arndt's view. This will be discussed later.
10. The strength of this barrier will, of course, vary depending on the ability of the two parties to speak each other's languages.

References

ANDERSON, B. 1991: *Imagined communities: reflections on the origin and rise of nationalism*. London: Verso.

ARDAGH, J. 1995: *Germany and the Germans*. New edition: *The united Germany in the mid-1990s*. London: Penguin.

BANCHOFF, T. 1999: German identity and European integration. _European Journal of International Relations_ 5 (3), 259–89.

BEST, S. 1996: The boundary rider: response to battle lines. In WELCHMAN, J. (ed.), _Rethinking Borders._ London: Macmillan Press Ltd., 65–70.

BOHNEN, K. 1993: Die „fremde Heimat" der Deutschen: Der „Mythos vom Norden" in deutscher Kulturtradition. In WIERLACHER, A. (ed.), _Kulturthema Fremdheit: Leitbegriffe und Problemfelder kulturwissenschaftlicher Fremdheitsforschung._ Munich: iudicium Verlag GmbH, 471–81.

BREUILLY, J. 1998: German national identity. In KOLINSKY, E. and VAN DER WILL, W. (eds), _The Cambridge companion to modern German culture._ Cambridge: Cambridge University Press, 44–66.

CHAPMAN, M. 1994: The commercial realization of the Community boundary. In GODDARD, V.A., LLOBERA, J.R. and SHORE, C. (eds), _The anthropology of Europe: boundaries and identities in conflict._ Oxford: Berg, 227–54.

CLIFFORD, J. 1997: _Routes: travel and translation in the late twentieth century._ Cambridge, MA: Harvard University Press.

COHEN, A. 1985: _The symbolic construction of community._ Chichester: Ellis Horwood Ltd.

COLOMINA, B. 1996: Battle lines. In WELCHMAN J. (ed.), _Rethinking borders,_ London: Macmillan Press Ltd, 51–64.

DEMANDT, A. 1991: _Deutschlands Grenzen in der Geschichte._ Munich: C.H. Beck.

DONNAN, H. and WILSON, T.M. 1999: _Borders: frontiers of identity, nation and state._ Oxford: Berg.

INGOLD, T. 1993: The art of translation in a continuous world. In PÁLSSON, G. (ed.), _Beyond boundaries: understanding, translation and anthropological discourse._ Oxford: Berg, 211–30.

KAVANAGH, W. 1994: Symbolic boundaries and real borders on the Portuguese-Spanish frontier. In DONNAN, H. and WILSON, T.M. (eds) 1994, _Border approaches: anthropological perspectives on frontiers._ Lanham, MD: University Press of America, 75–88.

KITCHEN, M. 1996: _The Cambridge illustrated history of Germany._ Cambridge: Cambridge University Press.

KOLINSKY, E. 1998: Non-German minorities, women and the emergence of civil society. In KOLINSKY, E. and VAN DER WILL, W. (eds), _The Cambridge companion to modern German culture._ Cambridge: Cambridge University Press, 110–31.

LLOBERA, J.R. 1994: Anthropological approaches to the study of nationalism in Europe: the work of Van Gennep and Mauss. In GODDARD, V.A., LLOBERA, J.R. and SHORE, C. (eds), _The anthropology of Europe: boundaries and identities in conflict._ Oxford: Berg, 93–112.

MANDEL, R. 1994: Fortress Europe and the foreigners within: Germany's Turks. In GODDARD, V.A., LLOBERA, J.R. and SHORE, C. (eds), _The anthropology of Europe: boundaries and identities in conflict._ Oxford: Berg, 113–24.

MARTÍNEZ, O. (ed.) 1986: _Across boundaries: transborder interaction in comparative perspective._ El Paso, TX: Texas Western Press.

MARTÍNEZ, O. 1994: The dynamics of border interaction: new approaches to border analysis. In SCHOFIELD, C. (ed.), _World boundaries._ vol. 1 _Global boundaries._ London: Routledge, 1–15.

O'BYRNE, D.J. 2001: On passports and border controls. _Annals of Tourism Research, A Social Sciences Journal_ 28 (2), 399–416.

PARKES, S. 1997: _Understanding contemporary Germany._ London: Routledge.

PRESCOTT, J.R.V. 1987: _Political frontiers and boundaries._ London: Allen and Unwin.

RICHARD, N. 1996: The cultural periphery and postmodern decentring: Latin America's reconversion of borders. In WELCHMAN, J. (ed.), *Rethinking borders*. London: Macmillan Press Ltd., 71–84.

SIMMEL, G. 1997: Bridge and door. In FEATHERSTONE, M and FRISBY, D. (eds) *Simmel on culture: selected writings*. London: Sage, 170–4.

TURNER, V. 1969: *The ritual process: structure and anti-structure*. Chicago: Aldine Publishing Company.

TURNER, V. 1982: *From ritual to theatre: the human seriousness of play*. New York: PAJ Publications.

VAN GENNEP, A. 1922: *Traité comparatif des nationalités,* vol. 1 *Les Éléments éxtérieurs de la nationalité*. Paris: Payot and Compagnie.

VAN GENNEP, A. 1960: *The rites of passage*. Chicago: The University of Chicago Press.

Websites

http://www.germany-info.org/ (Citizenship Laws in Germany)

http://www.mauer-museum.com/ (information about museum 'Haus am Checkpoint Charlie')

http://www.checkpoint-charlie.de/ (information about current projects on old site of Checkpoint Charlie)

2

German language: whose language, whose culture?

BY HELEN KELLY-HOLMES

The encounter with the German language happens in manifold ways. It may be an intercultural encounter that takes place in a multinational company or on a tourist visit to Germany, Austria or Switzerland; it may be random, a fleeting word or phrase overheard in the news headlines; it may occur in the most unexpected place, for instance, the menu of a restaurant in a Spanish holiday resort where the German version is, disarmingly, placed before the English. The more intensive encounter with German often takes place in the classroom, here too there are many possibilities. It may be motivated by the desire to maintain some link with the country of their forebears, as in the case of the heritage learner in Australia or Argentina; it may take place in the German for Foreigners classroom in any German-speaking country, where the encounter with German is a necessary hurdle for the immigrant or asylum seeker; or it may take place in one of the many foreign language classrooms of the English-speaking world, in which German is being taught. It is just such an encounter I would like to relate, before beginning our discussion of language and contemporary culture.

One day, in a translation class I was teaching, our deliberations on Peter Schneider's (1990) witty and thought-provoking study of German culture following unification in 1990 led to an insightful discussion on the dimensions of national culture. In the particular chapter we were translating, he uses the analogy of identical twins (i.e. East and West Germany) separated at birth to explore whether or not there is some sort of over-arching, primordial 'German' culture, which could have survived political and economic upheavals, ideological polarization and 40 years of isolation and separation. He further extends his hypothesizing to consider whether or not German-speaking Switzerland and Austria might not also share this 'original' culture. We decided to explore what this German culture might be and the white board at the top of the class was very quickly covered in suggestions: music; a literary canon; political experiences; folk and fairytales; geographical space; a governmental system; shared history; economic practices;

ideologies; religion. Finally, the German exchange student at the back of the class got the chance to intervene: 'I think you've forgotten the most important thing. For me, it would have to be the language.' 'Ah, yes, of course', the British students, all studying German, nodded in agreement. 'That's obvious. Why didn't we think of it? ....'

This story, I think, illustrates some fundamental differences between the role played by language in culture in German-speaking countries on the one hand and Anglophone or English-speaking countries, even Great Britain, the 'home' of the English language, on the other. Language may not be something that automatically counts as part of culture and identity in the Anglophone world, whereas I think this claim could be made with a good degree of confidence for the German-speaking world. This chapter is an attempt to estimate the role of the German language in contemporary culture. Language, like culture, is something lived, shared, cumulative, multifaceted, contradictory. It is imperfect, mongrelized; at one and the same time both natural and manipulated. It is not something we can put in a test tube in order to carry out experiments. It is instead something that is constantly changing – it is alive. And, it only lives through its speakers. Words themselves have no inherent meanings. Meanings are instead attached to them by members of a speech community, a culture. Thus, just like our random and not-so-random encounters with German, describing and discussing the language means taking a snapshot, different to one we could have taken yesterday, different to the one we might take tomorrow.

The chapter begins with a general discussion of the link between language, culture and identity before going on to look at the facts and figures of the German language. The third part of this chapter attempts to provide a brief outline of the recent historical context of the German language, before going on to look at linguistic diversity in German-speaking countries and how this both reflects and is reflected in cultural diversity in the fourth part. The fifth section looks at who 'owns' the German language and discusses the cultural impetus for and reactions against standardization and 'foreign' words. The final section addresses the issue of how the German language is experienced and perceived from outside of Germany and how these experiences and perceptions contribute to the understanding of German culture and identity beyond the German-speaking world.

Language and culture

The first thing we need to understand about the association between language and culture is that it is not a simple, one-way, cause and effect relationship. We should think of it instead as something two-way or circular or even multi-layered. We cannot say that language contributes to culture without acknowledging at the same time that culture contributes in turn to language. In order for a cultural or social group to exist, there must be a common language; in order for a common language to come into existence, a social or cultural group needs to create it. Likewise, the main vehicle we have for talking about and expressing culture is language. Through using this language, our links are strengthened, we become a more coherent cultural group, we learn more about ourselves, we evolve cultural practices and our common identity as members of that group may be reinforced. We can find examples of this in almost every minute of our daily lives. Television news, for example, is addressed to a national or local audience (a cultural group whose members identify to a greater or lesser extent with each other). Because of this, the presenter can take for granted that certain concepts and words do not need to be explained and that a certain level of common knowledge can be assumed because she/he is speaking to people who share some sort of culture and identity. They would have been through the same educational system, they experience a similar type of press in the newspapers they read, they may share the same or a related religion and have similar values and mores, they may have read some of the same books and seen many of the same films, they are talked to by the same politicians on the radio or television, they shop in the same shops where they buy the same brands, they see the same advertisements everyday, they watch the same television programmes, etc. Similarly, as a result of watching this news programme everyday, the national or local group has even more in common. They will discuss the events reported on with friends, family and workmates. They will bring new words and concepts which they hear on the news programme into their everyday conversation. Their culture and identity are reinforced by watching this programme.

This is, of course, a very great generalization. What about age differences, gender differences, ethnic differences, educational difference, religious differences, political differences, class differences, linguistic differences? It goes without saying that all of these occur within national frontiers. There is no such thing as a completely homogeneous linguistic and cultural group. However, despite this, we can still claim that sharing the German language and living in a country in which that is the language through which people go about their daily business – being part of what in German is called a *Kommunikationsgemeinschaft* or speech and communication community – does give people some sort of shared culture and identity. An important point here is that this 'membership' of a nation or country does not preclude membership of other cultural, identity and linguistic groups. For instance, we may speak a language other than the official or dominant one at home, making us part of a regional or ethnic minority speech community. If we are members of a football team, we share the language and experiences with other members of that team to a very great extent and members of other football teams in other parts of the country and even across the world too, to a greater or lesser extent, making up a kind sub-speech community and culture.

Another concept we need to acknowledge here is that language is not simply a code – anyone who has ever attempted anything but the most basic translation will already realize this. Because languages are inextricably linked to cultures, they invariably reflect this in their vocabulary, structures, rules about politeness, etc. A good example here is the difference between American English and British English. If a language were simply a set of scientifically derived and defined units of meaning, unaffected by the people who use them and the situations in which they are used, then there would be no differences in vocabulary, spelling, etc. between the USA and Great Britain. As it is, the many variations show how languages are the result of political, economic, historical, social, ideological and cultural processes. To take a fairly banal example, there is no Federal Reserve in England because England, unlike the USA, is not a federal country, the equivalent institution being called the Bank of England. Likewise, the name of the 'equivalent' German institution, the *Bundesbank*, is the result of a number of important aspects of recent and not so recent German history, for example, the fact that Germany has only been a unified group of *Länder* or states since 1871 and the fact that the Americans fitted some aspects of their federalism to German social, economic and political life during the post-war occupation and de-nazification. Something as basic as this, the way in which a country is governed and organized economically, politically and administratively may seem to have little to do with its language. But, when we look closely, we see that all of these processes naturally take place through the language and inevitably mould and develop it. An experience from another translation class may serve to illustrate this. In the text we were discussing the German '*Innenminister*' was mentioned. The student who was presenting his translation to the group had translated this as 'Home Secretary'. He argued that this was the British 'equivalent' and, as such was, the appropriate choice. There followed a lengthy discussion, at the end of which the student opted instead for the generic 'Minister of the Interior'. He had a point, to a certain extent, in that the British Home Secretary does indeed have some functions in common with the German *Innenminister* – however, while the former also has responsibility for Justice, his German counterpart does not, this task being allocated to a specific Minister for Justice (*Justizminister*) in Germany. Thus, the difference between these two terms reflects different ways of organizing matters of state – something which is both a product of and an ingredient in culture. Another argument against using the 'British' term was the fact that it would mean little to readers in English-speaking countries outside the UK, all of which have their own particular term for this office. Again, if language were indeed a code, like computer programming languages, then why would there be all these different words for what is a more or less similar function?

The German language – some facts

It is estimated that over 90 million people speak German as their first or second language (as opposed to learning it as a foreign language in school). If we broaden our definition of who speaks German, we could end up with a figure anywhere between 100 million and 260 million! (Stevenson 1997) In Germany, Austria, Liechtenstein and Switzerland, German has the status of an official language (in the case of Switzerland, it is co-official with French, Italian and Rhaeto-Romanic, but German has the greatest number of speakers). In the Eastern part of Belgium[1] which borders Germany and the Süd Tyrol area of Northern Italy, there are significant numbers of German speakers and the language has an official status within these regions and also at a national level in the case of Belgium. There are, however, groups of German speakers found in many countries throughout Europe. This reality reflects the fact that national frontiers are not set in stone and those around Germany and its neighbours were drawn and redrawn many times, particularly, in the late nineteenth century and the twentieth century. For example, in Alsace, in Eastern France, there is a collection of varieties, which together comprise Alsatian or *Elsässisch*, a dialect or linguistic variety of standard German – this is hardly surprising when we consider how Alsace was 'swapped' back and forth between France and Germany. There are also significant German-speaking minorities in Hungary, Romania, the successor states of the USSR, and many other countries across Europe and the world (e.g. in Argentina, Chile, Brazil, Canada and the USA).

What all of these facts and figures tell us is that when thinking about culture and its relationship with the German language, we need to think sometimes beyond Germany and the other primarily German-speaking countries. German is not just the official language of a number of Western European countries; it is also an international language and, like all languages, its status and significance are not carved in stone. For example, at the turn of the twentieth century, German was the international language of science and technology and it was considered a serious contender for official language in the USA, at the time when a language policy was being proposed for that country.

If we look back at the history and origins of the group of languages and linguistic varieties that make up the German language today, Sally Johnson's analogy with the family gives us a very useful way of looking at where the German language comes from, where it is today and where it is going:

> It goes without saying that it is not possible to identify a particular day several hundred years ago when a group of people suddenly decided to speak German .... Languages, like people, have parents, as well as sisters and cousins. In many cases, they even produce their own offspring.
>
> (Johnson 1998, 9)

In the case of the German language (and indeed many other languages which are spoken across Europe, Asia and America), the particular family is known as Indo-European. The reason for grouping all of these languages together is found in the fact that a basic concept such as mother is similar in all these languages – (e.g. *Mutter* (in German); *moeder* (in Dutch); *matka* (in Czech and Polish); *madre* (in Spanish and Italian); *matar* (in Sanskrit) – and appears to come originally from a common language which probably evolved in Eastern Europe around 3000 BC. When the Indo-Europeans broke up and moved to different parts of the continent, different language groups and languages evolved, German being part of the Germanic group. It is interesting to note that it was a German linguist, Jakob Grimm (perhaps better known for his collections of fairy tales), who was instrumental in identifying these links. In terms of sisters and brothers, offspring and cousins, German has Dutch (and Flemish), Afrikaans, Lëtzebuergesch, the Scandinavian languages and Icelandic, Yiddish and English.

The word *deutsch* or German, actually derives from the old (Middle High) German word 'tiutsch', which literally means 'voelkisch' or of the people, thus 'the language of the people' or the language spoken by the common people. Hence, the great diversity in spoken German that persists to this day and the fact that the standardization of the written language is a relatively recent phenomenon (see below). The German language as spoken and written today represents the evolution of many varieties in tandem with political, economic, cultural and social change.

The recent historical context of the German language

At this point, we are faced with a dilemma: our topic of interest is, after all, language in contemporary culture, so, where does 'contemporary' start and what should it cover? The end of the Second World War is perhaps a predictable and depressing place at which to commence our discussion of language and contemporary German culture. However, the post-war period represented such a major break with the Germany (in particular, but this also applies to Austria) of the time before this, that it is in this '*Stunde Null*' or 'year zero' that we can, with some justification, start our examination of language and contemporary culture. However, before moving to this more contemporary sphere, it is important to highlight some particularly important periods and events in the emergence of the contemporary language.

Martin Luther is probably one of the best-known Germans in the world – the revolutionary whose demands for reforms led to the Reformation and ultimately the development of the Protestant religion. However, Luther also carried out another important task with far-reaching consequences. In 1522 he translated the Bible from Latin to German, a formidable undertaking, since just as before 1871 there was no unified German state, so too was there no unified standard language, and comprehension between speakers from different – particularly geographically distant regions –was often problematic. There had been attempts to unify the language before, for example, in the service of commerce, the *Kanzleien* or chanceries who provided a system of administration for businesses in the medieval towns developed a standardized language in order to be able to communicate and thus facilitate trade. This was later used by the Hanseatic League – a trading confederation which included cities such as Lübeck, Hamburg, Bremen and Rostock – but which gradually fell into decline, until it disbanded in the seventeenth century.

Luther's ambition therefore was to write a language that could be read by people who spoke a range of different dialects (see below for more in-depth discussion of dialects). Although his motivation was primarily religious, he unwittingly laid the seeds for socio-linguistic change in German-speaking lands. For many languages, their major breakthrough in terms of status as a national or standard variety came with the translation of the Bible. Suddenly it became acceptable for a sacred text to appear in the 'vulgar' tongue, rather than in Latin, as had been the case up to now. If the Bible could be read, discussed and written about in German, then that language was capable of being a *Kultursprache*, a language of culture, literature and other 'higher' functions.

Another significant milestone in the cultural history of the German language was, interestingly, the result of a reaction against religious and monarchical absolutism and piety that led to *Die Aufklärung*, the German Enlightenment of the eighteenth century. This followed similar movements in France and England, and not only saw the dawn of new ways of thinking and discussing with philosophers such as Kant and Hegel, it also saw a revolution in printing and publishing in German. The extent of the Latin hegemony in this area up to that point in time is clear when we consider that about half of all books published in the late seventeenth century appeared in Latin, whereas this had declined to a tiny 5 per cent by the end of the eighteenth century. (Fulbrook 1990, 91) Not only did this mean that more texts by German authors were available to more people rather than just to the minority who could read Latin; it also meant that the German language was growing, expanding and becoming more enriched. Furthermore, the Enlightenment saw 'a veritable explosion in the production of newspapers, magazines and periodicals' (ibid., 91), marking the beginning of a shared body of texts in German, which in turn strengthened German linguistic culture.

The second half of the eighteenth century heralded another important period, in the form of a golden era for literature in German with the emergence of a whole host of major writers and the two foremost figures of the German literary canon, Johann Wolfgang von Goethe and Friedrich Schiller. The poetry and prose of this period showed how the German language was capable of the highest forms of art, of expressing beauty, emotion and elevated thinking – all of which were essential for the evolution in the status of the language in German-speaking culture. Germans could be proud of such a language; more than this, however, some writers and philosophers, such as Gottfried Herder, maintained that they *should*, that language was an inherent part of the *Volk*, the cultural nation.

The next significant event was the unification of the autonomous German states under Bismarck in 1871. It is worth pointing out that this could not really have happened without the German language and 'a belief in the possession of a common cultural and linguistic heritage' (Wright 2000, 41). As Florian Coulmas puts it: 'language was an indispensable tool' in the nation-building project of nineteenth-century Germany. Language, as the key medium of culture, 'was more likely than any other social feature to lend itself to the creation of a national myth' (1995, 57). Unification meant that German became a national language, the language of both a *Staatsnation* (a nation–state) and a *Kulturnation* (cultural nation) – the two becoming increasingly linked and interdependent in the writings of people like Fichte. A necessary condition for the success of linguistic nationalism is, arguably, a dose of chauvinism: the language in question (in this case German) has to be presented as something special, something superior.

In the humiliating and impoverished aftermath of the First World War, such notions of superiority were once more stoked up, this time in the cause of National Socialism. Although it has been argued that language was not seen by the Nazis as a primary factor in determining 'Germanness' and membership of the 'Aryan race' – as Florian Coulmas (1995) points out, many millions of those killed in gas chambers were in fact speakers of German or, more likely the Germanic language of Yiddish – the role of language in the cult and success of Nazism should not be underestimated. The entire Nazi project took place through the language, the German language was used and manipulated to persuade people of the necessity of this project, the language of the Nazi project filtered through to almost every level of spoken and written culture – at least in the public sphere. For example, consider the impact of the term '*Untermenschen*' – once this is uttered, then the dehumanizing of such people is already taking place. Goebbels claimed that propaganda was 'a first-class weapon'. His propaganda was inextricably bound up with language and the nazification of the German language was a major part of the Nazi arsenal. Consequently, public discourse came to be recognized as a vital tool in the National Socialist agenda and the need to alter public communication and language was recognized almost immediately in the post-war period. Overnight, radical changes took place in the meaning and associations of particular words. A very basic instance of this was the term '*Führer*' which was suddenly switched in public language (e.g. political and media texts) from having a very positive to a very negative connotation, something which has persisted in Germany and internationally to this day. The de-nazification process led to what Schlosser (1990) terms 'ein terminiologisches Vakuum in der offiziellen Kommunikation der Deutschen', a 'terminological vacuum' in the public communication of Germans. Given that certain words were now taboo and had come to be associated with a shameful period in Germany's history, the two fledgling states which grew from Germany's division (the Federal Republic or West Germany and the German Democratic Republic or East Germany) were now faced with the problem of filling this terminological vacuum. Not only were Germans, East and West, given a new state, with a new ideology and political, economic and international orientation, they were also given a new vocabulary to go with this. Initially, language and public discourse – in particular the media – were overtly controlled by the Allies (the British in Northern Germany, the Americans in Southern Germany, the French in Western Germany and the Soviets in Eastern Germany) as part of de-nazification. However, long after such controls were lifted, these important changes and influences meant that in future, too, public communication would inevitably be (directly and indirectly) determined by Soviet interests in the East and Anglo-American influences in the West. A good example of this lasting influence is the media. Many of Germany's most famous publications date from this period and were moulded to a great extent by the occupying authorities, particularly the British and the Americans. For example, Germany's flagship weekly news magazine, *Der Spiegel* was set up under an Allied licence and modelled on *Time* magazine. Likewise, *Die Welt* was modelled on *The Times* of London.

The debate about the extent to which official and public language in East and West Germany differed was contested by many German language experts for many years. While the final consensus would appear to be that 'no major structural differences took root in the standard varieties of the GDR and the Federal Republic' (Stevenson 1993, 350), it has been acknowledged that there were many differences in terms of vocabulary and meaning, particularly in the fields of politics, economics and social and public institutions, as Michael Clyne, among others, has pointed out. While West Germany's political friendship with the USA in the second half of the twentieth century meant an inevitable influx of English *Fremdwörter* into the West German language, the influence on German in the East came in terms of semantics from Russian, rather than specific Russian vocabulary items. On top of this, while the East German state promoted a separate *nationalsprachliche Variante*, the West German state saw itself perhaps as the original protector of German culture. The *Wende* of 1989, (the period leading up to the fall of the Berlin Wall and lasting until Unification in July 1990), and subsequent German unification created their own version of *Stunde Null* for many East Germans. Terms such as '*Volkseigener Betrieb*', 'people's own enterprise', which expressed a culture of, in this instance, common ownership, were replaced and citizens of the former GDR soon found themselves having to learn, rather rapidly, the language of what had up to that point been a foreign consumer culture. For example, research carried out in Leipzig in 1994 identified two substantial groups in society who were removed from this process of introducing the texts and vocabulary of the market economy to East Germany. One group, termed the 'victims' were 'bewildered, disillusioned and apathetic' in the face of the stream of advertising and other market and media discourses; the other group, termed the 'conscientious objectors' were openly and consciously hostile to the approaches of big business, despite their status as professionals, their income and their potential as consumers (Kelly-Holmes 1995, 1999). There is the temptation to dismiss the vocabulary of *Realexistierender Sozialismus* or actually existing socialism as '*würgende Wörter*' (Oschlies 1989) or choking or chaining words which rendered the citizens of the GDR incapable of free expression, however, this is to disregard our notion of language as a lived, shared reality. As Schäffner and Porsch (1993, 35) point out, 'we have to confess that such "choking words" were somehow, at least sometimes, "our words" ... a simple dichotomy of official (party) discourse and private (everyday) discourse would not do justice to the complex communicative practice in the former GDR'. The vocabulary of the unification process, the linguistic expression of what was happening politically, economically and ideologically, was also far from disputed. In particular the term '*Wiedervereinigung*' or reunification caused alarm in some circles. The argument here was that the united Germany as it is today has never really existed and thus the use of 're' could only refer to pre-war border configurations, something which showed an ignorance of Polish, Czech and French sensitivities.

Although unification inevitably led to a 'Westernization' of East German public language and culture, for example, the almost exclusive take-over of media in East Germany by Western companies, this is not to say that these aspects were totally wiped out nor that they no longer had validity in unified Germany.

Linguistic diversity, cultural diversity

On my first trip to Germany as a teenager I stayed with a family in Jülich (near Düsseldorf) who spoke German which was very familiar to me from my school lessons, books and tapes, I had few problems understanding them. One day we went to visit relatives who lived in the countryside about 50 miles away. Instantaneously, the father, a lawyer who spoke *Hochdeutsch* (or standard German), suddenly switched to what sounded like a completely different language when he greeted his cousins. He then proceeded to translate for me as I tried to get accustomed to their language, their version of the German language – alive and well and less than an hour away from where I thought I was learning to speak that language!

Although we have regional varieties of English in Anglophone countries, it is fair to say that they tend to manifest themselves mainly in terms of different accents. People may unconsciously modify this accent in certain conditions – for example, intensifying it when they return home to a region in order to feel a sense of belonging and be accepted, while modifying it and attempting a more standard pronunciation when they are in a different part of the country or in a different social setting. German regional (and national in the cases of Austrian German and, even more so, Swiss German) variation encompasses far more than simply phonological changes relating to pronunciation and accent. Sentence structure, meanings and vocabulary are all subject to change. These quite major differences are termed a dialect (as opposed to an accent) and there are many dialects found throughout German-speaking countries. There is of course an obvious question here, namely, what is the difference between a dialect and a language? One rather facetious but very telling answer which has been posited is that a language has a flag and an army or navy, and this makes some sense when we consider, for instance, that Dutch is defined as a language, whereas *Bayrisch* (Bavarian) or *Sächsisch* (Saxon) – both of which are far removed from Standard or High German – are all classified as dialects. Dialects are often defined sociologically, politically or economically rather than linguistically. Such dialects both reflect and reinforce a strong regional culture and identity, in the words of Schlosser (1983) they are 'eine Grammatik der Erfahrungen und Gefühle', 'a grammar of experiences and feelings'. When asked, many Germans will often refer first to their region, rather than to their country when defining their culture and identity. Knowledge of their dialect, the ability to speak a dialect and switch to and from it are all fundamental to identity and culture in many parts of Germany and, interestingly, in a country where few are prepared to profess a pride in their nation, many more feel comfortable expressing pride in a regional identity and culture.

It is important to remember, however, that the relationship with dialect is not the same throughout German-speaking countries. In some parts of Germany and Austria, for example in urban areas, dialect may be viewed as the preserve of older people, being for mainstream culture little more than a *Reliktsprache* or heritage language. Whereas, in other parts (e.g. Southern Germany), it is the main variety, used in all situations and non-speakers are forced to learn it in order to take part in the culture (Mattheier 1980). It should also be pointed out that perceptions of the standard language can also vary in different German-speaking areas. For example, as Moosmuller (1995, 259) points out, the use of the standard in the electronic media in Austria is 'widely perceived as artificial'. It is important, therefore, to look at the relationship between dialects and standard varieties on a case-by-case level in order to gain a thorough understanding of how dialects impact on local, regional and national culture.

Not only are dialects a means of expressing a lived, shared culture; their status also depends on their relationship – or perceived relationship – with culture. Braun (1998) claims that the evolution from dialect to *Kultursprache* or language of culture (and presumably to official or national language) depends on the particular dialect's changing relationship with 'high' culture. For many, dialect is concerned with 'low culture' (for example, terms such as 'vulgar speech' are often used to describe this way of speaking), and even though speakers may see the dialect in question in a positive way in terms of its social function – providing a means of convivial conversation – they and non-speakers may still view its relationship with culture (and here we mean 'high' culture) in a negative way. Unfortunately, research carried out by Bernstein in the late 1960s which concluded that children who spoke dialect or what he termed 'restricted code' rather than the standard language or in his words 'elaborated code' were disadvantaged in the education system and wider society was used to discourage parents from passing on the local dialect to their children. The consequences of this for dialects or *Plattdeutsch* in poorer parts of Germany, such as *Ostfriesland*, where migration to other parts of Germany was a fact of life, were quite devastating.

The transition to a written form is a key point in the movement from dialect to *Kultursprache*, since, by proving itself capable of expression of high forms of literature, such as original prose and poetry, the dialect shows that it is also worthy of being a vessel for containing and expressing culture. Once the dialect's credentials in the literary sphere have been established, it will then make inroads into other areas of public culture such as the media (television news), the administration, education and government. We can observe this process taking place for Swiss German and Lëtzebuergesch, having come from a situation where many people in Luxembourg were ashamed to admit they spoke the language in the wake of the Second World War.[2] Traditionally dialect was the preserve of spoken language, written texts – particularly public, media and official – being formulated in Standard German. However, in recent years, this diglossic situation (where different and distinct varieties of languages are used for different and distinct purposes) has changed somewhat and more and more dialect is found in public and media texts such as advertising and television. Interestingly, once the preserve of *Hochdeutsch* and a disseminator of the standard language, television has in recent years seen a relaxation in linguistic practice. It is now not uncommon to come across dialects and informal language in traditionally high-register domains such as news programmes. For example, MDR (*Mitteldeutscher Rundfunk*), the regional channel for Sachsen, Thüringen and Sachsen-Anhalt, has never tried to cover up its pride in its regional dialects (some of which are among the most maligned in Germany!) since it was set up following the post-unification reorganization of broadcasting in East Germany. In an advertisement for the East German *Glückauf* beer, the slogan 'Wo mit Glückauf gegrüßt wird, wird auch Glückauf getrunken' (Where people greet each other with *Glückauf*, they also drink *Glückauf*) makes specific reference to mining dialect in the *Erzgebirge* region of Saxony – the dialect being seen as linked with the local beer as part of local pride and culture. In Alsace, an increasing number of children's books are available in written Alsatian. This mini-revolution in using dialects in written texts and in contexts in which they would not have been used before (e.g. television news or by politicians making speeches) reflects a situation in which regional cultures and identities are intensifying and these linguistic varieties are seen as a way of expressing a culture and identity that are specific to a particular part of Germany or a German-speaking country.

Regional and national varieties and dialects are not the only ways of expressing identities and cultures, however. The use of slang or *Umgangssprache* is also an attempt to express an identity, usually tied up with being a member of a group, defined by age (teenagers, for example), occupation (for example, shop-floor workers), etc. *Fachsprache* or specialist language – what we might call jargon – also provides important varieties of German. In almost all professional, scientific and occupational areas there is a body of more or less specialized vocabulary and expressions shared by people who work in that particular sector and which makes them feel part of a particular linguistic group and culture. This notion – and perhaps more importantly awareness of and knowledge about it – is again, arguably, more developed in German-speaking than in English-speaking countries. When using this language such groups create their own mini-cultures, which can serve to include those who do 'speak the language' and exclude those who do not.

A group which has often felt excluded by the German language is women, in fact, it has been claimed that they are often rendered invisible by its patriarchal grammar. An example of this highlighted by Patrick Stevenson (1997) is the fact that only the masculine form of nouns such as '*Student*' and '*Lehrer*' can be used when talking about a mixed group of males and females or when not wanting to specify a particular sex. An alternative to this, which has been promoted by proponents of non-sexist language in Germany and which is in use in a number of sectors of society, is the capital I, as in, *StudentInnen* and *LehrerInnen*. However, this is not included in the revised Duden dictionary, published in 1996 to cover the spelling reform[3]. Furthermore, as one of the foremost feminist linguists, Luise Pusch (1997a), points out, the decision makers in this process of spelling and language reform, the three countries commission and the commission of the Institut der Deutschen Sprache in Mannheim, although representing the major German-speaking countries in Europe, were exclusively male. Despite these shortcomings, Pusch still concludes that 'the process of language change set in motion by women during the last twenty years is the most significant and far-reaching linguistic innovation of the century' (1997b, 323).[4]

If we were asked to think of a multilingual German-speaking country in Europe, Switzerland would perhaps be the first country to come to mind. However, even though Switzerland is officially a multilingual country, all the German-speaking countries are, in practice, multilingual to a greater or lesser extent. In certain regions of Germany, there are speakers of Frisian,

Danish and Sorbian. In addition, like all large economies, Germany has a substantial number of immigrants who have come to that country for a variety of motivations and have lived there for varying lengths of time. Consequently, there are significant numbers of speakers of other languages, for example, Turkish, Slavic languages (e.g. Serbo-Croat, Russian, Polish), Italian, Greek, Arabic and many other European, Asian and African languages. These groups of immigrants are collectively known as *Ausländer*[5] – the term itself is an interesting example, again, of how language reflects culture, legalities, ideologies etc. The word is frequently translated as 'foreigner'. For the English speaker, a foreigner is someone who comes from another country for a brief period of time, a visit or a holiday, however, many of these 'foreigners' were in fact born in Germany, the second or third generation of immigrants who came in the 1960s to fill Germany's need for *Gastarbeiter* (guest or migrant workers). Despite this fact, the term still continues to be used to describe people who have spent most or all of their lives in Germany, but who belong to a different ethnic group. The New Duden (1996) also gives the 'equivalent' for *Ausländer* as 'foreigner', 'alien'. We need to ask ourselves what the effect of using such a word has on the status of these individuals and groups within society. The most significant group of *Ausländer* comprises those individuals of Turkish origin, over 1.8 million. Although not all of these individuals will necessarily have equal competence in speaking the Turkish language or will use it on an everyday basis or even transmit it to their children, they still constitute a very significant minority language group in Germany with their own linguistic culture. For example, the leading Turkish-language tabloid, *Hürriyet*, sells over 400,000 copies in Germany (twice as many as *Die Welt*, for instance) and it is estimated that 86 per cent of Turkish origin households receive Turkish language satellite television programmes via TRT-International (Ohlwein *et al.* 1997, 178).

What all these examples of linguistic and cultural variation show us is that we cannot consider Germany to be simply a linguistically and culturally homogeneous country. While at a national – and indeed an international level – there is the unifying cultural and identity marker of the German language, groups, localities and regions all share various types of 'German' and construct and reinforce a variety of complementary and competing cultures and sub-cultures, the sum of which equate to German language and culture.

Whose German? Whose culture?

A subject like spelling might seem a long way removed from an exciting topic such as culture. However the debates about spelling reform in German which began in the late 1980s opened up a whole discussion of who owns the heart and soul of the German language.

It may seem absurd to the outsiders from the English-speaking world to have institutions and groups who are concerned with the defence and maintenance of those respective languages. Institutions which discuss how new concepts can be described and translated (usually from English) into acceptable forms; bodies which are concerned with domesticating foreign words, by giving them a gender for instance, and deciding when a foreign word has become part of the German language; linguists (and politicians) who are concerned with the 'purity' of the language; and who decide on spelling. To a monolingual English speaker, such issues might never have occurred. There would appear to be very little need to preserve or defend that language, since English is seen by French and German speakers, and in fact speakers of many more languages in the world, as the key culprit and triumphant conqueror here. The idea of a threat to Anglophone culture is as surreal as the actual threat to Francophone and Germanophone cultures is real. *Sprachkultur*, what Patrick Stevenson defines as 'the conscious attempt to cultivate the knowledge and use of the language as the embodiment of the German cultural tradition' (1997, 186), is a very real topic in contemporary German-speaking culture.

The original codification and standardization of German spelling were seen as an important part of linguistic and ultimately national unification from 1871 on. Up to that time, the individual states had had their own separate rulebooks. Karl Duden published his first dictionary in 1880 for all of Germany and in 1901 the rules that were in operation until recently were agreed. When proposals for reform and simplification of German spelling were unveiled in 1988, they 'resulted in media uproar. Every commentator, feature writer, and talk-show host was suddenly an expert on orthography' (Sauer and Glück 1995, 86). A modified version of these new norms is now being implemented on a gradual basis. However, spelling and language norms are not something removed from everyday culture. Spelling is not just the rules, but also how the rules are used in day-to-day communication – and the process is not simply one-way. As Sauer and Glück point out, there has been a good deal of relaxation in spelling norms, not least as a result of everyday use and experimentation with language in advertising and the media.

One thing that invariably strikes the visitor to Germany – in particular, but this applies also to the other German-speaking countries – or the casual viewer/reader of German media is the amount of English words and phrases. Advertising is an area in which the use of English is particularly prominent. Sometimes it may be a simple buzzword or slogan. In other examples, it will be a whole sentence or complex phrase which requires more than a surface knowledge of English. In a number of cases, English is used because the product or service being advertised is of British or American origin. For example, the British brand, Rover, uses the English slogan 'You're welcome' when advertising its cars in Germany. However, the extent of English usage in all areas of the media in German-speaking countries has meaning, use and significance independent of the countries in which it is spoken. Its use may be a symbol of globalism, of youth, of progress and modernity; at one and the same time, it can bear the properties of pan-Europeanness, Americanness and internationalism. For example, an advertisement for Rolf Benz, a furniture manufacturer, contains a number of English vocabulary items, such as '*unser Showroom*'. The text is set against a background graphic of a trendily dressed couple living in an apartment furnished with the most modern furniture. The atmosphere is sophisticated and worldly. The slogan sums this up: 'Rolf Benz: Living at its Best.' Conversely, advertisements for products aimed at an older audience tend to avoid foreign words in favour of their German counterparts in an attempt to appeal to a sense of traditional culture.

There are many reasons for the preponderance of anglicisms or English words in German, particularly in the media. One was the economic aid given to Germany by the USA through the Marshall Plan. This not only contributed to the *Wirtschaftswunder* or economic miracle of the post-war period, but also helped to cement German–American relations. Because of the Cold War and East Germany's allegiance to the Soviet Union, it became inevitable that West Germany would follow a Western orientation in its politics and economics and, in the second half of the twentieth century, this sphere was dominated by the USA. Probably the most significant factor for the quantity of anglicisms today is the omnipresence of American and Anglophone international culture and the status of English as a global lingua franca.

Attitudes towards these anglicisms and their impact on German-speaking culture vary greatly depending on age, education, linguistic abilities, experiences, etc. For every person who feels that they accommodate international communication and openness to other cultures, there is someone else who feels that they are the harbinger of *Denglisch* – the dreaded hybrid of Deutsch and English, spoken by a generation who will master neither language adequately. The Internet and its vocabulary appear for many to have consolidated the position of the English language in German linguistic culture and exemplify the German language's easy access policy regarding foreign words. As Dieter Zimmer (1997) points out, the Germans have only translated 57 per cent of IT and Internet vocabulary into German, far less than the Spanish (80 per cent), the Polish (82 per cent), the French (86 per cent) and the Finnish (93 per cent), despite the fact that German is one of the major European languages. The heated debates that take place on the Internet about these issues illustrate that the topic is hotly contested in Germanophone culture. The following sample of contributions about whether or not to translate the word 'site' speak for themselves:

> Die Fachleute verbinden mit den englischen Begriffen inzwischen klare Vorstellungen, waehrend eine deutsche Uebersetzung zunaechst einmal etabliert werden mueßte.

> (Experts working in the IT area know exactly what is meant by the English words, whereas a German translation would first of all have to become established and accepted.)

Die deutschen Sprachen sind also die Sprachen des Volkes und vielleicht sollte man dem Volk auch die Hoheit ueber die deutschen Sprachen ueberlassen. Oft ist das 'Volk' im Umgang mit neuen Kulturen und Woertern viel unverkrampfter als viele Intellektuelle und Sprachpuristen.

(The Germanic languages are, after all, the languages of the people and perhaps the people should be given control over these languages. Ordinary people are often much less inhibited than many intellectuals and language purists when it comes to new cultures and words.)

Es [kann] gar nicht so schwer sein, deutsche Begriffe fuer den Informatikbereich zu finden. Ich glaube, dass es oft einfach Faulheit ist, wenn wir die englischen Begriffe uebernehmen. Ein(e)(?) web-site waere schlicht und einfach eine Intenet-Adresse.

(It cannot really be that difficult to find German expressions for the IT sector. I think that it is often due to sheer laziness that English terms are used. A web-site is an '*Internet-Adresse*', plain and simple.)

Projekte, die amerikanisch geprägte und international etablierte Fachsprache der Informationstechnologie zu regionalisieren, kann man mit dem gleichen Humor betrachten, als wollten einige Germanisten den Medizinern das Lateinische und Griechische verbieten. Gegen die so entwickelten Sprachkraempfe schlage ich als Therapie freundliches Laecheln vor, solange man uns nicht mit der Kraft des Gesetzes dazu bewegen will, uns daran zu halten.

(Attempts to localize the internationally established language of IT which has been moulded by American English is as crazy as Germanists trying to ban medics from using Latin and Greek. Laughter is the best medicine for these linguistic spasms, just so long as no one is going to try to make us all abide by some rule about this.)

(http://www.dafnett.com.br/diskuss/site001.htm)

Language, culture and external perceptions

A few years ago, following a number of unpleasant incidents, the German School in London decided to issue guidelines to its pupils. One recommendation was to avoid acting provocatively in public, by, for instance, speaking German with each other. It is depressing to think that speaking German in a non-German-speaking country could be perceived as provocative, but it is not perhaps surprising when we consider external attitudes to the German language, particularly among people who have never learned the language and who have only limited encounters with it. Many will comment on what a 'hard' language it is (presumably as opposed to a 'soft' language such as French or an 'easy' language such as English). Mark Twain's famous quotations about the impossibility of the German language (it would, he claimed, take 30 years to master the language, as opposed to 30 hours for English, and 30 days for French), and his conclusion that many German compounds were not words but alphabetic processions, seem to ring true for many who have no knowledge of the German language. Value judgements about languages and the people who speak them are part of our own culture too. After all, how could we feel part of a particular culture if it did not exclude some other people? What would make it special? Many of these stereotypes are formed and fed by our own language via our media. It is hardly surprising that many people have a negative attitude to German, thinking it is an 'aggressive language', since, for most people, their first encounter with the language often takes place through films about the Second World War in which very nasty-looking German soldiers are played by Anglophone actors with a German accent! It may seem rather absurd that such images and encounters inform attitudes towards the German language, but we just have to consider the effect of inserting a German word (or an English word with a 'German' accent) into a sentence. Why does a speaker do this? What effect is s/he trying to achieve? For example, a very negative review of a German restaurant in London which appeared in *The Sunday Times* included vocabulary such as '*Herr*', '*Ja, Ja*' and '*übernationale* cuisine'. The inclusion of these words certainly added to the bilious tone of the review. In a television report about a Star Trek convention, one participant, when asked how to impersonate the fearsome Klingon race, advised that the best thing was probably to look very angry and shout something in German! People are all too familiar with the tabloid headlines in the UK which deliberately use German words, such as '*Achtung*' and '*Herr*' to conjure up negative feelings and associations.

On the other hand, a positive association which the German language appears to have for non-German-speakers internationally and which impacts on their perception of German culture is that of technology. Not surprisingly, this is an association German manufacturers have been keen to exploit when selling their products. As a result, we regularly come across German words in automobile advertisements. The best example of this is Audi's well-known slogan '*Vorsprung durch Technik*', a rather strange slogan which roughly means jumping ahead through technology. The decision was taken not to translate this for advertising in non-German-speaking countries and this clearly paid off for Audi, as it is now one of the best known and recognized advertising slogans and a standard 'German' phrase of the non-German-speaking Anglophone.

While all of these examples may seem fairly harmless, for someone who has little or no contact with German speakers and whose only exposure to the language is through such channels, these very minor encounters with the German language take on a very great significance, summing up for that person and whole groups of people, in a metonymic way, what German culture is. And, because of the history of the first half of the twentieth century, German is often a 'misunderstood' and misrepresented language. The very substantial financial and human resources allocated to cultural and linguistic institutions such as the Goethe Institute are intended to go some way towards improving knowledge and understanding of the German language and by extension German culture internationally.

In conclusion, to come back to the translation class mentioned at the beginning of the chapter, it is important to remember that the apparent coincidence of language, culture, nation, identity, etc. is not something that has existed in perpetuity. We should never make the mistake of assuming a sacred and ancient link between language, culture and identity. Once we start digging beneath what appears to be a prototypical nation–state, we will inevitably unearth someone's hand – politician, preacher, entrepreneur – who has manipulated this combination with some goal in sight, be it ideological, political, religious, economic, etc. Language may not always be the cause, but instead the effect of national culture. As with all languages, encountering German, learning the language and studying the culture are not really about seeking out the 'true' German language and culture; instead they involve opening up to the contradictions and inconsistencies that are the lived linguistic culture.

Notes

1. This is something of a simplification of the Belgian situation, since German is actually one of the three national languages of Belgium (along with French and Dutch/Flemish). For a detailed account of the status of German in Belgium, cf. Nelde and Darquennes (2000). Hogan-Brün (2000) also contains useful accounts of the role and status of German in the Süd Tyrol, Hungary, Alsace and a number of other countries in which German is spoken as a minority language.
2. For a comprehensive history of Lëtzebuergesch, cf. Newton (1996). Hogan-Brün (2000) also contains a chapter on the German language in Luxembourg.
3. The spelling reform is discussed in more detail below.
4. An important point to make here is that there is a danger when considering the important issue of sexist language in assuming that male or masculine language is the norm. A challenging and refreshing accompaniment to any exploration of feminist linguistics is *Masculinity and Language* (1997), edited by two Germanists, Sally Johnson and Ulrike Hanna Meinhof.
5. A number of immigrants, mainly from Russia and other states of the former Soviet Republics, but also from certain other countries in Eastern Europe are afforded special status as *Aussiedler* or ethnic Germans. This is because they come from German-speaking minority groups in these countries.

References

BERNSTEIN, B. 1971: *Social class, language and socialisation*. The Hague: Mouton.

BRAUN, P. 1998: *Tendenzen in der deutschen Gegenwartssprache – Sprachvarietäten.* 4th edition. Stuttgart: Kohlhammer.

CLYNE, M. 1995: *The German language in a changing Europe.* Cambridge: Cambridge University Press.

COULMAS, F. 1995: Germanness: language and nation. In STEVENSON, P. (ed.), *The German language and the real world.* Oxford: Clarendon Press, 55–68.

FULBROOK, M. 1990: *A concise history of Germany.* Cambridge: Cambridge University Press.

GLÜCK, H. and SAUER, W.W. 1995: Norms and reforms: fixing the form of language. In STEVENSON, P. (ed.), *The German language and the real world.* Oxford: Clarendon Press, 95–116.

HOGAN-BRÜN, G. (ed.) 2000: *National varieties of German outside Germany.* Oxford: Peter Lang.

JOHNSON, S. 1998: *Exploring the German language.* London: Arnold.

JOHNSON, S. and MEINHOF, U.H. (eds) 1997: *Masculinity and language.* Oxford: Blackwell.

KELLY-HOLMES, H. 1995: West German banks and East German consumers: a study in intercultural advertising communication., unpublished doctoral thesis, Aston University, UK.

KELLY-HOLMES, H. 1999: United consumers? Advertising discourse and constructions of German identity. In STEVENSON, P. and THEOBALD, J. (eds) *Relocating Germanness. discursive disunity in unified Germany.* London and New York: Macmillan.

MATTHEIER, K.J. 1980: *Pragmatik und Soziologie der Dialekte: Einführung in die Kommunikative Dialektologie des Deutschen.* Heidelberg.

MOOSMULLER, S. 1995: Evaluation of language use in public discourse: language attitudes in Austria. In STEVENSON, P. (ed.), *The German language and the real world.* Oxford: Clarendon Press, 257–78.

NELDE, P. and DARQUENNES, J. 2000: German in old and new Belgium. In HOGAN-BRÜN, G. (ed.), *National varieties of German outside Germany.* Oxford: Peter Lang, 121–38.

NEWTON, G. (ed.) 1996: *Luxembourg and Lëtzebuergesch: language and communication at the crossroads of Europe.* Oxford: Clarendon Press.

OHLWEIN, M., SCHELLHASE, R. and WOLF, B. 1997: Marketing and the marketplace. In REEVES, N.B.R. and KELLY-HOLMES, H. (eds), *The European business environment – Germany.* London and Boston: International Thompson Business Press, 160–211.

OSCHLIES, W. 1989: *Würgende und wirkende Wörter. Deutschsprechen in der DDR.* Berlin: Gebr. Holzapfel.

PUSCH, L. 1997: The New Duden: out of date already? In HERMINGHOUSE, P. and MUELLER, M. (eds), *Gender and Germanness: cultural productions of nation.* Providence and Oxford: Berghahn, 327–30.

PUSCH, L. 1997: Language is publicity for men – but enough is enough! In HERMINGHOUSE, P. and MUELLER, M. (eds), *Gender and Germanness: cultural productions of nation.* Providence and Oxford: Berghahn, 323–6.

SCHÄFFNER, C. and PORSCH, P. 1993: Meeting the challenge on the path to democracy: discursive strategies in government declarations in Germany and the former GDR. *Discourse and Society,* 4 (1), 33–55.

SCHLOSSER, H.D. 1983: Die 'Dialektwelle' – eine Gefahr für die Hochsprache? *Der Sprachdienst* 1983/3–4.

SCHLOSSER, H.D. 1990: *Die deutsche Sprache in der DDR – zwischen Stalinismus und Demokratie.* Cologne: Verlag Wissenschaft und Politik.

SCHNEIDER, P. 1990: *Extreme Mittellage – Eine Reise durch das deutsche Nationalgefühl.* Reinbek bei Hamburg: Rowohlt.

STEVENSON, P. 1997: *The German-speaking world.* London: Routledge.
WRIGHT, S. 2000: *Community and communication: the role of language in state building and European integration.* Clevedon: Multilingual Matters.
ZIMMER, D. 1997: *Deutsch und anders. Die Sprache im Modernisierungsfieber.* Reinbek: Rowohlt.

PART

II

THINGS TO SEE: SPACE, PLACE AND MATERIAL CULTURE

A culture can never be reduced to its artefacts while it is being lived

(Raymond Williams, *Culture and Society*)

Once over the threshold, be it physically, through crossing the German border, or interculturally, by engaging with German material objects, we move from one type of space and one kind of material encounter into another. Space and material culture are intertwined and, as David Harvey (1990, 203–4) has argued space 'has direction, area, shape, pattern and volume as key attributes, as well as distance . . . neither time nor space can be assigned objective meanings independently of material processes'. In the GDR the sharing of material resources equally was an important ideological goal, whereas in West Germany and in post-unification Germany the ability of the individual to amass and control material resources themselves, and for regional rather than state bodies to have some say in their use and allocation have been more to the fore. The relationship between space and materials has become an important aspect of cultural study.

Particular historical and cultural issues come to the fore when questions of space and material culture are asked in the context of contemporary German culture, using the tools of Cultural Studies. In this part such questions are traced, through survey and example, avoiding a reduction to the notion of a 'typical' German style of space or any 'standard' mode of using materials as ways of creating and representing culture. Instead our encounters with space and with material culture are examined for the way in which specific historical events, particular cultural policies and certain political ideologies have left their imprint. This is not to say that the built environment or the materials of German culture that surround us will determine our behaviour but it is to say that space is appropriated and reappropriated culturally in interesting ways that reflect contemporary concerns, uses of power, contemporary understandings of history and of our visions for the future. How we react to space, how we engage with cultural artefacts will also be largely influenced by our own experiences and life histories. Housing exemplifies this. Uniform tower blocks, housing estates, spacious suburban dwellings materialize domestic, everyday life in different ways and our particular experiences of these types of environment travels with us when we encounter other ways of organizing domestic space.

The anthropologist Mary Douglas (Douglas and Isherwood 1996, 67) sees material culture as neutral but the way materials are used as social. How we react to a piece of architecture, a domestic interior, an object on display or a landscape is affective, often occurring as a 'gut feeling' that processes, scans, compares and contrasts, reaching conclusions of liking and disliking in a momentary encounter. It is also important to remember that our experience of cultural artefacts and of the built and natural environment is constantly mediated, as Colin Riordan demonstrates in Chapter 3 on the German Environment and landscape. Our encounters may be mediated through literature, humour, media, history and our diverse cultural experiences. Understanding and critically evaluating these reactions, situating them historically and in the pattern of German culture, through cultural studies, is the aim of this section.

Our encounters with the German landscape and environment and attitudes in Germany towards these are shown in Chapter 3 to have important historical and political roots. In order to understand how a sense of 'Germanness' has been constructed and linked to landscape and the environment, this chapter traces the varied responses to the German environment through the ideologies of left and right into the contemporary period. The scale and significance of Germany as a culturally environmental nation are also discussed with the facts and statistics which point to environmental concern also tested and questioned. Germany may be largely experienced as a highly environmental culture but equally there are contradictions and paradoxes which help us to avoid simple assumptions about environmentalism in Germany. Literature, cartoons, film and media are all cultural artefacts through which we may encounter the complexity of German environmentalism and attitudes to the German landscape and these are discussed for their contribution to political ecology in Germany.

In Chapter 4 Gillian Pye engages with architecture and with public spaces in Germany. It discusses the importance of analysing the built environment in order to illuminate the dynamics of form and function, past and present, future and cultural vision. Again, we do not find a survey of 'typical' and stereotypical German form and style, but rather a questioning of such reductive notions through site-specific examples. Here we see the way in which an international and intercultural concern is shaping the face of contemporary Germany through two specific, yet differing examples. What the detailed analysis of these examples of the Jewish Museum in Berlin and the IBA Emscher Park Project gives us is a sense of current cultural concerns being give form and engaging with the past and shaping space for the future. Both projects provide excellent sites for Cultural Studies to engage with questions of identity, responsibility and power.

Major political and economic upheavals are felt in the spaces we inhabit – not only the public spaces but also in the homes and domestic spaces where we live our 'private' lives. Chapter 5 by Lois Weinthal examines some of the tensions and limits that the different configurations of domestic space may impose upon homemaking and the way in which the policies of those in power directly affected the kinds of homes that were built in the recent past and now survive in the contemporary period. Berlin's homes are selected as a focus for the discussion of issues of cultural identity and housing policy. The differences between the housing policies of East and West, magnified in the strategic and symbolic city of Berlin, thus provide a fascinating focus for a discussion of tangible expressions of collective and individual identities and of the changing sense of home and domestic space in post-unification Germany. Here the focus is not on lines of difference, of race, gender or class, but along the surviving, tangible lines of ideology. Theories of the difference between notions of 'space' and of 'place' and of affective ties to a home over time are also used to examine some of the complex issues at play in the development of new homes and a new sense of *Heimat* in contemporary Germany.

Museums, as Chapter 6 by Sharon McDonald demonstrates, make for intriguing sites of cultural study. In them are housed, in tangible form, objects specially and publicly selected to display our understandings of the past and of our cultural heritage. Museums help to make and materialize identities and they do so by providing specially constructed spaces for this purpose. Museums, like architecture, also provide a more lasting site of cultural expression than, for instance, theatre or the media, which are more ephemeral forms. This chapter provides a survey of the different types of German museum and the purposes they have served and continue to serve in the present. It shows how museums and their displays have been especially bound into ideas of national identity and how, as these questions have been problematized, not least in Cultural Studies, museums have themselves become sites of contest and debate, most especially in a culture where the last century has provided several occasions for a reconstruction of national identity.

References

DOUGLAS, M. and ISHERWOOD, B 1996: *The world of goods: towards an anthropology of consumption.* 2nd edn. London and New York: Routledge.
HARVEY, D. 1990: *The condition of postmodernity: an enquiry into the origins of cultural change.* Oxford: Blackwell.
WILLIAMS, R. *Culture and society.* London: The Hogarth Press.

|3|

Environment, landscape and culture in Germany

BY COLIN RIORDAN

In 1928 the left-wing German satirist Kurt Tucholsky wrote a parallel list of personal likes and dislikes. The dislikes included cauliflower, the likes, properly sharpened pencils. One word appears in both columns; under dislikes in inverted commas as '"Deutschland"', under likes simply as 'Deutschland' (Tucholsky 1985a, 7). What the writer and journalist hated was the chauvinist, militaristic parody of Germany portrayed by German nationalists and indicated by the inverted commas. What he loved about the country, it emerges from a later illustrated essay called 'Heimat' ('Homeland'), was the landscape; to be 'in den Bergen, wo Feld und Wiese in die kleinen Straßen sehen, am Rand der Gebirgsseen, wo es nach Wasser und Holz und Felsen riecht, und wo man einsam sein kann' (in the mountains, where field and meadow look into the small streets, on the edge of the mountain lakes, where it smells of water and wood and rock-faces, and where one can be alone) (Tucholsky 1985b, 313). Tucholsky here is using landscape to articulate a sense of belonging, an alternate sense of Germanness in a way which has been characteristic of German culture for centuries, and which can still be detected today. Landscape as a cultural denominator was perhaps an unfortunate choice, for whether Tucholsky knew it or not, the German landscape had long been used by the writer's right-wing opponents and their predecessors in order precisely to define what it meant to belong to the German nation. Nevertheless, while in today's Germany landscape is less often enlisted in debates over patriotism and nationalism, the natural and built environment are still crucial elements in the country's understanding of itself.

Environmental commitment in Germany

Modern empathy with landscape almost always implies a commitment to its protection in the face of the ravages caused by industrial development.

Commitment of that kind is everywhere apparent in contemporary Germany. Any traveller to the country is struck by the way in which the public is invited to dispose of litter in one of four colour-coded receptacles, dividing it into paper, packaging, glass and other to make recycling easier. What is even more striking to the anglophone observer is that people conventionally comply; Germany has the highest rate of paper recycling in the EU, according to 1999 figures (*Common Ground* 2/2000, 5). Any visitor would also notice the numbers of bicycles and dedicated cycle lanes: by the end of 1998, 65 million bicycles were owned in Germany, which represents one for every German able to cycle (*Common Ground Climate Special* 1999). While the presence of bicycles does not necessarily mean that they are used, nor that all bicycle use is related to concern for the environment, a regular survey on environmental consciousness conducted by the German government nonetheless shows a high level of environmental awareness in the country. In 2000, only 6 per cent regarded *Umweltschutz* (environmental protection) as of little or no importance. Germans, it seems, have accepted the *Ende oder Wende* (change or die) argument and are prepared to make personal sacrifices to achieve it: 71 per cent of those surveyed in 2000 were prepared to pay more for environmentally friendly products (Kuckartz 2000, 8). As Kuckartz puts it:

> Die Bevölkerung ist überwiegend von der Notwendigkeit des Umweltschutzes überzeugt. Die Mehrheit glaubt, dass die Grenzen des Wachstums erreicht sind und wir auf eine Umweltkatastrophe zusteuern, wenn so weitergewirtschaftet wird wie bisher.

> (The population is overwhelmingly convinced of the necessity of environmental protection. The majority believes that the limits to growth have been reached and that we are heading for an environmental catastrophe if we carry on the way we have been.)

> (ibid., 20)

Few, then, would disagree that the environment and its protection play a strikingly important role in contemporary German culture in the widest sense.

Yet it would be wrong merely to assume from this that questions of landscape and environment loom large in the lives of all the German population all the time. On closer examination, more ambivalent and differentiated attitudes can be detected. Although in September 1998 Germany elected a Green Party into government, Bündnis90/Die Grünen still only received 6.7 per cent of the vote, and owe their position in government to a coalition with the much bigger centre-left SPD (Social Democratic Party), made necessary by Germany's system of proportional representation. Moreover, despite an apparent commitment to the environment, there are still areas where many are reluctant to make the kinds of compromises that effective action on pollution and climate change would demand. For example, Germany's love affair with the motor car shows no sign of abating. There is still no majority in favour of speed limits on motorways, and 40 per cent remain against any speed limit on the motorway (Kuckartz 2000, 7). Even though more than 90 per cent favour the expansion of the public transport network, almost 40 per cent claim they would not change their behaviour even if the price of petrol were to be doubled (ibid., 58). The advance of the car in Germany, then, seems unlikely to be significantly obstructed in the near future.

Perhaps more seriously, there is less evidence than one might expect of a particular commitment to the environment among young Germans. A study designed to find out whether there is such a thing as an 'ecological conscience', carried out by the Heinrich-Böll-Stiftung, unsurprisingly found that environmental activists all over the world did recognize in themselves a sense of responsibility for the environment, and that there was a gap between the well-developed ecological conscience evident among younger people and comparative indifference about the extent of ecological crisis among adults. Notably, however, young Germans were singled out as the most pessimistic surveyed as far as the environment is concerned (Sohr 2000). Other studies show similar results. The best-known survey of youth attitudes in Germany is the regular *Shell Jugendstudie*, which attempts to convey the views of young people themselves, allowing them to set the agenda, rather than approaching attitudes among teenagers from a pre-conceived adult perspective. Surprisingly, the summary of the findings of the 2000 study mentions the environment in passing only once, while the study itself seems to suggest that mobile phones, Internet access and ultimately a good job followed by the chance to start a family are of much greater interest to most young people in Germany than is the future of the climate or Agenda 21 (Fischer 2000).

Environmental awareness among the general public in Germany, though demonstrably high, seems to show similar gaps. Familiarity with a key term such as *Nachhaltigkeit* (sustainable development) is a case in point. Sustainable development has existed as a concept since 1987, and was highlighted at the UN conference in Rio de Janeiro in 1992 as the most important plank of effective environmental action. When the two formerly separate environmentally concerned parties Bündnis90 (formed in the GDR) and the West German Die Grünen merged in 1993, their thoroughly revised programme based its whole social and economic policy on the principles of sustainable development. Yet the 2000 survey shows that '*Nachhaltigkeit*' is a term familiar to only 13 per cent of Germans (ibid., 68).[1] However, the survey also established that notwithstanding most people's ignorance of the term, there was overwhelming support for its central principles. Respondents gave massive assent to statements such as 'Es sollte Gerechtigkeit zwischen den Generationen bestehen, wir sollten die Umwelt nicht auf Kosten der nachkommenden Generationen ausplündern'

(There should be justice between the generations, we should not plunder the environment at the cost of succeeding generations) (Kuckartz 2000, 69). Clearly, people in Germany believe that their right to enjoy the natural world also imposes duties and responsibilities. This strong ethical sense does reflect the importance in German culture of nature and the way we treat it.

Although it is clear from the above that it would be a mistake uncritically to assume that all Germans are by nature environmentalists, it would not be an exaggeration to say that there is a cultural assumption in favour of nature and its protection which is particularly strong in Germany. A number of international studies have shown that 'die Deutschen in ganz besonderem Maße von Umweltängsten geplagt werden' (the Germans are particularly plagued by fears relating to the environment), and display a 'hohe Sensibilität für Umweltrisiken' (a high sensitivity to environmental risk) (ibid., 77). Indeed, it seems that so far as the environment is concerned, the fear and pessimism in Germany can reach apocalyptic levels:

> Mehr als 90% rechnen mit einer Erwärmung des Klimas und 86% damit, dass die globale Umweltverschmutzung zunimmt. Nur eine 1% Minderheit äußert dezidiert, dies werde nicht eintreffen. Auch andere Horrorszenarien werden von einer Bevölkerungsmehrheit für wahrscheinlich gehalten: Gutes Trinkwasser wird knapp und es wird kriegerische Auseinandersetzungen um Rohstoffe und Wasserreserven geben.

> (More than 90 per cent expect global warming to take place and 86 per cent believe that global environmental pollution will increase. Only a minority of 1 per cent express a clear view that this will not happen. A majority of the population also believes other horrific scenarios to be probable: good drinking water will become scarce and open hostilities will break out over natural resources and water reserves.) (Kuckartz 2000, 78–9)

Illogically, however, most also believe that the state of the environment will tend to improve in the future. Be that as it may, we can conclude that landscape and environment do indeed play a more important role in Germany than in other countries.

But is the role of the environment in Germany restricted to questions of pollution, health, quality of life and sustainable development? This chapter will show that it is not, and that issues of a broadly environmental nature actually have deep roots in German culture with connections to fundamental questions of what it means to be German. Although there is no question that environmental awareness has crept inexorably up the public agenda since the publication of the Club of Rome's *Limits to Growth* in 1972, elements of environmental awareness can be detected in Germany long before this.

Roots of environmental thinking

Elsewhere I have had this to say about the origins of environmental thinking in Germany:

> Everyday environmentalism is only the visible evidence of a more profound, enduring and well-established cultural phenomenon. Donald Worster has found that the science of ecology is, perhaps more than mathematics or thermodynamics, the product of 'specific cultural conditions' (Worster 1995, p. ix). In Germany, green ideas have a peculiar and complex resonance: their historical associations are diverse and splintered, ranging from Romantic nature-philosophy to anthroposophy, from anarcho-socialism to fascism, from heady nationalism to scientific apocalypse. A historical and contemporary consideration of the influence of green thought on German culture is, then, a product of the recognition that green thought is indivisible from German culture.
>
> (Riordan 1997, ix)

This is not the place to reiterate in detail the historical associations mentioned above, but it will be helpful to outline broadly the way in which environmental ideas have developed in German culture in the broadest sense. Raymond H. Dominick III has recorded the long history of conservation movements in Germany. His (1992) book *The Environmental Movement in Germany: Prophets and Pioneers, 1871–1971* has shown the way in which there have been organizations with a mass membership formed with the aim of protecting features of the natural environment in Germany for more than a century. Dominick traces the earliest protests as far back as 1715, and shows how they multiplied with the onset of industrialization. Ironically, given our modern concern for renewable sources of energy, hydroelectric projects were frequently targets because of their aesthetic impact on river and mountain scenery previously untouched by development. The result was, Dominick shows, that by 1914 there were 10,000 publications on *Naturschutz* (nature protection) (1992, 69). Membership of conservation groups remained high throughout the twentieth century, continuing during and after the Second World War. In 1954, for example, the umbrella organisation *Deutscher Naturschutzring* (German Nature Protection Association) comprised 62 groups numbering three-quarters of a million members (ibid., 121). It is clear from Dominick's research that large numbers of people in Germany have been mobilized in the defence of landscape for generations. The question is, why should this have happened? One of the reasons was the way in which landscape was used as part of the most important political debate of nineteenth-century Germany: that concerning the creation of a unified German state for the first time.

Before its unification in 1871, Germany had consisted of a confederation of more than 1800 states and statelets; some city-states, many princedoms and bishoprics, and some large states such as Bavaria, Württemberg and Prussia. One of the problems facing those arguing for national unity in the face of such diversity was how to define Germany, and what it meant to be German. Language was certainly a major unifying factor, although linguistic diversity militated against using this as an absolute measure, especially since it was clearly not a realistic political aim to unite every single German-speaking (or German-dialect-speaking) community in a single state (see Chapter 2). From the earliest part of the nineteenth century, then, landscape and a particular relationship with nature were pressed into service as defining elements in the German psyche; as distinctive markers of Germanness.

In 1819 Ernst Moritz Arndt, for example, an early vocal proponent of German nationalism, exhorted German youth to reject the degeneracy of urban life for the fields and the forest, valleys and mountains, since the Germans were characterized by 'Naturliebe, ein stilles Verständnis, eine innige Freundschaft und ein zarter Umgang mit der Natur' (Love of nature, a quiet understanding, an intimate friendship and gentle way of dealing with nature) (Arndt 1910–19, 246). His pupil Wilhelm Heinrich Riehl, in the middle of the century, argued that the continued existence of the forest and of wilderness in Germany was the guarantee of national success, by contrast with England and France, whose loss of forestry reserves had left them fatally weakened. By the 1880s, then, the musician and nationalist Fritz Rudorff was able to draw on tradition in asserting that the very essence of Germanness lay in the trees, forests, rivers and mountains of the new Empire (see Riordan 1997, 10 and 14).

But at the core of the nationalists' attitude to nature lay a grave paradox. The nationalist movement relied on the rise of the bourgeoisie for its ultimate success. It was only through the capitalist ventures of the middle classes that Germany could industrialize, and rapid industrialization was essential for the nationalist project. Any future unification of Germany depended on strong military power, and the efficient central administration of a new greater Germany was reliant on modern, efficient communication systems. The explosive growth of railways in the second third of the nineteenth century provided both the communications and the transport system for the very rapid economic and industrial expansion Germany needed if it hoped to catch up with the much earlier industrialization which had taken place in the chief competitors such as Britain and France. But as the century progressed, the negative effects of industrialization both on human health and on the landscape became increasingly apparent. Berlin, the capital of the new *Kaiserreich* after 1871, became a smoky city with heavily polluted waterways, for example, and tracts of previously untouched countryside were occupied by industrial developments. The nationalists were thus faced with a dilemma: the demands of the national economy versus the impact of economic expansion on a landscape venerated as a defining feature of the nation. As has so often been the case since, the economic demands almost always prevailed. But the central problem of political ecology under capitalism, that of how to expand the economy while reducing as far as possible the impact on nature, was certainly recognized in Germany as early as the nineteenth century, even if it was not acted upon effectively.

The association between conservative ideology and green ideas reached its most extreme form under National Socialism. There were a number of reasons for this. One was the legacy of the nationalist movement described above; the German landscape, its soil, became mystically intertwined with the soul of Germany. The farmers who tilled the land were held to embody the destiny of the race, and they were declared the 'new nobility' by an important early Nazi ideologue, Richard Walther Darré. Darré was to become the minister responsible for agriculture in the new Nazi state, and he attempted to introduce a policy of self-sufficiency through organic farming. His attempt was forestalled by Goering in 1942, but Darré was partly responsible for associating notions of low environmental impact and landscape protection with virulent racial hatred (see Bramwell 1985). Even before National Socialism, it was a short step from wishing to preserve the purity of the German landscape to wishing to protect the purity of the German race. Some people associated environmental pollution with racial pollution of Germans by immigrants (see Dominick 1992, 88). Nature conservation, then, was exploited in the early years of the regime to try to create a coherent basis for a set of ideas that was in fact wholly misconceived. In practical terms, however, environmentalism was accorded a much lower priority than the central demands of the economy and of military expansion. Although certain measures were taken, for instance to try to make the new autobahns fit as harmoniously as possible into the landscape, and to protect wild animals, the actual effects were very limited and far outweighed by the catastrophic human and environmental cost of the war.

As we learned at the outset, love of the German landscape was by no means solely the preserve of the political right. Today, green politics tends on the whole to be associated much more with left-of-centre attitudes, and indeed there is a long history of such an association in Germany. Both Marx and Engels stressed the importance of the relationship between human beings and nature, and the first leader of the SPD, August Bebel, had far-sighted views on matters such as deforestation and renewable energy sources. There was even a socialist environmental campaigning group, active at the beginning of the twentieth century, known as the 'Naturfreunde' (Friends of Nature). They protested against a variety of attacks on nature by industry, including the felling of forests, the building of factories, quarrying, and digging for peat. Moreover, it is possible to argue that the earliest recognizable forerunners of modern eco-warriors were active in Germany in the first 20 or 30 years of the twentieth century. One of the ways in which people began to react against the industrial revolution of the nineteenth century was in the form of 'back-to-nature' movements; a desire to abandon the trappings of modern life, to leave the city and to live off the land harmoniously with nature. This kind of reaction was particularly pronounced in Germany: the oldest members of the population at the beginning of the twentieth century would have had memories of when the country was still largely rural, and relatively untouched by the advance of industry. Some adherents of the settlement movement tried to combine the tenets of socialism with a respect for nature and a desire to inflict as little damage on it as possible. Green socialist revolutionaries such as Leberecht Migge and Paul Robien rejected industrial society altogether and proposed living in small communities using resources in a sustainable way. They argued for many of the elements that one would recognize today as part of a green credo: a reduction in consumption, animal rights, the preservation of wilderness, an international approach to environmental protection, organic cultivation and recycling (see Linse 1986).

Groups such as this, it has to be said, were very marginal and have largely been forgotten. It would be difficult to argue that they had any lasting influence, and the interest in the environment which we find in Germany today is actually a product of very different circumstances. Nevertheless, it is clear even from this brief outline of some aspects of German green history that recognizable elements of contemporary green ideas have been present in German culture for generations. Research is also increasingly beginning to show that assumptions, fears and prognostications related to the environment and the fate of the earth have actually been present in German cultural artefacts for generations also.

Environmental encounters in literature

In literature, it is not difficult to find expressions of unease at the way human beings treat nature. Even in the early nineteenth century we can find descriptions of damage to the natural environment, coupled with a lament for the loss of a natural idyll. Karl Immermann in *Die Epigonen* (*The Imitators*) (1836) describes how a character views the ravages caused to the landscape by dye-works in a beautiful valley:

> Diese anmuthige Hügel- und Waldnatur schien ihm durch sie entstellt und zerfetzt zu seyn ... Um alle Sinne aus der Fassung zu bringen, lagerte sich über der ganzen Gegend ein mit widerlichen Gerüchen geschwängerter Dunst, welcher von den vielen Färbereien und Bleichen herrührte.

> (The pleasant natural scene of hills and forests seemed to him to be distorted and ravaged by them ... Disrupting all the senses, a fog pregnant with disgusting smells hung over the whole area, having emanated from the many dye-works and bleaching grounds.)

> (Immermann 1836a, 20)

The ultimate reaction to this destruction of nature is profoundly pessimistic, however. There seems no hope of stopping the advance of industrialisation with all its environmental consequences:

> Mit Sturmesschnelligkeit eilt die Gegenwart einem trockenen Mechanismus zu; wir können ihren Lauf nicht hemmen, sind aber nicht zu schelten, wenn wir für uns und die Unsrigen ein grünes Plätzchen abzäunen und diese Insel solange als möglich gegen den Sturz der vorbeirauschenden industriellen Wogen befestigen

> (The present day is hurrying like the wind towards a dry mechanistic condition; we cannot stop its progress, but should not be scolded if we fence off a small green area for ourselves and our families, and fortify this island for as long as possible against the pounding of the industrial waves as they rush by.)

> (Immermann 1836b, 436)

At that stage, then, industrialization appeared as inevitable, the only recourse being conservationism, the preservation of a particular area of landscape on primarily aesthetic grounds.

Further similar examples could be cited from later in the nineteenth century and throughout the twentieth century. After the publication of the Club of Rome report *The Limits to Growth* in 1972 there was, as one would expect, a surge in the production of texts which bear the imprint of environmental concern. Strikingly, even in the contemporary enlightened period of ecological awareness and activism, expressions of impotence in the face of the advance of industry still dominate. The cultural pessimism of contemporary Germans with respect to the environmental future is amply reflected in German-language fiction since 1972. Even though modern writers have a vast armoury of fact and argument at their disposal, contemporary literature still has overwhelmingly negative implications so far as the environment is concerned. A text such as *Der Mensch erscheint im Holozän* (*Man Appears in the Holocene*) (1979) by Max Frisch (a Swiss writer, but operating to all intents and purposes in German culture) is a case in point. This text makes explicit reference to the global consequences of environmental damage, extrapolating not just from the local erosion and flooding of a Swiss valley, but also from the thought-processes of its senile protagonist to the whole of the human race in our relationship with nature. The approach, however, is diagnostic, not prescriptive. This is not a green political tract, but an exposure of the state of the human race in geological perspective, on the time-scale of the earth itself; a reminder of our insignificant status in the universal order of things. That is, the human race is in a much more precarious position than it realizes, or likes to think. This predicament is encapsulated in the phrase 'Die Natur kennt keine Katastrophen' (There are no catastrophes for nature) (Frisch 1979, 103). A 'natural catastrophe' is only catastrophic to us, not to nature.

The possibility of global catastrophe was a preoccupation in the 1980s, perhaps nowhere so much as in Germany. During that period the danger of nuclear warfare seemed acute, as indeed did the possibility of nuclear reactor meltdown and ecological apocalypse.[2] To name just two of the most prominent and well-known writers of the post-war generation, from the former East and West Germanies respectively, both Christa Wolf and Günter Grass gave expression to widely held fears of global environmental destruction. In her story *Störfall. Nachrichten eines Tages* (*Disruption: The News of One Day*) (1987), Wolf's narrator ruminates in the days following the disastrous reactor meltdown at Chernobyl in 1986, trying to discover how humankind ever got into a position whereby we cause such immense damage to ourselves and the environment. The whole story is shot through with cultural references which shed light on the way in which the relationship between people and nature was so violently disrupted during the course of the last century. Günter Grass's *Die Rättin* (*The She-Rat*) (1986) is a satirical dystopic vision of a world destroyed by nuclear war, but unusually in the genre, Grass leaves a window of hope in the possibilities of literature. In Grass's *Unkenrufe* (*The Call of the Toad*) (1992) the ecological question is presented in far less apocalyptic if equally satirical tones, but nevertheless broaches issues of contemporary concern such as global climate change, limited fossil fuel resources and the problem of transport. The view of the future here is not quite so bleak: the global nature of the environmental problem is matched by potential global solutions (though expressed with heavy irony) in the form of the disintegration of nation–states and cultural migration.

The above refers to only a small fraction of German literature with relevance to environmental issues. In common with other cultural artefacts, German literature offers no solutions to the problems of political ecology, but unlike some, it does have a number of diagnoses. In that way, perhaps, it is no worse and no better than much of Green politics. But there are other methods of cultural dissemination which have regularly focused on the environment; cartoonists in particular have found much material on which to sharpen their satirical knives.

Cartoonists on the environment

There is a valuable resource on cartoons about the environment in the form of a catalogue arising from an exhibition of German and British cartoonists mounted by the German Embassy in the UK, entitled *A Common Cause – Our Environment/Unsere Umwelt – eine gemeinsame Sache*, published by the Press Department of the Embassy of the Federal Republic of Germany, London (no date). In a brief introduction, Reiner Lukyen of the German weekly paper *Die Zeit* makes the following point:

Quite a few of the cartoons in this collection are dark prophecies of a looming catastrophe. They don't really stir you to laugh. Those British contributions which stick most in the mind are the funny ones. German cartoonists (and artists in general) wish permanently to 'bring about change'. Most British cartoonists in this exhibition are quite happy just to caricature human weaknesses. They don't want to change the world all the time. The cartoonists reflect a fundamentally different outlook in both countries

(p. 15)

That is perhaps rather unfair on the German cartoonists, but there is no doubt that a dark and pessimistic tone pervades the volume. The German cartoons do show a higher frequency of political satire as well as extreme scepticism about the prospects for real reform, but they tend on the whole to draw attention primarily to the plight of nature. The section on global climate change is perhaps the best example of this. Of the six cartoons reproduced, two were published in the British press, and four in the German press. Both of those which appeared in Britain satirize the hypocrisy of many of the participants in the global climate conferences in Rio (1992) and New York (1995). Louis Hellmann's cartoon shows the exhaust fumes produced by the hundreds of flights necessary to convey the '128 heads of state' which the caption says were due to attend the earth summit. Similarly Peter Schrank (a cartoonist of Swiss extraction working in London) shows Bill Clinton, driving a huge American car with seven exhaust pipes, roaring past the earth drawn as a hitch hiker vainly attempting to thumb a lift to the New York summit.

By contrast, three of the four German cartoons take a much more eco-centric approach, focusing on the plight of the earth and of the environment itself. Pepsch Gottscheber, on the occasion of the New York environmental summit in 1995, shows the earth as a rotten apple riddled with worms that are clearly the delegates to the conference. Although this is a satirical barb aimed at the industrialized nations, it is the earth itself which is placed centre stage. Similarly, Rolf Henn depicts the environment as a half-dead, hacked-about tree held together with crutches, bandages and sticking plaster. Dogs labelled 'World Economic Summit' and 'UN Conference' are relieving themselves on it. The contempt of such occasions for the genuine plight of the environment is all too apparent, but it is nature in distress which occupies the central position. Fritz Behrendt shows characters representing the world's nations queuing up to milk the world; the German 'Michel' sits dismayed on the milking-stool, only able to produce a few drops. This graphic illustration of the limits to growth does not even bother to attack the iniquity of humankind: the implication is that in exploiting nature beyond the limit, we will damage ourselves in a far more thorough-going manner than any cartoonist could hope to. The fourth German cartoon, by Heiko Sakurai, does highlight the futility of repeated talks at

summits with no effective action, in a series of three cartoons. Three delegates are shown around a table on a summit surrounded by sea. They sit
without speaking, arms folded. In the sea around them people are drowning
and reaching for help. The first picture, captioned Rio 1992, shows the level
some way from the summit. In the second, showing the 1995 climate conference in Berlin, the sea is much closer. The third, at some indeterminate
point in the future, shows the entire area submerged: only the tops of the
heads of the three delegates are visible. This is a graphic depiction of Max
Frisch's dictum mentioned earlier, 'Die Natur kennt keine Katastrophen'
(There are no catastrophes for nature).

Catastrophic flooding became a reality in Germany in January 1995 as
several German rivers broke their banks. Horst Haitzinger's reaction was
a cartoon rather similar to the one by Sakurai described above. In it, a
clueless politician sits on a pile of files on his desk, floating amid the
floods. The files are labelled 'Umweltpolitik' (environmental policy),
'Landschaftsverbetonierung' (concreting over the landscape) and
'Flussbegradigungen' (river-straightening). Next to them lies a rubber stamp
bearing the legend 'genehmigt' (permission granted). The contradictions
and confusions which characterize the policy mix in industrialized countries
are to be found in Germany just as elsewhere. The attitude to cars in
Germany, as outlined above, reflects the same problem. Our tendency to
believe that we have the policies necessary to keep environmental damage
under control is satirized by Erik Liebermann, who shows a man reading a
newspaper with the headline 'alles unter Kontrolle' (everything under
control). Behind him, however, is a huge net containing the detritus of
industrial society, from bottles to tyres to old TVs and computers. The net
is attached to a fuse and is clearly due to explode over the oblivious newspaper reader. Another cartoon by Horst Haitzinger argues that despite all
the environmental rhetoric, and the building of environmental topics into
the school curriculum, our attitude to the environment is characterized
mainly by complacency, in Germany as elsewhere. A teacher points to the
North Sea on an unlabelled map, and a pupil responds by calling it 'Totes
Meer' (The Dead Sea). The teacher is beaming as he confirms 'richtig'
(correct). The cartoonists, then, expose the contradictions, ineffectiveness
and resignation which underlie the rhetoric of world summits and individual governments.

Environmentalism in the German media

The German media have focused on environmental issues consistently since
the beginning of the 1950s. Raymond H. Dominick cites the popularity of
Otto Kraus's documentary *Natur in Gefahr* (Nature in Jeopardy), made in
1952, for example (Dominick 1992, 197). While it is commonplace today
for newspapers to have special environmental sections, reports and corres-

pondents, Dominick has analysed back issues to show that, for example, *Der Spiegel* contained much detailed, informed environmental reporting between 1957 and 1964, while the *Frankfurter Allgemeine Zeitung* reported more frequently on the environment in 1959–60 than it did in 1969–70 (ibid., 189 and 184). It was *Der Spiegel* which first broke the story of *Waldsterben* (forest die-back) in Germany in November 1981, causing a wave of public concern which fed the burgeoning Green Party. TV and films have continued to reflect and propagate such concern, both in fiction and documentary (see also Chapters 12 and 13). Werner Herzog is an exponent of both forms, and Tom Cheesman has shown how preoccupations with landscape, the problems of progress, environmental destruction and apocalypse characterize his films. Herzog's film-making, Cheesman argues, places nature at the forefront: 'his fascination with landscape, with the aesthetics of nature, distinguishes him from all his peers in the new German cinema' (1997, 292). Television, too, is a primary channel for the dissemination of opinion and information on the environment. The TV reporter and qualified theologian Franz Alt has specialized in making polemical programmes on environmental issues, transmitted on the ARD and 3–Sat networks with titles such as *Klimaschutz schafft Arbeitsplätze* (Climate protection creates jobs), and *Mobil ohne Auto* (Mobile without a car). Alt is more than a reporter on these matters; he is an eco-evangelist, synthesizing Christianity and ecology in his book *Der ökologische Jesus* (1999).

The prevalence of environmental issues in the media has been sufficient to prompt the founding of an institute to record and theorize its manifestations. Freiburg im Breisgau, which has long been a centre for green activism, is home to the Öko-Media Institut (Institute for Eco-Media), founded in 1984 in the belief that the media are the most important influencers of opinion. The institute's founders put it like this:

Um überleben zu können, müssen wir umdenken. Den Medien, vor allem auch den Bildmedien, kommt dabei eine zentrale Bedeutung zu, denn sie sind heute zu den wichtigsten Trägern von Information geworden.

Ökologisch orientierte und engagierte Medien, aber auch eine entsprechende Medienpolitik und Medienarbeit sind heute notwendiger denn je. Nur wenn sich bei der Bevölkerung und Regierenden gleichermaßen ein neues ökologisches Bewußtsein bildet, kann unsere Zukunft gesichert werden.

(In order to survive, we need to re-think. In that process the media, above all the visual media, are of central significance, since they are today some of the most important carriers of information.

Ecologically oriented and committed media, along with a corresponding media policy and operation, are today more necessary than

ever. Only when a new ecological consciousness is formed in the population and government alike can our future be secured.)

(Founding statement of the Öko-Media Institut, Freiburg,
11 April 1984)

In pursuit of these aims, the Institute has been holding a film festival annually since 1984, showing on average 30 films chosen from more than 400
submitted from all over the world. There are no prescriptions except that
the films should be creatively oriented towards nature, ecology and the environment. Prizes are awarded and a substantial archive has been built up in
the meantime. The best films tour the whole country, and there is a particular emphasis on work by and for young people. This kind of commitment to
the raising of ecological consciousness is emblematic of the importance of
such issues in Germany, despite all the contradictions and caveats mentioned above. For some, indeed, environmental commitment can become
the central determining factor of life.

Living the environment in Germany

In Germany as elsewhere in the world, there are communities where those
people gather whose decision to act ecologically expresses itself in the establishment of a whole new way of life. As described above, communities living
in harmony with nature have existed in Germany since the nineteenth
century, and the present-day international ecovillages movement is strongly
represented there too.[3] Ecovillages try to keep their environmental impact to
a minimum, and to live in a co-operative and mutually supportive way which
uses green design and technology to the limits. The precepts of sustainabil-
ity are paramount. Just one example of at least 15 such communities existing in present-day Germany is the Lebensgarten settlement near the village
of Steyerberg in Lower Saxony. Established in 1986, the settlement made
use of terraced housing originally built in 1938 for munition workers in the
Third Reich. The 4-hectare site is now home to 70 adults and 45 children,
who aim to live together in respect and tolerance both for each other and for
nature. The settlement has its own constitution which seeks consensus as far
as possible. The settlers have a communal building and a meeting hall
housing 200, and organize common tasks through distribution of responsibility. The houses have been renovated according to ecological practice. The
businesses run from the premises include a variety of educational enterprises
as well as a homeopathic practice, an ecological architect's practice and an
ecological builder's merchants. The inhabitants thus practise everyday
ecology, and their desire to live in harmony with nature informs all aspects
of their lives, from transport to food to waste management.

Naturally, consensus is not always possible, and in no sense can this form
of settlement necessarily be regarded as a utopian ideal. Lebensgarten, in

common with other such settlements, still depends to some degree on financial support in the form of sponsors or donors in order to continue the development of the site; it is simply not possible to live in a manner wholly detached from global capitalism. Nor is the ecological imperative absolute: although the inhabitants do strive to minimize their environmental impact, they nevertheless still use cars, though they have invested in electric automotive technology and pool the vehicles. What is interesting for our topic, however, is the way in which this community's holistic approach sees an intimate connection between ecological and cultural fulfilment. Artists and musicians live in the colony, while communal singing and dancing are an integral part of life there, as is meditation. Concerts take place in the hall, and have included a performance by the Stuttgart Chamber Orchestra. The same sort of connection can be seen in another experimental ecological colony, a site of approximately 15 hectares sited at Belzig, about 80 km south-west of Berlin, called ZEGG, which stands for Zentrum für Experimentelle Gesellschafts-Gestaltung (Centre for Experimental Forms of Society). Like Lebensgarten, ZEGG lays great stress on communal living and on techniques such as meditation to resolve conflicts and build consensus. At ZEGG, ecological values are inseparable from human values such as curiosity, contact, knowledge and love. ZEGG's experiment with ecological living extends beyond arrangements one might expect, such as a well-developed sewage-composting system, to embrace more novel concepts such as shelters made of living trees. The 80 adults and 20 children permanently housed at ZEGG regard culture as an integral part of life: art and music are central to the communal ideal, serving as a means for people to fulfil both their own creative potential and that of the community as a whole. The colony has its own music studios (where members have produced a CD of their own songs) and its own art gallery. It is perhaps the existence of settlements such as Lebensgarten and ZEGG that demonstrate most eloquently the interweaving of ecological and cultural practice in the German context.

Conclusion

Necessarily, this chapter has covered only a small fraction of the volume of potential material on interactions between landscape, environment and culture in Germany. Space has precluded detailed consideration of environmental issues in music and popular song and in the visual arts. It has not been possible to explore more than a small number of the many groups and associations devoted to nature and the environment, including those committed to environmental education such as the Arbeitsgemeinschaft Natur- und Umweltbildung (Working Group on Environment and Nature Education), based in Hamburg, or the Gesellschaft für ökologische Kommunikation (Society for Ecological Communication). Commitment to the environment takes as many forms in Germany as it does elsewhere in the world, from a minority of activists prepared to use violence in defence of nature if necessary, to New Age eco-warriors who believe passionately in peaceful protest. Engagement with environmental issues can, as elsewhere, range from passive mild sympathy to whole-hearted devotion. But engaging with German culture means engaging with landscape and the environment. That is made inevitable by the intertwining of landscape, nature and the environment with all aspects of German culture, whether in history, in everyday life, in the high cultural arena of the literary novel and the environmental poetry of the GDR, or in popular culture and the media. Nothing could better illustrate the principle that all adequate approaches to culture must be holistic. E.M. Forster's dictum 'only connect', originally conceived with human relationships in mind, is as true of culture as it is of ecology.

Notes

1. By contrast, 34 per cent claimed to have heard of the term in the UK in 1996/97 (*Digest of Environmental Statistics* 2001, table 10.17).
2. For more detail on this, see Goodbody (1997).
3. I am very grateful to my colleague Sabine Egger of the University of Limerick for drawing my attention to the ecovillages movement.

References

A Common Cause – Our Environment/Unsere Umwelt – eine gemeinsame Sache (no date). Exhibition catalogue. London: Press Department of the Embassy of the Federal Republic of Germany.
ALT, F. 1999: *Der ökologische Jesus.*
ARNDT, E.M. 1910–19: *Geist der Zeit IV* (*Werke*, vols 8–9). Berlin: Deutsches Verlagshaus Bong.
BRAMWELL, A. 1985: *Blood and soil: Walther Darré and Hitler's 'Green Party'*, Abbotsbrook.
CHEESMAN, T. 1997: Apocalypse nein danke: the fall of Werner Herzog. In RIORDAN, 285–306.
Common Ground 2/2000: Berlin: Federal Ministry for the Environment, Nature Conservation and Nuclear Safety.
Common Ground Climate Special 1999: Published on the occasion of COP 5. Bonn. Berlin: Federal Ministry for the Environment, Nature Conservation and Nuclear Safety.
Digest of environmental statistics 2001: London: Department for Environment, Food and Rural Affairs.
DOMINICK, R.H. 1992: *The environmental movement in Germany: prophets and pioneers, 1871–1971.* Bloomington and Indianapolis: Indiana University Press.
FISCHER, A. *et al.* 2000: *Jugend 2000: 13. Shell Jugendstudie.* Opladen: Leske + Budrich.
FRISCH, M. 1979: *Der Mensch erscheint im Holozän.* Frankfurt am Main: Suhrkamp.
GOODBODY, A. 1997: Catastrophism in post-war German literature. In RIORDAN 1997, 159–80.

IMMERMANN, K. 1836a: *Die Epigonen: Familienmemoiren in neun Büchern. Erster Theil.* Düsseldorf: J.E. Schaub.
IMMERMANN, K. 1836b: *Die Epigonen: Familienmemoiren in neun Büchern. Dritter Theil.* Düsseldorf: J.E. Schaub.
KUCKARTZ, U. 2000: *Umweltbewusstsein in Deutschland 2000: Ergebnisse einer repräsentativen Bevolkerungsumfrage.* Berlin: Umweltbundesamt.
LINSE, U. 1986: *Ökopax und Anarchie: Eine Geschichte der ökologischen Bewegungen in Deutschland.* Munich: dtv.
RIORDAN. C. (ed.)1997: *Green thought in German culture: historical and contemporary perspectives.* Cardiff: University of Wales Press.
SOHR, S. 2000: *Ökologisches Gewissen.* Baden-Baden: Nomos Verlag.
TUCHOLSKY, K. 1985a: *Gesammelte Werke*, vol. 6, 1928. Reinbek bei Hamburg: Rowohlt.
TUCHOLSKY, K. 1985b: *Gesammelte Werke*, vol. 7, 1929. Reinbek bei Hamburg: Rowohlt.
WORSTER, D. 1995: *Nature's economy: a history of ecological ideas.* 2nd edn. Cambridge: Cambridge University Press.

4

Constructing Germany: architecture and cultural identity

BY GILLIAN PYE

Not only does man make his world but the world makes the man.

(Ernst Bloch)

For around 300,000 years societies have been engaged in shaping their environments with buildings and, to both those living inside a particular social and cultural sphere, as well as those approaching it from elsewhere, built structure is a primary factor in the identification of and with place. The centrality of building to the definition of cultural identity can of course be most easily illustrated with reference to famous pieces of architecture which operate as indices of particular places. For example, even to those with the most rudimentary knowledge of the European cultural landscape, the Eiffel Tower has come to signify France. Similarly, in the case of Germany, features such as the Reichstag or the Brandenburg Gate have become figures of cultural shorthand connoting 'Germany', 'Germanness' and more recently the 're-united Germany'. On a more general level too, certain building types and styles are often associated with particular cultural spaces: the Swiss Chalet with the Alpine landscape, the *Fachwerkhaus* with medieval merchant towns and cities of Northern Europe. However, the immediacy of the connection often made between the built environment and a particular culture or nation–state (see also Chapter 6), masks the complexity of architecture's role in the construction, maintenance and projection of identity. In particular, it is not enough to interpret the forms of buildings as the 'face' of a culture. Consequently, this chapter does not seek to provide a reductive reading of German architecture by concentrating on certain styles, forms or buildings as 'typical' of the built environment in Germany. Equally, a historical survey of the development of German architecture is beyond the scope of this present chapter, and indeed there are many good introductions to this area (cf. Boyd-White 1998). Rather, this discussion aims to illuminate the dynamic way in which architecture may operate as both blueprint for and an imprint of cultural identity in Germany. For this reason, this discussion focuses on examples of the ways in which German culture has created spaces by balancing the relationship between form and function, between past and present, between future and eternity.

Defining architecture: space – function – time

The most common association evoked by the term architecture is built structure: enclosures or shelters constructed to fulfil human purpose. Equally important, however, is the concept of architecture as process – the design and construction of buildings in which the imaginary is united with the technological. Viewing architecture as both product and process is a useful starting point, which will be important in the following discussion of the way in which the built environment is implicated in cultural experience. However, in order to explore the cultural functions of architecture we must develop this definition a little further. In particular, it will be important to assess the role buildings play in the negotiation of time and human purpose and in the construction of space itself.

In the first place, then, a basic definition of architecture is the enclosure of a space with technical means (Berger and Berger 1999). That is to say, buildings imply the construction of boundaries which mark the difference between inside and outside, public and private, finite and infinite (see also Chapter 1). However, this process involves more than merely constructing walls around a pre-existing space. For Bill Hillier, spatial organization through the setting of boundaries is in fact, 'one of the principal ways in which culture becomes real for us in the material world' (1996, 29). Defining space is important because human activity acquires social meaning when it occurs repeatedly within a designated area. This means that space is not merely the pre-existing 'backdrop' for human activity, but is actually created in conjunction with it.

An oft-cited example of this process is the church or temple. The temple is not merely a building which houses a god. Rather, as an enclosure, it helps to create a sense of the god's existence. Entering a darker, contemplative space, decorated with signs and symbols, the worshipper's senses are heightened in anticipation of the sacred experience. However, in addition, the action of praying or leaving offerings, repeated again and again by worshippers at the holy place, defines the location as the space or place within which the god is present. Such repeated actions create the space: they construct it as a sacred place. As this example shows, architecture is not only about enclosing a space with technical means suited to a particular purpose, but it also involves the creation of space itself.

A second defining feature of architecture is that it is intrinsically linked to the notion of function. As we have already suggested, the enclosure of space is always related in some way to human activity or purpose. The interpretation of architecture is therefore virtually impossible without considering what occurs, or should occur, inside, or indeed outside, the immediate boundaries of a building or buildings. Admittedly, many buildings are multi-functional, and others have been created as 'follies' – structures that are unique because they seem to have no purpose at all. However, in the latter case, it is the seeming absence of function which is crucial, affirming again that in many ways it is the question of purpose which separates architecture from the other arts. Paintings or sculptures, textiles or poetry, may be associated with certain purposes (perhaps a moral message or a decoration for a wall). However, their primary value lies in their existence as imaginative human creations to be contemplated by individuals at certain moments in time. Most importantly, works of art often function by reference to other works and other experiences, reaching beyond the moment by stimulating the associative faculties of the beholder. As we have already seen, architecture is by nature a public phenomenon intimately associated with the setting of boundaries between social spheres and with the enacting of particular social rituals or functions. Like the piece of art, it may incorporate expressive elements – decorative, spatial or ornamental aspects that refer the viewer to another realm of experience. However, such aspects nevertheless depend on the question of purpose.

The way in which expressive and functional aspects relate to one another in architecture is a key to the understanding of the cultural significance of built structures. For instance, this leads us to ask the important question of exactly how a function of a building may affect its form. Can the form of a building be read as an indicator of social function and in what way is this relationship indicative of cultural context? Naturally, this involves an understanding not only of those particular cultural practices which create and are created by architectural space, but also implies an insight into the social, economic and technological conditions which dictate the construction process itself. Finally, the issue of the precise relationship between form and function is one which has certainly dominated twentieth-century Western architectural theory. This applies particularly to the case of modernist architecture, which drew much of its inspiration from German models. In what follows then, it will be important to consider the way in which German architecture has contributed to the construction of a culture in its treatment of the relationship between form and function.

The third distinctive element of architecture for discussion is its relationship to the concept of time. As immovable, public objects, buildings are closely associated with the concept of durability. In other words, with the obvious exception of deliberately temporary structures, buildings are a physical index of continuing cultural presence. This durable or eternal aspect is of particular importance in the construction of cultural identity and, as the ruins of ancient Greek temples testify, this may even extend beyond the life span of the complete building. Equally, however, as a response to cultural practice and technological advances, buildings are clearly creations of their own time. Perhaps more than any other creative process, they are testimonies to the way in which a particular culture responds to its own specific problems, needs and capabilities. At the same time, such a response not only presumes a reckoning with tradition (both in a technological and in a sociological sense), but – not least because buildings are constructed to last – with the future (see also Chapter 6). For this reason, architecture is an important means by which societies project images of their origins, hopes and aspirations. Of interest in this discussion is therefore the way in which architecture in Germany has responded to its own technological and aesthetic heritage as well as to the political and social legacies of the German, and wider European, cultural context. Finally, a further object of analysis will be the way in which architecture has been employed in the creation of identity through the projection of hopes and aspirations. In the following sections, this analysis will focus on two examples from German architecture around the turn of the nineteenth century, before proceeding to consider two further contemporary case studies from the late twentieth century.

Example 1: Architecture and temporality: historical models in the nineteenth century

Although all creative processes are bound to historical precedent in some way, architecture is perhaps more intimately affected by the past than any other. First, as a craft, building is even more reliant on the effective handing down of specific techniques and principles than the fine arts. Second, however, because buildings of different eras exist alongside each other in public spaces, because they are physically durable, and because they are less concerned with representation than with the accommodation of human purpose, they are in constant dialogue with the past. In the German cultural context, perhaps one of the clearest examples of this process is the fashion for historical ornament which began in the eighteenth century but reached its climax with stylistic eclecticism at the end of the nineteenth century. The accelerated process of industrialization and democratization, which accompanied the founding of the new German State naturally meant the need for more public building. More city living space was needed to house workers and the expanding middle classes, while the new offices of public institutions and services (banks, court houses, department stores, town halls) created the focal points of capitalist democracy. This increased architectural activity therefore indicates the way in which political and social developments are made material in the defining of space. In the 'lavish displays' (Boyd-White 1998, 284) of building which accompanied the birth of the nation–state, German society was drawing attention to its arrival on the world stage as a modern, industrial state (see Chapter 6).

Significantly, however, the majority of new buildings in this period were characterized not by association with Germany's future, but rather by conscious reference to the past. The columns, pediments and garlands of the ancient Greek temple, the pointed arches of the gothic cathedral, the rounded windows of the Italian renaissance palace adorned the façades of the new German banks, courts, universities, museums and apartment blocks for the rising middle classes. Examples of such buildings include the Polytechnikum in Munich (Gottfried Neureuter, 1866, Neo-Renaissance style), Hamburg's famous Nikolaikirche (Gilbert Scott, 1844, Neo-Gothic style), the Reichstag in Berlin (Paul Wallot, 1884–94, Neo-Baroque style) (cited in Boyd-White 1998, 285) and Stüler and Strack's National Galerie, Berlin (see Fig. 4.1) (Neo-Classical style 1865–9). By invoking the heritage of past cultures, such buildings indexed the desire of German society to trace its roots to great intellectual, political and cultural traditions as part of a drive to establish itself as a leading light in the Western world. Furthermore, the creation of new spaces and their embodiment of explicit references to the cultural triumphs of the past allowed a society increasingly dominated by its middle-class citizens to lay claim to a sense of luxury which, under feudalism, had been accessible only to the social and cultural elite.

Importantly however, such stylistic pretensions are not merely the translation of contemporary social and political needs or future aspirations to historical style. The extravagant eclecticism of the end of the century in fact

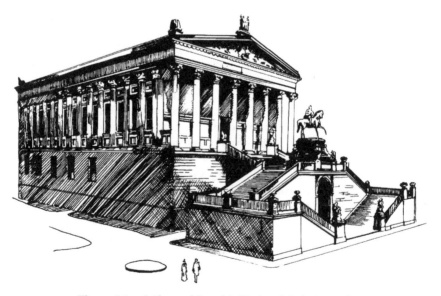

Figure 4.1   Stüler and Strack's National Galerie, Berlin

owed its existence to precisely the sort of modern intellectual and technological achievements which were to secure Germany's future as a modern
society. Without the new techniques of iron frame building (which meant
that the features of a façade need not necessarily carry the weight of a building, but could serve as decoration); without the application of relatively
modern industrial methods (for example, the mass production and marketing of architectural ornament); and without decades of field work by anti-
quarianists who had catalogued historical buildings and relics, the stylistic
variety which characterized much new building in German cities would not
have been possible.

From the turn of the century onwards, however, developments in German
architecture began to shift away from such a literal employment of historical models and to move towards a more explicit concentration on expressions of the culture of the present and the future. Primarily, this involved a
shift in paradigm to focus more closely on the relationship between form
and function, a shift which was to be crucial for the development of Western
architecture in general.

Example 2: Architecture and function: *Neues Bauen* and the Bauhaus

The turn towards an architecture which dealt more explicitly with function
can be seen, at least in part, as a direct response to the rampant historical
eclecticism discussed above. Architects and architectural historians were
critical of a built environment which attempted to project cultural identity
through conscious imitation of the past. In a technological sense, this trend
had in fact been a victim of its own success. Contemporary building and
design techniques were able to reproduce and mix historical models so effectively that their meaning had, to a certain extent, been undermined. As
already suggested, such buildings masked the reality of those industrial conditions – in particular, modern structural engineering and mass production
– which had enabled their construction. Accordingly, the emphasis shifted
towards the development of an architecture which would engage explicitly
– and therefore more 'honestly' – with the culture of industry. This architecture therefore sought to unite technological processes and contemporary
consumer ideals in order to promote a new aesthetic sensibility more representative of a modern industrial nation competing in a technologically
advanced marketplace. For the leading architects of this generation, the
solution to this equation lay in applying industrial methods to architectural
design. What was needed was a new formulation of the relationship
between the intended *function* of a building, the *materials* with which it was
to be built and its *spatial proportions*. Many of the leading proponents of
this new way of thinking, or the *Neues Bauen* (lit. 'new building') as it was

known, were working in Germany in the early years of the new century. There is no doubt that German architects such as Mies van der Rohe, Hans Scharoun, Hugo Häring, Walter Gropius, Peter Behrens and their Swiss colleagues Hannes Meyer and Le Corbusier, represent a generation of modernist designers who revolutionized international building culture.

One of the most famous movements in architectural modernism was the Bauhaus school of design. The Bauhaus operated from 1919 until its closure by the National Socialist regime in 1933, and was directed in turn by the architects Gropius, Mies and Meyer in the cities of Weimar, Dessau and Berlin. The school was founded to offer a modern design programme which would explore the advantages of contemporary industrial production and new building materials in a format which nevertheless emphasized traditional apprenticeship-based training. Students were instructed in subjects such as ceramics, textiles, colour theory, metal and woodworking by staff trained in both fine arts and more practically oriented crafts. Only the best students were permitted to progress to the study of architecture, which, as the discipline combining a broad range of skills acquired throughout the course, was considered the highest art. Although initially operating closely with Gropius' own architectural practice, the Bauhaus school did not begin to teach architecture until 1924 and even then, for a time students were required to study the more technical aspects of the subject at another institution. However, as the ultimate design art, architecture nevertheless remained at the core of the Bauhaus philosophy and the school engaged in pioneering building projects: notably experiments in cost-effective, prefabricated social housing, which was badly needed in the economically precarious inter-war years. However, it is perhaps the new Bauhaus school building, constructed after the move to Dessau in 1925, which provided the most prominent example of Bauhaus modernism (see Fig. 4.2).

The Dessau building stood in stark contrast to the historically eclectic façades which still dominated the buildings of most European cities in the early twentieth century. It comprised two L-shaped blocks with plain white rendered concrete walls and a flat roof (in contrast to the pitched or pointed roof more commonly seen in traditional northern European buildings), and, most spectacularly, a large curtain wall of glass. The bareness of the façade and simplicity of the geometry did not suggest a temple or palace but rather a warehouse or factory, built to accommodate practical needs. To a certain extent, this interpretation is borne out by the design aims for the school, which were derived not from an architectural pattern book, but rather from a set of functional requirements. The building was required to house workshops, teaching rooms, assembly, exhibition and eating areas. It was to provide as much light as possible for designers to work by and to create large flexible spaces which would accommodate the changing needs of the staff and students. Finally, in order to facilitate living and working together, the building was to provide for ease of movement between one space and another.

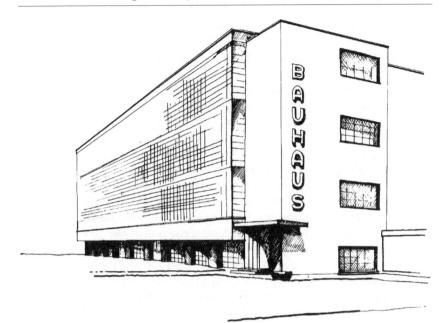

Figure 4.2   The new Bauhaus school building

These criteria are typical of the new way of thinking about design which did not rely principally on ancient models or traditional theories of harmony and proportion, but instead sought to rationalize the building process, developing design solutions which would allow a productive and logical relationship between user, function and space. Moreover, this application of scientific thinking was intended to suggest design solutions which would be valid for other buildings too. Technology had proven itself supremely capable of reproducing items on a mass scale. For the Bauhaus, however, the challenge was to suggest standardized designs which – at least in theory – because they were created with the user in mind, would not compromise on quality. In the Dessau building, then, the need for light was resolved in a large glass wall, which was possible due to new building techniques and materials – notably reinforced concrete which meant that the loading of a building need no longer rest squarely on its perimeter walls, but could be redistributed across the structure. The same technology allowed for the relatively free planning of interior spaces, which could be designed according to the needs of the user and not solely to restrictive structural principles.

On the one hand, this building seems to be the logical result of a series of functionally determined design criteria. However, it is in fact much more than this and demonstrates the way in which buildings are not only created in order to accommodate cultural and social functions, but are also involved in the construction and projection of social and cultural identity. The white walls, glass and simple geometry of the Dessau building are in fact as much an *expression* of functionality as they are a solution to rational design problems. The desire for an 'honest' relationship between building and industrial culture is expressed in the plain, warehouse-like form. The transparency of glass and the purity of the white paint actively promote the ideal of simplicity. That this is more than just a functional necessity is illustrated by the fact that part of the building was actually constructed with traditional masonry and then rendered with concrete and painted white (Naylor 1985, 126). The Dessau building is a projection of the Bauhaus faith in the ability of design, technology and co-operation to produce a better environment for the future of the masses. It is also a material expression of the desire to reconcile the traditional values of craftsmanship and individualism with the new conditions of mass-production and anonymity. The success of this project continues to be a subject of debate, however, its place at the heart of contemporary architecture is undisputed. In our late twentieth-century cities, dominated by the clean lines of concrete, glass and steel, the influence of architecture inspired by German modernism is clearly visible.

The preceding two examples have served to illuminate the way in which buildings may constitute a negotiation of cultural space by engaging in dialogues between past, present and future and between the needs, hopes and aspirations of users and designers. In the following case studies I will consider how two prominent examples of contemporary German architecture may illustrate some of the ways in which these dialogues are being conducted today.

Contemporary case study 1: Daniel Libeskind, Jewish Museum Berlin

Completed in 1998, Daniel Libeskind's Jewish Museum on the edge of Friedrichsstadt, formerly in East Berlin, is a useful case study for several principal reasons. In the first place, in an increasingly secularized Western world in which public building projects are at best scarce and at worst (one need only think of Britain's recent difficulties with the Millennium Dome) highly contested, the museum building provides architects with a rare opportunity to build for a broad public. In the second place, as Sharon MacDonald shows (see Chapter 6), museums offer an interesting insight into the temporal aspect of architecture because they seek to provide the public with a space in which to (re)visit their own cultural identities by engaging with a collection of historical artefacts. In the nineteenth century when many of these spaces were created, their designers espoused the values of education and self-improvement precisely by adopting the architectural styles of Greece, Rome, Renaissance or Medieval Europe discussed previously. In the late twentieth century, however, Libeskind's museum responds to history in quite a different way. The building does not offer an easy lesson in reverence for the past, but actually engages the visitor in an unsettling dialogue about a complex and brutal series of events which changed cultural perceptions forever. Needless to say, this building is absolutely bound up with the German cultural context. It is located at the heart of post-*Wende* Berlin, a city at the centre of Europe whose future direction must be determined through a reckoning with a difficult past. Equally, however, the construction of a Jewish museum at the heart of Berlin is indicative of the intercultural aspirations of contemporary German society. This project reflects the country's preoccupation with the need to renegotiate its identity not only in response to its own social and political past, but also to the pressures and opportunities of globalized culture in which virtual and actual mobility have developed at an unprecedented rate. This aspect is of particular interest in relation to architecture, which, particularly in its public manifestations, has always been characterized by international and intercultural exchange. In the past, as outlined above, such exchange was often reflected in the borrowing of architectural styles and traditions. Particularly since the beginning of the twentieth century, however, the architectural discipline has been especially characterized by international and intercultural collaboration and exchange. Hence, in post-*Wende* Berlin for example, it is significant that the vast rebuilding programme which constitutes one of Germany's most important cultural showcases, has been spearheaded by a significant number of architects from outside Germany. Alongside Libeskind, the high-profile involvement of architects such as Norman Foster (UK, Reichstag modernization) or Renzo Piano (Italy, Potsdamer Platz) reflects the centrality of intercultural exchange and international trade to constructions of contemporary German identity.

Design and conception

Proceeding from the brief to design an extension to the existing Berlin Museum – a baroque style building with a former life as a judicial court – Libeskind based his design for the Jewish museum not only on the functional requirements of a large museum extension, but on a series of philosophical principles. Briefly described, the result is a huge zigzag shaped, zinc-clad structure, criss-crossed by long, narrow slanting windows (see Fig. 4.3). Six 'voids', or empty spaces, of varying heights slice through the building at intervals along its length. Viewed on plan, they appear like the spine of the structure (see Fig. 4.4). Libeskind's extension is not connected to the main museum on ground level but by an underground passageway which emerges as a staircase boring into the old building. The only connection between the underground tunnel and the outside world is a door which leads into the Exilgarten (Garden of Exile), a series of 48 concrete pillars set

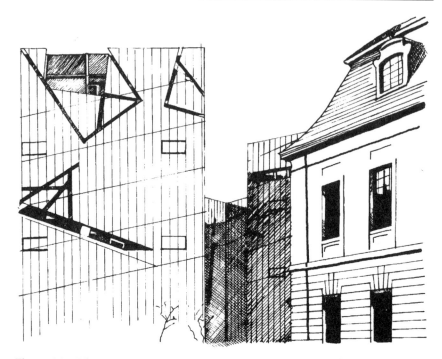

Figure 4.3   The new Jewish Museum standing alongside the existing Berlin Museum

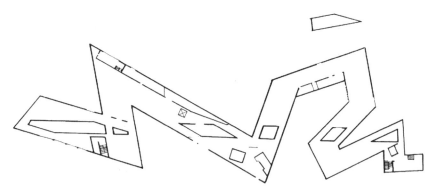

Figure 4.4   Plan of the new Jewish Museum

on a slanting base. The pillars are hollow and contain soil in which trees have been planted, producing an unusual and highly symbolic, urban garden.

Libeskind's building engages in a conscious dialogue about past, present and future in a number of ways and a detailed analysis is beyond the scope of this chapter. However, several areas are of particular interest in this discussion. In the first place, Libeskind determined the plan of the building and the elevation with its unusual windows, not by studying past architectural models or merely on the basis of functionally determined 'design problems', but in a rather more abstract, philosophical manner. Taking a map of the site and plotting points which marked the former dwellings of some of Berlin's famous Jewish citizens, he connected them together to form a matrix of lines which yielded the zig-zag shape (which also loosely resembles a fragmented Star of David) and the slanting windows which, in some places, cut across several storeys. In the second place, Libeskind deliberately planned the 'voids' – huge, empty concrete spaces which have no spatial or structural function other than their presence as emptiness. They are unheated and not all of them are accessible, even by viewing through a window. The largest void, however, which the architect designated as the Holocaust Tower, is lit by a small slanted window at the top and can be entered by the public.

In these two elements the building engages in a dialogue about presence and absence. The connections to absent Jewish Berliners are re-established in the shape of the building and in the windows which slash lines across its façade. At the same time, the voids are the material representation of absence. They testify to the loss of European Jews, not by creating a space which may be filled with exhibits to remind the visitor, but by constituting an emptiness which, because it cannot be filled or accessed, signifies the huge cultural rupture engendered by the Holocaust. In contrast to the two examples discussed earlier in this chapter, Libeskind's building does not evoke the past in imitation, nor does it reject it in a conscious adoption of radical style. Rather, in both the design process and the reality of the building, the ruptured and fragmented nature of history becomes material. Moreover, the fragmentation and disruption reflected in the central elements of the design are echoed throughout the building on a number of levels in a conscious rejection of architectural expectations. There is, for example, a disunity between inside and outside: as already mentioned, windows – which usually indicate to the viewer of a façade how the storeys of a building relate to one another – cut across several floors at odd angles. Libeskind also uses altering floor levels to disorientate and unsettle the visitor: in one of the main underground corridors for example, the floor height rises at one end although the ceiling height remains constant, altering the viewer's perception of space. In the Exilgarten, the floor of the area is slanted making the visitor uneasy as he/she walks through the dense forest of pillars. The Holocaust Tower itself, by its sheer size and emptiness and the single shaft of light emitted at its very top, may foster feelings of insignificance and isolation. As these examples show, this is a building which not only invites the visitor to enter and to consider a series of artefacts or objects, but also involves him/her directly in a sensual experience of disorientation and isolation which aim to encourage him/her to re-evaluate his/her own position in relation to the experience of the museum in particular, and to cultural and historical experience in general.

At the same time, what Libeskind's building may have in common with the two historical examples discussed earlier in this chapter – and perhaps this is a distinctive feature of architecture in general – is that it incorporates a desire to reconcile past with present, technology with aesthetics, the functional with the philosophical. However, in keeping with the self-reflexivity of late twentieth-century culture, Libeskind's building often does this in quite a self-conscious way. This is a technologically advanced building – it required revolutionary concrete casting techniques and seems to reject architectural precedent in its crazy zigzag shape – which is fitting for a city looking to the future. At the same time, however, it is created as a link to the past and quite literally has its roots in the history of Berlin. As such, its task is not only to evoke the fragmented relationship between past and present but also, by its very existence as a site of memory, to inspire possibilities for future reconciliation and understanding. This is indicative of the sophisticated manner in which a building may offer a means to construct, reconstruct and deconstruct cultural identity.

Contemporary case study 2: IBA Emscher Park Project

The Emscher Park scheme, initiated by the Internationale Bauausstellung (International Building Exhibition) is a landscape, planning and architecture project unprecedented in its extensive scope and innovative approach to the urban environment. The scheme, which officially ran from 1989–99, aimed to regenerate some 800 km² of industrial Nordrheinwestfalen, stretching between Bergkamen to the East and Duisburg to the West and involving some 17 towns and cities including Bochum, Essen, Bottrop, Oberhausen and Gelsenkirchen. Decades of heavy industry had left much of this landscape polluted and the closure during the 1980s of many of its steel and coal plants meant that large areas of this region were lying derelict. In addition, this is an extremely densely populated part of Germany with around 2 million inhabitants (in 1993 for example there were ca. 2000 inhabitants per km² compared to a national average of 224 per km²) (Wührl 1993, 30) from a wide variety of cultural and ethnic backgrounds. Clearly, a radical approach was needed to create new possibilities for living, working and leisure in this industrial heartland. The approach which the IBA adopted can be seen as a response to concerns which affect the entire post-industrial Western world. At the same time, in its conception and delivery, this project reflects very particular German conditions and again, offers Europe a new way of approaching the built environment.

At the core of the Emscher Park project was a rethinking of both the concept of the park and the idea of the architectural exhibition (*Bauausstellung*) – two key factors in the history of modern urban architecture. First, the project team (which included the IBA committee itself, an advisory committee of experts and representatives from the local authorities) aimed to bring together the notion of the park as nature, landscape or leisure area, with the modern concept of the industrial or business park as the focal point for the post-industrial economy. Second, they developed the idea of the building exhibition by extending it from its origins as a showcase for new technologies and materials (as in the 1851 exhibition in London which featured Joseph Paxton's revolutionary glass and steel Crystal Palace), and by building on its potential as a focus for modelling social architecture (as in Stuttgart 1927 or Berlin 1957). This was therefore an exhibition which not only sought to provide possible models for the future of building, but also to apply them in an integrated way which considered their ecological, social and cultural impact. Ultimately, it was hoped that this would help to support and develop the infrastructure and identity of an entire region of Germany. That this project was not merely about architecture in the sense of constructing new buildings is highly significant. The ca. 120 Emscher Park projects included the creation of a network of cycle and footpaths, the conservation and 'recycling' of industrial buildings, the cleansing of polluted waterways, the construction of new housing and business developments and the designation of tourist routes. In this way, this scheme demonstrates that at the beginning of the twenty-first century, a concern for the built environment now not only means the responsible construction of new buildings, or the provision of services for their inhabitants, but a sensitive response to the past, to the environment and a conscious awareness of the role of architecture and landscaping in the construction of social identity (see Chapter 3).

A detailed discussion of this vast project is clearly impossible in this introductory chapter. An example of a successful IBA project, the Duisburg Landschaftspark Nord, will, however, serve as an interesting case study. In 1985, the Duisburg Meiderich steelworks was closed down when market forces meant it was no longer competitive. This plant occupied more than 500 hectares of land, over which its furnaces and pipes, great machine halls and rolling mills sprawled. The logical consequence of the closure of the works would previously have been the demolition of the entire complex and this is certainly what happened elsewhere in Europe. For example, during the same period, in County Durham, North-East England, the complete demolition of the Consett steelworks did occur. This left a small town, which had been literally overshadowed for decades by huge industrial buildings, suddenly faced with a vast, empty area at the heart of its urban space. In an environmental respect of course, without the iron oxide which had spewed out of the plant, colouring the houses a dirty red, the town fared much better. At the same time, however, there was a huge sense of loss and the large grassy space where the steelworks had been seemed to physically embody the period of economic and social limbo in which, to a certain extent, the town still seems to exist almost twenty years on.

In Duisburg, however, the IBA planners and the local community adopted a different approach. Instead of spending an estimated 75 million Deutschmarks on the demolition of the buildings, they decided to spend the money on transforming the area into an innovative landscape and leisure park. This was possible not only because of the imagination of planners and architects but, first, because of a tradition of urban planning in Germany extending back to the beginning of the century, and, second, to a set of particularly German economic and political circumstances. In the latter case, this relates to the possibility of organizing and funding planning at regional level, the availability of national and European funds for urban planning, the emphasis on the environment and, perhaps most importantly, the possibility of buying land with public finances and holding it until plans have been drawn up for its redevelopment. Such structures which, crucially, were permitted to operate in conjunction with one another, allowed plans to be drawn up for the Duisburg plant. This opened up an area which, although it had previously dominated the skyline of the town and the lives of its citizens, had nevertheless only been accessible to those working inside its gates. The new plans for the site aimed to combine conservation with transformation. In some areas, gardens were planted in the walls of former buildings, providing a wonderful maze of garden 'rooms'. In other areas plants have been left to grow wild, creeping around the remains of the works and showing a gradual conquest of nature over man-made structures. Some of the buildings have been turned into eating, exhibition or concert areas and the Kraftwerkzentrale (power plant) has become a popular venue for concerts. The walls of the Möllerbunker are now used to train climbers and the cooling pools provide a diving club with a space to practise. Most impressively, the huge furnaces which tower above the park have been allowed to remain standing and visitors can climb up a stairway, through bundles of pipes and under huge metal girders, to reach a platform from which there is a breathtaking view over the whole of the area (see Fig. 4.5). At weekends and public holidays, a light installation illuminates these buildings turning them slowly from green through red to blue.

The significance of this project is that it involves a form of architecture which is concerned with intervening in minimal ways in order to re-evaluate existing buildings, opening them up to generate a dialogue about the function and aesthetics of built structure and about the relationship between the past and the future. Buildings created in iron and brick with only their industrial function in mind are now presented as monuments to a past industrial age which shaped the culture of Germany as a major industrial power. This is achieved in the first place by a redefinition of function. For example, at the base of the furnaces in the Landschaftspark there is a large square area bordered by iron columns and traversed by metal girders at ceiling height. This forms an excellent area for modern theatre performance,

Figure 4.5   The Duisberg plant

combining an enclosed space with eerie acoustics and an existing framework for a heavy lighting rig. At the same time, in exploring the site visitors
are naturally curious about the original function of each area and guided
tours – staffed occasionally by former steelworkers – exploit the educational
potential of the park. By adapting the site with a small amount of new structure (walkways, stairways, planting, and so forth), the designers have
invited visitors to engage in a dialogue with the building about its past,
present and possible future functions. In this way it is literally a space in
progress, a space which is being created by the many visitors who contribute
to its new identity by bringing new uses and interpretations to it.

Equally, the buildings of the Landschaftspark invite the visitor to consider
preconceptions about architectural beauty itself. The rusting iron of the
pipes and dirty brick of the sheds connote architectural ugliness: the purely
functional structure built to be used and then disposed of. However, once
still and emptied of function, once encroached upon by plant life, once lit up
at night, the buildings offer the viewer an entirely different aspect. One dis-
covers for example, a huge variety of colours in the rusting metal. The
patchwork of riveted metal sheets which covers some of the towers appears

to be decorative and no longer merely the result of expedience. The blue, red and green lights which illuminate the towers at night make them seem like unearthly gods, or, as the industrial monuments of the region have often been described, great 'cathedrals of industry'.

The imbuing of such buildings with new uses and the rethinking of what architectural beauty may mean are key elements in the maintenance and promotion of regional identity in the Ruhrgebiet and in this sense the IBA projects testify to the great importance of the built environment in the construction of cultural identity in general. In this type of project, urban architecture, once viewed as an ugly necessity of economic growth, is being transformed into a source of cultural and social development. The pride taken by the citizens of this region in the difficult and often dangerous work carried out by generations before them is made manifest in the transformation of gasometers and chimneys, furnaces or minewheels into 'cathedrals of industry'. At the same time, the values of flexibility and change are clearly being espoused in the transformation and aestheticization of these buildings. The clear message conveyed by these structures, both to local communities as well as to outsiders, is that this is a region capable of embracing huge change. In this way, the IBA project is one which engages with key problems facing Germany in the here and now, as it adapts and changes to the marketplace of the new millennium. With its next project, just beginning in Lausitz, the IBA is now set to take up the challenge of regenerating the industrial landscape of former East Germany. This project will be the IBA's largest undertaking to date and involves the transformation of an area ca. 5000km² which has been damaged by years of opencast brown coal mining. A central project in this building exhibition involves the controlled flooding of the pitted and scarred landscape with water to create a series of lakes, thus transforming an industrial region into a location for leisure and tourism. It remains to be seen just how successful this project will be, but it will certainly have a huge impact on the area. Some will read this project along with accompanying conservation schemes and employment initiatives (for example, the preservation of industrial buildings, the adoption of new energy sources and the creation of new industries) as symbolic of the ecological, economic and social hope being injected into the new *Bundesländer*. In particular, the apparent emphasis on local co-operation seems to reflect the wish to do this in a manner which is sensitive to the specifically East German heritage. On the other hand, however, some will doubtless observe that, particularly because it employs an approach first piloted in the Emscher Park and yet, unlike this model, proposes a radical transformation of the landscape, the Lausitz project underlines a perceived tendency to 'erase' rather than to preserve East German heritage.

What is significant about the IBA Emscher Park project is not merely that it provides a fascinating insight into architectural, social and economic culture in a very important, yet often overlooked region of Germany. Its value in the context of the debate about contemporary architecture is that it demonstrates that the architecture of the future is concerned neither purely with the creation of new spaces to accommodate the physical needs of generations to come, nor just with the preservation of the structures of the past to remind them of their origins. What this German pioneering project shows, is that it is also about redefining and developing the built environment in a way which consciously acknowledges its psychological importance in the maintenance and construction of social and cultural identity.

Conclusion

As the above examples illustrate, architecture has a crucial role to play in the construction of German cultural identity. However, this role does not consist merely in the creation of 'typical' buildings or styles which form a recognizably 'German' environment, nor does it revolve solely around the lives and work of German architects. Rather, as a creative activity which conditions and is conditioned by the social environment, architecture can provide both a blueprint of and for German culture. Axiomatic in this process is the way in which architecture constructs for the future by engaging in a dialogue about the needs and capabilities of the present, the aspirations of the future and the legacies of the past. Moreover, central to this dialogue is the question of how architecture balances its commitment to the physical needs of its users with both its technological limitations and its potential as an expressive medium. In the case studies explored in this chapter, German architecture may be seen to have responded to these challenges in a number of interesting ways.

In the first place, as an expression of Germany's future, architecture has not only explicitly engaged in pioneering work with modern materials and forms, but is also concerned to engage in conscious negotiation with the past. Libeskind's Jewish Museum and the IBA Emscher Park Project are significant examples because they employ new technologies to explicitly address architecture's role in the transmission and interpretation of Germany's political, economic and social past. In contrast to the rather hollow stylistic eclecticism of the late nineteenth century, these twenty-first-century schemes openly merge past, present and future. Both clearly embody contradiction, fragmentation, rupture and continuity: Libeskind's museum in terms of the continuing legacy of a terrible caesura in human history, the IBA as a reflection of the dynamic, yet rather mixed blessings brought to bear by huge industrial development. Both, however, project the importance of a self-reflexive attitude towards the past as a means of engendering future growth and development in Germany. In the case of the IBA, such future growth and development are projected through the 'recycling' of industrial buildings and environments in a spirit of co-operation and flexibility. A redefinition of architectural function and the reinterpretation of architectural beauty reflect the importance of these values. In the case of

Libeskind's Jewish Museum, the values of co-operation, reflection and tolerance – and not least the importance of Jewish history to German culture – are espoused in the construction of an aesthetically radical extension to an historical building at the heart of Berlin.

Finally, in both schemes, the values of intercultural and international exchange rank highly. The IBA project not only aims to provide focal points for the economically and ethnically diverse inhabitants of the Ruhrgebiet, but also to attract foreign tourists and to serve as a progressive building exhibition of international importance. Libeskind's building clearly aims to raise questions about intercultural understanding and to promote the essential and continued debate about the international significance of the Holocaust and its relationship to German identity. In this sense, both case studies are indicative of the international aspect to German architecture which is concerned not only with providing for its own citizens, but also with mediating their relationship to the European, and wider international community.

References

BERGER, R. and BERGER, E. 1999: *Bauwerke betrachten, erfassen, beurteilen: Wege zum Verständnis klassischer und moderner Architektur.* Munich: Augustus Verlag.

BLOCH, E. 1997: Formative education, engineering, form, ornament. In LEACH.

BOYD-WHITE, I. 1998: Modern German architecture. In KOLINSKY, E. and VAN DER WILL, W. (eds.) *The Cambridge companion to modern German culture.* Cambridge: Cambridge University Press, 282–301.

HILLIER, B. 1996: *Space is the machine: a configurational theory of architecture.* Cambridge: Cambridge University Press.

WÜHRL, E. 1993: Rettet die IBA den Emscherraum? *geographie heute,* 113, 28–35.

Further reading

Introductions to architectural aesthetics/critical and cultural theory

LEACH, N. (ed) *Rethinking architecture: a reader in cultural theory.* London and New York: Routledge

SCRUTON, R. 1979: *The aesthetics of architecture.* Princeton: NJ: Princeton University Press.

Architectural history

RISEBERO, B. 1982: *Modern architecture and design: an alternative history.* London: Herbert Press.

SCHNEIDER, R., NERDINGER, W. and WAND, W. 2000: *Architektur im 20. Jahrhundert:* vol. 8, *Deutschland.* Munich: Prestel.
SCHWARZER, M. 1995: *German architectural theory and the search for modern identity.* Cambridge: Cambridge University Press.

IBA Emscher Park

SACK, M. 1999: *Siebzig Kilometer Hoffnung: Die IBA Emscher-Park – Erneuerung eines Industriegebiets.* Stuttgart: Deutsche Verlags-Anstalt: Stuttgart.
SCHÄFER, R. (ed.) 1999: *TOPOS: European Landscape Magazine: Internationale Bauausstellung Emscher Park: IBA – a renewal concept for a region.* Munich: Callwey, March 1999, no. 26
IBA Emscher Park website: http://www.iba.nrw.de

Bauhaus

NAYLOR, G. 1985: *The Bauhaus reassessed: sources and design theory.* London: Herbert Press.
ROWLAND, A. 1990: *Bauhaus source book.* Oxford: Phaidon.

Daniel Libeskind's Jewish Museum

BINET, H. 1999: *Jewish Museum Berlin.* Amsterdam: G + B Arts International.
SCHNEIDER, B. 1999: *Daniel Libeskind, Jewish Museum Berlin: between the lines,* Munich, London: Prestel.

5

Domestic spaces: homes in the Heimat

BY LOIS R. WEINTHAL

The typical German postcard is filled with narrow cobble-stoned streets, traditional brick and stucco façades, and clay tile roofs. The postcard as a snapshot in time projects an image of a typical European townscape. This encounter with an image enables the viewer to draw conclusions regarding the types of places where German people live. Yet, upon closer inspection of the façades, the cohesion of the buildings is broken, revealing the presence of the new within the old. How did it come about that the presence of this new architecture is situated within the picturesque townscape of the early twentieth century? What can this juxtaposition of the new and the old within the German landscape tell us about the nature of the German home and domestic spaces? What do these romantic German postcards mask from the viewer concerning the current state of the German home and domestic space? What these postcards do not reveal is the image of the overwhelming and dense concrete prefabricated housing complexes, called *Plattenbauten* built from the 1960s to the 1980s throughout East Germany. Unlike the traditional postcard that captures our imagination of the German home, the *Plattenbauten* made up 50 to 80 per cent of the housing stock throughout the German Democratic Republic.[1] Similar to the immersion of the new architecture within the typical German streetscape (e.g. Berlin), these new façades reflect the major political and economic changes that have taken place in the nineteenth and twentieth centuries such as the industrial revolution, the Second World War, the division of Germany and then its unification. Parallel to these political and economic changes, the German home and domestic spaces have undergone similar transformations.

This chapter examines the major political and economic events of twentieth-century Germany in order to understand their impact on the nature of interior spaces of the German home. Simply put, the home is a representation of its occupants; the home, moreover, can reveal cultural, religious or political affiliations owing to the tangible objects within it. German unification has forced the former East German citizens to redefine their notion of the home; specifically, the encounter with new objects that are part of a capitalist society. As part of the transition to a capitalist society, the East Germans can now adopt new objects that represent capitalist values, but that now call into question their previous identity with socialism. By investigating the changes Germany has undergone, it is possible to use the interior as a gauge of how the individual identifies with ones home, surroundings or moreover, his or her Heimat (meaning the homeland).

Home as identity

German architecture concerning homes and domestic spaces has mirrored Germany's different political regimes, especially the split between East and West Germany. As the German political system has undergone periods of change, the design of the German home and domestic spaces in the East and West has similarly undergone extensive renovation. To the extent that history shapes the emergence of new political regimes, the foundation of homes and domestic spaces likewise retain structures encapsulating the history of the previous regime. In particular, Germany's domestic architecture at the onset of the twenty-first century reflects this split between the East and West. In response to the split between East and West, the German government is carrying out renovations to erase both the physical legacy of East German architecture and the political, economic and cultural differences created by the erection of the Berlin Wall.

The construction of the Berlin Wall in 1961 and its demolition after 1989 are the starting points for this chapter as the Wall's construction and demolition enable us to map the changes in homes and domestic spaces that are characterized by the dense prefabricated housing in Berlin and adjacent areas to the east. This chapter focuses on domestic spaces in Germany over three different time periods: before the construction of the Berlin Wall, during the Cold War where the Berlin Wall symbolized the physical split between East and West, and after its demolition.[2] The Berlin Wall as a reference point marks the monumental political and economic changes that took place in Germany in the twentieth century, but more so, the Berlin Wall reveals the divisions between the East and West regarding homes and domestic spaces after the Second World War. The Berlin Wall has had its greatest impact upon East German architecture with the construction of the *Plattenbauten*, which were built by the German Democratic Republic. As one travels through the former East, these *Plattenbauten* dot the East German landscape and can be seen in cities such as Rostock in the north, and eastern Germany such as Berlin, Leipzig, Dresden and Jena. Although unification has been an issue more tangibly related to the East with the housing as reminders of the GDR system, the country as a whole has felt the effects of renovation. Prior to unification both West and East Germany received substantial subsidies from the former Allied countries and the

Soviet Union respectively; yet with unification these subsidies dramatically decreased. The German government has had to raise domestic taxes to replace this loss in subsidies in order to close the gap between the former East and West. Many of these taxes have been designated for renovation in the East that would specifically change the façade of socialism.[3]

The *Plattenbauten* in the East stand as a strong contrast to housing in the West. Whereas the *Plattenbauten* reflect a functional form of building, the homes and apartments that were constructed in the West in the 1990s speak of variations in modern design, materials and methods of construction. For example, in the West newly constructed multiple dwellings were integrated into the fabric of older homes and buildings by remaining at their original height, and using a common element found in most multiple dwellings that can be seen from the turn of the century: the courtyard.

The realm of housing such as the *Plattenbauten* is, moreover, connected to our understanding of domesticity – the shaping of one's home to reflect the occupant(s), and his or her character. Domesticity can refer to an individual's personal interests that are manifested in objects seen on the interior or his or her allegiance to a homeland that also appears as cues in their personal spaces. The concept of domesticity allows us to focus on the following issues: memory as a means to claim a home that no longer exists; interior space as a reflection of the individual; the amount of freedom that an individual has to alter his or her physical home; and the concept of personal possessions in light of the existence and disappearance of the Berlin Wall (see Chapter 1). Berlin and its outlying vicinities will be the areas of primary focus to reveal how politics have shaped and reshaped the dense housing stock located in these areas.[4]

Before the Berlin Wall

Architectural changes in Germany have been in tandem with periods of economic prosperity. During a period of economic growth in the late 1800s, architects were forced to respond to the rise in urbanization whereby the growing cities were overwhelmed by an influx of inhabitants and a lack of suitable housing. The more prosperous Germany was, the more possible it was for German architects to experiment with new and innovative housing types. The economic boom in Berlin in the late 1800s that resulted in an increase in factory work led to a specific housing type called the *Mietskaserne*, which sought to resolve the housing shortages in Berlin as people moved from rural areas to the city in search of work. The development and building of these urban housing blocks characterized this period from 1860–1914 and organized the layout of housing and city blocks. The Mietskaserne buildings were five stories high with façades that extended 50 to 100 feet across the length of the city blocks. They bordered the edge of the street on all sides and contained courtyards in the center (Ladd 1997).

Overall, they resembled long rectangular blocks with courtyards punched out evenly throughout the solid mass. On the one hand, the *Mietskaserne* helped resolve a housing shortage, but on the other hand, the design of these buildings also created the conditions for disease to flourish because the buildings did not allow light to penetrate and air to circulate. Simply put, the combination of small courtyards and the height of five stories resulted in limited space for proper ventilation. To make conditions worse, little care was given to the needs or desires of these occupants, as they were the poor working class (ibid.). Over time, the *Mietskaserne* became the typical building footprint throughout Berlin, defining the city center from the rural landscape of individual homes.

With the advent of industrialization in the nineteenth century, socially conscious architects made several advances with building materials and urban planning that were intended to rectify the persistent housing problems. By the 1920s, German architects, such as Walter Gropius and Bruno Taut were at the forefront in the development of the Modernist Movement that recognized the importance of industry, utilitarian design, and the possibility for design to also be expressive (see Chapter 4). The 1920s' Modernist Movement approached housing as a model for applying this new style consisting of industrial materials and for bringing it to the public through housing. In addition, utilitarian products such as lamps and chairs were designed for the home with these new materials, which contrasted to the previous traditional vernacular forms (Curtis 1987). Frankfurt, in particular, became the site for experimentation in housing. One of their major contributions was the 'Frankfurt Kitchen' that was an extremely compact and exceptionally functional kitchen (ibid., 167). Modernism was also a reaction by German architects to the *Mietskaserne*, with their limited light and air ventilation. Advanced materials, such as steel and glass, allowed housing to address cleanliness, along with the ability for fresh air and sunlight to penetrate. In addition, the new housing estates met the needs of occupants by bringing the element of close proximity to home and work. This would later set an example for the development of suburban housing in the 1950s in the United States, where homes were constructed close to the work place (Kelly 1993).[5] These new housing forms were given names such as the Gross-Siedlung Britz, where *Siedlung* refers to 'estates'. This term 'estate' would later contrast with housing types called 'complexes' such as the housing complexes built in East Germany during the socialist period of the 1970s and 1980s. These two terms, 'estate' and 'complex' reveal the political ideals of the systems under which they were built and reflect the differences in economic class and issues of ownership. The term 'estate' is associated with homes that one would invest in, own and become permanently attached to, as opposed to the 'complexes' that spoke about a community of ownership rather than the individual as owner.

Another example of the Modernist Movement is the Bauhaus architecture that is also associated with Walter Gropius (see Chapter 4). The Bauhaus style is most evident in the city of Dessau, where Walter Gropius opened up the school of design in 1926. Examples of the Bauhaus style include a series of homes that were built for the Bauhaus school. Yet, soon after the first Bauhaus buildings were erected, opposition to the Bauhaus movement appeared in Dessau, which included supporters of the Nazis. In response to the highly modern style, those opposed to the style began to build in the traditional vernacular German style with the intention of overshadowing the strong presence of the Bauhaus. Therefore, due to the change in political climate, the Modernist Movement in Germany was forced to stop building.[6]

The Second World War brought tremendous destruction to Germany's homes and its occupants. In particular, the demolition of Berlin left its remaining inhabitants without food, shelter, sanitation, and created a housing shortage. When the four powers (Great Britain, France, the Soviet Union and the United States) gained control of Germany and established their respective sectors of control, they began to provide subsidies to German occupants who were without food and shelter. Shortly afterwards, the Soviet Union changed its policy toward isolationism from the three other powers. This separation from the three other powers first materialized physically as a wire on the ground, which then served as a visual reference for the newly established border that divided Berlin into two parts. At that time, people in the Soviet sector could still visit and shake hands with their former neighbors (Wyden 1989). By 1961 the division, however, had became more distinct and permanent with the construction of the Berlin Wall. This was in part a reaction to the two million East German occupants who had fled to the West by 1961, leaving the East with a shortage of skilled workers.[7] The solid concrete wall blocked the visual connection between the East and West, and moreover, it obstructed any chance of physical contact between people in the separate sectors. In short, the Berlin Wall symbolized the physical division in what had once been a unified city.

Before the construction of the Wall, people could still choose to live in the East under Soviet control while also retaining a sense of a unified Berlin owing to the visual and verbal connection that existed in their daily activities as they went to and from their homes. The building of the Wall challenged the allegiance of the occupants in the East and their decision to affirm their attachment to the homes they had already established before the division. They transferred their notion of the home to a new homeland: specifically, their homes became part of the East and the Soviet sphere of influence. This attachment to the home conveys a strong statement about the attachment of the individual to his or her private interior space, and to his or her connections to neighbors and place. In particular, the simple act of choosing objects to place in the home creates a sense of belonging for the individual. Similarly, the maintenance of the home creates a sense of belonging to the neighborhood in which the home is located. A person's attachments are thus represented by the simple balance of home and neighborhood cohesiveness. Even those who fled from the East to the West before the Wall was built were still forced to leave behind family and physical possessions. As a result of this separation from the home, they were forced to draw upon their memories of their previous home in order not to lose ties to their past. Moreover, for those Germans (both in the East and West) whose neighborhoods were destroyed, they also relied upon the memory of these places by recalling objects and colours in their homes and neighborhoods (Kaiser and Führe 1996).

The presence of the Berlin Wall

The presence of the Berlin Wall and the close proximity of the Allied powers to the Soviet sector placed Berlin in the public view as a strategic international centre, overshadowing other cities in Germany. The completion of the Berlin Wall separated the East and West into two distinct zones, with both facing issues of serious housing shortages. However, the different solutions taken by the East German and the West German governments to deal with the housing shortages reflected the different political and economic trajectories emerging in the two countries. The housing built in the East and West during the 1970s and 1980s can be seen as symbols of each sector's political structure. The development and building of housing in the West spoke of the openness to individual expression. In the 1980s in the West, for example, the government commissioned famous German and international architects to design and build new housing structures. This contrasts starkly with East Germany in which architecture was anonymous, speaking about the collective, but never the individual. The West German architect Josef-Paul Kleihues was the most prominent of these architects. Overall, these architects received much publicity for their work in the post-modern style of the 1980s. In contrast, the architects who built much of the Socialist housing in the 1970s in the East were not recognized for their work. The Socialist housing was seen by the West, particularly with the media, as a brutal approach to defining home.

The new housing built in West Berlin in the 1980s followed shortly after the construction of the *Plattenbauten* in the East. These developments were the largest impact of housing construction since the Second World War and currently remain unrivalled by new housing construction. Before the housing filled the streetscapes, the picturesque postcard image was destroyed by the war. Two factors can be seen as contributing to the rebuilding of homes in West Berlin: first was the assemblage of famous architects by the West German government; second, illegal occupants known as squatters were already occupying war-damaged buildings and beginning repairs on their own. At the same time, the West German government was encouraging people to move to Berlin from other parts of the country.

The group of famous architects planning the new housing chose to build upon elements of the streetscapes that had previously existed such as block sizes and building heights that were previously established by the dimensions of the *Mietskaserne*. The streetscapes would now recall the urban space of the pre-war picturesque postcard but with new façades that would fill the gaps between surviving buildings. The West German government sympathized with the squatters who were slowly renovating buildings on their own and encouraged the group of international architects not only to build new housing but to renovate existing buildings.

In contrast to the West, the East chose to build new urban towns outside of central Berlin. The East was also faced with a similar situation of having bullet-scarred *Mietskaserne*. Rather than renovating these buildings and filling in the gaps as the West chose to do, the urban planners under Soviet influence chose to abandon the scarred housing in favour of building new satellite cities outside of Berlin. Erich Honecker, a former leader of East Germany, pushed for the housing complexes in the satellite cities of the East. At the same time, it is important to note that unlike the West, individual architects in the East usually never received credit for building and designing these housing complexes. Rather, the image presented was that the housing was part of the government collective and did not need to specify names of the designers.

With the closing of the East from the West in 1961 by Walter Ulbricht as head of East Germany and in alliance with Nikita Khruschev (head of the Soviet Union), the two leaders had to deal immediately with the housing shortage in the East by providing a home and place in society for those under the East German political and economic system. At that time, much of the existing housing had been destroyed in the war. The large housing complexes later built under Erich Honecker and the Sozialistische Einheitspartei Deutschlands (Socialist Unity Party) left their mark as a way of building to monumental proportions and solve a housing shortage at the same time. The socialist political system enforced by the Soviet sector in the East is clearly reflected in the architecture for these housing complexes. The satellite cities, Marzahn, Hohenschönhausen, and Hellersdorf, housed one-third of East Berlin's residents by 1989, with Marzahn alone housing 56,000 apartments (Ladd 1997, 190–1). These buildings are constructed of concrete panels and possess a uniform exterior based on a grid with regular

---

Figure 5.1   The streetscape at the top of the page shows the traditional *Mietskaserne* housing built at the turn of the twentieth century. The war-damaged *Mietskaserne* can still be found in the former East Berlin neighbourhoods and are currently being absorbed into the capitalist market as they are under renovation by private ownership. The *Plattenbauten* at the bottom of the page shows the typical pre-fabricated concrete panel system as a solution to the East German housing shortage in the 1970s and 1980s. The *Plattenbauten* can be found throughout cities in the East such as Dresden and Berlin. Although the *Plattenbauten* are also under renovation, the issue of ownership differs as the Berlin government is funding the renovation.

Former East Berlin Streetscape

Plattenbauten in the satellite city of Marzahn

repeating floor plans, depicting an equality similar to the stated goals of the political system. The resulting housing reveals the importance of the immediacy to build first rather than to consider the types of housing being built and their ability to become homes. Because of the immediacy, pre-fabricated building systems developed by engineers in the Soviet Union enabled East German builders to use the same kit of parts that had been applied to a range of other building programs such as office buildings and schools located in the Soviet Union.

The East had to find new ways to build efficiently and fast, thereby, looking to the Soviet Union for methods of construction, and replacing men with cranes, and brick and stucco with concrete. The assemblage of pre-fabricated parts did not require the skilled craftsmen and needed fewer workers owing to the use of cranes to put the parts into place. This was important to the East German government for two reasons: first, many skilled laborers had fled to the West before the borders were sealed; second, the East felt the need to show the West that they could develop new progressive housing systems.[8] This new pre-fabricated housing was desirable for East Germans as it had central heating which was very modern for the time and no longer contained the coal ovens that were still in use shortly after unification in the *Mietskaserne*. Later, a result of implementing the anonymous kit of parts meant that there was no typology used to define the shape of homes. The housing reveal the absence of the role of an architect whose discipline is to recognize and solve problems through the knowledge of programmed space, the interaction of people, the site and materials. In the case of these large housing complexes, the architect is absent. Instead, engineers without any training in housing design were given the authority to define the home, and as a result, the housing complexes of the East do not take into account the desires of the occupants. This lack of attention to small detail and to individuality characterized much of East German architecture. The original planning of these complexes contained a range of programmed spaces to fulfil the needs of the occupants. Among these spaces were schools, parks, sports complexes, cultural centres, and shopping centres, but as housing was the most necessary element, many of the social support spaces were not built. As a result, the hope of creating neighborhoods situated in districts known as *Bezirks* where an occupant could find everything they needed close to their home, was impossible.

The interior of a building, moreover, illuminates the relationship between the political system and its citizens. In East Germany where the citizens were considered 'equal', the housing was also built to be anonymous, uniform and equal. The floor plans of these buildings do not lend themselves towards the personal. The most personal space these buildings offer are windows and balconies that allow one to see out; they also provide a place to put window boxes. The anonymity extends from the planning of the complexes and reaches every scale down to the standard-issued front door.

The planning of buildings and streets is similar to a large-scale maze where issues of orientation are a concern when one is walking through the uniform blocks. Because the housing blocks are similar in appearance, in order to help children find their way home among the rows of identical blocks, bright murals were painted around the doors (McElvoy 1992). In addition, the street names did not offer any more guidance in orientation (ibid.).

In the *Journal of Environmental Psychology*, Jonathon D. Sime writes in his (1986) article 'Creating Places or Designing Spaces': 'the term place, as opposed to space, implies a strong emotional tie, temporary or more long-lasting between a person and a particular physical location'. There are specific elements that allow the occupant to have a sense of place over space. The architectural writer, Christian Norberg-Shulz, defines genius loci, a place as 'space plus character', where 'the existential purpose of building is therefore to make a site become a place, that is to uncover the meanings potentially present in the environment' (ibid.). Accordingly, it is the role of the architect to make the space, and then the occupant makes the place. From these definitions, it is, moreover, possible to establish the differences between homeland and home. The homeland belongs to the collective, to the group of citizens who can claim their country as a community. It is a general term similar to the more anonymous term 'citizen' that is used to describe an individual. The homeland is an overall space as opposed to a place. The uniform and repeating plans of the Socialist housing estates reflect the term space on the exterior, whereas the occupant can transform the interior into a place. It is this distinction, where the broader architectural realm reflects space, and the interior personalized area reflects place.

Kevin Lynch writes of urban issues in 'The Image of the City', and looks at the physical features of a location and how an individual identifies with that space. Two important factors are orientation and identification, the latter being able 'to identify himself with the environment, that is he has to know how he is in a certain place'. This returns us to the exterior of the housing complexes and the cues that are offered to the occupants by the architects and planners to identify with that space. Immediately after the Wall came down, Westerners perceived a problem with the housing as being too uniform and vast. They found themselves continuously getting lost in the mazes of building blocks, leading them to suggest the housing should be torn down. For the outsider, the plan is a space, unlike for the inhabitants where the signals, such as the brightly coloured murals signify location, orientation and become a place. Assisting in this proposal to demolish the housing was the West German media that reported negatively on them, inferring that they were more similar to housing 'projects' or temporary housing for people with low incomes. Before the Wall came down, these housing complexes were occupied by people of different economic and professional levels, where a labourer could be a neighbor of a doctor. The previous system did not separate professions because the ideal of socialism was to make the home equal and available for all of its citizens. The psychologists Brown and Perkins (1992) have studied attachments to places and have noticed that one can become attached to a place over time without being conscious of the ties he or she has formed to that place. Once the attachment has been established, an identity is formed that expresses the relationship of the individual to a specific place and also the relationship of the individual to the larger community. At present, the occupants of the *Plattenbauten* are torn between two worlds because their identity is being restructured. They now have two parallel and often conflicting identities. The first identity belongs to the place where they have lived for decades. The second represents their identity within a new country. This new identity is pushing for these occupants to adopt a new lifestyle that is associated with the West and capitalism. Thus, although these residents have remained in the same housing they must acclimate to a new citizenship and redefine their understanding of the home in a new homeland.

Within this realm of shifting identities, architecture must mediate between the old and new and between the previous places made by the occupants and the imposition of a new space caused by the change of political systems. The major housing complexes located in the east of Berlin have undergone renovations, where new façades have been added to the buildings and thereby erasing the uniform grids that form the visual fabric of the socialist cities. By 1990, 50 per cent of East Berlin residents were living in these housing complexes. Since unification, up to 20 per cent of the residents have left. The number is decreasing as the renovations have helped to keep people in their homes.[9] This is especially important for those residents who have grown up in these complexes and have formed bonds with their homes, neighbors, and the environment. The renovations allow the past to be preserved in its current physical structure while simultaneously seeking to create a new future within this same structure, rather than demolishing the memory. The places made by the occupants reveal a personal detail that has the ability to start from the interior and reach to the exterior, where the first marks made are the simple window boxes that reveal a life behind the anonymous wall. Is it only when the individual makes that generic space into a place that an identity is formed and becomes more personalized.

Within the interior of these homes, the GDR sought to complete the spaces with furniture that could also be mass-produced using modern methods of fabrication and be highly functional. The furniture similarly reveals a design sensibility similar to the production of the *Plattenbauten*. Furniture was based on modules that could be matched to other parts with easy assemblage to form chairs, sofas, beds, tables, and cabinets. To promote this, design magazines were published in the GDR such as '*form + zweck*' that kept readers in the design industry up to date on current methods of mass production (for domestic objects and industrialization) along with GDR design principles and aesthetics. Images from the magazine show the assemblage of these parts to make domestic spaces such as the bedroom, living room, and kitchen. Much of the furniture was moulded from plastic as it could take on many forms. It is possible to imagine the contrast of aesthetics upon the interior as East German citizens had placed this mass-produced furniture alongside antique furniture that they owned before the war. Witold Rybczynski writes in his book *Home*, that '*Stimmung*, is a characteristic of interiors that has less to do with functionality than with the way that the room conveys the character of its owner; that is, the way that it mirrors his soul' (1987, 43). *Stimmung* first occurred in Northern Europe and was present by the sixteenth century in Germany. With the imposed aesthetics of the East German government into the interior spaces of the home, the *Stimmung* would now be absent as the imposed aesthetics no longer represented the individual, but rather the collective. This notion of *Stimmung* would now stand in contrast to the individual character that existed throughout the rest of West Germany.

In contrast to the housing of the 1970s in the East, and the absence of architects as designers, the West saw the housing shortage as an opportunity to make new buildings public and famous. The most recognized new housing in the West after the Second World War took place from 1984–87 as the International Building Exhibition (IBA). West Germany's most successful architects and well-known international architects such as Rob Krier, O.M. Ungers, Alvaro Siza, Aldo Rossi, and Peter Eisenman designed and built new housing developments in West Berlin and the adjacent areas. The outward recognition of this list of famous architects reveals the capitalist trend toward the development of housing in the West. The architects chosen to design the housing were fully aware of the devastation Germany had experienced during the war. The architects took this into consideration, and in turn, their designs responded to the people and their needs. These new buildings also corresponded to the growth in the German economy and did not reflect a one-dimensional solution to a housing shortage such as that seen with the overnight development of the satellite cities on the East. One of Germany's most prominent architects at that time, Josef-Paul Kleihues, became the program director of new construction for the IBA. A general theme was developed for the housing called 'Living in the Inner City'; the goal was to redevelop West Berlin (van Vunckt 1993). The IBA presented design competitions as the means to attract the most famous architects and offered them the opportunity to work among their colleagues in the reconstruction of Berlin. At the onset of the competitions, a clearly defined goal was stated for the reconstruction of West Berlin that addressed social issues beyond the goal of fulfilling a housing shortage. Issues of urban planning, transportation, landscape, and gardens were brought to the foreground as these elements would make West Berlin a more habitable city where one would want to live. The architects building for the IBA in West Berlin were able to learn from the large housing complexes in the East that the building of homes and domestic spaces without architects were a mistake.

Architects designing for the IBA acknowledged landmarks that were part of the Berlin cityscape before the war. These demolished landmarks were important in that they defined the city of Berlin and acted as reference points for its occupants. The West acknowledged and made the decision to continue the recognition of landmarks specific to the city such as zoos, parks, and public buildings that were present before the war. Whereas some were in ruins, the architects were still responsive to the history and memory of the city. In contrast, in the East, the older landmarks were demolished or forgotten about in order to make way for new landmarks that spoke explicitly about the new Socialist state. This issue of choosing to remember and keeping a landmark, as opposed to demolishing and relying upon memory comes into play here as two different political and economic systems had to confront the remnants of a previous time. Today, the *Plattenbauten* in the East have become landmarks owing to their significance as a commentary on housing after the Second World War but not in the positive sense that the West views landmarks before the war.

The architects of the IBA were given sites around West Berlin to develop for housing, which would fill in the empty pockets among buildings that were destroyed in the war. Unlike the East, the West chose to re-build in the city rather than solely locate new satellite cities outside of Berlin. Each architect was given the freedom to express his or her ideas and interests, allowing for variations of housing schemes in the city. This gave a different texture to each neighborhood. The architects would have the same issues to address along with similar themes of reference and problems to solve; yet unlike the housing in the East, the IBA architects could use their own individual language of architecture to bring variation and individuality to the city.[10] The presence of famous architects in the 1980s designing housing in the West can be seen as the beginning of Germany's ability to put emphasis on architecture and housing as a departure from the past and to build a new future. The fall of the Berlin Wall marks the next phase in changes affecting the housing of East and West and the attempt to find a balance between the two divided cities.

After the Berlin Wall

The fall of the Berlin Wall in 1989 has revealed a sharp contrast between West German and East German housing. An early priority for the Berlin government was to minimize this contrast. As the former residents of the East and West began to freely cross the border they also recognize the differences between the two styles of architecture. Indeed, when the housing of the IBA in the West was compared to the *Plattenbauten* in the satellite cities of the East, the contrast was amplified. Moreover the western media portrayed the *Plattenbauten* negatively, which in turn made the occupants question the quality and worth of their homes. However, it should not be forgotten that after the war, the occupants in the East had little choice in finding a home and were faced with either living in demolished buildings or in the new complexes made from the pre-fabricated building components.

This negative projection from the West to the East after the fall of the wall needed to be resolved. In order for the housing to remain useful and prevent the wealthier occupants of higher income levels from moving out, the negative attitudes of the residents needed to be lifted so the housing would not fall into disrepair. City planners sought to prevent the *Plattenbauten* from becoming slums.

Since the early 1990s, the Senatsverwaltung für Stadtentwicklung (Senate Department for Urban Development) has acknowledged the problem of the large housing estates in the East. Renovations have currently been implemented to modernize the façades, providing landscaping that was never completed, and renovating the interiors to be more environmentally compatible to resolve the problem of poor insulation. A study of place attachment by psychologists reinforce the need to renovate the housing complexes as 'housing renovation is an example of an activity that changes the environment ... if people fail to make the changes in their environment that provide support for their desired identities and goals, then attachment can erode' (Brown and Perkins 1992, 279–304). The exterior renovations include in-filling empty lots of land between the large housing blocks with façades similar to housing in the West. Indeed, the exterior renovations remind us of the new slots of housing one finds in the picturesque postcard of Berlin. The choice of the façade is a commentary on the original design of the housing complexes, whereas the original façade of the housing does not reveal the individual, but rather their Soviet production. The new in-fill, instead, makes reference to modern architecture in the West. This process of in-filling can be interpreted as the West's commentary on the East and the West's dislike of the old housing and desire to erase the *Plattenbauten*. In short, the new government has sought to erase the original façade.

The contemporary architect, Daniel Libeskind, who has recently completed the Jewish Museum in Berlin (see Chapters 4 and 6), has said: 'To produce meaningful architecture is not to parody history but to articulate it: it is not to erase history but to deal with it. For example, one must take the existing context in the former GDR seriously, not because one likes the ill-conceived buildings, but because its history and its people must be respected' (Balfour 1995, 36). The current renovation of housing in the East is similar to the previous change in political systems. Like the anonymous façades of the 1970s' Socialist housing, the new Berlin government is expressing its absorption of the East through housing.

In summary, the changes made to the homes and domestic spaces of a unified, divided and re-unified Berlin can be seen through the conception to the demolition of the Berlin Wall. At the present, the public architecture and the image of Berlin through the current media are increasing as famous architects are re-creating Berlin. But it is also a city where the relationship of occupants to home and government is revealed. Currently, the picturesque postcard of Germany will continue to evolve as the streetscapes of the East and West become unified.

Notes

1. Interview with Monica Schümer Strucksberg and Barbara Hoidn, Senate Department for Urban Development, Berlin, 7 June 2001.
2. I recognize that the East and West are not the only way to study German interior spaces. It is also possible to study North (Protestant) and South (Catholic) but at the same time, the East–West best captures the extent to which political and economic events have shaped domestic spaces.
3. Interview with Monica Schümer Strucksberg and Barbara Hoidn, Senate Department for Urban Development, Berlin, 7 June 2001.
4. Berlin in specific is the main focus for this chapter since it reveals issues of homes and domestic spaces currently evolving with unification.
5. Levittown is a similar example that focuses more specifically on the development of American suburban home development.
6. Interview with Andreas Butter, Humboldt Universität, Berlin and Dessau, June 2001.
7. Interview with Dr. Martin Wimmer, Dipl.-Ing. Architeckt BDA-AIV, Berlin, 8 June 2001.
8. Interview with Dr. Martin Wimmer, Dipl.-Ing. Architeckt BDA-AIV, Berlin, 8 June 2001.
9. Interview with Monica Schümer Strucksberg and Barbara Hoidn, Senate Department for Urban Development, Berlin, 7 June 2001.
10. Lotus International 41, Milan, Industrie Grafiche Editoriali.

References

BALFOUR, A. 1995: *World cities: Berlin*. New York: Academy Editions, St. Martin's Press.

BROWN, B. and PERKINS, D. 1992: Disruptions in place attachment. *Human Behavior and Environment: Advances in Theory and Research*, 12, 279–304.

CURTIS, W.J. 1987: *Modern architecture since 1900*. Oxford: Phaidon Press Limited, 118–31.

KAISER, F.G. and FUHRER, U. 1996: Dwelling: speaking of an unnoticed universal language. *New Ideas in Psychology* 14, 3, 225–36.

KELLY, B.M. 1993: *Expanding the American dream: building and rebuilding Levittown*. Albany: State University of New York Press.

LADD, B. 1997: *The ghosts of Berlin*. Chicago: The University of Chicago Press, 99–102.

McELVOY, A. 1992: *The saddled cow*. London and Boston: Faber and Faber Limited.

RYBCZYNSKI, W. 1987: *Home: a short history of an idea*. New York: Penguin Books.

SIME, J.D. 1986: Creating places or designing spaces? *Journal of Environmental Psychology* 6 , 49–63.

VAN VUNCKT, R. (ed.) 1993: *International dictionary of architects*. Detroit: St. James Press, 463–4.

WYDEN, P. 1989: *Wall: the inside story of divided Berlin*. New York: Simon and Schuster.

6

Museums and identities: materializing German culture

BY SHARON MACDONALD

Museums are, among other things, public statements of what counts as significant or 'worthy' culture. Making such statements is not only a matter of assigning value to cultural stuff, however. It is also a means of defining and asserting identities through material culture. In other words, museums help to make identities – our sense of who we are – tangible: they help to *materialize* identities. Museums are always explicitly or implicitly 'of' some population or other, e.g. of the nation, the city or locality. However, that 'of' is as much an aspiration as a fact; it is as much part of the business of creating, defining and redefining a perhaps only partially realized identity as it is of reflecting upon one that is already established and well-defined. As such, museums are of interest to cultural studies not only in terms of the subjects to which they explicitly address themselves but also for what they can tell us about the identities which they are said to be 'of' and which they imagine through their displays. Defined as special and even 'sacred' cultural arenas (set apart from ordinary 'everyday' spaces), museums have much to tell us about the ways in which those who create them see themselves and the world. This is one reason why museums have been called 'contact zones' (Clifford 1997) – spaces of cultural encounter. Any visit to a museum inevitably involves an encounter with the knowledge, identities and cultural assumptions of those who created the displays.

The museum is not, of course, an exclusively German cultural form. The birth and initial development and spread of the public museum can be said to be especially European, with Germany as one of its most significant sites (Bennett 1995; Horne 1984). While many of the developments in the history of German museums can be seen elsewhere (especially elsewhere in Europe), Germany is a particularly interesting case because it became a nation–state relatively late, maintained strong regional identities and has divided and reunified. The development of museums in Germany is intimately interwoven with this identity complex; and the contours of the museum landscape today bear the imprint of earlier entanglements.

While identity definition and performance are important roles of museums, this does not exhaust the cultural work that they do or the meanings that they help articulate. Museum displays are also generally expressions of scholarly and disciplinary knowledge and thus may tell us about predominant academic classifications – classifications which may to greater or lesser extents be shared by the lay-public and/or academic traditions in other countries. Museums are premised on certain cultural assumptions about objects and material culture which, again, may or may not be widely shared. And museums entail particular assumptions about the public – its social constitution, capacities and shortcomings, about learning and communication, and about the kind of experience that a museum visit should generate, which may be more or less culturally specific. These are some of the other, often related, concerns which museums raise and which contribute to making museums fertile investigative ground for cultural studies (see Macdonald and Fyfe 1996; Sherman and Rogoff 1994). Below, I touch on some of these, especially where they connect with my main focus on museums and identity formation and struggle.

From the *Wunderkammer* to the public museum

As elsewhere in Europe, the birth of the public museum in Germany can be seen to have antecedents in the earlier, sixteenth- and seventeenth-century traditions of the princely collections and curiosity cabinets. The latter were collections of what may seem to us to be rather heterogeneous groupings of artefacts but which were based on certain ways of ordering the world at that time, such as drawing connections of similarity of form or of relationship between nature and culture. In what was to become Germany, these curiosity cabinets had a rather specific formation – the *Wunderkammer* or *Kunstkammer*. Like the princely collections of art works, *Wunderkammern* and *Kunstkammern* belonged to wealthy political rulers and served to signal the power and wealth of their owners (Hooper-Greenhill 1992: Chapters 4 and 5). Eminent persons permitted to visit and view the cabinets often brought objects to be added to the collection, thus entangling those visitors in the web of socio-political relations that the cabinets also expressed. The capacities of cabinets to represent knowledge of the world in miniature, to express identities of their owners and to implicate viewing subjects were all ones which would be important to museums, though not in precisely the same ways.

In 1764 Frederick the Great constructed what has claims to be the first public museum in Germany: the art gallery in the Orangerie at his Sans Souci palace in Potsdam. Located at some distance from the main palace, Frederick made his collection open to the public. The founding in the 1820s and 1830s of the complex of Berlin museums which grew out of the royal collections was a more fully 'public' example of the presentation of great art works in that it was not intended to reflect the glory of a particular individual but that of Prussia and Berlin, and to some extent that of the as yet unconsolidated Germany. These museums, especially the Altes Museum, were arranged not simply as splendid eclectic collections but on educational (mostly historical) principles. This allowed for a practice of including reproductions (especially plaster casts) to fill in gaps in the educational-historical stories (Joachimides 2000; Marchand 2000). While this was particularly prevalent in German museums by comparison with their other European counterparts, it was by no means uncontested and existed alongside the attempt to acquire and display authentic originals.

As elsewhere in Europe, the birth and expansion of the public museum were bound up with the formation of the nation–state. In Germany the nation–state, formed from many smaller states, was officially founded in 1871. Despite the fact that it has become so ubiquitous and apparently 'natural' today, the nation–state is a historically rather unique form. Rather than being simply a political unit (a state) to which citizens have a kind of contractual relationship, the nation–state entails the idea that its members share a sense of belonging and identity – an emotional, 'meaningful' relationship. That this sense of felt identity was accorded such importance was very much influenced by Romanticism – a literary-philosophical movement which was largely German in origin (see Introduction). Reacting partly against the rationalizing and bureaucratizing tendencies of modernity, the Romantics emphasized emotional sensibility, tradition and the vernacular, and the importance of distinctive identities at both the individual and national or *Volk* levels. In addition, the nation–state was also characterized by the idea that its citizens are equally members in their own terms rather than this being mediated through hierarchical social relationships. None of this is to say that all of those living within the boundaries of the nation–state felt equally as though they belonged or that hierarchies and forms of social exclusion were absent (see Chapter 1). Rather, these were some of the key, aspirational, elements on which the notion of the nation–state was founded. Because of the importance accorded to the sense of belonging, judicial and political organization alone could not effectively define national subjects and subjectivities. Nor could social organization, in this case because of the fact that nation–states are too large for their members to know one another directly or even semi-directly. Shared cultural forms, and especially those capable of telling stories of nationhood and involving members of the population as national subjects, therefore became crucial for creating a sense of shared belonging and national distinctiveness. Moreover, within the romantic-influenced nation–state world-view, culture came to be seen as the mark of a distinctive identity – the outer expression of 'deep' difference. Museums, as 'culture houses' open to the public, were cultural forms *par excellence* for the identity work entailed in nation building – for creating the *Kulturnation*. Coupled with the spread of the idea of the museum as an expression of cultural identities of other kinds too (e.g. cities and regions), and competition between nations, cities and regions through the medium of the museum (Penny 1999), this led to an explosion of museum-founding in the late nineteenth century.

Materializing national identity

In the period leading up to the official formation of Germany, a number of public museums were established which can be seen as attempts to present some kind of 'German' identity through material culture (though representing regional identities also characterized the period). In 1852, for example, both the Römisch-germanisches Zentralmuseum (the Roman-Germanic Central Museum) in Mainz and the Germanisches Nationalmuseum (the Germanic National Museum) in Nuremberg were founded. As the names of both indicate, they involved an attempt to speak from a 'Central' or 'National' position and to represent a culture that could be said in some sense to be 'Germanic' – an adjective whose referent was still to some extent uncertain in this pre-nation-statist period. Museums such as these were in many respects perfect cultural forms through which to try to define and proclaim the kind of nascent identities which characterized nation-statism. The artefacts which the museums brought together both presented tangible evidence of the existence of 'national' culture (which, whatever it was exactly, was regarded as evidence in turn of 'national' identity) and of the historical depth of that culture. The Germanic National Museum concentrated particularly upon artefacts from the Middle Ages while the Roman-Germanic sought to press 'German' or 'Germanic' identity even further back into classical times. Based on the model of the princely collections and curiosity cabinets, museums also performed the idea that those in whose name they were formed were important – and their architecture often alluded to palaces or temples to emphasize the point (see Chapter 4). Moreover, by opening themselves up to a voluntarily visiting public, the museums helped to materialize the notion of a national citizenship itself. Made visible in the interior spaces of museums were not only encased objects which could be claimed as products of the nation, but also citizens sharing – albeit not necessarily simultaneously – the experience of communing with national culture.

The Römisch-germanisches Zentralmuseum and the Germanisches Nationalmuseum were two particularly prominent examples of a widespread museum-building programme in cities in the years leading up to unification. In the immediate pre-unification years and the decades which followed, most major cities in the new nation–state established museums which, even if they did not include such terms as 'national' in their titles, frequently presented historical and material evidence to give credence to a German identity. Historical and material data employed in museums were not restricted to the prehistoric, classical and mediaeval artefacts favoured by the two 1852 museums, and nor necessarily to the 'high cultural' examples of art collections such as the Altes Museum. The romantic vogue for folk culture, and the significance which this was accorded as part of national identity, were reflected in displays of relatively recent and even contemporary folk-life material as in the Museum of German Popular Dresses and Everyday Life in Berlin (founded in 1889). Museums did not, however, only display items which could be said to be German and indeed the ambition of being 'universal' was important to many museums. Ethnological museums, for example, such as those founded in Leipzig in 1869, Berlin in 1873, Dresden in 1876, Hamburg in 1879 and Stuttgart in 1884, presented displays of cultures from around the world (especially areas colonized by Germany) – sometimes with German folk culture alongside (Voges 2001). In their presentation of discrete 'cultures' through material things, however, such museums helped instantiate the naturalness of the idea of separate and distinctive cultural identities – with 'German' naturalized alongside Melanesian, Polynesian and other 'Others' as part of a broader depiction of 'humanity'.

This kind of representation was also a manifestation of a broader and expanding enthusiasm for classification and typology which distinguished museums from their *Wunderkammer* predecessors. Museums themselves were divided into different types – ethnology, archaeology, art, science and so forth; and their internal spaces and collections were divided and subdivided into taxonomic schemes of various sorts. This concern to order and map the world served also to demonstrate mastery over it; and there was competition between museums at the international, state and city levels to possess the most comprehensive collections. Museums of art, geology, natural history, and industrial technology, also enabled a dual task of showing 'stuff' characteristic of Germany as well as the German, regional and, or, metropolitan capacity to represent and possess the world. Moreover, new evolutionist ideas transformed many displays not only in natural history but also in other types of museums. Thus, the 'cultures' in the ethnological museums came to be presented not only as discrete 'species' but also arranged as part of an evolutionary chain of development in which, as in industrial-technological museums (such as the Deutsches Museum in Munich, Butler 1992, Mayr *et al.* 1990), the German was almost always implicitly or explicitly the culmination.

The whole and the Heimat

One significant feature of the late nineteenth-century museums boom in Germany was the construction of hundreds of local history museums – *Heimatmuseen* – in small towns. Heimat, generally translated as 'home' or 'homeland', is a term which carries a good deal of affective weight and significance in Germany, conveying senses of belonging and community (see Chapters 1, 9 and 10). While the larger museums based in larger towns and cities were generally set up by the upper classes, Heimat museums were more likely to be established by the newly expanding middle classes; and while national and metropolitan museums tended to emulate a sacred, aristocratic and regal aesthetic, the provincial Heimat museums, with their emphasis on ordinary life and persons from the locality, made more secular, rural and homely aesthetic references.

One explanation for the great expansion of Heimat museums in the late nineteenth and early twentieth century might be that they helped articulate identities opposed to that of the new nation–state. However, as Alon Confino (1997) convincingly argues, they are better understood as part of, rather than oppositional to, the newly forming national identity. Heimat enthusiasts were generally also nationalists – mostly middle-class Burgers who saw their work on the Heimat front as part of a recovery of the *'Eigenart'* (the specificity or peculiarity) of which national identity was ultimately composed (Applegate 1990, 86). Thus, the concept of Heimat – which could, after all, be used to refer to both the locality and the nation – was part of the means by which an understanding of 'German history as a network of interconnected local identities' (Confino 1997, 153) came to be expressed and spread. In the historical narratives represented in many Heimat museums, the story of the locality was often related through more 'national' categories: thus, material culture might be arranged beginning with 'the Germanic tribes, such as the Franks and the Alemanni, represented in the archaeological exhibits, advancing to the Middle Ages, with displays of weapons, coats of arms, and heraldic figures, progressing to the life of hometown inhabitants in the early modern period, and finally to the recent past' (ibid., 143). In this way, the local town expressed its identity through the same Germanic ancestors and historical antecedents as were found in the displays in national museums. More generally, as Confino observes, despite the emphasis on local specificity, Heimat museums tended to draw on similar stereotypes (e.g. of a people with respect for nature but willing to embrace aspects of modernity) which had the cumulative effect of conveying a sense of 'national character' through an idiom of local difference.

Rather than depicting localities as irreducibly different from other localities, then, Heimat museums expressed local particularity within a broader depiction of similarity; and rather than being cast as an alternative to national museums and the identities that these articulated, Heimat museums seemed to be regarded as parts that constituted a wider whole. The understanding, then, was of a nesting hierarchy of mutually supportive identities, all expressed by museums, ranging from the local to the national (with various kinds of regional museums in between). Heimat museums, which like their national counterparts sought to make belonging tangible and root it in a material past, were part of the means through which the new way of thinking about national identity was also brought home.

One of the characteristic features of German national identity, in contrast to some other European cases, is that it seems to exist relatively comfortably alongside regional and local identities. The web of museums – Heimat museums, national museums and regional museums – that emerged in the years leading up to the formation of the German nation–state and in the decades which followed, as the national idea was diffused through society, illustrates how this was possible. It also highlights the significance of the museum as a cultural form in enabling this conception of interconnected and mutually supportive identities.

From consolidation to Nazi use

The museum expansion ushered in by national unification continued fairly unabated up until the First World War; and the inter-war period saw the establishment of some further museums along the same general principles, though at a considerably reduced rate compared with the pre-war period. What had been written into the cultural landscape was a conception that any place of any kind of significance should be recognized through having a museum. Marking this significance was important not only for self-identity but also for the growing tourist economy which was connected with the expansion of the middle class (see Introduction). Places came increasingly to signal their distinctiveness – through museums of local history, of famous events, of famous persons (many places, for example, managed to make and museumify connections with Goethe and Schiller), particular industries and products (e.g. the motor-cycle museum at Augustusburg). Moreover, as spaces dedicated to 'things', museums provided apt sites for implicit (and sometimes explicit) discourse on relationships to material goods and consumption – relationships which were often experienced as problematic and contradictory for the new middle classes in this period of capitalist expansion. Museums, which removed objects from the usual cycles of production and consumption, helped to express the idea that things could be about more than monetary value alone (see Chapter 8).

The symbolic and communicative potential of museums was well recognized by the National Socialists when they came to power in the 1930s. Many works of modern art and masterpieces by Jewish artists were claimed 'degenerate' and removed from public display (or, as in the Degenerate Art exhibition of 1937, brought together and exhibited as evidence of depravity (Grasskamp 1994)). Nazi-approved artworks – often neo-classical in style and focused upon idealized 'Aryan' bodies – took their place. Other types of museums were also influenced by Nazi ideology and even established along fascist principles. The latter particularly included archaeological museums – especially open-air versions, the numbers of which grew under the Nazis. As Henning Haßmann explains:

> Pre- and protohistory was a good vehicle for important ideological messages: the cult of race, the Führer cult, the cult of motherhood, the

family, idealization of country life, feelings for the homeland, glorifi-
cation of death, the idea of the Reich, territorial expansion, self-
sacrifice, heroism, loyalty to leaders, honour, fidelity, uprightness.

(2000, 109)

Although not all museums followed the Aryan supremacist line that was
officially propounded by the organization in charge of archaeology at the
time, museums were undoubtedly important public sites for disseminating
these ideas. In museums, artefacts could be used not only to illustrate the
messages but also to provide material substance and the gloss of academic
credibility to make claims appear incontrovertible.

Post-war, pre-reunification

After the Second World War, de-nazification led to the removal of obvious
signs of Nazi influence (such as swastikas) in museum displays and to
attempts to restore confiscated treasures as well as those which had been
stored in order to preserve them from allied bombing. Nevertheless, where
Nazi ideology was deeply embedded in superficially scholarly displays (as in
some of the archaeological museums) these sometimes remained in place for
decades (Haßmann 2000, 123). Doris Schmidt suggests that in the Federal
Republic there was an unspoken ranking order of institutions to be recon-
structed and given public funding, and that museums featured low on this,
beneath theatres and libraries as well as more obvious priorities such as hos-
pitals and schools, and the same is likely to have been the case in the East
which had greater economic difficulties (1989, 270). Nevertheless, in the
West especially, an immense effort to reconstruct historic buildings, including museums, was launched, sometimes almost immediately post-war, suggesting that the rebuilding of museums had a significant psychological
function in this period of disrupted and dislocated identity. Reconstructing,
say, the house of Albrecht Dürer (which was also a museum of his work) in
Nuremberg (which was completed by 1949, before all of those whose
homes had been destroyed had had new homes built for them, see also
Chapter 5), was an important symbolic statement of the possibility of recov-
ering that which was of value in the German past and of rebuilding for the
future. Resurrecting the pre-war landscape was also in part a means of
drawing seamless lines of continuity between pre- and post-war and thus
'skipping' the Third Reich period.

The German Democratic Republic was premised much more thoroughly
and explicitly on the sense of having made a distinct break with the past;
and there the problem was often more one of what to do with 'bourgeois'
cultural forms and heritage. Museums were often revised on explicit ideological lines, as part of an official didactic museological philosophy – an
approach which sometimes entailed displaying 'bourgeois' works specifi-

cally as such, as well as, say, introducing more commentary on, and artefacts pertaining to, working-class life into displays. The organizations
running Heimat museums, for example, were replaced by the 'Cultural
Association for the Democratic Renewal of Germany' and such museums
were at least partly revised, though those in charge of running them were
often not Party members (Coblenz 2000, 327). In a rather wonderful
harking back to the *Wunderkammer* tradition, and in recognition of the
potential of the museum form in identity construction,

> [a]ll large factories, military bases and businesses constructed a
> *Traditionskabinett* or 'tradition room', which showed a brief history
> of the German workers' movement, the Communist anti-fascist resis-
> tance, the liberation of Germany by the Red Army and the foundation
> of the GDR.

> (Richie 1998, 740)

On a larger scale, the East German regime also used museums to sanctify the
new state and its political leadership, most notably in the museums of
German History and of the Communist Party which were established in the
Russian sector of Berlin. East Berlin also inherited the 'museum island'
complex of museums with their splendid collections (of Egyptian and classical treasures among others) and although the buildings remained war-
damaged and to some extent dilapidated, these museums continued to
function partly as they had previously: as signs of prestige, scholarship,
touristic value and state power. It should also be remembered, however, that
those who visit museums do not necessarily only interpret them in the ways
intended by those who have created them – indeed, collections of objects are
perhaps open to alternative and various 'readings' to a greater extent than
are other cultural media. In East Germany, rates of museum attendance (an
activity which is often a matter of personal choice) were in this period considerably higher than those in West Germany (Kirchberg 1999), suggesting
that the appeal of museums may have cut across political affiliations.

In the Federal Republic, museums in the post-War decades seem to have
tended at first towards the academic and apolitical (Schmidt 1989, 267–70).
Beginning in the 1960s, however, the museum emerged as an important site
of identity politics and cultural debate. New museums – over two hundred
in the 1960s and nearly three hundred in the 1970s (Maier 1997, 123) –
sprang up and older ones were often revised and mounted new exhibitions.
A similar museums boom was also seen in other western nations and has
been understood, among other things, as a search for stability and certainty
in a world experienced as increasingly fluid and uncertain, as well as part of
the 'package' of cultural techniques for presenting and marketing 'place'
and 'identity'. In Germany, it also had particular inflections – most especially the degree of concern over the German past and how this should be
represented.

The most high profile examples of attempts to represent history in West German museums were the Haus der Geschichte (House of History, more usually called the Museum of Contemporary German History in English) in Bonn and a German Historical Museum (Deutches Historisches Museum) proposed for a site near the Reichstag in West Berlin. Official proposals for both new museums made in the early 1980s, at a time of greater rapprochement between West and East as well as at a time of growing European cooperation; and both, especially the Berlin proposal, provoked considerable debate about how the past – especially the Nazi past – and 'German identity' should be represented. One notable feature in the proposals for both museums was an emphasis on the place of Germany in *Europe* – the museums would, it was suggested, be able to show the centrality of Germany within European history and at the same time would show Germany to be reflecting on the difficult aspects of its own identity (Till 2000). Moreover, in a period when German reunification was on the agenda, these museums of German history provided the possibility of reminding the public of the shared past and identity of the two states. In the end, neither museum opened until after German reunification: the Haus der Geschichte in 1994 (see below) and the opening of the German Historical Museum, which has now taken over the site of the East Berlin Museum of German History (Museum für Deutsche Geschichte), is due in late 2002.

Another interesting example of struggles to deal with the past in relation to identity, and different treatments by East and West, is the 'museumification' of sites of Nazi terror (Reichel 1999). Occupying troops in both East and West sought, to varying extents, to preserve some of the sites of Nazi atrocity, particularly concentration camps, partly in order to provide 'historical lessons'. In the Democratic Republic, as at Buchenwald, for example, the 'lesson' became a conventionalized account of the persecution of political prisoners which served as a clear ideological story in which opponents to the Nazi regime are depicted as precursors to the existing socialist state. This form of representation effectively framed the East German state as having superseded Nazism – unlike its Western neighbor. In the West, such a neat story was less readily available, and there was sometimes local resistance to being reminded of the brutality – and even existence – of the camps at all. At Dachau, for example, an exhibition mounted by the American forces of photographs of atrocities committed during the war was removed in 1955 after sustained local opposition; and there were complaints from those living in the area that the site was being used for American 'anti-German propaganda' (Young 1993, 64) and that it should be razed completely. Later, however, a group of former prisoners succeeded in creating a small provisional museum on the site, though it was not until 1965 that a more permanent exhibition and memorial were opened. Even after this, controversy over the representation of the site rumbled on. As in the East, concentration camps in the West tended to focus on political prisoners rather than other kinds of internees, especially Jews, particularly prior to the

1980s (Reichel 1999). In both Germanies, then, the museumification of concentration camps was not simply an attempt to 'remember' the past and heed its warnings: it was also concerned with 'containing' the past and in many ways only rather evasively addressing the awkward identity question raised by such sites: namely, 'Are "we" the same Germans who committed these crimes?'.

Post-unification

The decade since German reunification has been marked by what has been called a 'museum mania' – an explosion of museum revision and founding that has superceded even the expansion of the 1970s and 1980s. One particularly notable feature of this epidemic has been a widespread sweeping away of existing displays in East German museums and the creation of new ones. The removal of socialist ideological exhibitions was often effected extremely swiftly post-unification – an indication of a readiness to divest the East from such public signs of its former political identity.

The transcendence of the Nazi past in East German representations of history was a particular bone of contention in the West, no doubt especially as this also implicitly represented Nazism as a 'Western' matter. Moreover, in the West, rather psychoanalytic understandings of the relationship between past and present had become widespread especially since the 1970s – represented, for example, in the concept of 'historical consciousness' (*Geschichtsbewußtsein*) (Macdonald 2000). From this perspective, the avoidance of 'repression' – the failure to face up to and acknowledge the past – was seen as vital for psychic health and especially for preventing the same from happening in future. To 'Wessis' (West Germans), then, the 'Ossi' (East German) way of dealing with the Nazi past, as in the concentration camps, looked like an example of repression that could even contribute to the rise of neo-Nazism. Revising museum displays which gave evidence of such a perspective was, then, regarded as crucial not only in addressing Germany's 'new' reunified identity but also in helping to safeguard the nation in the future, as well, some may argue, as colonizing the former East with perspectives on history rooted in Western capitalism and traditions of psychoanalysis.

However, the drive to push East Germans to reflect critically on the way that the past had been presented in their museums and on what this had to say about how they had defined their identities also highlighted the fact that West Germans had not always 'faced' the past in an exemplary fashion themselves. Many sites of Nazi activity – so-called 'sites of perpetrators' (*Orte der Täter*) as well as 'sites of victims' (*Orte der Opfer*) – had only rather minimal and inadequate exhibitions or were even not made publicly visible at all. One reason for this was Germany's regionalism, the responsibility for such exhibitions generally being at the regional or local level and many regions and localities having no wish to single themselves out as having more Nazi pasts than others. Nuremberg, which I have studied in detail, is a case in point. Lying just outside the city centre, is a collection of marching grounds and vast monumental fascist buildings, which were used for National Socialist rallies. It was not until the mid-1980s that any kind of information for visitors was available at the site and although proposals were made for more extensive museological and didactic treatment, substantial funding was not forthcoming from the city or Bavarian governments as these argued that the site was 'national' and not the responsibility of the city and region (*Land*) alone. Only in the late 1990s did the central government agree to contribute alongside the city and *Land* governments to the creation of a permanent exhibition at the site (which is currently under construction). Funding for the post-unification revision of concentration camps has also come in large part from the central government. This is an acknowledgement of the problem of *national* identity in the new Germany. One way of expressing the fact that the 'new' Germany is not a reconstitution of the 'old' German identity which is regarded as having led to Nazism, is to explicitly and critically reflect upon the past. Museums – already well recognized as 'identity institutions' in various senses – provide ideal spaces for the public acknowledgement and 'working through' of the past, which is considered as a psychic necessity for the health of the new Germany.

The Haus der Geschichte is an apt case in point. Near the beginning of its displays is a panel entitled 'The Ever-Present Past' which says 'Many Germans do not want to discuss the recent past and their own complicity. The burden of National Socialist Crimes accompanies Germany through to the present day.' Inside a small room in the centre of the ground floor exhibition space, names of those who perished in the Holocaust are projected onto the black walls, so placing this destruction at the centre of the account of contemporary Germany. The narrative continues, spiralling up through the floors of the Museum, through denazification, division, the different trajectories of the two Germanies (this is a central juxtaposition), greater participation in European politics, and reunification. This account, repeated in large measure in the new eastern Haus der Geschichte which opened in Leipzig in 1999 as well as in numerous smaller exhibitions, manages to both acknowledge the place of the Holocaust in German identity and also to create a narrative of transcendence of both fascism and totalitarian socialism through democratization. The emphasis given to Europe in these exhibitions is also of interest in terms of identity, for sometimes the narrative almost suggests that German and European identities have become synonymous, the former 'dissolving' into the latter. That proposals for a new Museum of European History have come from the director of the Haus der Geschichte – and that he has suggested that the Haus der Geschichte might offer a suitable model for such a museum (Schäfer 1999) – could, perhaps, be regarded as a logical continuation of this equation.

Another expression of the struggle over identity in Germany is the considerable expansion in numbers of Jewish museums or museums of Jewish history and culture. These include not only the celebrated new Jewish museum in Berlin (in a building designed by architect Daniel Libeskind, see Chapter 4), and well known examples such as the synagogues which have been turned into museums in Berlin and Essen and Frankfurt's Jewish museum – all of which opened in the late 1980s/early 1990s, but also, increasingly, numerous smaller museums and exhibitions, in smaller towns and even rural locations. As Elizabeth Beck-Gernsheim (1999) points out in her discussion of the more general vogue for Jewish culture that has blossomed in Germany over the last decade, these have not necessarily always entailed much Jewish involvement in their construction and running. Their existence is not, therefore, only a matter of Jewish identity (or German-Jewish/Jewish-German identity) but also of the struggle to reflect upon, debate and express what it is to be a non-Jewish German today (ibid.; see also Lackmann 2001). At the same time, such museums are also a recognition of the complex and multicultural nature of German identity; and exhibitions addressing German identity – as, for example, the German Pavilion at Expo 2000 – may strive to conjure up images of an ethnically and culturally mixed nation and depictions of identity that are fluid and dynamic.

Sites of identity reflection and debate

Museums and exhibitions today are much more likely to be concerned with difficult and contested issues – and to be sites of debate and controversy – than were their forebears. Rather than confidently proclaiming identities (though some still do), today's museums are more likely to be sites of reflection and questioning. Thus, the Haus der Geschichte (effectively Germany's national museum of contemporary history and identity), while on the one hand presenting a fairly confident narrative about German identity, also leaves space for sometimes controversial questioning of it. For example, an exhibition which opened in 1999, entitled 'Krauts, Fritz, Piefkes ...? Deutschland von Aussen', highlighted lots of stereotypes about Germans (including garden gnomes, Nazism and tennis stars) and provocatively raised the question of how Germany is seen, and sees itself, today.

Reflection, uncertainty and controversy – and complex, reflexive, multiple and fragmented identities – may also be represented through innovative exhibitionary strategies. This includes the use of provocative art in non-art museums – as in an aircraft exhibition in the Deutsches Museum – Germany's major science and technology museum (Fehlhammer 2000), as well as non-linear and interactive displays – all of which indicate a move away from the typological and evolutionary formats of the past. As in earlier periods, however, by no means all museums and exhibitions today deal with questions of identity, and providing a space for debate on what it means to be German is only one of the many uses to which museums are put. There remain many different kinds of museums and exhibitions – many of which reflect dominant ideas of earlier periods. In addition, there are new hybrid variants that may or may not 'count' as museums (for example, the Centre of Media Art – Zentrum Kunst Medien – in Karlsruhe). Museums today are likely to use multi-media techniques – including video and computers – alongside artefacts and, sometimes, to raise questions about the status of that which they display (Dufresne 1999). While new museum buildings do not generally emulate palaces and temples as did their forebears, they nevertheless generally seek to make striking architectural style statements and perhaps – as, famously, with Stuttgart's New State Gallery or Berlin's Jewish Museum – provocative self-referential allusions. Such museums, through the panache and innovativeness of their displays and architecture as much as through their collections, are, like earlier museums, proclamations of the significance of the places in which they are sited and also, increasingly, part of a set of acknowledged cultural strategies through which image is brought to bear to channel capital in the direction of those places. This, together with the many other kinds of cultural work that museums can do, takes us some way towards accounting for the continued increase in numbers of museums – now totalling more than 3,000 – in Germany. It also helps us understand why 'today, at the beginning of the century, the Museum is the subject of debate as never before' (Schneede 2000, 15).

References

APPLEGATE, C. 1990: *A nation of provincials: the German idea of Heimat.* Berkeley, Los Angeles and Oxford: University of California Press.

BECK-GERNSHEIM, E. 1999: *Juden, Deutsche und andere Erinnerungslandschaften.* Frankfurt: Suhrkamp.

BENNETT, T. 1995: *The birth of the museum.* London: Routledge.

BUTLER, S. 1992: *Science and technology museums.* London: Leicester University Press.

CLIFFORD, J. 1997: Museums as contact zones. In Clifford, J. (ed.) *Routes: travel and translation in the late twentieth century.* Cambridge, MA: Harvard University Press.

COBLENZ, W. 2000: Archaeology under Communist control: the German Democratic Republic, 1945–1990. In HÄRKE, H. (ed.) *Archaeology, ideology and society: the German experience.* Frankfurt: Peter Lang, 304–38.

CONFINO, A. 1997: *The nation as local metaphor: Württemberg, imperial Germany, and national memory, 1817–1918.* Chapel Hill, NC: University of North Carolina Press.

DUFRESNE, S. 1999: Des fantômes qui en disent long: la relation virtualité et interprétation au musée. In GEVEREAU, L. (ed.) *Quel Avenir pur les Musées d'Histoire?*, Paris: Association internationale des musées d'histoire, 137–44.

FEHLHAMMER, W.P. 2000: Communication of science in the Deutsches Museum: in search of the right formula. In LINDQVIST, S. (ed.) *Museums of modern science.* Canton, MA: Science History Publications, 17–28.

GRASSKAMP, W. 1994: 'Degenerate Art' and documenta I: modernism ostracized and disarmed'. In SHERMAN, D. and ROGOFF, I. (eds) *Museum culture*. London: Routledge, 163– 94.

HAßMANN, H. 2000: Archaeology in the 'Third Reich'. In HÄRKE, H. (ed.) *Archaeology, ideology and society: the German experience*. Frankfurt: Peter Lang, 65–139.

HOOPER-GREENHILL, E. 1992: *Museums and the shaping of knowledge*. London: Routledge.

HORNE, D. 1984: *The great museum: the re-presentation of history*. London: Pluto.

JOACHIMIDES, A. 2000: The museum's discourse on art: the formation of curatorial art history in turn-of-the-century Berlin. In CRANE, S.A. (ed.) *Museums and memory*. Stanford: Stanford University Press, 200–19.

KIRCHBERG, V. 1999: Boom, bust and recovery? Arts audience development in Germany between 1980 and 1996, *Cultural Policy*, 5.2, 219–54.

LACKMANN, T. 2001: *Jewrassic Park. Wie baut man (k)ein Jüdisches Museum in Berlin*. Berlin and Vienna: Philo.

MACDONALD, S. (ed.) 2000: *Approaches to European historical consciousness: reflections and provocations*. Hamburg: Körber.

MACDONALD, S. and FYFE G. (eds) 1996: *Theorizing museums: representing identity and diversity in a changing world*, Oxford: Blackwell.

MAIER, C.S. 1997: *The unmasterable past. history, holocaust, and German national identity*, Cambridge, MA and London: Harvard University Press.

MARCHAND, S. 2000: The quarrel of the ancients and the moderns in the German museums. In CRANE, S.A. (ed.) *Museums and memory*. Stanford: Stanford University Press, 179–99.

MAYR, O. *et al.* 1990: *The Deutsches museum*. London: Scala.

PENNY, G. 1999: Fashioning local identities in an age of nation-building: museums, cosmopolitan visions, and intra-German competition, *German History*, 17, 4, 489–505.

REICHEL, P. 1999: *Politik mit der Erinnerung. Gedächtnisorte im Streit um die nationalsozialistische Vergangenheit*. Frankfurt: Fischer Verlag.

RICHIE, A.1998: *Faust's metropolis: a history of Berlin*. London: HarperCollins.

SCHÄFER, H. 1999: Museum of European history. In Haus der Geschichte, *The culture of European history in the 21st century*. Berlin: Nicolaische Verlagsbuchhandlung Beuermann, 227–30.

SCHMIDT, D. 1989: Bildende Kunst. In BENZ W. (ed.) *Die Geschichte der Bundesrepublik Deutschland. Kultur*. Frankfurt: Fischer Verlag, 243–89.

SCHMIDT, M. 2000: Archaeology and the German public. In HÄRKE, H. (ed.) *Archaeology, ideology and society. the German experience*. Frankfurt: Peter Lang, 240–70.

SCHNEEDE, U.M. 2000: Einführung. In SCHNEEDE, U.M. (ed.) *Museum 2000 – Erlebnispark oder Bildungsstätte*. Cologne: DuMont Buchverlag, 7–17.

SHERMAN, D. and ROGOFF, I. (eds) 1994 *Museum culture: histories, discourses, spectacles*. London: Routledge.

TILL, K.E. 2000: Verortung des Museums. Ein geo-ethnographischer Ansatz zum Verständnis der sozialen Erinnerung. In BEIER, R. (ed.) *Geschichtskultur in der Zweiten Moderne*. Frankfurt and New York: Campus, 183–206.

VOGES, H. 2001: Das Völkerkundemuseum. In FRANÇOIS, E. and SCHULZE, H. (eds.) *Deutsche Erinnerungsorte*. Munich: C.H. Beck.

YOUNG, J.E. 1993: *The texture of memory. holocaust memorials and meaning*. New Haven and London: Yale University Press.

III

EVERYDAY CULTURAL PRACTICES

A culture, while it is being lived, is always in part unknown, in part unrealized.

(Raymond Williams. *Culture and Society*)

In his seminal work *The Practice of Everyday Life* (1984), the French ethnologist and cultural historian Michel de Certeau maintains that 'everyday life invents itself by poaching in countless ways on the property of others.' De Certeau's approach to understanding popular culture has been influential, especially in its focus on practices, their strategies and tactics in everyday life. In his work he draws on other cultural historians and ethnologists most notably Foucault and Bourdieu, and on their differing approaches to the study of culture. In this section we see countless examples of 'poaching' on other cultures, on history, on basic assumptions as different spheres of everyday life and work – education, business, food consumption – are brought to our critical attention. De Certeau's work demonstrates a concern with 'the very ordinary' alongside a concern for politics. As the chapters in this section demonstrate, the 'fixed' ideas and assumptions that we find on the surface, when we encounter everyday German culture, in whatever sphere, may be mined for other understandings. What on the surface appears as an egalitarian education system, or a smooth running business culture will appear very different when viewed from other angles and when commonplace assumptions are questioned critically. Indeed, the 'very ordinary' often appears so obvious as to seem self-explanatory, even unworthy of closer scrutiny. In this section, however, questions are asked of how certain practices have come into being, what assumptions have shaped them and how they have been formed into artful, seemingly obvious ways of living, eating, learning, consuming, working, remembering and celebrating.

A dominant aspect of our experience of life in late capitalist, postmodern society, is compulsory education. Although education has a long history, it was, until the last century, mainly the preserve of the elite and leisured classes. Access to education has therefore historically been a mark of class and its fruits seen as giving access to economic and social status and prestige, what Bourdieu (1984) terms 'cultural capital'. Germany's current education system is not its own product, but a system set up under the Marshall Plan after the end of the Second World War. Chapter 7 by Susan Tebbutt maps out the contemporary legacies of this system with a cultural studies concern for the inequalities in the system, particularly those relating to gender and ethnicity. In this chapter we also see how Germany's past is inscribed in the educational process and the way that schools are important sites of memorial, recalling significant authors or historical figures in the names they bear. One of the ways in which education is represented is through literature and film, especially for young people, and this chapter offers some pertinent examples of the images of education that occur in films and fiction in German, seeing these as 'hyperhighways' – as alternative ways of understanding and engaging with education in German culture, that are no less valid routes to understanding than sociological surveys or statistics.

In recent years the work of Jacques Derrida, a French theorist particularly concerned with the approach known as deconstruction, has had a profound influence on the field of cultural studies. Deconstruction may be understood as a critical attitude towards sets of assumptions that attempt to fix meaning. The world of business and the world of consumption are constituent parts of everyday life in contemporary Germany. Germany, like many western countries, is a consumer society and, since the fall of the Berlin Wall, has often been understood as a giant example of the triumph of capitalism. Chapter 8 by Gavin Jack uses this important critical attitude to look at the sets of assumptions that pervade popular consciousness in relation to the 'fixed idea' of 'German business'. It does so in particular by focusing on the wealth of literature and social scientific approaches that have grown up to describe German business practices and German business attitudes, in particular those studies which attempt to show that there will always be a 'fixed' and 'German' way of doing business. The way our assumptions about German business are constructed is carefully and clearly deconstructed here, using critical tools to question the foundations of our knowledge and carefully replace these shaky foundations with other ways of seeing and understanding German business.

In Chapter 9 by Simon Richter we are introduced to the dialectics of the German culinary landscape through the pleasures and the pathologies of German 'foodways'. The focus is particularly on understanding attitudes towards food and how, in different cases, the relationships to regional cuisines, Turkish cuisine and questions of identity may be explored through food and drink. Descriptions of attitudes towards digestion provide an important focus for an exploration of

German food. The author of this chapter relies particularly on psychoanalytic approaches to culture, opening with reference to Freud and to the promising way in which fears, troubles and neuroses of consumption may bring certain distinctive cultural behaviours and assumptions to light. Psychoanalytic approaches to culture and particularly to questions of cultural identity have been productive and significant in the development of cultural studies. Through specific examples, such as BSE, the Döner Kebab, and the distinctive phenomenon of urine therapy, this approach is exemplified and both the cultural history of food and the contemporary issue of food contamination are analysed together to suggest fruitful ways of understanding food consumption in German culture.

References

BOURDIEU, P. 1984: *Distinction: a social critique of the judgement of Taste*. London: Routledge.
de CERTEAU, M. 1984: *The practice of everyday life*. Los Angeles and London: University of California Press.
WILLIAMS, R. 1993 *Culture and Society*. London: The Hogarth Press.

|7|

Schools, colleges and universities: from major routes to hyper-highways

BY SUSAN TEBBUTT

Mapping the education system

Encountering contemporary German culture means encountering attitudes and experiences shaped and formed in part by educational systems. Just as race, gender, class and language all influence culture, so too does education, yet this powerful influence is often neglected in cultural studies analyses. In order to chart the terrain of this cultural studies analysis of schools, colleges and universities in Germany I will produce three overlapping 'maps', the first focusing on major routes and dead-end streets, the second on common ground, and the last on 'hyper-highways'. The aim is to explore the location of power, be it clearly signposted or taken for granted. The focus is on signs of inclusion and exclusion, shared spaces and subcultural identity, traces of and links with past and foreign cultures and images of education in literature and film.

Major routes and dead-end streets

What is education? The German term *Bildung* encapsulates the private and the state concept of education, since it means both 'growth/formation' and 'education' in the formal sense.[1] Over the centuries formal education has been the preserve of a small minority, and compulsory school education is less than two hundred years old in Germany.

Whereas most studies of education systems are of a socio-historical nature, I am interested here in a cultural perspective: I follow in the footsteps of French cultural historian Giroux (1992), who reads education oppositionally, deconstructs historical knowledge as a way of reclaiming an identity for hitherto excluded or marginalized groups, and argues against a romanticization of dominant power structures: 'A more critical version of cultural studies raises questions about the margins and the centre, especially around the categories of race, class and gender' (1992, 202).

Just as Burns sees the *Bildungsbürgertum* (educated bourgeoisie) as the 'acknowledged exponents of the classical conception of German culture' (1995, 16), so there is a tendency for academics to take a canonical approach to the culture of German education.[2] I would like instead to adopt a cultural studies approach, and to provoke debate on issues of inclusion and exclusion within the German educational system.

The discrepancy between the official image of education and the underlying reality is perhaps nowhere more evident than in the Nazi period, when education was overtly hijacked by propaganda propagation, with each lesson beginning and ending with the children and the teacher saying 'Heil Hitler'. Ideological indoctrination was omnipresent in the curriculum, even in subjects such as physics, maths or music.[3] Jewish teachers were banned from teaching German or History as from 17 May 1933 and from 1938 onwards Rust, the Education Minister, banned all Jews from attending school. On 15 June 1939 a decree was introduced which allowed for the expulsion of Romany children from school if they represented a danger for their German fellow pupils (Ortmeyer 1996, 132–7). The racial and racist agenda within schools was closely linked to the work of the *Hitlerjugend – HJ* – (Hitler Youth) and *Bund Deutscher Mädel – BDM* – (League of German Girls); which also served to educate/indoctrinate young people.[4]

After 1945 cultural power was easily located: it resided initially with the Allies. Hearnden (1978) illustrates the influence of Britain on the education system and on Anglo-German relations. Once the two German states were formed in 1949 the ideological manipulation was more explicit and visible in the education system of the GDR than the FRG. Where once Hitler's face looked down from classroom walls, the gurus of Marxism-Leninism cast their imperial gaze on the *Sozialistische Einheitspartei Deutschlands* (*SED* – Socialist Unity Part of Germany) controlled classrooms of the former GDR. In the *Polytechnische Oberschule* (form of comprehensive school for all pupils from age 7 upwards, lit. 'polytechnic upper school'), the principles of Marxism-Leninism were taught, religion was not. Access to higher university was free to all, but some were more equal than others, since priority was given to children whose parents were working class or party members.[5]

Major routes

Before attempting to negotiate some of the dead-end streets I would like to plot the 'major routes', or educational highways through the German system (see Table 7.1).[6] Even after unification in 1990 *Kulturhoheit* (cultural autonomy) lies with the *Länder* (federal states), who are responsible for legislation regarding education, such as the curriculum, recommended course books and exams, but there is some cooperation between the federal states. This cultural federalism means that educational provision is not the same in, for example, Brandenburg and Bavaria. Vestiges of the former differences between the new and the old federal states are found in the fact that pupils in the old federal states still do 13 years of compulsory schooling, whereas those in the new do 12.

Table 7.1 Progression through the German educational system

	Approx ages 6–11	Approx ages 11–16	16+
Grundschule/Volksschule	X		
Hauptschule		X	
Realschule		X	
Gymnasium		X	X
Berufsschule			X
Volkshochschule (VHS)			X
Fachhochschule			
Technische			X
Hochschule/Universität			
Universität			X

Where do the major routes run? Most pupils start their compulsory schooling at a *Grundschule*, formerly also referred to as *Volksschule* (primary school), at the age of six, and attend an educational institution for twelve years, of which the last three can be part-time.[7] At approximately the age of ten or eleven they start the so-called *Orientierungsstufe* (orientation stage) of secondary education. They then opt for one of three types of institution, a *Hauptschule* (a school for those less academically oriented – at the start of the new millennium only some 30 per cent of pupils attend this type of school), *Realschule* (intermediate school) or *Gymnasium* (grammar school) which leads up to the *Abitur* (A levels) specializing in four subjects from three obligatory categories.[8] Failure to achieve adequate grades (1 is the best, 6 the worst), means that pupils have to *sitzen bleiben* (repeat a year, lit. 'remain sitting') and may not finish school till they are in their early twenties.

As Ostermann and Schmidt point out (1998, 106), there is little mobility between the three school types, and the *Gesamtschule* (comprehensive school) does not offer much flexibility either. The 'cooperative' comprehensive has the three separate school types grouped together physically: there were about 200 such schools in the mid-1990s, particularly in Hessen, Bremen (where it was known as a *Schulzentrum*, lit. 'school centre') and Lower Saxony. The 'integrated' comprehensive is more like the British comprehensive, that is, integrated in terms of education and organization:

according to 1996 figures there were about 800 of these, notably in Brandenburg, North Rhine Westphalia, Brandenburg and Saxony (Führ 1997: 125–31). In any case neither type of *Gesamtschule* is truly comprehensive, since neither includes those who are disabled, who have to attend a *Sonderschule* (special school), known in Bavaria as a *Förderschule*.

The *Duales System* (dual system) of vocational training consists of some three to three and a half years of practical instruction side by side with theoretical training once a week at a *Berufsschule* (vocational college). The system is monitored by the local *Handelskammer* (Chamber of Commerce), which vets companies and their training programmes. The *Berufsfachschulen* (Vocational Colleges of Higher Education) were introduced in the 1980s, and attempts have been made to introduce more training places (Ostermann and Schmidt 1998, 110–11) but many large firms such as Siemens run their own training workshops and programmes.

Can people rejoin the highway further along? Those without the *Abitur* can follow the *Zweiter Bildungsweg* (alternative access route to higher education), but within the further and higher education sector there is again a hierarchy, with some 300 institutions of higher education, 90 per cent of them run by the federal states. The *Fachhochschulen* (degree-awarding colleges of higher education – roughly equivalent to the former polytechnics in Britain) have over 400,000 students (Ostermann and Schmidt 1998, 115) and complement the provision for 1.4 million students who in 1994/5 were studying at a *Technische Hochschule* (technical university) or *Universität* (university). Specialized higher education is provided by *Pädagogische Hochschulen* (colleges of education), *Kunsthochschule* (art colleges) or *Musikhochschule* (music colleges).

At universities students gain a *Schein* (certificate) per module, attending *Vorlesungen* (lectures), *Proseminare* (seminars) and *Hauptseminar* (advanced seminars), progress to the *Zwischenprüfung* or *Vordiplom* (halfway stage exam) then *Diplom* (degree) exams, which include a viva. The *Staatsexamen* (degree with a pedagogical component, lit. 'state exam') entitles the holder to teach, but further in-service training is then provided before a teacher is fully qualified.[9] Graduates can proceed to a *Magisterarbeit* (roughly equivalent to a MA), or *Doktorarbeit* (PhD) and even *Habilitationsschrift* (effectively like a second PhD), which may lead to a professorship, although this is not guaranteed.

Since the University Rectors' Conference in 1992 moves are being made to encourage faster completion rates, since apart from courses such as *Betriebswirtschaftslehre* – *BWL* (business studies) with fixed study periods, students may take up to ten years to graduate.[10]

Other highways to learning include over a thousand *Volkshochschulen* (College of Adult Education, lit. 'people's university') over the whole FRG, offering courses on anything from local history and language learning to flower arranging and furniture-making. Whereas anyone can access special radio and TV education programmes (running since the 1960s), the

Fernuniversität (Open University) in Hagen, opened in 1975, is expensive and attracts mainly middle-class students. Correspondence courses are run by over 180 organizations (see Führ 1997, 206 and 223–4). With the introduction of American/British-style league-tables for educational institutions, which grade elements such as employability of students and research successes, people are begin to question traditional concepts of the status of different institutions, but there are still problems with access to the system.

Dead-end streets

In theory the major educational routes are always open. I would like to examine the extent to which certain factors – namely gender, religion and ethnicity, disability and wealth – may prevent pupils or students from travelling down these routes and lead them instead into a dead-end street.

Gender issues

Until the nineteenth century access to higher education was denied to women. 1850 saw the opening of the first institute of female higher education in Hamburg, the *Hochschule für das weibliche Geschlecht* (The Academy for the Female Sex). The first woman to be awarded a PhD was Käthe Windscheid in 1894 (Burns 1995, 18). From 1910 to 1990 the percentage of women studying had shot up from 4.4 per cent to 42 per cent but at the start of the twentieth century there was a reluctance to recognize women's talents not only in universities but also in vocational institutions (see Kolinsky 1995, 33–9). For Gabriele Münter, for example, later to be a key member of *Der Blaue Reiter* (Blue Rider) group of Expressionist artists based in Munich, it was hard to gain a place at art college. In 1912 the director of the Munich Academy of Art is quoted as arguing:

> Vor 100 Jahren mußten die jungen Fräuleins Nähen und Stricken lernen; jetzt tun das die Maschinen; aber die Damen waren damals beschäftigt. Selbstverständlich wollen sie auch jetzt eine Tätigkeit haben und werfen sich deshalb sehr häufig auf die Kunst. Wenn auch vielleicht zehn Prozent von ihnen ein wirklich ernstes Streben haben, 90 Prozent ist es doch nur darum zu tun, die Zeit herum zu bringen, bis ein glücklicher Gatte kommt, der sie von der Kunst wegholt. (Kleine 1994: 88–9)

> (One hundred years ago young ladies had to learn to sew and knit. Nowadays machines do that job, but in former times the ladies were at least kept busy. Of course nowadays they still want to have something to do, and that is why they very often throw themselves into art. Even if maybe 10 per cent of them really have serious intentions, it is

still the case that for 90 per cent it really is merely a matter of killing time until a suitable husband comes on the scene to take them away from the world of art. [NB. All translations are my own])

Despite many improvements to the law less than 4 per cent of professors in Germany are women today.

Gender issues in education do not only relate to participation by females. There are wider implications. Even at the start of the twenty-first century many features conspire to make it difficult for a German woman with children of school age to work unless she has very good child-care. Whereas the state-run *Kindergarten*[11] in the former GDR was an integral part of the state policy to enable women to work, in the West families had to pay to send their child first to a *Kindertagesstätte* (children's day centre)[12] for very young children, and then between the ages of three and six to a *Kindergarten*.[13]

The structure of the school day has implications for families. It is hard for both parents to have full-time jobs, since most schools start at 8 in the morning and finish at 1 p.m. or 2 p.m., with some pupils having to set off at 6 a.m. or even earlier. In the mid-1990s there were over 52,400 schools in Germany, but only 992 were *Ganztagsschulen* (schools which pupils attend the whole day), of which 312 were private schools (Führ 1997: 86–7).[14] Although *Vertretung* or *Sprungkräfte* (supply teachers) are employed in Germany, pupils are often told 'die Stunde fällt aus' ('the class is cancelled') if teachers are absent. Furthermore, if the temperature rises above a certain level, pupils have *hitzefrei* (no classes because of the heat) and may be sent home early. There are some *Schülerlotsen* (equivalent of the British 'lollipop man or woman' or 'crossing guard'), but many pupils cycle to school or take public transport and are thus not dependent on their parents for being taken to school (see Chapter 3).

Religious and ethnic issues

Religious institutions, formerly the main physical site of education, still play a major role in the German-speaking world. In Germany today the Protestant Church has 28.5 million members, the Catholic Church 28 million, and religious affiliation influences the religious holidays which schools have in each federal state. The great majority of schools in the north and east are Protestant, whilst those in the south and west are Catholic, yet there is now a significant minority of pupils in Germany who are Muslims.

Where there is a mismatch between the culture of the school and the culture of the home it is important that teaching should 'encompass a more multicultural philosophy and curriculum, as well as a culturally relevant manner of educating' (Nixon-Ponder 1998, 71). Although there are no all-

Muslim schools, many Muslim children attend a Koran school in the afternoons or on Saturdays. Similarly, children from religious and ethnic minority groups frequently attend sessions of instruction in their own culture, be it Polish, Turkish, Jewish or another culture. There are Jewish private schools in Berlin and Frankfurt am Main.

The constitution makes provision for promoting the languages of the autochthonous minorities in Germany (ethnic groups which have been settled there for a substantial period of time), that is the Danish, Frisian, Sorb and Romany minorities, but in practice this is not always feasible within the official system. In Schleswig-Holstein, near the Danish border, there are now 53 private bilingual schools and 62 kindergartens, and 20 per cent of pupils in Flensburg go to schools in which Danish is the language of instruction (Barker 2000, 145). After unification the Frisian and Sorb language minority (the former in the north-east of Germany, the latter in Lusatia, in the former GDR), have a weaker sense of national identity in relation to the majority German population than do the Danes or Romanies, because the two latter groups have a stronger lobby (see Chapter 2). Nevertheless Sorbian language instruction is still going strong in Upper Lausatia, whereas 'Lower Sorbian has almost died out in the younger generation as a living language, despite the establishment of a Lower Sorbian grammar school in Cottbus in 1991' (ibid., 143). The case of the Romanies is complicated by the lack of a standard written form of the language.

The Romanies' lack of success in educational terms is attributed at least in part to low school attendance rates and the low level of education of the parents. As Hundsalz points out: 'Während die schulpflichtigen Kinder der übrigen deutschen Bevölkerung nur zu etwa 3% die Sonderschule besuchen, sind es bei den Sinti etwa 25 bis 30% der Kinder' (1982, 57) (Whereas some 25 per cent to 30 per cent of Sinti children required to attend school go to a special school, the figure for all other children required to attend school is approximately 3 per cent.). Since there is no support system similar to the Traveller Education Service in Britain, initiatives tend to be limited and local.

At the beginning of the twenty-first century some 10 per cent of Germany's population are *Ausländer* (foreigners), and many children whose mother tongue is not German end up in the *Hauptschule* alongside children from nomadic families or those who are not regular attendees at school. It is hard to find a way out of what appears to be a dead-end street:

From the mid-1970s onwards, the presence of non-German children in the educational system improved the chances of German children to gain [sic] advanced educational qualifications. The lowest tier of a selective school system which would at best equip for low-status employment in the future was increasingly populated by non-German children. The low socio-economic status of parents was perpetuated across the generations through the low educational opportunities of their children. In 1994, one in four young non-Germans and only six percent of young Germans failed to gain a school leavers' certificate.

(Kürsat-Ahlers 1996, 128)

In the higher education sector the picture is no better, as Kürsat-Ahlers points out:

> 0.8 per cent of students at German universities were Turks with German educational qualifications ... Given that university education has become the required route to the professions and to elite positions, even the best-educated young Turks in Germany continue to be penalised because of the background of their parents (1996, 131).[15]

Disability and other issues

The most common reason for attending the *Sonderschule* – called *Förderschule* in Bavaria – (special school) is that a pupil has failed two successive years at school. Others attending may have a visual, hearing or speech impairment, be *Legastheniker* (dyslexics), have learning difficulties, behavioural problems or a mental or physical disability. The special school is separate from mainstream provision, and unlike in Britain, there are no special units for pupils who are blind, deaf or have another disability located within a school for pupils without a disability.

Stress, often refereed to as *Leistungsdruck* (lit. pressure to perform well) may affect performance. There is pressure to pass the year and avoid having to *sitzen bleiben*, even though this enables pupils to have a second chance. Indeed, the competitive nature of the school system may lead to bullying and/or violence, and whole editions of newspapers and magazines have been given over to *Schulstress* (stress at school) and the suicide of schoolchildren. One source of stress which is associated more with Britain and the USA than Germany is schoolgirl-pregnancies. A possible reason for the lower incidence in Germany may be that it is quite normal to find condom-vending machines in school toilets, acknowledging the fact that many pupils are sexually active.

Financial issues

Can money buy privilege in the cultural space occupied by the education system? There are some 2000 private schools in Germany, of which just over half are Catholic. Private schools include grammar schools, schools for the disabled (usually with boarding facilities) and vocational schools. The percentage of pupils attending private school, about 6 per cent, is a relatively low compared to France, the Netherlands or Belgium (see Führ 1997, 168–73).

There are also a number of *Freie Waldorfschulen*, the equivalent of the anthroposophist Rudolf Steiner schools in Britain, which offer more emphasis on creativity and less on academic cramming.

German education is, however, not entirely free, and all pupils are expected to buy their textbooks, which is why each federal state has a limited number of approved works from which schools may select, to ensure standards are maintained. Students may receive *BaFöG* (a grant) to support them through their studies, but most students study in or near their home area, live at home and work part-time or in vacations to finance their study.

The common ground

The term common ground refers in local planning terms to land which is accessible to all. It can also refer to physical or intellectual space shared by two or more people. I will use this analogy to examine first the physical shared spaces and then the subcultures which develop in these areas.

Shared spaces

The classroom is the most obvious example in the education system of common ground. In Germany the primary and secondary class tends to remain most of the day in one classroom, apart from when studying art or laboratory subjects, which helps create a greater sense of group identity than if a class only meets twice a day to be registered, as tends to be the case in British secondary schools. There is a *Klassenbuch* (register and class logbook) in which each teacher records absences, notes misdemeanours and allocates appropriate punishments where necessary.

It is hard to think of other locations within the school which could be said to common ground. Given the low number of German *Ganztagsschulen*, the school canteen is a rarity, but pupils tend to gather instead round small kiosks or spaces where drinks and snacks are on sale at break-times (see Chapter 5). Further subcultures within subcultures may emerge since many secondary schools actually have a room or *Raucherecke* (smokers' corner) designated for smokers.

Since most German universities suffer from severe overcrowding they may initially seem physically hostile. *Numerus clausus* (restriction on admissions) operates in certain types of courses, notably law, medicine and subjects with laboratory places, and it is not uncommon to have up to 1000 students in a *Hörsaal* (lecture theatre). Even when students select courses from the semester's *Vorlesungsverzeichnis* (official list of lectures/seminars on offer), their first choice way well already be full up. Lecturers post details of their *Sprechstunde* (consulting hour) outside their office, but it may prove hard to make an appointment.

Students do, however, negotiate spaces for themselves. The *ASTA* (Students' Union) with its rabbit-warren of offices is a central meeting point. The *Schwarzes Brett* (noticeboard) contains countless notices offering anything from *Mitfahrgelegenheit* (sharing cost of a lift to another city) to accommodation or help in essay writing. Students are usually prepared to eat cheap food in the *Mensa* (canteen) since it is possible to linger there for hours without being thrown out. Many students, particularly foreign visiting students, live in a *Studentenheim* (student hostel) or form a *Wohngemeinschaft* (flat-sharing group) and mark out their collective living space as their territory by painting and decorating it.

Subcultures and (sub)cultural identity

Within the culture of the school or university subcultures develop. To mark the first day at school parents give the *ABC-Schützen* (a term which has no English equivalent – lit. the 'ABC-marksmen') a giant paper cone full of sweets, which they carry to school. This ritual marks them out as the new arrivals and helps to create a common identity. Unlike Britain, children do not have a school uniform, perhaps because of the negative connotations of uniforms and the Hitler youth, but the *Schulmappe* or *Schulranzen* (satchel) has to have regulation reflective strips to make the wearer more visible when heading to school on dark winter mornings.

There is a far stronger sense of camaraderie within a class than there often is in Britain. Each class has a *Klassensprecher* (class spokesperson) and *Klassenlehrer* (class teacher) and usually organizes its own annual *Klassenfahrt* (class trip) sometimes to a *Schullandheim* (roughly equivalent to an education authority residential centre in the countryside) or to a foreign city, and may organize *Klassentreffen* (class reunions) or even *Jahrgangsfeier* (celebrations for a whole year group) in later years. At the end of the summer term many schools organize a *Projektwoche* (project week) when the normal timetable is suspended, and a class does an interdisciplinary project.[16]

The *Schülermitverwaltung* (SMV) (Pupils' council) is a by-product of the 1968 student revolution and the wish for pupils and students to have more say in the decision-making processes. Once pupils are approximately 16 it is common for teachers to start addressing them in the polite *Sie* form, to acknowledge that they are no longer young children. Pupils may, however, request that they still be addressed informally as *du*.

Whereas the SMV empowers pupils and encourages democratic procedures, the *Bundeswehr* (Federal Army), a key educational structure, even having its own *Bundeswehrfachschulen* (Army Training Colleges) and once referred to in 1969 as the 'Schule der Nation' by Chancellor Kiesinger (Küpper 1990, 745)[17] facilitates male bonding, but is strictly hierarchical in structure. All males have to do *Militärdienst* (military service) for 15 months, whereas those choosing the alternative *Zivildienst* (community service) for 18 months may well find themselves working in a hospital, youth centre or centre for the disabled.

Despite the overcrowding mentioned above, there are subcultural groupings to be found in universities, where there are countless religious, sporting and hobby-based organisations and societies. In some of the more traditional universities such as Heidelberg or Göttingen predominantly right-wing *Burschenschaften* (fraternities), some of which still involve duelling, survive. Self-help groups may meet to discuss academic work, and in the student hostels social events such as film evenings or barbecues may be organized. The *Wohngemeinschaft* often survives as a group even after some have completed their studies.

'Hyper-highways'

Just as hypertext is a feature of the computerised world, so there are what I term 'hyper-highways' within the culture of German education, highways which link up German educational culture with other cultural spaces (see Chapter 6). I would like to look first at the links between the names of educational institutions and the cultural heritage, then at links with foreign cultures, and finally at links between the educational culture and images of education in literature and film.

Institutional names as cultural space

Just as the culture and history of a city can be traced in the names of its streets, so the names of many schools, colleges and educational institutions bear witness to people, predominantly male, who have figured prominently in the city, region or country's past. Women are, however, also remembered, and the education connection is seen, for example, in the naming of schools after Anne Frank, born in Frankfurt, but best known for her diaries, and Sophie Scholl, executed for her part in the *Weiße Rose* (White Rose) Munich student resistance movement.[18]

The classical period in German literature, art and music features highly, with Goethe, Schiller and Mozart among the most common names, especially for a grammar school, e.g. 'Goethe-Gymnasium'. Yet the twentieth century is not forgotten. In the former GDR famous socialist or communist activists such as Ernst Thälmann were honoured. At the start of the twenty-first century it is possible to find people from many different spheres of public life whose name is attached to a school or university, from businessmen such as Porsche or Siemens to literary figures such as children's author Erich Kästner (most famous for his *Emil und die Detektive* series).

The erection of commemorative plaques may also link cultural memories to the fate of young people who were killed before they were able to complete their education. One of the most unusual forms of physical tributes to the past was installed in 1988 in the Munich square (now called *Geschwister-Scholl-Platz*) outside the university buildings in the Ludwigstraße. Facsimiles of the leaflets distributed by the resistance group were reproduced on ceramic tiles and cemented into the pavement so it looked as if the leaflets had just been scattered on the ground. Throughout Germany there are many other memorial sites marking the suffering of pupils, from that commemorating the 39 Gypsies from the orphanage in Mulfingen who were deported to Auschwitz, of whom only four survived,[19] two plaques erected in 1985 at the main entrance to the Moltke grammar school in Krefeld to commemorate the deportation or murder of Jewish pupils, or the plaques at the *Volkshochschule* in Bad Homburg and vocational college in Essen commemorating a Jewish school which stood on that site. The hyper-highways may even lead to foreign parts. In the schoolyard of the Maxschule in Ludwigshafen a plaque commemorates the fact that this was one of the three central gathering points from which Ludwigshafen's Jews were deported to Gurs internment camp in the south of France (Puvogel and Stankowski 1995, 278, 542, 593, 673).

Links with foreign cultures

On a more positive note, the *Klassenfahrt*, school and university exchanges and the growing use of English language as a means of instruction offer special opportunities for interaction with other cultures. Great emphasis is placed on language learning in the German system, with all students studying at least one foreign language to a relatively advanced level, English in most federal states, followed by French or Spanish. In the former GDR Russian was the first foreign language (see Chapter 2).

Some 120 schools offer bilingual education. Approximately half are taught in German/English, just under half are German/French, and three or less are German/Russian, German/Dutch, German/Spanish or German/Italian. About 80 grammar schools, thirty *Realschulen*, eight comprehensives, three *Hauptschulen*, and a school centre participate with a total of over 11,000 pupils (Führ 1997, 235). In addition, there are European schools in Karlsruhe and Munich, and many German schools have twinning arrangements with Great Britain, France, the USA or other countries.

There are many European university links with Germany through the SOCRATES scheme, set up in 1995 and formerly called the ERASMUS programme, although more Germans wish to do a foreign exchange and improve their intercultural competence than the number of British wishing to go to Germany.[20] Opportunities for student exchanges and cultural encounters for young people from many countries are sponsored by organizations such as the Goethe-Institut, the DAAD (Deutscher Akademischer Auslandsdienst – German Academic Exchange Service) and the Alexander-von-Humboldt-Stiftung, which gives some 600 grants every year for research in Germany (Moos, *et al.* 1992, 235–43). Kuhn and Wilhelm (1979) list some 200 organizations which facilitate exchanges, whether linked to music, the arts, theatre, literature, journalism, the media, cinema, religion, archaeology, sport or the peace movement.

This globalization is in turn having an impact on German universities, which now not only provide summer university programmes in German for foreign students but offer degree programmes in English to attract more students from abroad and collaborate with foreign institutions to offer jointly validated dual degrees (Ostermann and Schmidt 1998, 121).

Images of education in literature and film

The world of education may be reflected in works of German-language literature or films created by adults or young people. Works by adults far outweigh those by young people, and there is only room here to mention a very small selection. It is important to look at both the outsider and the insider perspective on the different stages of education.

By far the largest number of works relate to secondary school education. Examination pressure is central to Frank Wedekind's ground-breaking play *Frühlings Erwachen* (1891), about grammar school pupils, puberty and teenage pregnancy. In many respects it remains as topical as when it was first produced. As Moritz, one of the main schoolboy anti-heroes of the play complains: 'Wozu gehen wir in die Schule? – Wir gehen in die Schule, damit man uns examinieren kann! Und wozu examiniert man uns? – Damit wir durchfallen' (1967, 15) ('What's the reason we go to school? – We go to school, so that they can examine us! And what's the reason they examine us? – So that we fail.')[21]

Failing in society is a central theme in the *problemorientiertes Jugendbuch* (problem-oriented teenage novel) which developed into a sub-genre of teenage fiction from the 1960s onwards. Whether about ethnic minority groups, bullying, or addiction to alcohol or drugs, these uncompromising, ideologically critical works question the cultural authority of adults in power and the way the school system has failed teenage pupils.[22] The title *Die Einbahnstraße* (*One-way Street*) of Klaus Kordon's 1979 novel about a group of teenage pupils, one of whom dies of a heroin overdose, could be taken as paradigmatic for many of these novels, which demonstrate how hard it is to move from the culture of a disadvantaged group into mainstream education, once people have started out down a 'one-way street'.

The dead end may also be encountered by people doing apprenticeships, as in Swiss playwright Max Frisch's parable *Andorra* (1961), in which the

friction between the apprenticeships and their educators has racial under-
currents, and Ulrich Plenzdorf's novel *Die neuen Leiden des jungen W.*
(1973) in which the friction is between the expected conformity to the
socialist brigade and GDR anti-hero Wibeau, the rebellious apprentice,
weary of the cultural claustrophobia of the GDR system.[23]

Criticism of indoctrination plays a key role in Ödön von Horváth's
Jugend ohne Gott (1937), set in a Nazi Germany in which the humanitarian
goals of education have been marginalized. The headmaster tells the schoolboy narrator, who is soon to take part in a Hitler Youth camp: 'Wir müssen
von der Jugend alles fernhalten, was nur in irgendeiner Weise ihre zukünfti-
gen militärischen Fähigkeiten beeinträchtigen könnte – das heißt: wir
müssen sie moralisch zum Krieg erziehen. Punkt' (von Horváth 1937, 9),
(We have to keep everything away from young people which could in any
shape or form possibly be detrimental to their future military skills – in
other words, we have to prepare them morally for war. Full stop.)

The dramatic consequences of weaknesses in the education system are
apparent in both Austrian writer Erich Hackl's novel *Abschied von Sidonie*
(1989) and Bernhard Schlink's best-selling, controversial novel *Der Vorleser*
(*The Reader* 1995).[24] In the former an abandoned Gypsy girl is adopted by
an Austrian family and starts school in 1939. Derogatory statements by the
village primary school head contribute to the decision to deport her to
Auschwitz in 1943. Schlink's novel revolves round the relationship between
the illiterate Hanna, a former guard in a Nazi camp, and Michael Berg.
Hanna's inability to read plays a key role in the novel. Critics talk of
'humanizing' the perpetrators of Nazi crimes and of the dehistoricizing of
the Holocaust, but little attempt has been made to explore the 'humanizing'
of the woman who is illiterate, with Schmitz even referring to Hanna's illiteracy very melodramatically as 'her terrible secret' (2000, 262).[25] Both
works are examples of how one link may lead to another, since they both
open up further links to writing about the Holocaust and the complicity of
Germans and Austrians.

Many of the above works of literature have been filmed, providing further
'hyper-highways' traversing the world of education. Three examples of
intertextuality (or perhaps intermediality might be a more appropriate term)
are Josef von Sternberg's classic *Der blaue Engel* (1930) (see Chapter 13),
based on Heinrich Mann's *Professor Unrat* and starring Marlene Dietrich
and the music of Friedrich Hollaender, the film of Robert Musil's *Die
Verwirrungen des Zöglings Törleß* (1905) directed by German New Wave
film director Volker Schlöndorff (1965/66), and Egon Günther's film *Die
neuen Leiden des jungen W.* (1976), based on Plenzdorf's 1973 novel, itself
a reworking of Goethe's *Die Leiden des jungen Werthers* and strongly influenced by American cult writer Salinger's *Catcher in the Rye*.

Whereas the above films revolve round secondary school and apprenticeship, the results of poor education are highlighted in *Christiane F.*, one of
the hundred greatest cinema box-office hits of the 1980s, seen by 4.6 million

cinema-goers (Jacobsen, *et al.* 1993, 292), and a cultural phenomenon in its own right. The film was based on a book, which in turn was based on tape recordings made at the end of the 1970s by *Stern* reporters Hermann and Rieck with schoolgirls in Berlin who had been sucked into the world of prostitution and drug abuse.

Christiane F forms the bridge between works by adults and works by young people, since it was written by adults, but relies heavily on the transcripts of conversations with young people. In the 1990s a number of works have been published by schoolchildren for young people. They may be the result of local competitions, part of a *Projektwoche*, or initiated by specific ethnic, religious or city-based groups, but they generally only reach a restricted audience. Three examples of works which reached a national audience are the Wolfsburg secondary school collective production of a detective story, *Was ist denn schon dabei?* (1994),[26] an anthology by Jewish schoolchildren edited by Alexa Brum *et al.*, *Ich bin, was ich bin, ein Jude: Jüdische Kinder in Deutschland schreiben* (1995) and an anthology about Hamburg, *Kinder sehen ihre Stadt: Hamburg* (1997).

Conclusion

On examining the three 'maps' of the German education system the major highways are clearly marked, yet the 'slip roads' are often hard to access. As has been shown, many people are excluded from easy initiation to higher education as a result of their ethnicity or disability, although the constitution exists to protect them and supposedly guarantee equality of opportunity.

The hierarchical model of separate school types seems to promote a self-perpetuating exclusion, yet within this system there are very strong sub-cultural spaces which help the individual to find a cultural identity within institutions, to have a sense of cultural belonging.

Clicking on the links to the hyper-highways takes the explorer to inter-cultural, cross-cultural spaces, to traces of the cultural past, to intersections with other cultures and explorations of cultural forms, completing the loop back to the culture of education. Placed together, the three maps provide a multi-dimensional network of insights into the complex landscape of the German education system and its spaces and places. Yet the intrepid explorer need not despair: the landscape is constantly changing and there is still much uncharted territory.

Notes

1. See Burns (1995, 16–21) for an overview of the 'cultural education of the public' from the 1870s to the present day. Note that '*geschult*' meaning 'schooled' is normally used to mean 'practised' or 'expert'. The phrase '*Schule machen*' means 'to set a precedent', lit. 'to make school'.

2. See Ostermann and Schmidt (1998, 105–23) for an overview of the system, based almost entirely on articles in *Der Spiegel* and *WirtschaftsWoche*.
3. See Blackburn (1985) for a study of the pervasive influence of Nazi ideology in the representation of history of the 'mystical community: The Volksgemeinschaft' (1985, 116–37). See also Ortmeyer (1996) on the everyday culture of school during the Nazi period, with many first-hand recollections of school life, from the treatment of Jewish teachers and pupils and acerbic comments written on essays, to the deportation of Jewish and Sinti and Roma children to concentration camps. Ortmeyer devotes the final two parts of the book to the treatment of this period in schools after 1945 and the obstacles to researching this field. Giles (1985) gives a comprehensive overview of the oppositional activities of students.
4. Erika Mann's biting satire of education under the Nazis, *Die Schule der Barbaren* (*School for Barbarians* 1936) was republished in 1989 under the title *Zehn Millionen Kinder: Die Erziehung der Jugend im Dritten Reich* (*Ten Million Children: The Education of Young People in the Third Reich*), almost as though it were a documentary account.
5. See Husner for a survey of the structures of study programmes, but also interestingly on use of non-study time and the extent to which free time was regimented by the state (1985, 79–87).
6. Table 7.1 shows the passage through the German educational system.
7. Parents have the right to withhold their child if they feel he or she is not *schulreif* (ready for school) in either intellectual or social terms.
8. It is possible to do the *Abitur* in technical subjects. Pupils follow a separate programme for the two years leading to the exam.
9. Only German nationals can attain *Beamtenstatus* (civil servant status), which gives job security but forbids them from striking.
10. Many students take the odd semester off to earn money or to pursue a hobby, such as skiing.
11. See Allen (1997) for an account of the importance of Swiss pedagogue Johann Heinrich Pestalozzi and of Friedrich Froebel's development of the *Kindergarten* in the 1840s.
12. Commonly abbreviated to *Kitas*.
13. There are positive links between child rearing and feminism, as Allen points out, since the kindergarten: 'was a challenge to conventional public/private boundaries. It brought women and small children out of the home into an institution, but it also created an institutional culture based on private, or familial, values' (1997, 117), in contrast to the predominantly authoritarian methods of the time.
14. See Kappler (1996, 450–80) for an overview of schools, vocational training and research in Germany.
15. See Führ (1997, 30–1) on foreigners and foreign pupils and their distribution across different school types. Tan and Waldhoff (1996, 151–2) analyse the limited success of Turkish students in the German university system.
16. Roer (1986) describes how to run a project week based on Gudrun Pausewang's prize-winning novel *Die letzten Kinder von Schewenborn* (1983), exploring the connections between literature, film, peace education and environmental issues.
17. 27 June 1969. Since then some have jokingly referred to TV as the *Schule der Nation*.
18. See Vinke (1980) for a work of teenage literature, itself a subculture, which makes the culture of student resistance to the Nazi regime accessible to young people.
19. See Meister's article (1987) and Krausnick (1995, 95–124) for information about the intersection points of education, culture and commemoration.

20. See Parker and Rouxeville (1995) for articles on cross-cultural training and the impact of ethnographic training. See Opper *et al.* (1990) on the cultural impact of study programmes abroad and the importance of global awareness.

21. See Burns (1995, 18–21) for an analysis of images of education in German-language literature. Note that the term *Bildungsroman*, which has no English equivalent, revolves round the development or maturing of a character over the course of the book.

22. See Tebbutt (1994, 62–76) for an account of the rise of 'das problemorientierte Jugendbuch'.

23. See Peltsch on the role of hope in Plenzdorf's novel (1995, 204–7).

24. The novel has also become a best seller in English.

25. Long (2000) analyses Berg's 'retreat into moral relativism' (2000, 53). Parkes (2001, 94–101) explores the extent to which Hanna's guilt is explained in terms of her illiteracy. See also the film *Das schreckliche Mädchen* (1990), directed by Michael Verhoeven, about a schoolgirl who begins to investigate the Nazi past of her home-town of Passau, where Eichmann had lived and Himmler's father was a teacher.

26. See Tebbutt (2000, 227–32) for an overview of writing by young people for young people.

References

ALLEN, A.T. 1997: Feminism and motherhood in Germany and in international perspective 1800–1914. In Herminghouse, P. and Mueller, M. (eds), *Gender and Germanness: cultural productions of nation*. Providence, Oxford: Berghahn, 113–28.

ANWEILER, O., FUCHS, H-J., DORNER, M. and PETERMANN, E. 1992: *Bildungspolitik in Deutschland 1945–1990*. Opladen: Leske and Budrich.

BARKER, P. 2000: Autochthonous minorities in the German-speaking countries: an overview. In JORDAN, J. and BARKER, P. (eds) *Migrants in German-speaking countries*. London: CILT, 137–55.

BENZ, U. and BENZ, W. (eds) 1992: *Sozialisation und Traumatisierung: Kinder in der Zeit des Nationalsozialismus*. Frankfurt am Main: Fischer.

BLACKBURN, G.W. 1985: *Education in the Third Reich: a study of race and history in Nazi textbooks*. Albany, NY: State University of New York Press.

BRUM, A. et al (eds) 1995: *Ich bin, was ich bin, ein Jude: Jüdische Kinder in Deutschland erzählen*. Cologne: Kiepenheuer and Witsch.

BURNS, R. (ed.) 1995: *German cultural studies*. Oxford: Oxford University Press.

DROSDOWSKI, G. and SCHOLZE-STUBENRECHT, W. 1992: *Duden – Redewendungen und sprichwörtliche Redensarten: Wörterbuch der deutschen Idiomatik*, Mannheim, Leipzig: Duden.

FOCKE, H. and REIMER, U. 1979: *Alltag unterm Hakenkreuz: Wie die Nazis das Leben der Deutschen veränderten*, Reinbek bei Hamburg: Rowohlt.

FRISCH, M. 1961: *Andorra*, Frankfurt am Main: Suhrkamp.

FÜHR, C. 1997: *The German education system since 1945*. Translated from the German by HEIDINGSFELD, V. and NEVILL, T., Bonn: Inter Nationes.

GILES, G.J. 1985: *Students and National Socialism in Germany*. Princeton, NJ: Princeton University Press.

GIROUX, H.A. 1992: Resisting difference: cultural studies and the discourse of critical pedagogy. In GROSSBERG, L., NELSON, C. and TREICHLER, P.A. (eds) *Cultural studies*. New York, London: Routledge, 199–212.

HACKL, E. 1989: *Abschied von Sidonie*. Zurich: Diogenes.

HEARNDEN, A. 1976: *Education, culture and politics in West Germany*. Oxford: Pergamon.

HEARNDEN, A. (ed.) 1978: *The British in Germany: educational reconstruction after 1945*, London: Hamish Hamilton.

HERMANN, K. and RIECK, H. (eds) 1990 (32. edn.): *Christiane F.: Wir Kinder vom Bahnhof Zoo*. Hamburg: Gruner + Jahr.

HORVÁTH, Ö. VON [1937] 1974; *Jugend ohne Gott*. HUISH, I. (ed.) London: Harrap.

HUNDSALZ, A. 1982: *Soziale Situation der Sinti in der Bundesrepublik Deutschland*. Stuttgart: W. Kohlhammer.

HUSNER, G. 1985: *Studenten und Studium in der DDR*. Cologne: Verlag Wissenschaft und Politik.

JACOBSEN, W., KAES, A. and PRINZLER, H.H. 1993: *Geschichte des deutschen Films*. Stuttgart: Metzler.

KANT, H. 1966: *Die Aula*. Berlin: Rütten and Loening.

KAPPLER, A. (ed.) 1996: *Tatsachen über Deutschland*. Frankfurt am Main: Societäts-Verlag.

KINDER SEHEN IHRE STADT 1997: *Hamburg; Die schönsten Geschichten aus dem Hamburger Erzählwettbewerb*. Weinheim: Beltz and Gelberg.

KLEINE, G. 1994: *Gabriele Münter und Wassily Kandinksy: Biographie eines Paares*. Bonn: VG Bild-Kunst.

KOLINSKY, E. 1995: *Women in 20th-century Germany*. Manchester: MUP.

KORDON, K. 1979: *Die Einbahnstraße*. Stuttgart: Spektrum.

KRAUSNICK, M. 1995: *Wo sind sie hingekommen?: Der unterschlagene Völkermord an den Sinti und Roma*. Gerlingen: Bleicher.

KUHN, G. and WILHELM, H. (eds) 1979: *Deutsche Partner im internationalen Kulturaustausch: Verzeichnis deutscher Institutionen*. Baden-Baden: Nomos Verlagsgesellschaft.

KÜPPER, H. 1990: *Pons-Wörterbuch der deutschen Umgangssprache*. Stuttgart: Klett.

KÜRSAT-AHLERS, E. 1996: The Turkish minority in German society, in HORROCKS, D. and KOLINSKY, E. (eds) *Turkish culture in German society today*. Providence, Oxford: Berghahn, 113–35.

LONG, J.J. 2000: Bernhard Schlink's *Der Vorleser* and Binjamin Wilkomirski's *Bruchstücke*: best-selling responses to the Holocaust, in WILLIAMS. A., PARKES, S. and PREECE, J. (eds) *German-language literature today: international and popular?*, Oxford: Peter Lang, 49– 66.

MANN, E. 1989: *Zehn Millionen Kinder: Die Erziehung der Jugend im Dritten Reich*. Munich: dtv (1st publ. in New York as *School for Barbarians* in 1936, and later that year by Querido Press in Amsterdam as *Die Schule der Barbaren*).

MEISTER, J. 1987: Die „Zigeunerkinder" von der St. Josefspflege in Mulfingen. In *Sonderdruck aus 1999: Zeitschrift für Sozialgeschichte des 20. und 21. Jahrhunderts*, 2.

MOOS, D., PILTZ, T. and ELSBERGER, S. (eds) 1992: *Kulturelles Leben in der Bundesrepublik Deutschland*. Bonn: Inter Nationes.

NIXON-PONDER, S. 1998: Teens and schools: who is falling through the cracks and why. In EPSTEIN, J.S. (ed.) *Youth culture: identity in a postmodern world*. Oxford: Blackwell, 56–73.

OPPER, S., TEICHLER, U. and CARLSON, J. (eds) 1990: *Impacts of study abroad programmes on students and graduates*. London: Jessica Kingsley.

ORTMEYER, B. 1996: *Schulzeit unterm Hitlerbild*. Frankfurt am Main, Fischer.

OSTERMANN, H. and SCHMIDT, U.E. 1998: Education, training and the workplace. In JAMES, P. (ed.) *Modern Germany: politics, society and culture*. London and New York: Routledge.

PARKER, G. and ROUXEVILLE, A. (eds) 1995: *'The year abroad': preparation, monitoring, evaluation,* London: CILT.

PARKES, S. 2001: Die Ungnade der späten Geburt: the theme of National Socialism in recent novels by Bernhard Schlink and Klaus Modick. In SCHMITZ, H. (ed.) *German culture and the uncomfortable past,* Aldershot: Ashgate, 87–101.

PAUSEWANG, G. 1983: *Die letzten Kinder von Schewenborn,* Ravensburg: Otto Maier (Transl. N.M. Watt, 1988, *The last children of Schewenborn,* Saskatoon, Saskatchewan: Western Producer Prairie Books).

PELTSCH, S. 1995: Edgar Wibeau, Frank Mosman und andere: Jugendliche auf der Suche nach einem Platz in der DDR-Gesellschaft. In RAECKE, R. and BAUMANN, U.D. (eds) *Zwischen Bullerbü und Schewenborn: Auf Spurensuche in 40 Jahren deutschsprachiger Kinder- und Jugendliteratur.* Munich: Arbeitskreis für Jugendliteratur.

PLENZDORF, U. 1973: *Die neuen Leiden des jungen W.* Rostock: Hinstorff.

PUVOGEL, U. and STANKOWSKI, M. (eds) 1995, 2nd rev. edn.: *Gedenkstätten für die Opfer des Nationalsozialismus.* vol. 1. Bonn: Bundeszentrale für politische Bildung.

ROER, W. 1986: *Ein Buch macht Schule.* Lichtenau: Göttingen.

SCHITTENHELM, K. 1999: Ungleiche Wege in den Beruf: Geschlechterdifferenz und soziale Ungleichheit in der Aneignung und Verwertung von Bildung. In TIMMERMANN, H. and WESSELA, E. (eds), *Jugendforschung in Deutschland: Eine Zwischenbilanz.* Opladen: Leske and Budrich, 133–49.

SCHLINK, B. 1995: *Der Vorleser.* Zurich: Diogenes.

SCHMITZ, H. 2000: The return of the past: post-unification representation of National Socialism: Bernhard Schlink's *Der Vorleser* and Ulla Berkéwicz's *Engel sind schwarz und weiß.* In FLANAGAN, C. and TABERNER, S. (eds) *1949/1989: Cultural perspectives on division and unity in East and West.* Amsterdam, Atlanta/GA: Rodopi, 259–76.

SCHOLL, I. 1986: *Die Weiße Rose,* Frankfurt: Fischer (extended edition, 1st publ 1955).

SCHÜLER der Klasse 10a der Ferdinand-Porsche-Realschule Wolfsburg. 1994: *Was ist denn schon dabei?* Weinheim: Beltz and Gelberg.

SIEFKEN, H. (ed.) 1991: *Die Weiße Rose: Student Resistance to National Socialism 1942/1943.* Nottingham: University of Nottingham.

STEEDMAN, C. 1997: Writing the self: the end of the scholarship girl. In MCGUIGAN, J. *Cultural Methodologies.* London: Sage, 106–25.

SZYDLIK, M. 1999: Jugend zwischen Studium und Beruf. In TIMMERMANN, H. and WESSELA, E. (eds) *Jugendforschung in Deutschland: Eine Zwischenbilanz.* Opladen: Leske and Budrich, 133–49.

TAN, D. and WALDHOFF, H-P. 1996: Turkish everyday culture in Germany and its prospects. In HORROCKS, D. and KOLINSKY, E. (eds) *Turkish culture in German society today.* Providence, Oxford: Berghahn, 137–56.

TEBBUTT, S. 1994: *Gudrun Pausewang in context: socially critical 'Jugendliteratur', Gudrun Pausewang and the search for utopia.* Frankfurt am Main: Peter Lang.

TEBBUTT, S. 2000: Bridging the cultures: German contemporary *Jugendliteratur.* In WILLIAMS, A., PARKES, S. and PREECE, J. (eds) *German-language literature today: international and popular?* Oxford: Peter Lang, 221–36.

TIMMERMANN, H. and WESSELA, E. (eds) 1999: *Jugendforschung in Deutschland: Eine Zwischenbilanz.* Opladen: Leske and Budrich.

VINKE, H. 1980: *Das kurze Leben der Sophie Scholl.* Ravensburg: Otto Maier.

WEDEKIND, F. 1967 (1st publ. 1891): *Frühlings Erwachen: Eine Kindertragödie, Der Marquis von Keith.* Munich: Goldmann, 11–78.

8

Critical encounters with representations of German business

BY GAVIN JACK

Vorsprung durch Technik

For many students of German, especially in Britain, and for many car enthusiasts too, Volkswagen's famous advertising slogan for its Audi range has been a source of enduring fascination since its entry into the public sphere in 1982. For those learning German language, it presented an interesting problem of translation: just how best should the notion of *Vorsprung* be rendered in English? (see Chapter 2). For car enthusiasts, by contrast, its significance lay not so much in the translation conundrum as the use of the German language as a cultural signifier (i.e. as being symbolic of German culture). Here, the deployment of a German slogan in an English-speaking target market served to enhance the reputation of Audis as a technologically advanced automobile. It drew upon traditional notions of German strength and prowess in the area of engineering and technical production in order to endow Audi cars with connotations of reliability and efficiency. The slogan was a cultural signifier for the strong reputation of the manufacturing base of the German economy. It was constructed from and subsequently became emblematic of the 'Made in Germany' national brand, a sign of the country's (West Germany's at least) economic and political resurgence on the world stage propagated by the *Wirtschaftswunder* of the 1960s and early 1970s.

It is through such images of manufacturing strength, technological efficiency and economic success that everyday understandings of 'German business' are commonly encountered and mediated. In addition to these images, the traditional strength of German manufacturing has also been mediated in the everyday material cultures of cars, computers and pharmaceuticals as German brand names pervaded the mass consumer markets of the USA and the UK during the 1970s and 1980s. The borders of German business do not just pertain then to the domestic German market – they are more extensive and less rigidly demarcated than that. Against this background of economic prowess, the 'Germans' are stereotypically represented as markedly logical, unfailingly reliable and fiercely efficient in terms of their managerial practice, sometimes blunt and always direct in terms of their communicative style. Like all stereotypes, however, these images are just short-hand mental notes for the construction of a cultural Other and as such, they require qualification and exploration lest they remain at the level of popular myth. Within the discipline of management studies, research into Anglo-German business[1] has gone significantly beyond these stereotypical notions of German management (at least rhetorically) in attempting to understand and explain the philosophy, values and practices which differentiate the conduct of business in the UK and Germany. This chapter will provide a critical introduction to some of this literature on German business originating principally from the management studies sub-discipline of comparative management.[2]

With studies of comparative management involving Germany as its object of inquiry, then, the aim of this chapter is twofold. First, the chapter will begin by introducing two key frames of reference (or theories) which are predominantly deployed by researchers. These are labelled the *institutional* and the *culturist* frames respectively and they help us describe and explain what it is we encounter in this notion of 'German business'. As such, rather than providing an inevitably bland, broad-brush and freeze-frame description of 'how the Germans do business', this first objective sets out to provide an understanding of a 'way of seeing'[3] German business, rather than a 'particular picture'.

The second objective is based on the first and is more critical in intent. Having outlined these two principal frames of reference, the chapter seeks to undermine the very premises and possibilities of such frames. It poses reflective questions about the knowledge which the deployment of these frames constructs and in suggesting tentative answers to these questions offers criticisms of and challenges to these ways of seeing. In this spirit, the final section of this chapter presents data from a research study which offers an alternative frame for thinking about German business (a social constructionist frame). The data provides an interpretation of a real example of an encounter with 'German' business, one which emphasizes the provisional and shifting nature of the categories of knowledge used to understand the 'German' as a cultural Other. In order to achieve these critical aims, the chapter draws upon concepts from the disciplines of sociology and cultural studies such as reification, codification and reductionism. The intention here is to introduce a set of ideas with which to scrutinize the various ways of seeing the cultural Other instantiated by previous research on German business.

The concept of business culture and the institutional view

The institutionalist school of thought appears in various guises in the discipline of management studies, ranging from the study of disparate 'National Business Systems' (Whitley 1992), or the 'societal effect' of management (Maurice 1979) to the investigation of 'business cultures' (Randlesome *et al.* 1993). Binding together these various strands of institutional theory is a common concern to investigate and document how organizational structures/strategies/practices and societal/institutional arrangements are interrelated and, based upon this, how these relationships differ between nations like the UK and Germany. To give a brief illustration of what this means, take industrial democracy in Germany, i.e. the ways in which workers' voices are mobilized, organized and heard by their employers. The concept of *Mitbestimmung*, or co-determination, is key to understanding the philosophy and practice of industrial democracy in Germany. Derived from the broad philosophy of Germany's social market economy and its reproduction through societal institutions like the Federal government, the concept of *Mitbestimmung* has a determining influence on industrial relations policy for organizations (both corporations and private limited companies) which employ more than 2000 workers.[4] Enshrined in the 1976 Co-determination Act (*Mitbestimmungs-Gesetz*), the law makes it a statutory obligation for these organizations to have a supervisory board comprising half shareholders' and half workers' representation. At least in principle, then, workers should have an active and co-constructive role in the determining of its organizations' strategies and policies. Through this example we can see the main concerns of institutional thinkers, namely, the ways in which organizational strategies, structures and practices are determined by societal arrangements for organizing, in this case, industrial relations and human resources. Of key importance then is the fact that the institutional frame of reference foregrounds a *societal* explanation for the conduct of business in a particular country and looks at the determining influence of a society's institutions on its businesses.

In elaborating our understanding of the institutional frame of reference we move now to consider the concept of business culture, mentioned earlier. This concept has emerged as a key metaphor within the institutional perspective for understanding and explaining the societal contingencies of business. Of particular note here is the work of Collin Randlesome, a well-known writer on business culture in Germany. In the second edition of his edited text (Randlesome *et al.* 1993), Randlesome gives a comprehensive account of the business culture of Germany, providing readers with differing pictures of its features in western and eastern Germany. In his text, Randlesome defines business culture in the following way:

If a country's 'culture' can be defined as 'the state of intellectual development among a people', then 'business culture' might be held to be 'the state of commercial development in a country'. But the concept of business culture surely embraces this and much more: it also takes in the attitudes, values and norms which underpin commercial activities and helps to shape the behaviour of companies in a given country. These companies, in their turn, develop their own individual 'corporate cultures' which, put simply, manifest 'the way we do things round here'.

(ibid., xi)

For Randlesome, business culture is a concept which includes not only the levels and types of commercial activity in a country, but also the set of values and attitudes which underpin those activities. At the beginning of his text, Randlesome cites some specific examples of such values and attitudes. First, he states that much of (western) German business culture is based on the fundamental assumption that organizations are not 'in business to make profits which will subsequently be distributed to shareholders as dividends: they are in business to generate surpluses to stay in business' (ibid., 1). This 'ethos' of German business culture is a reflection of its latent conservatism and strength, and is positively manifest, Randlesome argues, second, in the following: the significant contribution of its manufacturing industries to Germany's GDP; its high levels of investment in research and development and human resource training, and the noteworthy commitment of private commercial banks to non-financial companies. On the negative side, by contrast, Randlesome points to ways in which the conservatism of German business culture has resulted in a tendency for its companies to be risk-averse, publicity-shy and lacking in entrepreneurial spirit (see Chapter 10). Having taken time to identify and pin down these key values of German business culture at the beginning of his text, the remainder of Randlesome's account would simply appear to be a 'description' (a thorough description, but a description nonetheless) of the various institutions and structures of (western) German business culture. He offers commentary, for example, about the relationship between business in Germany and *inter alia* the Federal and state governments, various economic actors like manufacturing industry, the law and its system of regulation, financial and labour markets, vocational training systems and industrial democracy, etc. His text is a veritable treasure-trove of information on the key and changing features of these different faces of German business.

At the heart of Randlesome's account of German business would appear to be an explanation of the ways in which Germany's societal institutions like Federal and state governments determine the philosophy and practice of business. From this we might infer that the aforementioned values which Randlesome nominates as central to German business culture and its 'commercial activities' would seem to be *societal* values i.e. values which under-

pin the creation and functioning of its institutions. In other words his way
of seeing German business through the metaphor of business culture is one
which foregrounds German business as a societal institution whose functioning is determined by its relationship with other societal institutions
(state governments, trade unions, etc.) which, together, make up the social
structure of Germany. German business culture is a construct of German
society.

While Randlesome's work is interesting, comprehensive and brimming
with 'facts', and therefore particularly useful for those with little knowledge
of the nature of business and management in Germany, an examination of
his frame of reference invites us to ask some difficult questions. For
example, what exactly is the nature of this 'thing' called business culture? Is
it possible that the nature of all German businesses and business interactions
can be described by this all-encompassing concept? Is accounting for
German business simply a question of explaining how societal values determine business practices? Where are the people who work in German businesses in this equation? What role do they play in it? What happens when
non-Germans work for German business both in Germany and outwith
Germany? Does this make a difference? Just what kind of frame of reference
is this anyway?

To address some of the issues raised by these questions, it is helpful to
introduce two terms from the disciplines of sociology and cultural studies –
functionalism and *reification*. In the next few paragraphs, we will develop
the argument that what we are being offered by institutionalist writers such
as Randlesome is a *functionalist* frame of reference which serves to *reify* its
core concepts of society, business and culture with problematic consequences. Beginning with reification, the *Oxford Dictionary of Sociology*
defines it as: 'the error of regarding an abstraction as a material thing and
attributing causal powers to it – in other words the fallacy of misplaced concreteness. An example would be treating a model as if it were a description
of a real individual or society.'

While Randlesome does not explicitly claim to be offering us any kind of
'model', his account of business culture works in the same ways as models
do – it provides us with a template for sketching, understanding and
explaining the key features and functions of its chosen object of study. In
offering us this quasi-model, Randlesome's account does exactly what the
above quotation is pointing to – it treats a very partial and personal 'model'
of a particular aspect of a German society as if it were a description of a real
society. Yet the idea of a German business culture, just as much as the idea
of a German society, is essentially an abstraction – a mental concept which,
in this text at least, is removed from the everyday workings and personal
experiences of the very thing it purports to describe. However, through the
language he uses, he gives this essentially abstracted concept the quality of a
material object. Even at the very beginning of his chapter with the title 'The
business culture in Germany', his use of the definite article serves to place a

set of boundaries and thus give definition and presence to something called German business culture. Somewhat crudely then, Randlesome writes about business culture as if it were a table or a chair, a kind of concrete object whose contours are easily definable, and whose function and meaning are clear and easily accounted for. In writing from an institutional perspective with its emphasis on 'big concepts' like society and social structure and deploying very factual, descriptive language, Randlesome's frame of reference has the unfortunate effect of reifying these central concepts – giving them a misplaced concreteness. As a consequence of this process of reification, Randlesome's way of seeing German business culture renders it a *monolith*, a gigantic, impenetrable and unitary social institution whose function and meanings are (purportedly) imprinted upon and thus shared unequivocally by all its members. The ways in which members of this German business culture come to understand these functions and meanings are not clear in Randlesome's text. Nor is the possibility that this monolith might in fact be a highly differentiated social institution, i.e. one which is constructed and experienced by different people in different ways. In fact, apart from the implicit assumption that business people in Germany passively and unitarily ingest its business culture, they are barely present in Randlesome's account. How has this come about?

To suggest how, it is instructive to note that a key consequence of writing about ideas like society as if they were 'real objects' is that in the process, these ideas become dislocated from the humans that create them. Reified concepts *appear* to exist of their own accord, independently of human perception or language – they are written about as if they existed externally to the human, untouched by their constructions of everyday reality. Importantly, we fail to see the many different ways in which the idea of business culture, just as the idea of society, can be understood. Reified concepts present very homogeneous (monolithic) visions of German society and culture which fail to explore the diversity of meanings which might be ascribed to these concepts. This diversity is contingent upon whether one constructs and experiences German society and culture, say, as a man or a woman, as an immigrant, second generation Turk or a 'German national', or as a 'Wessi' or an 'Ossi', as a gay man or a straight woman, etc. Notions of German society, culture and business culture are heterogeneous and dependent upon one's perspective. Randlesome's account of German business culture fails to mention the many different meanings which it might have for those who work within it, the different interests which shape these meanings and importantly omits any comment about how people experience these different interpretations. Reifying German business culture certainly tidies things up for us – it provides us with an 'ordered picture of things' – at the expense of a more complex, variegated, 'disordered' notion of the workings of German business culture. And reification is precisely what happens when we are confronted with stereotypes of German business in the media.

This impulse of Randlesome's work to 'tidy things up' and provide an 'ordered' picture of things where business and society work in mutually beneficial and cohesive ways is largely the result of the functionalist assumptions which underpin his frame of reference. In relation to the literature on German business, we might illustrate this regulative and cohesive characteristic of functionalist thought with reference to the following quotation taken from Ebster-Grosz and Pugh's (1996) book entitled _Anglo-German Business Collaboration: Pitfalls and Potentials_. Here they talk about the relationship between societal infrastructure and industrial culture:

> The whole infrastructure of Germany ... has been considerably fashioned to suit the requirements of industry; for example, the banking system, the system of vocational education, and the new graduate's job opportunities are all well integrated. This institutional cohesion and support of the environment underpins German industrial success, which could not have occurred solely through effective management. The nature of the social environment in which a company operates has a major impact on the nature of its organizational behaviour ... The structured nature of environmental relationships typical for German industrial culture affects the style of management, the attitudes to work and the interpersonal relationships associated with work activities in Germany.

> (1996, 122)

The aim of Ebster-Grosz and Pugh's book is to provide a comparison between different aspects of business e.g. marketing, organizational behaviour, collaborative relationships, in Britain and Germany. Although they use the term 'industrial' culture, rather than 'business' culture, as Randlesome does, they too approach their study from a largely institutional perspective (i.e. one which emphasizes societal values) and a functionalist theoretical framework. Like Randlesome, their work examines the relationship between German business culture and other social institutions, like its system of vocational training, which together form the social structure of Germany. A simple linguistic analysis of this quotation reveals how the functionalist way of seeing implicit in its writing serves to create monolithic and reified social structures whose function is to promote the cohesion and stability of German industrial society. For a start, the quotation contains a set of clearly nominated subjects and objects, presented as distinctly demarcated, discrete and homogenized phenomena: 'the infrastructure of Germany', 'the social environment', 'German industrial culture'. These are further examples of reified concepts. More than this, however, these monolithic subjects and objects stand in a causal and deterministic relationship with one another in this quotation. This interpretation might be gleaned by examining the nature of the verbs deployed to link them and in particular, the consistent use of the active voice by the authors. For example, the quotation refers to the way in which:

'the nature of the social environment . . . *has a major impact on* the nature of its organizational behaviour'; or the way in which 'the structured nature of environmental relationships . . . *affects* the style of management'. Such verbs create a definite intransitivity on the part of these objects, thus denying them the possibility of standing in a reciprocal and co-constructive relationship with their subjects. In other words 'organizational behaviour' and 'style of management' become mere functions of their environment rather than partners in a symbiotic relationship.

Not only does a functionalist way of seeing work then with problematic reifications and monoliths such as business culture, but also with problematic assertions about the determining influence of such social structures and the ways in which these structures function to stimulate societal and cultural cohesion. The way of seeing deployed by writers like Randlesome and Ebster-Grosz and Pugh presents an all-too-ordered and tidy picture of unitary social structures determining and regulating individual behaviour in ways which promote the maintenance of a purportedly German business culture. But what about the disorder of German business culture? What about the parts of the picture that are less cohesive? Surely conflict and dissent belong to this picture? Yet curiously this is not apparent to Randlesome.

The concept of codes and the culturist view

In this section we consider the culturist school of thought which came to prominence during the 1980s as an alternative way of looking at diversity in business organizations between nations. The fundamental difference here is that while the institutionalists emphasize society as their key concept for explaining difference, the culturists regard *national culture* as a more appropriate vehicle for understanding international management and organization. In the case of German business, then, to put it simply, institutionalists would view it as a function of German society, while culturists would rather regard it as a function of German national culture. This division between culture and society as the foundation for competing explanations of human life is central to many of the theoretical debates in the literatures of sociology and more especially anthropology. Indeed, in the latter discipline, two different types of anthropology (social and cultural) have emerged out of this division of the societal and the cultural, emphasizing differing and often contradictory views on various aspects of human existence. Although it is notoriously difficult to define either, and even more so the interrelationship of the two, anthropologist Thomas Eriksen offers a starting point for understanding the divergent notions of culture and society: 'Culture refers to the acquired, cognitive and symbolic aspects of existence, whereas society refers to the social organisation of human life, patterns of interaction and power relationships' (1995, 9).

Here, we foreground the culturist way of seeing German business which emphasizes the 'acquired, cognitive and symbolic' rather than the 'institutional' aspects of management and organization in Germany. Within comparative management, this culturist perspective is most commonly associated with studies of 'cross-cultural management', which take differences in national culture[5] as the source for the divergent nature of business practices across the globe. In this section, we are introduced to the culturist way of seeing German business at the centre of which lies the concept of *codes*. It is the intention of this section to illustrate how cross-cultural researchers have gone about *codifying* notions of cultural difference and to offer some criticism of such acts of *codification*. To begin, we need to understand what is meant by the concept of a code.

In everyday life, we might think of the Highway Code, the legal code or sporting codes of conduct which exist to regulate the ways in which we drive, conduct our private and public lives in the eyes of the law and interact in sporting contexts. They provide us with sets of rules, practices and conventions for desirable behaviours – a kind of framework with which to make sense of the everyday conduct of our lives. Cultures can be seen as codes in so far as they provide its members with a set of common values, meanings and social practices which bond them together and allow them to identify with each other. Hippies, surfers, clubbers, the Ku-Klux-Klan, prisoners, punks, mods, university colleges *inter alia* can thus be said to have their own cultures because they have a set of codes which provide their members with common sources of identification (think also of the Code Red in the film *A Few Good Men*). This notion of a code as a shared framework which allows its members to identify with each other is well documented and theorized in the disciplines of cultural studies, and media and communication studies. The concept of the code is central to a semiotic understanding of culture as demonstrated by the following quote from John Fiske. He argues that codes

> constitute the shared centre of any culture's experience. They enable us to understand our social existence and to locate ourselves within our culture. Only through the common codes can we feel and express our membership of our culture. By using the codes, whether as an audience or a source, we are inserting ourselves into our culture and maintaining that culture's vitality and existence. A culture is an active, dynamic, living organism only because of the active participation of its members in its codes of communication.
>
> (1990, 82)

As Fiske's quote makes clear, if we wish to understand the nature of a particular culture, we need to ascertain and become part of the codes through which membership of that culture is achieved. We might say therefore that codes provide us with membership of a cultural group – when we encounter cultures, we encounter codes.

For researchers who are interested in studying cultures, a key way of investigating them involves immersing oneself in different cultural milieux in order to understand *from the inside* what codes its members draw upon to identify themselves. This idea of immersing oneself in a culture in order to understand that culture is commonly referred to as *ethnography* and is the linchpin of anthropological fieldwork. In the discipline of comparative management, however, the use of ethnography as a means of studying the codes of a culture has until very recently been extremely limited. Only in recent years have the disciplines of management and business studies begun to open themselves up to some of the ideas and methods of other social science and humanities subjects like sociology and anthropology. Rather than using ethnographic study, mainstream culturist research on cross-cultural business has, as a convention, made use of large-scale surveys and statistical techniques to gain access to the codes which underpin cultural differences. In order to illustrate how mainstream management researchers have approached the study of cultural codes, we now move to consider the work of Dutch organizational anthropologist Geert Hofstede, the most famous name of the culturist school.

Hofstede's work in the area of cross-cultural management research is vast and varied, but it is for his 1980 publication *Culture's Consequences: International Differences in Work-Related Attitudes* that he is best known. The aim of Hofstede's research reported in *Culture's Consequences* was to explore differences in the work-related *values* of managers from 40 different nations. Based on two sets of survey material yielding an impressive 116,000 questionnaires from a sample of managers from the IBM corporation, Hofstede ran rigorous and elaborate statistical tests on his data to identify key trends and patterns amongst the participants' responses. These statistical tests revealed four main dimensions along which, Hofstede asserted: 'dominant value systems in the 40 countries can be ordered (and) which affect human thinking, organizations, and institutions in predictable ways' (1980, 11).

The four main dimensions along which the national cultures in his study were found to differ can be summarized as follows in Box 8.1 (for further explanation, please consult Hofstede's original text).

For Hofstede, these four dimensions acted as yardsticks which provided the basis for comparisons of national cultures to be made and thereupon cultural differences in work-related values between nations to be established. The idea of a yardstick is crucial because it suggests that difference between cultures could be measured – and this is indeed what Hofstede did in his study. Hofstede referred to the dimensions above as 'indices', thereby making them a tool for gauging and measuring different aspects of culture. Hofstede used these indices to assign national cultures particular scores based upon the questionnaire answers of the managers, thereby quantifying the work-related values he asked about in the questionnaire. The result of this process was that it made differences in national cultural

---

Box 8.1   Hofstede's Dimensions

Individualism versus collectivism (IDV Score): the concern within a culture for the individual's own needs, goals and achievements as opposed to the social group's norms and benefits. This dimension purports to give an indication of the extent to which, in a given society, individual identity is determined by individual choices as to how to act and by one's obligation to the groups or collectives to which one belongs.

Power distance (PDI score): measures the concentration and distribution of authority, influence, power and equality within a culture. This dimension distinguishes countries where relations between superior and subordinate are close and informal, versus distant and formal and also pertains to the degree of hierarchy or level of participation in decisions. These first two dimensions of individualism-collectivism and power distance are closely related and, as Smith (1992, 40) points out, much subsequent research has distinguished between those countries which are individualistic and low on power distance from those which are collectivist and high on power distance.

Uncertainty avoidance (UAI score): relates to the extent to which a culture accepts ambiguity, risk or deviant behaviour. It thus pertains to the need for stability and conflict reduction and distinguishes national cultures which emphasise meticulous forward planning to those in which risk-taking and leaving things to chance are more prevalent.

Masculinity versus femininity (MAS score): according to Hofstede, cultures are relatively more masculine or feminine, that is they purportedly exhibit either more masculine values such as assertiveness, challenge and ambition or more feminine values such as caring, co-operation or security. This relates to a basic dichotomy between rational, aggressive, success-driven task orientation which is purported to be more masculine in nature, and the emotional, affiliation, passive, relationship orientation which is purported to be feminine.

---

values quantifiable and thus easily measurable. To illustrate this, let us look at the cultural differences in work-related values between 'British' and 'German' national cultures established by Hofstede's study.[6] These have been extracted from his text and are presented in Table 8.1.

Table 8.1   Values of the four indices for Great Britain and Germany

Country	PDI	UAI	IDV	MAS
Germany (F.R)	35	65	67	66
Great Britain	35	35	89	66

Source: Adapted from Hofstede (1980, 315)

For the foreign manager, Hofstede's dimensionalization of German national cultural codes rendered German business more accessible – it made it easier to understand, explain and thus predict. German business was rendered open for decodification. As with Randlesome's work, however, we can pose a number of problematizing questions about Hofstede's work. For example, as with Randlesome, is it possible that such an all-encompassing, reified concept like national culture can really explain all the facets of German business practice? Is accounting for German business simply a matter of consulting Hofstede's indices and applying its insights in practice? Can national culture be pinned down as easily as Hofstede suggests it can? What are the problems of 'measuring' culture? In the next few paragraphs we will develop the argument that what Hofstede is offering us. is a purportedly 'scientific' approach to studying culture which is reductionist and reificatory and which, like Randlesome's account, ignores the multiplicitous ways in which national culture can be interpreted and experienced.

At a simplistic level, there are a number of commonly articulated difficulties with Hofstede's work. First, his data were all collected from the same organization which arguably limits the generalizability of his work. Second, they were collected at the end of the 1960s and early 1970s, thus limiting their applicability to studies of management and organization some thirty years later. Third, there is the criticism that his concept of national culture is based on a problematic conflation of nation–states with culture. In other words, Hofstede assumes that Germany possesses something called a 'German' national culture and that Great Britain has a 'British' national culture, etc. While not unaware of this homogenizing tendency to ignore the multicultural nature of many of the societies which he studies, Hofstede is still content to present these broad-brush pictures of culture. These criticisms are themselves, however, only a small part of a more problematic picture constructed by Hofstede's way of seeing culture as an object capable of scientific inquiry. The bigger problem lies with the way in which Hofstede *represents* his object of inquiry using the language and practices of science.

Consider first of all the object which Hofstede is attempting to represent: is it the coded value set of the individual manager or is the object of inquiry something 'bigger' than that? To answer this, Hofstede asserted that a manager who lived and worked in Germany should most profitably be as an example of German 'national' culture writ small. In fact for any national culture, he regarded his participants as instantiations of the wider national cultural code to which he believed they singularly belonged. In short, then, one might argue that his unit of analysis, i.e. the thing he was trying to 're-present' was not the individual manager but national, or to use Hofstede's terminology, 'country cultures'. It is at this point that common criticisms emerge between the institutionalist work of Randlesome and the culturist work of Hofstede.

Like Randlesome, Hofstede *reifies* the notion of national culture. Although he did base his study on the questionnaire responses of individual managers, his unit of analysis as pointed out above was national culture, a concept he believed could be *abstracted* from these individual questionnaire responses. Hofstede views national culture as a Durkheimian social fact, that is something which pre-exists us and which we inhabit during our lives. As with the metaphor of business culture, Hofstede's national culture takes on a misplaced concreteness which curiously empties his account of the individual managers on which it was based and reduces them to a function of wider national cultural codes. Hofstede's way of seeing offers us therefore not a reified form of social organization as Randlesome's does, but a *reified semiotic concept* of national codes.

Furthermore, Hofstede's work is also problematic because it is scientifically reductionist. In his book *Modern Philosophy*, Roger Scruton (1994) gives an interesting definition of reductionism. Reductionist research, Scruton suggests, asks questions about 'problematic entities', like national culture and 'answers them by reducing those objects to the evidence which leads us to believe in them' (ibid., 26). According to Scruton's view of reductionism:

> We should suppose the existence only of those things that we *need* to assume, in order to explain our experience. Entities which are not needed should be excised from our world view, or else 'reduced' to other necessary things.
>
> (ibid., 26 emphasis in the original)

Hofstede's work is reductionist because he assumes that national culture is constituted by codes of values (or value systems) and takes this as his sole object of inquiry, eliminating anything else which might constitute culture from his world view. For national culture to exist, Hofstede has necessarily reduced the concept to the values articulated by its members. The boundaries of Hofstede's assumptions about national culture thereby come to define the existence of national culture. In other words national culture cannot exist outside the evidence which Hofstede has decided constitutes its essence – evidence of national cultural values. In relation to Hofstede, then, national culture cannot be anything outside his notion of a mental programming, a reductionist tendency which ignores the multifaceted and contradictory notions of (national) culture found in the disciplines of sociology, anthropology and cultural studies.

The second point of critique of Hofstede's scientification of culture relates to the statistical processes he engages to ascertain his dimensions of culture. Hofstede claims that the statistical tests he uses simply bring to light the a priori existence of differences in national work-related values. In other words, he believes that the questionnaires exhibit cultural differences in values which his statistics simply reveal through some fancy number work, thus making them visible for description to the reader. He assumes, as do many social scientists, that statistics are 'neutral' and 'passive' research tools which access secrets about the social and cultural worlds which are 'out there waiting to be discovered'. A contrasting view on statistical testing is that it, in fact, acts in ways which *create* or *force* similarities and differences in the data, rather than merely reflecting them. In other words they play an active role in constructing the evidence. Griffeth and Hom (1987) for example, have criticized comparative management researchers for precisely this point. In relation to the well-known comparative studies of Haire *et al.* (1966) and Ronen (1986), they point out that if these authors had used different statistical methods to classify national culture, the results they would have obtained and the countries which they would have deemed culturally similar would have been vastly different. This is a consequence of the way in which statistics work. What they do is to split empirical phenomena like national culture down before re-integrating them in a way which produces a 'group effect', creating specific similarities between different parts of the data depending on the particular test chosen. As such, we should be wary of the active role played by the deployment of statistical testing in constructing particular versions of the social and cultural world.

A further point about the number-crunching of Hofstede relates to the way in which he calculates the mean points of all the completed questionnaires as a basis for his delineation of the four dimensions. By focusing on the mean points of his data, Hofstede is attempting to define the essence of British or German managerial behaviour by focusing attention on the average point calculated from the questionnaire. What this does is to divert attention away from responses which lie far from the mean scores or the averages, the so-called statistical 'outliers'. These outliers subsequently become marginalized from the pictures of national culture painted by Hofstede's way of seeing. As a result, Hofstede ignores so-called 'standard deviations' in his data simply because they puncture the smooth pictures of national culture constructed by his study. He consequently opens up himself to the accusation that his characterizations of national cultures are no more than stereotypes based on average statistical scores which pasteurize the full diversity of his data. Any form of diversity, individuality, uniqueness, complexity contained within Hofstede's data is thus squeezed out. As Hollway (1989, 15) points out in relation to research of the Hofstedian type: 'The concern for mass generalization and the requirement to use large numbers for statistical manipulation together produce knowledge which does not address the complex conditions of people and their conduct, either in their uniqueness or their commonality.'

In sum then, these last few paragraphs have attempted to point to some of the problems of Hofstede's approach to understanding the cultural contingencies of business and management. His work suggests that when we encounter German business, we are encountering a set of German national cultural codes which manifest themselves in the behaviours and social practices of German managers. The problems pointed to in this chapter are not so much problems with the concept of national culture *per se*, but with the things which Hofstede's way of seeing does to the concept. To reiterate, Hofstede's way of seeing national culture is one which views it as an object of scientific inquiry, that is one which can be identified, measured and explained using ideas and practices from the natural sciences. The two principal problems with this way of seeing are, first, that, like Randlesome, it results in a reification of the concept of national culture which is inherently reductionist. In other words, it 'tidies up' the messiness and complexity of cultural relations by defining too rigidly what should and should not count as evidence of national culture. That national culture is seen to be such an easily demarcated and identifiable concept is a result of the scientistic frame of reference which Hofstede applies to it. The second problem with this scientification of culture relates to the ways in which the use of statistics produces normalized pictures of national cultures based on the averages of numerical figures. The consequence of this patterning of data is that the very thing that Hofstede purports to seek, 'difference', becomes marginalized. The statistical act of breaking down the data and building it up again into normalized pictures of national culture serves to paint over the 'outliers', i.e. those which lie far from the statistical norm.

The concept of leaky boundaries: a social constructionist view of identity and difference

The previous two sections have presented a critical encounter with German business by means of a deconstruction of two of the most influential pieces of literature in the area. Such an act of deconstruction raises an important question, however. If both these frames of reference are so problematic, what other ways exist for looking at German business? Can we say anything about German business if all attempts at representation, such as those instantiated by Randlesome and Hofstede, are ultimately doomed by the conditions of their existence? Is there a more constructive space from which to articulate an understanding of German business, one which might synthesize the potential dialectic between these two authors? In this final section of the chapter, empirical data are presented from a research study[7] carried out by the author (Jack 2000) which suggests a different way of theorizing 'German business'. In this section, we are introduced to a social constructionist interpretation of a 'real' i.e. empirically derived encounter with German business. Deploying this constructionist frame, it is argued that any notion of German business, the German manager, or any attempt at understanding how 'the Germans are different' is essentially fluid, provisional and an everyday production of social actors, not rigid, immutable or a taken for granted as social fact. Any construction of the German as a cultural Other will involve sets of moving and leaky boundaries, contingent upon their context of production.

This third approach to 'German business' contrasts with the previous ones in two respects. First, it explores these 'leaky boundaries' not as the product of an extensive literature review (Randlesome) or overly complex statistical manoeuvring (Hofstede), but as a central facet of the everyday social processes through which managers construct their cultural identities in professional contexts. Understanding German business or management then becomes a problem of investigating managerial identity as part of the practices of everyday social life. The data presented in this section come from the recording and observation of 'real' managers doing 'real' business as part of their professional lives. Connected to this different methodological approach to the study of German business, second, is a set of different theoretical assumptions (i.e. a different frame of reference) about the nature of identity and difference. These assumptions are neatly summed up in the following quotation from Stuart Hall:

> Identity is not as transparent or unproblematic as we think. Perhaps instead of thinking of identity as an already accomplished fact, which the new cultural practices then represent, we should think, instead, of identity 'as a production', which is never complete, always in process, and always constituted within, not outside, representation.

> (1990, 222)

Two aspects of this quotation are worth underlining. The first is that identities and differences are seen to be actively constituted by social actors rather than passively determined by one's insertion in an already existing and reified set of social (Randlesome's broad approach) or cultural structures (Hofstedian approach). Actors can determine, at least to some extent, the contours of their similarities to and difference from others. The other noteworthy point is Hall's insistence on seeing identity-work as an on-going process in which we are continuously engaged. Identities and differences are therefore not unified, singular or immutable social facts, but social processes which take form in the relational space between the self and the other and are always shifting, sometimes conflictual and based on a multiplicity of different social and cultural materials.

Deploying this frame of reference, the Self thus becomes 'one fragile moment in the dialogic circuit that connects 'us' with our 'others' (Gilroy 1997, 315).

We move now to look at some of these 'leaky boundaries' in action by considering Box 8.2 which contains a summary of a piece of conversation recorded from one of the various business meetings. It was the first meeting I attended and this conversation, held with four of the five main protagonists of my study, was their first real opportunity to ask about my research. It took place during a natural break in the main proceedings of the meeting between important agenda items. In reading Box 8.2, ask yourself the question, just whose boundaries are leaking?

Reading Box 8.2, it might be suggested that there are two broad sets of 'leaking' or 'shifting' boundaries, both of which are indicative of a critique of Hofstede's work. The first relates to the Hofstede's assumption that national cultural codes are the main resources which differentiate the philosophy and practice of business across nations and that, as such, these should be privileged in understanding how the 'Other' does business. Consider, however, Dieter's assertion that there are some things in business which 'transcend cultural boundaries' (which he goes on to call the 'technical point of view') or Cameron's suggestion that 'the common denominator of business is 'money-making'. What Dieter and Cameron are doing here is bringing into play a division between aspects of their business relationship which they viewed as being determined by national culture and those which, in their opinion, had nothing to do with national culture, but were part of a commonly shared, cross-national and therefore 'a-cultural' code of 'good management'. Cameron neatly sums up this division in the following way:

> I would rather look at the thing as a business association with business problems and get the problems on the table and deal with them rather than accentuate the cultural thing. One of the best things to learn from a business perspective is to stand alone. We are simply struggling with resource and priorities of things.

Contrary to Hofstede's implicit assumptions, then, these managers were able to articulate a rigid distinction between differences in their relationship which they considered 'cultural' and those which were purely business-related, as expressed in Dieter's 'technical point of view' or Cameron's 'levelling off'. The majority of differences which structured their relationship were not cultural in nature but related to the technical and commercial aspects of conducting business. Theoretically, as researchers with an interest in cultural studies, we might well critique Dieter and Cameron's assertion that there could ever be a category of knowledge which is ever 'culture-less'. But this is not the important point. What is vital here is that this division between 'culture and business' is a fundamental resource through which all the managers in the study constructed a sense of self and alterity. It is impor-

---

Box 8.2   The technical point of view

Lines 1–20:   Dieter asks me what I am studying, what I expect to find and what I will do with my work. I reply that I am interested in the role of culture and cultural stereotypes in business. I give examples of punctuality and precision as stereotypes of Germans. I assert the view that these stereotypes are barriers to good business.

Lines 21–37:   Somewhat cryptically, Dieter suggests that there are aspects of business which transcend cultural boundaries. He goes on to ask whether the project belongs to the discipline of economics or psychology. I reply it belongs to international management and attempt to clarify his previous utterance on this 'culture-less' part of business. Dieter then asks whether I will build the results into a management training course. I reply 'Partly', but suggest that its findings are primarily of academic value.

Lines 38–47:   Cameron interjects and suggests that the common denominator of business is money-making and this imperative serves to level the cultural terrain. I respond positively to Campbell's suggestion.

Lines 48–61:   Dieter asserts that research on the differences between Europeans and Indians, Indonesians and Chinese would be more complicated. Fritz gives an example of the differences between a typical German banker and an American one. I tell them that much research has been done into US-Japanese and Chinese cultural difference.

Lines 62–72:   Cameron asks me about research into Scottish and English cultural difference and suggests that there are no differences between him (a Scot) and Pete (an Englishman). Pete notes differences between Glaswegians and Edinburghers. I then note differences between Prussians and Bavarians. Dieter responds to this and then talks about Koreans.

---

tant to them, a part of their professional realities and as such this division needs to be taken seriously. This is not to suggest that talk of cultural differences in the more expected form of 'the British being like this and the Germans that' did not exist. It did, but it was limited and restricted to particular contexts.[8] However, the point is that this division between the cultural and the non-cultural as a resource drawn upon by the managers in their social and professional relations causes a rupture in Hofstede's smooth pictures of national culture.

The second set of leaky boundaries also relates to Hofstede's picture of self-contained and clearly marked national cultures. Referring to Box 8.2, we see that the conversation starts with talk of stereotypes of Germans, moves into this division between culture and business and ends with the articulation of several instances of cultural heterogeneity within the national borders of the UK and Germany (the Scots versus the English, the Glaswegians versus the Edinburghers, the Prussians versus the Bavarians). What this would seem to demonstrate is the ease with which the purportedly unitary and contained borders of a national culture can easily be collapsed and re-ordered in the process of everyday conversation (see Chapter 1). To order and therefore fix pictures of cultural difference into a rigid frame of national culture is to mask the fluid boundaries and multiplicitous forms which social actors' expressions of cultural identity might well assume. A further point worth noting in this conversation is that some 'differences' are thought to be more marked and more 'complex' than others, as summed up in Dieter's comment on the 'Europeans versus the Indians, Indonesians and Chinese'. This expression of more complex differences is partly a function of physical distance and psychological proximity (the further away a culture is geographically, the further away it is purported to be psychologically). But perhaps more so, it is a function of the way in which Western Europeans and Americans exoticize difference, partly with reference to the 'Orient' (see Edward Said's, 1978 _Orientalism_).[9] In any case, even in this restricted set of turns we see the emergence of multiple ways for marking one's identity ranging from the national cultural, to the regional and local. Of course these are not the only sources for marking a sense of identity and difference. The remainder of the research study explored the ways in which identities and differences are constructed at the _intersection_ of a number of different social and cultural divisions, e.g. divisions based on religion, the body, one's professional and occupational position, ideas of gender, race and ethnicity, age and generation, and sexuality. In exploring how social actors combined these divisions and thereby constructed a myriad of different identities and differences, the study demonstrated that privileging national culture as the main vehicle for looking at identity and difference in Anglo-German business serves to obscure, mask out and therefore suppress the gendered, racialized and sexualized nature of identity-work in these contexts. Taking a cultural studies-based approach to the study of German business encourages us to theorize 'more than one difference at once' and to begin to think about the changing and heterogeneous identities of managers in the intercultural workplace. Does this mean that Randlesome and Hofstede's respective works are of no value? In short, no. Talk of societal and institutional structures and national culture is still meaningful, but only when drawn upon as a resource by social actors in their articulations of self. These concepts are still useful. The problem lies in the ways the theoretical frames applied by Randlesome and Hofstede give us a highly restricted view of how they come to exist in social relations.

To come back to the earlier question, then, just whose boundaries are leaking? Even in this small conversation we can see that leaking boundaries are a part of everyday conversation, part of the social process of being in the world and that as such, everybody's boundaries are leaking, even Hofstede's. To present all too orderly and unitary a picture of our social and cultural identities is to suppress the simultaneous disorder and disunity which characterize the very process of the social ordering of self and other. In order to capture this, this third approach to German business is suggesting that research might be better focused on everyday social processes and contexts of identity production rather than the completion of structured questionnaires with categories pre-determined by the researcher. This would allow us to explore how we, as social actors, go about ordering and disordering our identities and differences in the eternal hope of closure.

Conclusion

This chapter has introduced *three* different ways of looking at German business, one which takes the relationships between societal institutions as its key explanatory vehicle (the institutional view), the other foregrounding the concept of national culture (the culturist view) and the latter emphasizing the leaky boundaries of everyday social processes of identity formation (social constructionist view). Despite the ostensible difference between the first two schools of thought, instantiated in this chapter by the work of Colin Randlesome and Geert Hofstede, it was argued that they could both be criticized for the reificatory and reductionist tendencies of their functionalist and scientistic frames of reference. The consequence of applying these frames of reference to their respective concepts of societal and cultural differences in the ways business is conducted between nations, is that these concepts become highly sanitized and homogenized monoliths. The French social theorist Bruno Latour refers to such concepts as 'black boxes' which he defines as follows:

> The word black box is used by cyberneticians whenever a piece of machinery or a set of commands is too complex. In its place they draw a little box about which they need know nothing but its input and output ... That is, no matter how controversial their history, how complex their inner workings, only their input and output count.

(1987, 2–3)

Studies of German business such as those by Randlesome and Hofstede deal in the very black boxes which Latour describes. Accounts of German business, seen either as a societal institution or a product of German national culture, have been framed by Randlesome and Hofstede in ways which ignore their complexities and their location in the processes and experiences of everyday interaction. Instead, understanding German business has come to be regarded as simply a matter of identifying and subsequently managing its inputs (societal arrangements, cultural values) and its outputs (national institutional differences, culturally specific managerial behaviour). We should be clear that when we talk about German business, society or culture, that we can never give a full, impartial and purely reflective account of its nature, a point which also applies to the latter social constructionist approach. Accounts will always be partial and framed by the perspective of the writer. We can only gain more or less complex understandings of chosen facets of German business through the frames of reference which we apply, in the knowledge though that this will always involve a sense of loss of the aspects of social reality which inevitably escape us. On a closing note, we turn to the sociologist Zygmunt Bauman who argues that any attempt to 'order difference' (including all three accounts given in this chapter, to differing extents) will be a vain exercise since all it serves to do is: 'To replace diversity with uniformity, ambivalence with a transparent order – and while doing so this turns out unstoppably more divisions, diversity and ambivalence that it has managed to get rid of' (1991, 5). The simple act of ordering any category of knowledge, including that of 'German business', while giving the impression of making all difference known and transparent, merely serves to hide and mask the heterogeneity contained within its boundaries.

Notes

1. Anglo-German management research refers principally to the study of differences in the values and practices of companies and managers in the UK and Germany.
2. Comparative management research is a particular type of business studies research which explores the similarities and differences in the business systems, philosophies and practices of management and organization in different nations.
3. The choice of the term 'Way of Seeing' is not coincidental. It reflects the similarly titled book by John Berger (1972) on art and the ways in which the historical, cultural and social position of the person looking at a piece filters and therefore affects what they see and how they see.
4. Companies employing between 500 and 2000 workers have supervisory boards with two-thirds shareholders' representatives and one-third workers representatives.
5. National culture refers to the idea of a culture which is shared by those who live within the boundaries of a particular nation state. Thus Germany has a German national culture, France a French national culture, etc.
6. Hofstede's work referred only to *West German* managers – the surveys were conducted at the end of the 1960s and early 1970s, a significant time before re-unification.

7. This section of the chapter is based on the author's doctoral research.
8. Constructions of national cultural difference i.e. the British are like this, the Germans are like that, did not appear randomly during the research study. They were patterned, locally emergent and contextually contingent.
9. This point about the exoticization of the Other, particularly 'Orientals' (to use a phrase derived from Said) is one which flags up issues of discourse, power and colonization. These are issues which have, intentionally, been sidelined in this chapter in order to communicate ideas about the shifting nature of identities. The interested reader is advised to consult the works of Foucault (especially *Discipline and Punish*, 1977) and Said (*Orientalism*, 1978) as a more theoretically advanced starting point for considerations of the relationship between power and identity formation.

References

BAUMAN, Z. 1991: *Modernity and ambivalence*. Cambridge: Polity Press.
BERGER, J. 1972: *Ways of seeing*. London: Penguin.
EBSTER-GROSZ, D. and PUGH, D. 1996: *Anglo-German business collaboration: pitfalls and potentials*. Basingstoke: Macmillan Business in collaboration with the Anglo-German Foundation.
ERIKSEN, T.H. 1995: *Small places, large issues: an introduction to social and cultural anthropology*. London: Pluto Press.
FISKE, J. 1990: *Introduction to communication studies*. 2nd edition. London: Routledge.
FOUCAULT, M. 1977: *Discipline and punish*. London: Penguin.
GILROY, P. 1997: Diaspora and the detours of identity. In WOODWARD, K. (ed.) *Identity and difference*. London: Sage in association with the Open University, 299–346.
GRIFFETH. R.W. and HOM, P.W. 1987: Some multivariate comparisons of multinational managers. *Multivariate Behavioural Research* 22, 173–91.
HAIRE, M., GHISELLI, E.F. and PORTER, L.W. 1966: *Managerial thinking: an international study*. New York: Wiley.
HALL, S. 1990: Cultural identity and diaspora. In RUTHERFORD, J. (ed.) *Identity: community, culture, difference*. London: Lawrence & Wishart, 222–37.
HOFSTEDE, G. 1980: *Culture's consequences: international differences in work-related values*. Beverley Hills, CA: Sage.
HOLLWAY, W. 1989: *Subjectivity and method in psychology: gender, meaning and science*. London: Sage.
JACK, G.A. 2000: *The politics of identity and difference in intercultural management communication: an Anglo-German study*. Unpublished PhD thesis, School of Management, Heriot-Watt University, Edinburgh.
LATOUR, B. 1987: *Science in action*. Cambridge, MA: Harvard University Press.
MARSHALL, G. 1998: *Oxford dictionary of sociology*. 2nd edn. Oxford: Oxford University Press.
MAURICE, M. 1979: For a study of the 'societal effect': universality and specificity in organization research. In LAMMER, C.J. and HICKSON, D.J. (eds) *Organizations like and unlike*. London: Routledge and Kegan Paul, 42–60.
RANDLESOME, C., BRIERLEY, W., BRUTON, K., GORDON, C. and KING, P. 1993: *Business cultures in Europe*. 2nd edition. Oxford: Butterworth-Heinemann.
RONEN, S. 1986: *Comparative and multinational management*. New York: Wiley.
SAID, E.W. 1978: *Orientalism: Western conceptions of the Orient*. London: Penguin Books.

SCRUTON, R. 1994: *Modern philosophy: an introduction and survey*. London: Mandarin.

SMITH, P.B. 1992: Organizational behaviour and national cultures. *British Journal of Management*, 3 (1), 8–15.

WHITLEY, R. 1992: *European business systems, firms and markets in their national contexts*. London: Sage.

|9|

Food and drink: Hegelian encounters with the culinary other

BY SIMON RICHTER

Not what we eat, but what we digest, benefits and nourishes us.

(Christoph Wilhelm Hufeland)

When the geographer of the unconscious Sigmund Freud (1933) introduced the general public to his tripartite model of human consciousness in a lecture entitled 'The Dissection of the Psychical Personality,' he argued that pathology, 'by making things larger and coarser, can draw our attention to normal conditions which would otherwise have escaped us'. This same principle proves useful for cultural analysis. If we wish to arrive at a distinct and specific conception of German foodways, the German culture of food and drink, the most promising avenue is to focus on the 'culinary pathology' of Germany, the traumas, hysterias, and neuroses of consumption, in order to reveal the normal conditions of German culture, which might otherwise escape us.

As it happens, the beginning of the twenty-first century has been particularly traumatic for Germany and other European nations. Not only have these cultures had to contend with the ongoing process of Americanization, the vagaries of EU trade and agriculture policies, and the globalization of the marketplace, the outbreak of mad cow disease or bovine spongiform encephalopathy (BSE) on farms throughout Europe has led to drastic governmental and consumer responses. While the facts of BSE will doubtless prove indisputable and be valid for all of Europe, the cultural responses to this wide-ranging trauma necessarily vary according to the distinct make-up of what might be called the culinary unconscious of each country. In Germany, BSE has confirmed a long-standing and deeply held suspicion regarding the fundamental indigestibility of all things and nullified the efficacy of cultural mechanisms evolved over centuries to render food acceptable to the stomach. On the level of the culinary unconscious, German culture is essentially Hegelian; in other words, a dialectic structures the encounter between the consuming subject and the object to be consumed in ways that emphasize the threatening otherness of the culinary object and call for measures to render or conceive of food as *magenfreundlich* – friendly to the stomach. BSE, along with two other food-related phenomena, the assimilation of the Turkish döner kebab and popular willingness to entertain the benefits of urine therapy, together constitute extreme instances of the culinary other and hence comprise ideal pathological circumstances for exploring the essence of German food culture. Although this analysis will begin with a description of the German culinary landscape in broad terms, the focus will be on discerning a specifically German pattern of food-related behaviors and beliefs. The culinary German described in this chapter will, of course, necessarily be a projection and not the 'average' German. Indeed, Germans may dispute the description's accuracy. Nonetheless, it is hoped that readers will find answers here to aspects of German food culture that otherwise remain puzzling.

The German culinary landscape

During a century that saw the tempo of culture in most areas accelerate to breakneck speeds, the cultures of eating, even in Western Europe, have submitted to change at a slightly slower pace. Even if the Americanization and globalization of culture working in tandem have made substantial inroads into traditional German foodways, there is nonetheless a strong sense in which food culture functions as a repository of age-old values, tastes, and habits of body and mind (Tolksdorf 1993). Studies of German immigrant groups living abroad have shown that they sooner part with their language than with the customs of their table (Rubner 1913). One may mock the provincialism of the German tourist for whom the German butcher or baker is a beacon whether at a beach resort in Italy, the Canary Islands, or Naples, or Florida. Seen from another perspective, these are profound attachments that indicate the extent to which food is invested with cultural meaning. Germany is certainly not the only European country to feature the proverb, 'Was der Bauer nicht kennt, das frißt er nicht' (what the farmer doesn't know, he won't eat) – the point is that it's a German *Bauer*, indeed, German foodways that are here under investigation.

Of course, as Sidney Mintz has argued (1996), national cuisine is always a dubious construction, based on adaptations from more authentic regional cuisines. The German cuisine familiar to residents of the UK and North America from excursions to restaurants with names like Edelweiss, Würzburg Haus, and Rathskeller tends to be a version of Bavarian and Austrian fare with a few generic sausages, Sauerbraten, and other things thrown in for good measure. In Germany itself, regional differences matter in the same way that local dialects are regarded by many as a point of pride. Part of the reason Germany is the undisputed king of sausage with over 1500 varieties of sausage on the market has to do with the incredible regional variety. By the same token, German bread is distinct for its density, strong flavor, and hard crust – yet there are over 200 varieties and a great deal of regional variation. *Brötchen, Schrippen, Semmeln,* and *Wecken* are just a few of the words used for a simple breakfast roll. As one moves from region to region, one encounters different flavors, staples, and specialties. In Swabia the restaurant will feature *Maultaschen* or perhaps *Spätzle* prepared with cheese and caramelized onions or served with lentils and wieners. In a Bavarian town one may order a *Leberknödelsuppe* or consume a *Weisswurst* with sweet mustard. In any part of the former GDR, one may be fortunate enough still to find *tote Oma* on the menu: *Grützwurst* (a type of blood sausage containing grits), *Leberwurst,* potatoes, and *Sauerkraut* together on a plate, a dish also known as *Verkehrsunfall* (traffic accident) – citizens of the GDR were renowned for a sense of humor sharpened by their everyday interactions with the state. Whereas in Bamberg, the local brew is a *Rauchbier* (a beer with a distinctly smoky flavor because of the smoked barley or malt, depending on the process) and in Reutlingen the barkeeper may add a few grains of uncooked rice to the *Weizenbier* (or wheat beer), along the Rhine, Mosel and Main rivers one finds ancient regional wine cultures with their distinct glasses, bottles, and customs. These are but a very few of the delights that await the visiting *Schlemmer* (German for gourmet), yet they indicate both the great diversity of regional cuisine and its comparative ability to withstand the homogenizing forces of a global economy with no patience for difference.

Regional and national cuisines increasingly co-exist with ethnic cuisines. As a country that up until very recently insisted in its law and in public pronouncements from then Chancellor Helmut Kohl (1982–98) that it was not a 'country of immigration', Germany has nonetheless since the 1950s admitted several million foreigners initially as guest workers, but in fact as quasi-permanent residents, not to mention the thousands who have entered as refugees and made their slow way through the bureaucratic mills that more often than not refused their applications and summarily initiated deportation (a fine food film that addresses this issue is Jan Schütte's 1987 *Dragon Chow*). Thus despite its long-standing rhetoric, Germany has in fact seen significant immigration and shows a distinct multi-cultural aspect. In the city of Frankfurt, for instance, one in three residents is not German. For years Greek, Italian, and Turkish restaurants (the three primary groups of guest workers) have been staples on the German culinary landscape, though of course with little regard for regional specificity and with considerable accommodations to German taste. Nonetheless, these institutions of cultural encounter, where a dominant culture steps out of its customary orbit and is served by an exotic minority culture, have enabled complex and dialectical processes to take place. Even if Germany was not prepared to naturalize its guest workers, Germans conferred a *de facto* citizenship on their cuisine and made it their own. In the meantime, other waves of immigration have washed across Germany, nor is it any longer necessary for an ethnic group to attain a substantial critical mass before launching yet another exotic restaurant. Asian restaurants of all kinds, Slavic and South American have taken hold in Germany. Germany's palate has been globalized. The McDonald's, the pizzeria, the shish kebab joint, and the local restaurant featuring *bürgerliche Küche* co-exist in an uneasy tension.

The döner kebab and the culinary other

The most astonishing feat of assimilation in gastronomical terms has been the triumph of the döner kebab, an oversize Turkish sandwich consisting of pita bread, thin slices of marinated roast lamb, raw red cabbage, tomatoes, and a garlicky yogurt-based sauce topped with paprika. Introduced to West Germany in the 1960s, the döner 'has become Germany's new national dish and a thriving industry that provides 50,000–60,000 jobs'. With an estimated annual turnover of DM 5 billion, 'Döner vendors take in more than all the country's other popular fast-food outlets combined – McDonald's (26 in Munich), Burger Kings, Pizza Huts, Wienerwalds, and countless wurst stalls.' Every day approximately 250 tons of döner meat are consumed. With such volume it is not surprising that döner factories, where the cones of marinated meat are prepared, have been set up throughout Germany, 30 in Berlin alone (Thornhill 1999).

But what sort of cultural transaction is repeated every day as millions of Germans step up to a stand at their local market and order a döner? In an essentially Hegelian move, food anthropologist Sidney Mintz points out in the title essay of *Tasting Food, Tasting Freedom*, a nuanced exploration of the powers of emancipation subtly at work in the food-related activities of Caribbean slaves, that a subordinate culture pressed into the service of a master culture nonetheless attains a measure of freedom through its mastery over the skills, ingredients, and cuisine of its invention. This is fundamentally a version of Hegel's master-slave dialectic. In Mintz's (1996) words:

> Dealing in food was dealing in freedom at many levels. Working in the emergence of cuisine legitimized status distinctions within slavery, both because the master class became dependent upon its cooks, and because the cooks actually invented a cuisine that the masters could vaunt, but could not themselves duplicate. The ideological space between what the slaves *were* and what the ideology *said* that they were was repeatedly enlarged by the activities of the slaves themselves.

Turning to the German situation, the encounter between the German customer and the Turkish vendor is similarly bilateral, complicated, and fraught with a latent tension. Vendors may banter with their patrons or remain laconic; German customers may be disarming or more likely taciturn. It does not matter. The point is the structure and result of the negotiation. The vendor wields a two-foot long razor sharp knife with which he delicately scrapes slices of meat from the cone, which fall into a handheld pan and are placed on a pita. Although the blade is not curved, on an unconscious level, our German patron may associate the knife with the Turkish scimitar – the threat of violence is at hand. For his part, the vendor has a wary sense of the xenophobic violence that might at any time be unleashed, not in all likelihood by this particular customer, but certainly in relation to his otherness of which the döner is a provocative sign. He solicits the customer's wishes with respect to the sauce and other toppings, a gesture accommodating German tastes. This is a crucial negotiation: does the customer want his sauce with or without *Knoblauch* (garlic)? For Germans, garlic has long been a culinary sign of the despised other. Turks and other people from the Mediterranean are still disparagingly called *Knoblauchfresser* (garlic-eaters). Increasingly, however, the German does choose garlic, overcomes a national food aversion, and strikes a modest blow against xenophobia. As the Turkish vendor tucks away his DM 6, the German customer bites into the döner. As his body's digestive processes assimilate the Turkish fare, and a stereotyping niche is reinforced for his Turkish compatriot, the vendor too gains a subtle and precarious victory in the form of increasing financial independence, and a knowing if ambivalent pride that the food of his homeland has so profoundly penetrated German culture. Most Germans may still not count Turkish people among their friends, but rare is the German not prepared to ingest a döner.

For all its complexity, the story of the döner kebab presumes that it is identifiable as what might be called the culinary other *vis-à-vis* the regional and national fare that is distinctly German. On a superficial level, this binary opposition may seem stable and indeed important for organizing the German food universe. But to remain on this level ignores the interpenetration of the culinary self and other and maintains the clichés of German gastro-cultural xenophobia. Analysis of two scenes from Werner Maria Faßbinder's film *Angst essen Seele auf* (1974; released abroad as *Ali: Fear Eats the Soul*) will allow us to move beyond these clichés. Faßbinder was a master at conceiving complex scenes of cultural encounter and misunderstanding with a distinctly German flavor (see also Chapter 12). *Fear Eats the Soul*, about the ill-starred and unlikely relationship between an elderly German cleaning lady and a somewhat younger Moroccan *Gastarbeiter*, was one of the earliest post-war films to focus on the complexities and ambiguities of otherness in a German context. Incongruously but successfully modeled on Douglas Sirk's *All that Heaven Allows*, Faßbinder's film initially plays out their relationship in terms of their joint isolation and ostracism from her German family, friends, and society, and then, as their marriage nonetheless finds acceptance, Faßbinder explores Ali's resistance to this assimilating and objectifying embrace. Not surprisingly, food is often the locus for dispute and cultural misunderstanding. In a scene immediately after their civil wedding, Ali and Emmy are in a celebratory mood and at Emmy's suggestion make their way to an Italian restaurant frequented, as Emmy claims by way of recommendation, by Hitler during his Munich years. The irony is enormous: an elderly German woman and younger Moroccan celebrate their miscegenation by entering an Italian restaurant favored by Hitler. A hostile German waiter holds them in his cold and supercilious gaze. Emmy's and Ali's festive spirits are not proof against the waiter's icy courtesy. The menu itself poses considerable challenges and the waiter's surly multilingual explanations only intensify their unease. Steak Chateaubriand can be ordered English style or medium – the latter is mispronounced as an English word and is unintelligible to Emmy. The cultural and linguistic confusion that should by rights parallel their own relationship and serve to destabilize German superciliousness, does not. Emmy and Ali are brutally cowed.

Later in the film, Emmy and Ali are in their small apartment at the point when her community is in the process of selfishly accepting their marriage and Emmy is basking in renewed respect. Ali asks her expressly for couscous, but Emmy is re-infected with German cultural obstinacy. 'You can't always eat couscous,' she says. 'You have to adjust to German cuisine.' Ali leaves the apartment in a sulk, and makes his way to the bar where he and other Moroccan compatriots commiserate, indeed, where he first met Emmy quite by chance. Though the bar is closed, he knows where to find the owner and barkeeper, a buxom German blonde, in her apartment nearby. When he sees her he merely says, 'I want couscous.' Remarkably, Faßbinder elides the cooking and eating (if there were any) and jumpcuts to a scene of sexual intimacy between Ali and the barkeeper. Once again, Faßbinder introduces confusion where we would expect clarity. Couscous is a metonymy for both sexual infidelity and cultural identity. Indeed, Faßbinder may be playing on the phonetic indistinguishability of couscous and *Kuß-Kuß* (the German word for kiss-kiss). Clearly, Ali is troubled by the process of assimilation that seems to be sweeping him up and mounts a resistance by his choice of food and its implied infidelity. Yet the couscous will be prepared not by Arab hands, but by a fulsome German woman, and may not be food after all. He escapes one German embrace only to enter another. With Walter Abish (1979), we may justly ask how German (or foreign) is it? By the end of the film, as Emmy and Ali reconcile on the most practical of grounds, Ali falls to the dance floor at the bar, writhing in pain caused by a perforated ulcer. In metaphorical terms, his plight was more than he could stomach.

Friend or foe: the dialectics of digestion

The German response to gastro-cultural otherness is merely an extreme instance of a general disposition with regard to food. At the deepest level of the German culinary unconscious, there is an overriding suspicion with respect to all food. Whereas many Americans tend to regard their stomachs as iron cylinders proof against almost any culinary onslaught, many Germans are intensely aware of the varied and putative effects of different foods on their digestive systems. In other words, many Germans are inclined to regard all food as other to their body and a potential hazard that must through any of several means either be neutralized or avoided. In conjunction with this suspicion, Germans have over the centuries developed an unusually fine-tuned visceral and cultural awareness of the digestive tract and a habit of classifying all food types with respect to their relative digestibility, their ease of assimilation. Both of these depend on a specialized but widely shared vocabulary of gastrointestinal judgment. The more than casual observer of German culture will soon notice the attention paid to the condition and combination of foods introduced to the gullet (temperature, quality, relative acidity, place of origin, consistency, etc.), predictions as to the foods' digestibility (*Bekömmlichkeit*), and the remarkable specificity with respect to imagining the process of digestion. Whereas the digestive awareness of most Americans and Brits is limited to a dim sense of the stomach and possibly the intestine, many Germans can imaginatively pinpoint such organs or body parts as the *Schleimhaut* (stomach lining), *Zwölffingerdarm* (duodenum), and the *Bauchspeicheldrüse* (pancreas). The sheer corporeality of these German terms as compared to the distant Latin features of English underscores the intensity of the experience.

Categorization of foods and dietetic regimes are premised on digestibility. There is *Kinderkost* (a regime suitable for children), *Rohkost* (a regime of raw vegetables and fruits), *Schonkost* (a 'light' diet intended to spare the stomach), and *Trennkost* (a regime that allows only certain combinations of foods and prohibits others). The key modifier in all matters, however, is *magenfreundlich* – whether a food is friendly to the stomach or not. A cursory stroll through the aisles of a grocery store or a *Reformhaus* (healthfood store); perusal of magazines with copious food advertisements; or simply a keyword search on the Internet yields a large sample of claims regarding the *Magenfreundlichkeit* of a host of products. A mineral water asserts that it is *magenfreundlich* and stimulates the *Stoffwechsel* (metabolism), the *Kreislauf* (circulation), and the digestive system. A wine promises to be *bekömmlich*, *magenfreundlich*, *gut verträglich* – all essentially synonyms – even in the event of immoderation. While coffee in general has the reputation of not being *magenfreundlich*, country of origin, roasting process, and other procedures are touted as ways of rendering it acceptable to the stomach. Liquors such as *Heilschnäpse* (schnapps for the health) and *Magenbitter* (herbal bitters for the stomach) are promoted for their medicinal effects on the digestion. A caraway liqueur promotes digestion, while a gentian schnapps has a high quotient of bitter ingredients and is therefore particularly *magenfreundlich*.

Underberg, a Swiss firm, sells a high percentage bitters in dosage-size bottles at the checkout in almost all grocery stores; the consumer imbibes strictly for the purpose of assisting digestion. A baker prepares special herbal whole grain bread and avers its friendliness to the liver, gall bladder and stomach. A small Austrian firm manufactures a meat massage system which pre-processes (pre-digests, as it were) pieces of meat. Such meat is, of course, especially *magenfreundlich*. Doctors recommend that their patients lead lives that are *magenfreundlich*: selecting foods carefully, eating six small meals a day instead of three large ones (a practice already shared by many Germans who enjoy a *zweites Frühstück* [second breakfast] or *Vesperbrot* mid-morning and *Kaffee und Kuchen* [coffee and cake] mid-afternoon), limiting stress, and otherwise sparing the stomach. *Magenfreundlich* is on the verge of becoming a metaphor for any non-threatening, stomach-sparing, moderate pleasure. A snippet of prose from a gay website illustrates its expansive tendencies: 'As I'm writing to you, Mr. Gately warbles *magenfreundlich* and *kuschelig* (cosily) from my stereo.' In due time, *magenfreundlich* may become an all-purpose adjective of the order of the Dutch word *lekker* (delicious).

The best formulation of what transpires in the German culinary unconscious is to be found in Hegel's account of the dialectics of digestion in *The Philosophy of Nature*. For Hegel, digestion is an important instance of assimilation, indeed, the first on a developmental scale that requires and affords a modicum of self-consciousness on the part of the eating subject. Some have wondered at the quaintness of Hegel's obvious fascination with digestion (Findlay 1970). Others, like Alexandre Kojève (1969), realize that eating is a telling instance of the dialectic at work:

> The being that eats, for example, creates and preserves its own reality by the overcoming of a reality other than its own, by the 'transformation' of an alien reality into its own reality, by the 'assimilation,' the 'internalization' of a 'foreign,' 'external' reality.

Every culinary other is a foe, a potential enemy of the stomach, unless the culinary subject succeeds in extinguishing the other's identity and making it his or her own. Anger, hostility and violence permeate the interaction between the subject and the culinary other, from the seizure and killing of food with instruments of battle and the ferocity of mastication to the total transformation into chyle in the digestive tract and the eradication of all specific qualities (Richter 1998).

Against this gastro-philosophical background, *magenfreundlich* designates foods or modes of preparation that over the centuries have proven to lend themselves readily to easy and effective assimilation. For the most part these foods and methods should be domestic. Christoph Wilhelm Hufeland (who provided the epigraph to this chapter), a medical doctor in Goethe's Weimar and author of the best-selling *Makrobiotik oder die Kunst, das menschliche Leben zu verlängern* (Macrobiotics, or the Art of

Extending Human Life, 1796), writes that 'domestic vegetables are milder and healthier than foreign'. French cooking, which observes aesthetic principles and aims foremost at pleasing the tongue, was held in particular suspicion. Karl Friedrich von Rumohr, another of Goethe's contemporaries and author of *Geist der Kochkunst* (The Spirit of the Art of Cooking; 1822), called Paris 'the seat of foolish pleasures'. The controversial meat broth containing osmazoma, the concentrated liquid essence of pounds of animal flesh, was regarded as a triumph by the French (cf. Brillat-Savarin), but frowned upon by Hufeland and Rumohr. The latter claims to own an original receipt from the household of Louis XV from which he deduces that two-thirds of all meat purchased was used for the purpose of preparing broths. According to Hufeland many believe there is a virtue in bypassing the teeth and the stomach and injecting such an essence of nutritive juice directly into the blood, as it were; on the contrary, the digestive process is crucial to transforming foods into a quality homogenous and similar to our nature. Broths introduce foreign bodies into our body and result more in our consumption than our restauration. The French art of cooking, say Hufeland and Ramdohr, should therefore be regarded as an enemy of our life, invented for the purpose of converting God's gifts into insidious poison.

BSE

If French cooking and its German imitation were regarded as pernicious for the health and well-being of Germans in the eighteenth and nineteenth centuries, in the late twentieth and early twenty-first it was at first the UK that seemed to have introduced a devastating virus that went straight to the heart of German culinary identity. In the meantime, Germans have had to acknowledge the enemy within – even Bavarian cattle herds have been identified as BSE infected. On 29 November 2000, the *Berliner Zeitung* published a lengthy table under the heading, 'What can I eat without fear?' Germans were confronted with the horrible fact that almost all of their beloved sausage varieties were suspect. A 1995 list of sausages containing 'innards' (liver, heart, tongue without mucous membrane, gullet without mucous membrane, lung, brain, spleen, kidney, stomach and rumen without mucous membrane) first published by *Stern* with the title 'Guten Appetit' was re-released in 2000 with the addition of sausage varieties containing *Sepfleisch*, i.e., meat separated from the bones including the spine through a mechanical process. It is in the brain and spinal cord that the prions that trigger BSE and its human variant Creutzfeldt-Jakob may be found. The list is endless and relentlessly records the impact on regional diversity: *Frankfurter Leberwurst, Rheinische Leberwurst, Berliner Preßwurst, Sächsische Blutwurst, Debreziner, Nürnberger Rostbratwurst, Westfälische Grützwurst*. Even the sacred pork sausage provides no consolation. The use until recently of 'cadaver flour', feed that contains cattle parts, as well as the circumstance that pork sausages by law may contain beef byproducts have tainted pork and other meats too.

BSE has had a devastating effect on the meat industry and the German economy. These effects can be measured in euros and lost jobs. The cultural effects, however, are of a different order and touch virtually every German (excepting vegetarians and those who have consistently eaten *Biofleisch*, i.e., meat from livestock not fed cadaver flour nor treated with hormones). The tainting of any food supply is discomforting. But when the food in question is at the same time central to the culture's cuisine, indeed, crucially involved with the culture's identity, the initial effect is trauma. In an article entitled 'The Hysteria of Decent People', *Der Spiegel* explores the deep psychological connections between three outwardly unrelated shocks to the German population: the murder of a Turkish child by neo-Nazi skinheads, the collapse of the Kyoto Accords regarding the greenhouse effect, and BSE (2000). In the face of xenophobic violence, the impending doom of the environment, and a tainted food supply, nothing is safe anymore. Morning talk show hosts report the coinage of a new motto that says it all: 'Zum Inder statt Rinder' (go to an Indian, i.e., non-beef-serving restaurant, instead of eating beef). The searing irony of this expression is its echo of a rightwing phrase that swept Germany only a year earlier when the government proposed relaxing immigration laws in order to bring in computer-savvy Indians: 'Kinder statt Inder' (bear children, instead of importing Indians). Food hysteria and xenophobia are tragically linked.

As I have tried to show, the German trauma is all the more profound for having confirmed a deeply held cultural suspicion with regard to all food. Germany will recover, as will the other European nations. The long-term effects of BSE on regional and national cuisine are uncertain, though some tendencies are evident. Certainly a heightened awareness and renewed suspicion will accompany every German on his or her trip to the supermarket and butcher. The BSE epidemic may have salutary consequences for the preservation of regional cuisine. Germans will return to what they know. More Germans will shop at local butchers and require assurances about the origin of the product and its ingredients. The *Stiftung Warentest*, a consumer advocacy group similar to the Consumers Union in the USA, puts it simply: 'Buy meat from your own region. Ask questions, and purchase only from butchers you know and trust.' Initiatives involving sustainable local agriculture, use of whole foods, organic farming, and the 'slow food' movement, may all receive considerable impetus. BSE is already popularly associated with agribusiness, the EU, globalization, and American models of food handling. If Germans seemed reluctantly willing to stomach the abandonment of the Deutschmark in favor of the Euro, the plight of the sausage may prove enough to rally Germans in effective opposition against some of the capitalist imperatives of the global economy.

No place like home: urine therapy in Germany

For many readers, urine therapy – the practice of regularly consuming one's own urine in the belief that it contains unique and potent healing powers – may be an unappetizing novelty, never before encountered. At the same time, readers should know that I am not asserting that the average German drinks his or her urine on a regular basis, or at all for that matter. It would be very difficult to gather reliable statistics on urine consumption under any circumstances and we will have to be content with less solid evidence. What I am arguing, however, is that German culture is uniquely predisposed to entertain the idea of urine therapy, indeed, that it is indigenous to German culture, and that urine therapy nicely fits into the patterns and logic of the German culinary unconscious.

Beliefs associated with the virtues of urine have existed for thousands of years and the practice of urine therapy can be found in non-western countries such as India, perhaps as a form of tantric religion. Given the popularity of alternative medicine, non-western spirituality and new ageism, it is not surprising that one finds a literature on urine therapy in most western countries. In the United States numerous books are available, but exclusively from specialty presses with limited retail exposure (Inner Traditions International, Life Science Institute, Water of Life Institute, etc.). One would be hard-pressed to find a title such as *Urine: Your Body's Secret Elixir of Health* in the shelves of a mainstream bookstore. In Germany, the situation is different. Whereas many of the American titles are actually translations, German books on urine therapy tend to be written by Germans and are published in inexpensive paperback format by major presses (Ullstein, Goldmann, and Piper, for example). A stroll through the self-help and medicine aisles of a bookstore will turn up titles such as *Urine the Ur-Nectar: The Inexhaustible Healing Power of Your Body's Own Pharmacy* or *Urine: A Very Special Juice*. There is evidently a niche market in Germany for what in most other countries would seem an object of revulsion.

Further indirect evidence comes from the circumstance that while the First World Conference on Urine Therapy was aptly held in India in 1997, the second just as aptly took place in Gersfeld, Germany, a spa town some 150 km east of Frankfurt, in 1999. Three days of scholarly presentations and workshops were followed by a day of public programs. The Internet record of the conference shows pictures of a public toilet identified as the pharmacy with a cup dispenser and the invitation to treat oneself. A second photograph shows a wastebasket full of empty cups. There seems to be no record of a toast.

Proponents of urine therapy claim that urine contains nutrients, proteins, amino acids, enzymes, hormones, minerals, vitamins and, most importantly, antibodies. The regular consumption of the middle portion of one's morning stream promotes good health, strengthens the auto-immune system, and combats a long list of ailments, diseases, and conditions ranging from sore throat to AIDS. The morning urine offers the individual body the precise cocktail required and initiates a process whereby urine and body are mutually purified.

The scientific jargon often deployed in contemporary claims for urine therapy may cause one to surmise that the German willingness to entertain the idea is linked to a general openness to homeopathic and other alternative forms of medicine presently in vogue. But in Germany, folk medicine has been cultivated for generations, if not centuries, and the favorable predisposition to urine therapy has been present for as long. Johann Heinrich Zedler and Ludovici's *Großes Vollständiges Universallexikon* (Great Comprehensive Universal Lexicon) of 1747, for instance, contains an eight-page article under the title 'Urin Arzneyen' in which numerous remedies are proposed involving the urine of animals, young boys, and one's own.

At the root of the German susceptibility to the idea of urine therapy stands a fantasy that responds to the dialectic of digestion, the uneasy tension between the subject and the culinary object. If, as the extreme cases of the döner kebab and BSE have illustrated, the German culinary unconscious is deeply convinced that all food is other to the body, potentially threatening and only assimilated with due caution and suspicion, one's own urine–far from being repulsive and foreign to the subject – is more a part of oneself already than almost anything else could be. The fantasy of a sustainable auto-digestion that elides the encounter with the culinary other, or reinforces the subject in its necessary encounters, has a distinctly German cultural appeal. What could be more *magenfreundlich*?

Eating with Hegel

The culturally inquisitive visitor to Germany should by all means savor the regional and ethnic variety of German culinary offerings, maintaining a due wariness with respect to BSE, of course. By the same token, there is no question that Germans still eat their foods with pleasure and gusto. Even in these traumatic times, a semblance of the normal conditions of food culture prevails. Our focus on German culinary pathology was not meant to put anyone off their appetite, or to characterize Germans as particularly neurotic. Every culture has its own pathology – one need only think of obesity, anorexia, and cholesterol panic in the USA, for example. But as the visitor interacts with Germans in restaurants, sausage stands, grocery stores, markets, bars, and in their homes, he or she may notice telling details that betray the persistence of a distinctly German culinary unconscious. The visitor may leave these details in isolation or, in a more speculative vein – and that has been the nature of this chapter – entertain a gastro-psychological context for them. In the face of culinary trauma – and what could be more traumatic than the recent ordeals – German foodways will rally and be reorganized along the dialectical lines already indicated. Key among the organizational principles will be the belief that it is not what one eats, but what one digests that counts.

References

ABISH, W. 1979: *How German is it?* New York: New Directions.

BUCKMAN, R. 1999: *Urine: your body's secret elixir of health.* Woodstock: Beekman.

FINDLAY, J.N. 1970: Foreword. *Hegel's philosophy of nature.* Oxford: Clarendon Press.

FREUD, S. 1965 (1933): *New introductory lectures on psychoanalysis.* New York: W. W. Norton.

HARNISCH, G. and WILLIAMS, C. 1996: *Ursaft Urin: Unerschöpfliche Heilkraft aus der Apotheke Ihres eignen Körpers.* Bietigheim: Lorber & Turm.

HEGEL, G.F.W. 1970: *Hegel's philosophy of nature.* Oxford: Clarendon Press.

HOLZHÜTER, R. 1995: *Urin Heilt: Das neue Therapie-Spektrum.* Berlin: Ullstein.

HÖTING, H. 1995: *Lebenssaft Urin: Die heilende Kraft.* Munich: Goldmann

HUFELAND, C.W. 1984 (1796): *Makrobiotik oder Die Kunst, das menschliche Leben zu verlängern.* Frankfurt a/M: Insel.

KOJÈVE, A. 1969: *Introduction to the reading of Hegel.* New York and London: Basic Books.

MINTZ, S.W. 1996: *Tasting food, tasting freedom: excursions into eating, culture, and the past.* Boston: Beacon.

RICHTER, S. 1998: Hegel and the dialectics of digestion. *Nineteenth Century Prose* 25, 11–25.

RUBNER, M. 1913: *Wandel der Volksernährung.* Leipzig: Akademische Verlagsgesellschaft.

RUMOHR, K.F. [1822] 1998: *Geist der Kochkunst.* Frankfurt a/M: Insel.

TEUTEBERG, H.J. and WIEGELMANN, G. 1986: *Unsere tägliche Kost: Geschichte und regionale Prägung.* Münster: F. Coppenrath.

THOMAS, C. 1999: *Ein ganz besonderer Saft – Urin.* Munich: Piper.

THORNHILL, R. 1999: Turkish delight: forget Bratwurst and Big Macs – Döner Kebab is Germany's fast food. *German Life.*

TOLKSDORF, U. 1993: Das Eigene und das Fremde: Küchen und Kulturen in Kontakt. In WIERLACHER, A., NEUMANN, G. and TEUTEBERG, H.J. (eds) *Kulturthema Essen.* Berlin: Akademie, 187–92.

ZEDLER, J.H. and LUDOVICI, C.G. [1732–50] 1961–82: *Grosses vollständiges Universal-Lexikon.* Graz: Akademische Druck- u. Verlagsanstalt.

Websites

http://www.goethe.de/gr/dub/projekt/deipess0.htm (a Goethe Institute website focused on German food and food customs)

http://userpages.fu-berlin.de/~dittbern/BSE/Facts1.html (German information regarding BSE, including a list of sausages considered risky)

http://utopia.knoware.nl/users/cvdk/urinetherapy/conference.html (the official website for the Second World Conference on Urine Therapy 1999)

P A R T

IV

CREATIVE CULTURAL PRACTICES

A culture, essentially, is unplannable.

(Raymond Williams: *Culture and Society*)

Cultural Studies opens up the field of creative practices. Cultural Studies does not look inside the language of literary works or inside their authors' biographies for its questions or its final explanations. Instead of constructing a canon of literature and other forms of 'high art', Cultural Studies, as the chapters in this part demonstrate, examines relations of power, of production and distribution, and problems inherent in the representation of race, gender and class. Cultural Studies exercises a belief that explanations for works of art need to be sought and examined in the contexts of their production and of their influence, that is to say in the system of social and cultural relations that sustain them. How a work is produced, who funds it, what markets it is consumed in, who contributes to its make-up and its prestige? These are all questions which concern the authors of the chapters in this part. The concerns here lie in the first instance with the culture industry – as conceptualized by Adorno and the Frankfurt School – and with the consumption of its products. But the analyses here do not end with the now somewhat commonplace understanding that works of art may be produced, packaged and consumed. The complex relationship between a diverse body of consumers and an equally diverse body of products its not simply one way. Different creative practices interact, they reference each other intertextually, they provide sites for the making of multiple and contested meanings, they are powerful vehicles for gaining access to power, influence and capital. Works of art are symbolic of social life and interwoven with the material conditions that enable them to come into being. This is not to say that material conditions will directly determine a work of art, but it is, importantly, to say that, in Cultural Studies, questions of access to power and money are highly significant and are important stakes in the culture industry.

Some aspects of contemporary German culture suggest immediate images, tangible objects, clear practices to those outside of the culture. Others, such as popular German music, do not. Chapter 10 by Osman Durrani begins with the puzzling absence of popular German music that has travelled beyond its borders, focusing on the rare examples that have had international acclaim, examining some of the aspects of the music industry that mitigate against wider distribution, and then giving a detailed survey of the trends in popular German music and its relationship to mass production and mass consumption. What emerges from the survey is a view of a diverse and hybrid music, drawing on a wide range of traditions, populated as a genre with many non-German singers, looking beyond its own borders to the exotic, and within to politics as well as to its own regional roots and dialects. The approach in this article is one that attends carefully to detail, examining and displaying the lyrics of songs for their range of humour, banality, politics and complexity.

Theatre has always been a public place where the values, beliefs, conflicts and concerns of particular cultures have been represented, live. Gaining a critical, cultural understanding of German theatre, from an anglophone perspective presents certain difficulties. Distanced encounters with German theatre, through surveys, reviews and academic work are all used in Chapter 11 by Meg Mumford and Alison Phipps, both to give an overview of some of the trends in contemporary German theatre, and also as perspectives that are highly contextualized and require critical reflection. In this way claims that German theatre is in crisis, or that German theatre has no concern with cultural identity are shown to be questionable and to have their roots in the struggles for vested interests in different microcosms of German theatre. Theatre is presented, not as the work of creative genius, but as rooted in the concerns of everyday life. The traditional oppositions between amateur and professional, audience and ensemble, high and low culture are replaced with understandings of the work of theatrical production taken from Bourdieu. This helps to situate divisions historically in the class-based distinctions that emerged during the nineteenth century as well as illuminating the differences inherent in the contemporary German theatre scene.

Contemporary German film has undergone something of a 'scene change' when compared to its famous, serious art-house predecessors. Chapter 12 by Dickon Copsey presents three crucial characteristics of the new film scene from the perspective of identities, those of the New Germany and post-*Wende* films, those of gender and finally of race relations. In each case several films are taken as examples and analysed for their place in the construction of new identities. Film provides a form of collective culture that displays some of the narratives and images of the times. The move from aesthetic film to commercial cinema with the development of home-produced Hollywood-style blockbusters is set alongside the growth of a focus on alternative themes. Questions are asked of films which purport to focus on feminist concerns but which, upon closer analysis, are at best ambiguous. This chapter gives us critical cultural readings of contemporary German films. It is not concerned to produce a canon or hierarchy of films according to their relative review status or 'high art' merit, but rather to ask questions of the way identities are made, unmade and remade on screen and how the contemporary film scene in Germany is one in which different groups, claiming different identities attempt to resist dominant discourse.

Drawing on Appadauri's concept of a 'scape' Chapter 13 by Holger Briel examines the contours of production and dissemination of images and narratives that make up the German mediascape. The examination of German media here relies on quantitative methods, with statistics presented to point to the large-scale trends and to show the level of consumption of different forms of media, be it print culture, television, film or Internet technologies. As with other chapters in this book, the claim to any distinct 'Germanness' in media practices is shown to be highly problematic and the trends in the statistics are used to point to the development of both international and also significant regional biases in the German mediascape. Equally, however, the structures of the media industries are examined in detail for the struggle to gain influence, power and capital. The study of German media is also set in context and, like the discussions of film, music and other creative and mass cultural forms, is shown to have been highly influenced by canonical understandings and hierarchies of media products. The influence of Cultural Studies on the study of German media is readily apparent in this chapter, however, with attention paid to gendered patterns of consumption, to the heterogeneity of German media, and to the question of power and equality in the structures of the culture industry.

10

Popular music in the German-speaking world

BY OSMAN DURRANI

The crisis of twentieth-century German popular music

From Bach to Mozart, from Beethoven through Brahms and Bruckner to Wagner and Strauss, most of the great composers who shaped the classical music of Western Europe were from a German-speaking background. This dominant influence came to an abrupt end in the twentieth century, and music no longer appears to constitute a major element of Germany's contemporary culture. The closer one looks at popular tastes in the post-war period, the more obvious the absence of German musical talent. Where one might expect *chansonneurs* who could match the successes of Edith Piaf and Charles Aznavour in France, Jacques Brel in Belgium, or Serge Reggiani in France and Italy, not to mention Anglo-Saxon star performers such as Bob Dylan and John Lennon, there appears to be a void. No one of comparable stature has emerged in the German-speaking world.

There are several ways of accounting for this anomaly. The unfamiliar and strange-sounding language may have had some effect. Two world wars severely reduced Germany's status as a cultural beacon. Attempts to generate or re-invent 'original' German culture were doomed to fail at home and abroad, as the GDR did when attempting to create new dance steps as alternatives to the products of Western consumerism. The 'pop' industry that owed its success to the portable record player and tape recorder did not bypass Germany, but it relied more heavily there than elsewhere on translations and imitations of Anglo-Saxon and other models. Non-Germans might be surprised to learn that there was a thriving local music industry post-1945, and they will be hard put to name the leading groups and soloists. The home-grown *Schlager*, which will be investigated in this chapter, had next to no following outside the German-speaking nations, at a time when most other European countries were producing international celebrities whose fame spread far across the continent and beyond: Françoise Hardy, Rita Pavone, Melina Mercouri, to name just a few of the mega-stars of the 'swinging sixties'. Germany's dismal record in the Eurovision Song Contest is another of many indicators of her failure in this respect (Fessmann *et al.* 1998). For this reason, it seems particularly important to attempt a survey of the main trends and influences, not merely to record what went on, but to show how a particularly German response to a global phenomenon came about and trace how it evolved. People may laugh at the antics of Guildo Horn and Stefan Raab, but the figures who hit today's headlines are merely the most recent exponents of a long process of adaptation in which social and other factors played a decisive role (Hilbk 2000).

It would be an over-simplification to suggest that the German mind is not well attuned to the production of lightweight and ephemeral products such as dance music. Germany had a very vibrant and successful light music industry up until and during the Second World War: Marlene Dietrich, Zarah Leander and Lale Andersen are remembered as stars who acquired an international following with songs sung in German. They were made up of simple but catchy tunes and of lyrics that lost nothing in translation. After the war, the German popular music industry, now represented by powerful companies such as Polydor, Electrola and Telefunken, was not idle for long. It resumed working to capacity soon after the end of hostilities, but was to encounter insurmountable problems in trying to win back international audiences.

Some rock groups, including Kraftwerk, have evidently been successful abroad and are recognized for their pioneering electronic techniques rather than for their lyrics. BAP have been touring for 20 years and were one of the first western rock groups to appear in China. Innovative non-vocal ensembles like CAN have been playing to large audiences overseas for many years. Claiming to be 'at least three steps ahead of contemporary popular music', CAN succeeded in entering the UK Top 30 in 1976 (Haring 1984, 36–41, 104–8). Yet these are the exceptions, and Germany's isolation is most obvious when one considers mainstream popular music, as exemplified by the *Schlager*, which played a dominant role in the youth culture of the post-war period.

Long before Stefan Raab and Guildo Horn made their dubious contributions to the Eurovision Contest, many observers viewed the German-language *Schlager* as the most lightweight and transitory of all art forms, suitable at best only for an occasional airing at so-called 'bad taste parties'. (Helmes 1996, 62; Hilbk 2000, 13). Its fortunes are nonetheless closely bound up with a series of phenomena characteristic of late twentieth-century German popular culture. Its ups and downs reflect the fluctuating mood of the country. Its themes engage, initially, with public uncertainties as to where Germany was heading during the period of reconstruction. As the *Wirtschaftswunder* gathers momentum, the discovery of the work ethic and the creeping Americanization of German life are conspicuous factors beneath the glitter of canned entertainment. From the 1960s onwards, a more confident tone evolves, and the homespun *Volkslied* gives way to imported country, blues and rock music. But as 'beat' gains in popularity, the *Schlager* suffers a setback, and during the period 1965–80, it functions as a bland placebo rather than as a stimulus. Germany's unexpected triumph in the Eurovision stakes at Harrogate in 1982 marks a further turning point, as foreign influences face a challenge from the '*Neue Deutsche Welle*'. In recent years, the German scene has experienced the advent of rap musicians, in consequence of which many marginal groups who would otherwise lack a voice have engaged with public discourse on front-page topics including immigration, youth culture, the 'ghetto' concept, feminism, and post-unification politics.

The origins of the *Schlager* are buried somewhere in the late nineteenth century; its forebears include the music hall hit and the *Gassenhauer*: an aria from a light opera that caught the imagination of the masses and reappeared in popular renditions. The word seems to have originated in Vienna some time around 1870, and then as now it covered a variety of semi-distinct genres: folksongs, humorous couplets, arias and concert music, often used as the basis of topical texts. (Helmes 1996, 63). These early examples were different from today's products in one important respect: they had little or no commercial value. Everything changed with the advent of the gramophone. 'Der *Schlager* als Gattung setzt dort ein, wo er zur Ware wird, seine Herstellung und sein Vertrieb zum Geschäft werden' (Bardong *et al.* 1992, 9). (The *Schlager* became an independent genre when it became marketable and its production and distribution were commercialized.) This, in turn, is recognizable as a small part of a much wider process in which the world's culture ceased to be determined by individual artists and became a 'mass' culture. The most immediate consequence was that industry began to play a significant role in reducing the autonomous status of all art, with the consequence that 'The seriousness of high art is destroyed in speculation about its efficacy' (Adorno 1991, 85).

The 1930s are remembered as the Golden Age of German light music. Many songs of the period were romantic in their mood and import. The best-known example is probably Friedrich Hollaender's 'Ich bin von Kopf bis Fuß auf Liebe eingestellt', sung by Marlene Dietrich in the film *The Blue Angel* (1930). Other songwriters found themselves engaging with politics. There were musical numbers that appealed to the political left (Kurt Weill's 'Mäcki-Messer Song'); others were closer to the aspirations of the right ('Warum ist es am Rhein so schön?'). Both of these were major hits in 1928. The Nazis clamped down no less ruthlessly on musicians than on any of the other arts (Levi 1994, 48). The distinctions are often blurred; Fritz Löhner may have penned the text of 'Ich hab mein Herz in Heidelberg verloren', but he wrote his last *Schlager* in a concentration camp, as 'O Buchenwald, ich kann dich nicht vergessen' (Bardong *et al.* 1992, 15). The fortunes of German fans of American-style 'Swing-*Schlager*' during the Nazi years have

been charted by Michael Kater. Although the picture he paints is not one of
uniform opposition, there were countless victims among *Schlager*-writers as
in all other walks of life; to cite one example, Erich Knauf was executed for
making allegedly defeatist remarks, despite having penned the words to
several of the Nazi regime's favourites, 'Mit Musik geht alles besser' and
'Heimat, deine Sterne'.

The latter stages of the Second World War saw the rise of a new type of
Schlager, the so-called *Durchhalte-Schlager*; with titles that scarcely conceal
a subtext of frustration and despair: 'Davon geht die Welt nicht unter'
(Zarah Leander, 1942), 'Ich weiß, es wird einmal ein Wunder geschehn'
(Zarah Leander, 1942), and 'Es geht alles vorüber' (Lale Andersen, 1942).
The story of 'Lili Marleen' (Lale Andersen, 1939), so successful among
German troops that Anne Sheldon and Vera Lynn were soon prevailed upon
to record it for the British, has been well documented, not least in the film
Lili Marleen (Rainer Werner Fassbinder, 1980). These songs represent a last
flowering of the spirit of the Weimar Republic; a beautifully muted lyrical
pessimism determines their quality and must account for their popularity
among soldiers on both sides during and after the war.

The lure of the exotic

The quality that immediately comes to mind when considering the songs
that entered the charts in the early years of the Federal Republic is the preponderance of exotic references. Dreams of distant places, idyllic sunsets in
the tropics, white schooners ploughing the seven seas: such are the ingredients that occur most regularly in the texts of the period. Their popularity
can be traced back to one single record, 'Caprifischer', which had been produced by Deutscher Film Verlag in 1943. But it could not be released at the
time, because after Mussolini's downfall in the autumn of that year
Germany and Italy were at war. Instead, it was stockpiled. Two years later,
it so happened that this was the only 'new' record available in large quantities, and it immediately became a bestseller and set the tone for the future
production of 'hit music' in Germany:

> Wenn bei Capri die rote Sonne im Meer versinkt
> Und vom Himmel die bleiche Sichel des Mondes blinkt,
> zieh'n die Fischer mit ihren Booten aufs Meer hinaus
> und sie legen im weiten Bogen die Netze aus. (Port le roi, 36 f.)

> (When the red sun sinks over Capri, and the pale crescent of the moon
> glitters overhead, the fishermen head out in their boats and cast their
> nets in a wide arc.)

This tendency continues as the post-war *Schlager* reaches its peak in the
early 1960s (Kraushaar 1983, 53–9). By 1960, the German chart is entirely

dominated by three types of material: foreign-language songs by foreign artistes, German-language songs by foreign artistes, and German-language songs by German artistes posing as non-Germans. These included the Italian coal miner Rocco Granata singing his homespun 'Marina' in Italian; square-jawed Freddy Quinn posing as a deracinated traveller; Croatian Ivo Robic giving lessons in love to the very young; Swiss Hazy Osterwald with their lively tangos; Greek Jimmy Makulis who gave up his job in the British embassy in Athens to become a celebrity in Munich; and, last but not least, Bill Ramsey, born William McCreery Ramsey into the world of rhythm 'n' blues in Cincinnati, who abandoned his studies at Yale to train in the Frankfurt Jazz-Keller and perfect the art of reciting comic numbers in a well-honed transatlantic accent. All the above were in the 'top ten' during January 1960 (*Hit Bilanz*, 86).

The great debate which we shall repeatedly revisit in these pages revolves around a simple issue: are these songs purely ephemeral, or do they have a wider significance as indicators of cultural processes? Do they focus or distort reality? Are they, as 'virtual' paradises, capable of yielding insights into the underlying preoccupations and problems of the age? To this day, there are those who maintain that '*Schlager* do not tell lies' (Port le roi, title), while others see the medium as a distorting mirror in which reality is replaced by wish fulfilment (Mäsker 1999, 90). Are they accurate 'barometers' of what goes on on a wider stage? Or do they reproduce a fractured and unstable image of what is not and never can be? Even as musical curiosities, the German products are not easily approached by the novice. Yet they have found a following in certain specific circles. It should be mentioned that, for reasons discussed by Chotjewitz (1971) and Kraushaar (1983, 117f.), the *Schlager* enjoys a generally positive reputation in Germany's gay and lesbian circles. If the reader is to benefit from intercultural encounters involving German popular music, it will be necessary to look closely at the texts of representative examples from the past 40 years. Only in this way can we hope to gain an understanding of the variety of artistic and socio-political factors that have shaped this rapidly evolving genre.

In Freddy Quinn's 'Unter fremden Sternen' (No. 1 for 6 weeks, 21 November–26 December 1959; total sales 4 million copies), two contradictory elements are significant: the apparent confidence conveyed by the grittiness of Quinn's resolute delivery, combined with an underlying uncertainty, as Quinn oscillates between *Fernweh* and *Heimweh* and ends up profoundly disoriented between the familiar and the exotic worlds. There is something about this tension that both mimics Faustian restlessness and, more importantly, reflects the moral disorientation of post-war Germany. Is the country to open itself up, to abandon its isolation ('dort wo man lebt, scheint alles viel zu klein'), or is it to continue cultivating an inward-looking love of its own traditions? Whither Germany? seems to be the underlying question here. The transitional qualities of Germany (and

Britain) in the 1950s and 1960s can be perceived in this and other songs whose subtext is anti-Establishment (Hall and Whannel 1990, 27–37).

Quinn's success was spectacular. He was the most popular of all German singers and his record 'Heimweh' was the all-time best-selling *Schlager* (8 million copies sold). Quinn's simple rhymes broach epic themes, which are then resolved in three minutes:

> Jimmy Brown, das war ein Seemann
> und das Herz war ihm so schwer;
> doch es blieben ihm zwei Freunde:
> Die Gitarre und das Meer.

> (Jimmy Brown, he was a sailor, and his heart was so heavy; yet he had two companions: his guitar and the open sea.)

Quinn is important for another reason. Most Germans saw him as the boy from next door masquerading as an itinerant sailor or mercenary, but his background turned out to be very different: the son of an Irish salesman and an Austrian mother, born in Vienna, he was raised in New York, then in Vienna, where he was adopted by Baron Rudolf Freiherr Anatol von Petz, ran away from school, worked in a circus, became fluent in seven languages, sailed round the world, actually joined the Foreign Legion, and ended up as an entertainer in Hamburg's Reeperbahn (Bardong *et al.* 1992, 283). Far removed from his image as a 'home-grown' poser, he could be described as an intercultural mediator at a time when Germany was striving to shake off its historic insularity.

The opposite seems to be the case with René Carol. He was born in Berlin as Gerhard Tschierschnitz and acquired a reputation as a parodist. A foreign-sounding name helped him to recast himself in the image of a Latin lover, whereupon he went on to embody German nostalgia for the South ('Rote Rosen, rote Lippen, roter Wein', 1958). His best-known song takes the title of one of Germany's most sentimentally patriotic ditties ('Kein schöner Land in dieser Zeit ...' (No country more beautiful right now ...)) and stands it on its head: 'Kein Land kann schöner sein' (No. 3 for 3 weeks, 11–25 June 1960; in the charts for a total of 36 weeks) extols not the linden trees of Rothenburg or the elms of Hirsau, but the open spaces of Argentina, where the roving gaucho feels truly free and at home. This, significantly, at the precise point in time when Argentina was a haven for mass-murderers, the most notorious of whom, Adolf Eichmann, was captured and brought to justice while Carol's gaucho song was in the charts.

Carol's fame was enhanced by his foreign looks; he is reported to have escaped from a French POW camp by posing as an Italian (Anon 1994, 119). But alongside the bluffers and the impostors came 'genuine' artistes from abroad, who attracted a following by singing in broken German about their own native microworlds. So successful were they that many chose to settle temporarily or permanently in Germany. This is true of Mina, Gus

Backus, Connie Francis, and Bill Ramsey, to name but a few. Greece's future Minister of Culture vied with veteran Lale Andersen and relative newcomer Caterina Valente to cover the enormously popular Hadjidakis number 'Ein Schiff wird kommen' from the film *Never on a Sunday* (No. 1 for 10 weeks, 22 October–24 December 1960). Notable for its mantra-like liturgy of inaccessible destinations ('die fremden Schiffe aus Hongkong, aus Java, aus Chile und Shanghai'), it also possesses a powerful erotic dynamism, which, on close inspection, presents a number of puzzles. The woman initially presents an image of utter fidelity:

Ein Schiff wird kommen,
und das bringt mir den einen,
den ich so lieb' wie keinen,
und der mich glücklich macht

(A ship will arrive, bringing me the one and only, whom I love more than all the rest and who will bring me joy)

only to undermine this by slyly introducing a note of longing for someone else:

Ich bin ein Mädchen aus Piräus, und wenn
eines Tages mein Herz ich mal verlier'
dann muß es einer sein vom Hafen, nur so
einen Burschen wünsch' ich mir.

(I'm a girl from Piraeus, and if I should ever lose my heart to someone, then that someone will have to be one of the men from the harbour; I only wish for that type of lad.)

Here the woman simultaneously longs for her 'one and only' partner and while envisaging the day when she will lose her heart to another. Feminist readings tell us that this is a male fantasy image of a woman who is both utterly faithful and simultaneously available to any sailor who sets foot in her harbour. Following Julia Kristeva, it could be read as embodying a 'significant' contradiction, indicating the imminent break-up of the code of social norms (Hebdige 1990, 60), although at this time, lyrics were only noticed when intrusive.

On the fragmentation of experience, there could be no more fitting text than Bill Ramsey's 'Souvenirs' (Polydor, 1959). This held the position of No. 1 for 6 weeks, from 10 October–14 November 1959. Ramsey, famous for his 'ansteckend gute Laune' (contagious cheerfulness) (Anon 1994, 183), eagerly exhorts all and sundry to purchase the cast-offs of the rich and famous:

Souvenirs, Souvenirs, kauft ihr Leute, kauft sie ein,
Denn sie sollen wie das Salz in der Lebenssuppe sein!
Von der Gitarre eine Saite, die Elvis schlug,
Und den Verschluß der Bluse, die die Lolo trug.

> (Souvenirs, souvenirs: you've just got to snap them up, because they
> are said to put the salt in the broth of life! A string from the guitar that
> Elvis played, and the fastener from the blouse that Lolo wore.)

What is this other than an invitation to seize hold of whatever seems fashionable at the time, regardless of its value or use, in the hope that it will add
spice to an otherwise dull existence ('wie das Salz in der Lebenssuppe')? A
remarkable number of *Schlager* revolve around money. Jupp Schmitz had
broached the topic in lachrymose tones in his 'Wer soll das bezahlen?',
which was clearly relevant to the German situation in 1949. The homely
virtue of looking after one's own is now vividly contrasted with lure of spec-
ulating for profit on the world's stock exchanges. The utterly negative 'Wir
versaufen unsrer Oma ihr klein Häuschen' (originally written by R. Steidl
during the inflation of 1922, and reissued by W. Rose in 1962) and the
Swabian evergreen 'Schaffe, schaffe, Häusle bauen' (Ralf Bendix, 1964)
may allude to the traditional virtue of parsimony versus profligacy, but the
Swiss Hazy Osterwald group's 'Konjunktur-Cha-cha cha' (Polydor, 1960)
introduces a new and exotic world of high finance in a then fashionable
rhythm, dispensing a few easy lessons in how to play the stock market, as
though the mysteries of high finance could be learned like some new dance
step.

The discovery of youth

The 1960s not only embraced capitalism with unprecedented fervour, but
discovered, or maybe re-invented, youth as a huge, hitherto much underval-
ued source of consumer activity, of which the *Schlager* itself is one manifestation among many. The young were crying out to be discovered, no one
more so than an 11–year-old child prodigy known as Gabriele, whose
chirpy little number 'Vielleicht in 3,4,5,6 Jahren' (No. 7 for 2 weeks, 11–18
October 1958), once attacked as *'jugendgefährdend'* (likely to corrupt
young people), summed up the hopes of the young and precocious. Philippe
Ariès may have argued that the discovery of childhood came at a relatively
late stage in the history of western civilization, but Gabriele proves him
wrong: children are raring to abandon their special status and become just
like the grown-ups. This includes playing at mummies and daddies. Trude
Herr's outrageous 'Ich will keine Schokolade' bears this out:

> Ich will keine Schokolade
> ich will lieber einen Mann!
> Ich will einen der mich küssen
> und um den Finger wickeln kann!

> (I don't care for any chocolate, I would rather have a man! I want
> somebody who can kiss me, and hold me in the palm of his hand.)

Conversely, there are plenty of boys around eager to demonstrate that they can provide the desired qualities. Peter Kraus attempted rather pathetically to yelp and stutter like Elvis. (Haring 1984, 15) Ted Herold's 'Ich bin ein Mann' consists of little more than the endlessly repeated affirmations of the singer's manhood:

> Warum behandelst du mich wie ein großes Kind?
> Meine Küsse brennen heißer als Wüstenwind.

> (Why do you treat me like a grown-up child? My kisses burn hotter than the desert wind.)

The *Schlager* works in different ways, at times seeming to encourage promiscuity, at times praising domesticity. This is the subtext to countless *Schnulzen*, slow waltzes and other tempi that lend themselves to the turgid sentimentality of the likes of Heidi Brühl ('Wir wollen niemals auseinandergehn'). One way in which singers could opt out of the furious debates between antithetical moral codes (as exemplified in the public debate about rock and roll) was to opt for parody and pastiche. Old tunes could be subverted in a playful manner that robbed them of their original connotations. The folksong appears to be targeted in this way, when diminutive American Gus Backus (born in New York as Donald Edgar Backus) rhymes 'Edeltraut' and 'Sauerkraut' in his hilarious 'Sauerkraut-Polka':

> Ich esse gerne Sauerkraut und tanze gerne Polka,
> und meine Braut heißt Edeltraut, die denkt genau wie ich.
> Sie kocht am besten Sauerkraut und tanzt am besten Polka,
> deshalb ist auch die Edeltraut die beste Braut für mich.

> (I love to eat sauerkraut and I love to dance the polka, and Edeltraut, my bride-to-be, feels just the same as me. She cooks the best sauerkraut and dances polka best, which is what makes Edeltraut the champion bride-to-be.

It is here that we come full circle: Germany imports an American to bring its music up to scratch, and the American ends up celebrating the sheer Germanness of *Sauerkraut*, with only his accent to give him away. While treading a post-modern tightrope between celebration of and scorn for his chosen medium, Backus emerged as a somewhat tragic figure, compelled by Polydor to conform to the role they imposed upon him as a *Stimmungskanone* (purveyor of instant cheerfulness 'on demand'). Nonetheless, he was to manage an almost unique achievement, by singing in Bavarian dialect with an American accent ('I bin a stiller Zecher', 1961). The importance of the *Schlager* in dialect must not be underrated, as it indicates a regional identity which is still strong in most parts of Germany today (see BAP, EAV below). A similar inversion occurs when fellow-American Bill Ramsey, in 'Zuckerpuppe', posing, *malgré* his accent, as a German visitor to an oriental night-club, becomes enamoured of a belly-dancer with a suspiciously familiar quality about her:

Die Zuckerpuppe / aus der Bauchtanztruppe / kannte ich aus Wuppertal!

(That sugar baby from the belly dance troupe was an acquaintance – from Wuppertal!)

Despite its claim to cosmopolitanism, the *Schlager* is self-evidently 'Made in Germany' and nowhere else. A comparison of Gene Pitney/Rick Nelson's 'Hello Mary-Lou' with the German cover version produced by 'Die Ricky Boys' bears this out: the rough edge of this song is completely lost in the prettified translation.

Hello Mary-Lou. Hello Mary-Lou,
Sweet Mary-Lou, I'm so in love with you.

becomes the very limp:

Hello, Mary-Lou, sieh mal an,
dein Kleid ist schick, und schick sind deine Schuh.

(Hello, Mary-Lou, well, well, your dress is smart and so are your shoes)

This 'clean-living' image of the German pop idol might puzzle non-German observers. Despite the occasionally dubious subtext ('Am Sonntag will mein Süßer mit mir segeln gehn' (This Sunday my sweetheart has promised to go sailing)), there is an essentially upbeat and edifying quality about the German *Schlager*. This may partly have been a consequence of the editorial policy of that important organ *BRAVO* ('die Zeitschrift mit dem jungen Herzen' (the young-at-heart magazine)), whose ageing editor Liselotte Krakauer, pursued a distinctly conservative line. Young readers were shown in Freddy Quinn an unselfish if solitary sailor, Elvis earned praise for being promoted to the rank of sergeant on account of personal bravery, and even the *gamine* Conny Froboess obeyed her parents unquestioningly when they asked her to postpone her nuptials. Those who disobeyed their elders or, worse still, ended up in the divorce courts, were denounced, as happened to Brigitte Bardot (Herrwerth 1997, 18). The battle to keep popular music wholesome was to have unexpected consequences in the late 1960s, when the *Schlager* became the refuge of ultra-conservative forces. Freddy Quinn led the way with a series of patently 'rightist' titles ('Hundert Mann und ein Befehl', 1966), and actually used the *Schlager* ('Wir') to attack the idle layabouts of the day (Herrwerth 1997, 104: Kraushaar 1983, 87f.).

The shadows lengthen

By the time of the oil crisis of 1973, only a few singers, particularly those who worked as independent song-writers, were still struggling to put across a very different message, in German, from that of relentless purveyors of *gute Laune* (instant cheerfulness). One such independent songwriter was Gunter Gabriel, a kind of German Woody Guthrie, who managed to break with the clichés of the *Schlager* and address himself directly to the man in the street whose life no longer promised limitless possibilities such as had been projected by the previous generation's musicians. Alcoholism ('Papa trinkt Bier', 1977), loneliness ('Ein Sonntag im Bett', written for Norwegian starlet Wencke Myhre, 1976), divorce ('Hey Yvonne, warum weint die Mami?'), unemployment and other social problems surface regularly in his work. His commitment is to 'Lieder, die jeder versteht, Musik von Hand gemacht' (songs that everyone can understand, hand-made music).[1]

By 1974, there were few people with whom Gabriel's most famous hit, 'Hey Boss, ich brauch mehr Geld' did not strike a chord:

Jeden Morgen fahr ich mit'm Fahrrad in' Betrieb,
und schaffe mich und tue meine Pflicht.
Und wer da glaubt, daß ich da nur 'ne ruhige Kugel schieb',
bei mir da gibt es solche Sachen nicht.
Ich bin doch einer, der die Firma stützt und der sie hält,
der nie auf krank macht oder so, der sich noch richtig quält.

(Every morning I ride my bike to work and make an effort to do my duty. And if anyone thinks I'm slacking, that just doesn't enter into it in my case. I'm one of those supportive types that keeps the firm going and never takes time off, I really put my back into my work.)

These lines present a stark contrast to the brash, forward-looking optimism of Hazy Osterwald's celebration of 'Konjunktur'. The virtual paradise has crashed, the 1970s and 1980s see new forms of realism entering popular song. Juliane Werding represents the interests of the fragile, insecure working woman and mother. Her album 'Jenseits der Nacht' (Warner, 1987) contains several sensitively worded tracks expressive of deep-seated fears of surveillance and domination. 'Hab keine Angst mein Kind', text and music by Werding herself, is a modern lullaby, in which a mother tries to reassure a child who has half understood a news item about the nuclear disaster at Chernobyl:

Mamma, dieser Mann in der Tagesschau
hat gesagt es wär ganz schlimm
Was Schreckliches ist dort passiert
Mamma, hör doch draußen rauscht es laut
können das die Strahlen sein
und sag mir was dann aus uns wird

(Mummy, that man on the news said something really awful has happened over there. Mummy, just listen to the noise outside, could that be the radiation, and tell me what's going to happen to us)

Another successful singer/composer determined to protect the independence of his art against the incursions of mass productions and technology is Reinhard Mey, whose 'Ein Stück Musik von Hand gemacht' ('Alleingang', Intercord 1986) sets out a programme for all those who still have ambitions to compose 'real' music:

> Zur Blütezeit der Fastfood-Zivilisation,
> der Einheitsmeinung, der Geschmacksautomation,
> der Plastikgefühle und der High-Tech-Lust,
> der Wegwerfbeziehung mit dem Einwegfrust,
> zur Zeit der Fertigträume aus der Traumfabrik,
> der Mickymauskultur und der Steckdosenmusik ...

> (At the height of our fast-food culture, surrounded by identikit sound-bites and automated fads, there were plastic emotions, there was high-tech lust, relationships were disposable and everyone drowned in junk; ready-made dreams from the dream factories, a Mickey Mouse culture and music on tap ...)

Three factors ensured the revival of the German-language text in the early 1980s: the efforts of one single individual (Udo Lindenberg) played an important part. Lindenberg was the first authentic German-language rock star, whose 'Alles Klar auf der Andrea Doria' of 1973 was the first attempt to address the rock-hungry youth of the day through the medium of the German rather than the English language. That a young girl from Saarbrücken could convince the world that a simple German song was worth anything more than 'deux points' in the Eurovision Song Contest (1982) was the second. The third and most controversial concomitant was the West German tour by the GDR group Puhdys in 1979, which showed the Federal Republic that 'beat auf Deutsch' was alive and kicking on the other side of the Elbe, so why not give it a go? A common factor was the use of German to promote peace and understanding in a more direct manner than this could be achieved through the medium of English, at least as far as the German-speaking youth of the day were concerned.

Seventeen-year-old Nicole from Saarbrücken captured the hearts and minds of several million viewers with 'Ein bißchen Frieden', first sung in Harrogate in 1982. *Schlager* on the theme of 'peace' had in fact been popular since the early 1970s; cf. Katja Ebstein: 'Ein kleines Lied vom Frieden' (1971). A large number of groups sprang up, as it seemed, from nowhere, ready to rock in German on the subject of peace and love. One of the most played was Geier Sturzflug, with the 'big hit' of 1983: 'Bruttosozialprodukt'. This ostensibly marks a return to the brash optimism of 'Konjunktur Cha-cha-cha', now enriched with a new dynamism. Workers have become automatons, determined to keep the wheels of industry turning. Even the machines seem to be enjoying themselves ('Und die Stechuhr beim Stechen lustvoll stöhnt' (And the check-in clock sighs with pleasure as it checks you in)). But taken as a whole, the song brings out the failure of the economic miracle on a personal level. A world in which amputees and frail granddads slave away like zombies is a blatant parody of the tireless work-ethic of the past. What is the point? is the underlying question. Songs of this type had been circulating since the early 1970s; cf. Udo Jürgens' 'Lieb Vaterland' of 1971:

> Für Krankenhäuser fehlen die Millionen,
> Doch unsre Spielkasinos scheinen sich zu lohnen.
> Lieb Vaterland, magst ruhig sein,
> Die Großen zäunen ihren Wohlstand ein ...

> (There's a deficit of millions when it comes to building hospitals, but the gambling casinos seem to pay their way. Rest peacefully, dear fatherland, while the tycoons build fences round their wealth ...)

Popular songs in dialect

Given the range of German dialects, it is not surprising that they have been put to many different uses by individual singers and groups. There are more or less straightforward romantic numbers that foster a sense of Heimat: Nicki's 'Wenn I mit Dir tanz' from the album 'Ganz oder gar net' (Virgin, 1986) was readily intelligible across Germany and had no difficulty getting into the charts and the disco repertoires. But the situation is more complicated in cities like Cologne and Vienna that have a lively cabaret tradition, where satirists had long availed themselves of a strong local dialect without really bothering about whether or not they would be understood throughout the German-speaking world. Few groups have attained the fame enjoyed over a period of more than 20 years by the Cologne rock group BAP, whose songs, often unintelligible beyond the Rhineland, have a wide appeal. 'Waschsalon' from the album 'BAP für Uszeschnigge' (EMI, 1981; Niedecken 1999, 51) is typical: a young man serenades his girl-friend not, as one might expect, for her good looks but for her uncanny ability to work the machinery in the local launderette:

> Su wie de opptritts in dämm Laade
> un tirek en leer Maschien entdecks
> un die Jebrauchsahnweisung nevvenbei
> met einem Blick affchecks
> Dozo kann ich nur saare: ‚Frau dat hätt Format, ich benn perplex!'

> Ich jonn su unwahrscheinlich jähn
> met dir en der Waschsalon,
> weil, do häss Ahnung vun dä Technik,
> vun der ich nix verstonn.

(The way you enter the shop and pick out an empty machine straight away, checking the instructions with a casual sidelong glance; all I can say is: 'Girl, you've got class, and I'm gobsmacked.'

I just love it when we go off to the laundry together, 'cos you are into technology, which I can't get to grips with.)

The Austrian group Erste Allgemeine Verunsicherung (EAV) continue in the footsteps of cabaret artists such as Georg Kreisler, Gerhart Bronner and Helmut Qualtinger. Their song 'Burli', a cautionary ballad about the consequences of a mishap at a nuclear power station, created a major stir; German radio stations refused to play it on the grounds that it trivialized the problems of physical disability:

> Es geht DIE ZEIT, der Burli nicht,
> er sitzt nur stui am Schammerl
> mit seim Wasserkopf
> und spuit si mit seim Schwammerl.

(Time passes, but Burli doesn't learn to walk, he just sits quietly on his stool with a bulbous head and plays around with his little sponge.)

The embarrassment surrounding this song was probably more to do with the implied critique of nuclear power stations post-Chernobyl than with concern about the portrayal of disadvantaged children.

The rise of hip hop

The increasing successes of German-language groups such as Kraftwerk and Münchner Freiheit have been charted by Haring (1984) and others. But far away from the limelight surrounding the multinational record companies, a new kind of music arose independently in many parts of Europe during the 1980s. Rap, or as it is more widely known in Germany, Hip Hop, is associated especially with the urban young and was strongly influenced by a variety of migrant cultures. Groups, more properly referred to as 'crews', of very young people, scarcely into their teens, proudly describing themselves as 'Ghetto-Kids', quickly attained a measure of notoriety in provincial backwaters such as Lüdenscheid, 'eine fucking langweilige (boring) Stadt' in the opinion of its younger inhabitants (Verlan and Loh 2000, 30). The astonishing manner in which these kids were able to make their mark on mainstream music has often been charted (Toop, 1984). The essence of rap lies in the personal, confessional presentation of monologues of a private nature which are both autobiographical and exemplary. 'Schüsselkind' by Cora E (EMI Electrola, 1996), for example, charts the experiences of a modern urban waif:

warum soll ich mich schäm'n für das was geschah
ich wäre heut nicht wie ich bin wär es nicht gewesen wie es war . . .

Ich lebte vor mich hin kaum was machte Sinn und dachte
nicht im Traum darüber nach womit ich meine Zeit verbrachte
was kennt man vom Leben
wenn man Leute Freunde nennt die ihren Joint an Kinder weitergeben
ich bin geflogen von den Schul'n der Stadt
meine Mutter schleppte mich zum Psychologen doch der hat
wenig Chance weil seine Mühen so gut wie umsonst sind
an einem Kind das denkt dass mit ihm alles stimmt

(Why should I be ashamed of what happened? I would not be who I
am if it had not been the way it was . . . I just took things as they came,
most things made no sense, and I didn't dream of thinking about what
I was doing. What d'you know about life, when the people you call
your friends pass their joints on to kids? I was expelled from the
schools in town, my mother dragged me off to the shrink, but he can't
do much with a kid that thinks that all is hunky dory.)

Never before has youth spoken as directly of its immediate concerns as
happens in the rap texts of the 1980s and 1990s. The 'ghetto' experience is
a fundamental characteristic of this kind of recital. 'Plastikghetto, ich hab
dich satt/ Plastikghetto – Neonstadt' (Plastic ghetto, I've had enough, plastic
ghetto, neon city) is Klischee's response to Hanover. The term proved
equally useful in expressing the frustrations of the gay community: 'Ich will
raus aus dem Ghetto/ Ich kann da nicht mehr rein' (Ton, Steine, Scherben)
(I want out of the ghetto, I can't live there no more). The term 'ghetto'
gained wider relevance when close-circuit television cameras started appear-
ing in city centres; people walking out of Leipzig station could now read, in
two languages: 'The Police Directorate of Leipzig is supervising this area by
video in order to prevent punishable acts' (Möbus and Münch 1998, 59).

But even this attempt at radical protest was quickly absorbed into mainstream culture. The economic interests of producers within the established
music industry were no less active here than elsewhere (Fiske 1989, 23–32).
The multinationals offered lucrative contracts to some rappers, which led to
a loss of street credibility; and new, 'all German' groups appeared and presented a cleaned-up version of the genre to the nation. What had started as
a 'holy alliance between rap, breakdance and graffiti' (Verlan and Loh 2000,
13) was quickly absorbed by the marketing managers of MTV. 'Die fantastischen Vier' ('Fanta Vier') from Stuttgart subverted the medium further
by presenting themselves as *konsequent deutsch* not only in language but
also in their choice of theme and presentation, which was surprisingly close
to the *Schlager* of the early post-war years. (Jürgens 1999, 47) As some tried
to turn rap into a *konsequent deutsch* product, many non-German rap
groups felt squeezed out, although sales of hip hop albums increased five-

fold in 1993 (Verlan and Loh 2000, 176). In Fanta Vier's clever little sketch 'Die da', a cluster of men ogle the talent in a bar and discuss their preferences in trendy but syntactically correct German:

> Hey, ist es die da, die da am Eingang steht?
> Oder die da, die dir den Kopf verdreht,
> Ist es die da, die mit dem dicken Pulli an, Mann?
> Nein, es ist die Frau, die freitags nicht kann ...

> (Hey, is it that one over there, standing by the door? Or is it this one, the one who has turned your head? Is it her over there, man, in the chunky sweater? No, it's the woman who is never available on Fridays ...)

This parody was itself soon parodied by a feminist group calling itself 'Die galaktischen Zwei' in their number 'Der da'. Further contributions to the genre include the controversial black group Tic-Tac-Toe with their ambivalent salutation 'Verpiß dich ... ich vermiß dich' (BMG Ariola, 1995). Whether or not the identity of the new woman emerges anywhere in *Schlager*-Musik remains a matter for debate (Thelen 1993; Mäsker 1999). The post-feminist incantations of Lucilectric provide many reasons for celebrating the inherent superiority of 'das ewig Weibliche'; or, in the words of one web-page author: 'Wer kennt es nicht, das Lied "Weil ich ein Mädchen bin", das zeigt, daß Emanzipation nicht nötig ist, wenn *frau* ihre Weiblichkeit richtig einzusetzen vermag!' (Who hasn't heard the song 'Because I'm a girl', which demonstrates that a woman does not need to be emancipated to make full use of her femininity!)[2]

> Komm' doch mal rüber, Mann, und setz' dich zu mir hin,
> Weil ich 'n Mädchen bin, weil ich 'n Mädchen bin.
> Keine Widerrede, Mann, weil ich ja sowieso gewinn,
> Weil ich 'n Mädchen bin.

> (Come over here, man, and sit down beside me, because I'm a girl, 'cos I'm a girl. Don't contradict me, 'cos I'm going to get you anyway, 'cos I'm a girl.)

Another, more insidious feature of some texts perceived as trendy is the extensive use they make of the vocabulary of the ruling class, as if seeking empowerment by this means: 'Ich bomb dich wie Vietnam' is hardly appealing, and 'Ich schalt die Radios gleich, wie die fuckin' Nazis' is suggestive of political naivety at the very least (Verlan and Loh 2000, 246). Yet it is beyond doubt that the music of the masses can have a strong and positive social influence. One singer who did much to politicize the *Schlager* and tried to promote a kind of music that was halfway between traditional pop and the more metallic strains of rock, was Udo Lindenberg. His thumping 'Mit dem Sonderzug nach Pankow' (1983), based on 'Kötzschenbroda-Expreß', and ultimately on Glenn Miller's 'Chattanooga Choo Choo' of

1941 ('Pardon me boys, is that the Chattanooga Choo Choo? (Yes Yes) Track 29! Boy you can give me a shine'), asks for an explanation as to why he, Lindenberg, is not allowed to perform in the GDR, something of a recurring issue in Lindenberg's early work (Köster 1998, 50–4). Here, Lindenberg attempts to show up the artificiality of the German–German border, by suggesting that people on both sides have similar musical tastes; see Durrani (2000) for a comprehensive account of progressive music in the GDR. Simultaneously, Lindenberg delivers a hard-hitting attack on the regime for failing to practise what it preaches:

> Honey ich glaub, du wirkst doch eigentlich auch ganz locker.
> Ich weiß tief in dir drin, bist du doch eigentlich auch 'n Rocker.
> Du ziehst dir doch heimlich auch gerne mal die Lederjacke an
> Und schließt dich ein auf'm Klo und hörst West-Radio.

> (Honey, I think you're basically quite a laid-back type. Deep down inside, you are a rocker like the rest of us, I'm sure. Don't you sometimes put on a leather jacket in secret, and lock yourself into the loo to listen to western radio?)

Bunte Republik Deutschland

The theme of immigration had been introduced into the *Schlager* most memorably by teenage prodigy Conny Froboess in a curiously patronizing little ditty 'Zwei kleine Italiener' of 1962 (No. 1 for 6 weeks, 13 March–6 May).

> Zwei kleine Italiener, am Bahnhof, da kennt man sie,
> sie kommen jeden Abend zum D-Zug nach Napoli.
> Zwei kleine Italiener, die schaun hinterdrein.

> (Two little Italians, we recognize them at the station, they turn up every evening for the express train to Naples. Two little Italians, they watch it as it leaves.)

While the well-to-do were beginning to travel to Italy for extended vacations in the sun, Froboess's Italian guest-workers are recognizable ('da kennt man sie' is ambiguous, implying that they are 'known quantities' rather than that the locals have any deep 'knowledge' of them) as constituting Germany's new underclass, alongside the Turks and other nationalities that followed and eventually replaced the Italians condemned to hanging around railway stations watching more fortunate people depart for sunny climes. Are they as unhappy in their new homeland as Froboess claims?

> Eine Reise in den Süden ist für andre schick und fein,
> doch die beiden Italiener möchten gern zuhause sein.

O Tina, o Marina, wenn wir uns einmal wiedersehn,
O Tina, o Marina, dann wird es wieder schön.

(A journey to the south is trendy and posh, but these two Italians just
long to be back at home. O Tina, o Marina, when we meet again, o
Tina, o Marina, that's when things will improve.)

Many subtexts can be read into the wistful lyrics. That they should be presented as 'little' Italians is suggestive of their insignificance and places them
in proximity to the familiar cliché of the *Spaghettifresser*. That they should
spend every evening at the station gives a clear indication that they are not
integrated and that their hearts will forever be filled with longing for their
true home and their 'little women' Tina and Marina, the latter presumably
named after the Rocco Granata hit of 1959. But at least an effort is being
made here to move away from the cultural imperialism of the 'Casa mia pic-
colina, kleines Häuslein im Tessin' approach to Italy, which probably
reached its nadir in Peter Alexander's embarrassingly trite and chauvinistic
rendering of Domenico Modugno's 'Bambina' in 1958 (Hügel and Zeisler
1992, 76).

Udo Lindenberg's 'Bunte Republik Deutschland' (Polydor, 1989) shows
just how much had changed between the 1960s and the 1980s. Here we
have a song in which the topic of immigration is addressed head-on from a
much more positive angle. The railway station is no longer somewhere for
people to brood about their roots, but a place where Germans should go to
welcome each new arrival:

Wir steh'n am Bahnsteig und begrüßen jeden Zug,
denn graue deutsche Mäuse,
die haben wir schon genug.

(We stand here on the platform, welcoming each train, as for grey mice
from Germany, there are more than enough of them.)

Germany is colourless by comparison with the variety of types that are
arriving every day:

Egal, ob Du 'n Aficooler bist,
oder 'n Afrikaner.
Egal, ob Du 'n Indoneser bist,
oder 'n Indianer.
Ob Kapuziner, Argentiner, Franziskaner oder Franzose ...

(It doesn't matter whether you're Afri-Cool or an Afri-Can. You can
be an Indonesian or an Indjan. Capucine Friar or Argentine,
Franciscan or Frenchman ...)

And the time has come for the 'foreign' Italian (*'Italjener'*) to shake off his
alterity and see himself as a local (*'Italdieser'*).

Many groups now proudly display a multi-ethnic component through the medium of German. Tahir Cevik, known as Tachi, later Tachiles, founded the group Fresh Familee in 1988, which was soon to win the *Düsseldorfer Nachwuchspreis*. The group's first EP, 'Coming From Ratinga' appeared in 1991, and featured a track 'Ahmet Gündüz', in which life is portrayed from the migrant's point of view:

> Mein Name ist Ahmet Gündüz, laß mich erzählen euch
> du muss schon zuhören, ich kann nix sehr viel Deutsch
> komm von der Türkei, swei Jahre her
> und ich viel gefreut, doch Lebne hier is schwer
> zur Arbeit Chef mir sagen Kanake, hey wie geht's?
> ich sag dann hadi siktir lan doch Arschloch nix versteht

> (My name is Ahmet Gündüz, lemme tell you somet'ing, you muss lissen coz I no speak German, come from Turkey two years live here and was very happy but this life is hard Boss says hey nigger how you doing? I say *hadi siktir lan* but the asshole no understand.)

This was one of the first attempts to use rap as a platform for the voice of the migrant worker; as Tachi was later to comment, sound-bites from the group were much in demand as long as outrages against migrants were in the headlines (Verlan and Loh 2000, 134–9). A more sustained attempt to speak out against German prejudices can be seen in Kanak Attack's 'Diese (*sic*) Song gehört uns' (2000):

> Aus mir spricht nur der Hass, den ihr geschaffen habt.
> Logisch, dass ein normaler Mensch in Deutschland überschnappt,
> wenn man sieht, wie Unterschriften gesammelt werden
> von geistigen Brandstiftern, die mit Integration werben ...

> (Mine is the voice of hatred, which you have created. It's quite normal for ordinary people to go crazy in Germany, when you see how the spiritual arsonists go round collecting signatures and campaigning for integration ...)

See Verlan and Loh (2000, 159–65). Other teams, such as Cartel, a loose association of the groups Karakan from Nürnberg, Da Crime Posse from Kiel, and Erci E from Berlin, sing principally in Turkish and, deliberately placing themselves on the 'other' side of the German/Turkish cultural divide, have probably enjoyed greater success in Turkey than in Germany (ibid, 153f.).

The final item in the present survey was directed against former Chancellor Helmut Kohl. Kohl was Chancellor for 16 years, longer than any other politician since the war, and will be remembered for steering Germany to ever greater prosperity during the 1980s, eventually engineering the unification of East and West Germany in 1990. However, many suspected that behind the veneer of gentility and bonhomie there lurked a guilty secret. A larger-than-life figure, Kohl always appeared slightly sinister, and it was with considerable foresight that, in 1994, the radical rock group Ärzte brought out an album called 'Ab 18' which contained the track 'Helmut Kohl schlägt seine Frau'. Although banal by the standards of some of today's satirical television shows, the song was felt to be too offensive to be broadcast and was quickly deleted from the album:

> Hannelores Tag ist grau, denn Helmut Kohl schlägt seine Frau
> Es macht die Runde in der Koalition
> Selbst Rita Süssmuth weiß es schon
> Hannelores Tag ist grau, denn Helmut Kohl schlägt seine Frau

> (Hannelore's days are bleak, because Helmut Kohl is a wife-basher. It's doing the rounds in the Coalition, and even Rita Süssmuth has picked it up: Hannelore's days are bleak, because Helmut Kohl is a wife-basher.)

The reasons for this brutal treatment are spelt out. On the one hand, Kohl is portrayed as 'ein Mann, genau wie wir, tief in ihm, da steckt ein Tier', i.e. no less aggressive than anyone else, but there is also a specifically German preoccupation with table manners:

> Neulich ließ die Hannelore mal etwas auf dem Teller,
> Zur Strafe lud sie Helmut ein in seinen Folterkeller.
> Er ist ein Mann wie ich und du: Helmut Kohl schlägt wieder zu.

> (The other day Hannelore didn't quite finish what was on her plate. Helmut punished her by making her step into his torture chamber. He's a man like you and I: Helmut Kohl lashes out once more.)

This is a grotesque reminder of the old saying: 'Was auf den Tisch kommt, wird gegessen' (What is served at table must be eaten), allowing Kohl to appear as the petty tyrant who tortures his family if they don't obey the age-old house rules. The ironic effect is enhanced by the knowledge that the real Hannelore Kohl was a multi-talented professional woman fluent in four languages, who sacrificed her personal ambitions to further her husband's political career, and ended up publishing, of all things, a cookery book.

The observations as set down above do little more than show that paths taken within one important subdivision of modern culture are so diverse as to range from the banal *Schnulze* to the focused political tract. As we noted at the beginning, German popular music is not 'world class', despite its variety and vitality. That many of its leading proponents seem to stagnate rather than develop is often blamed on the legal machinations of the established record companies (Herrwerth 1997, 'Platten-Oldies'). The doyen of the indigenous pop scene, Freddy Quinn, is unquestionably a singer of international stature, but there is little doubt that Polydor used blatant strong-arm tactics to prevent him from breaking out of the seafaring 'Seemannslos' mould in which they preferred to cast him (Quinn 1999). The German music industry operates like the German motor industry: it resists change and puts its faith in the maintenance of consistent standards. This lack of flexibility has proved a winning formula in the motor industry, but is less of an advantage in a fast-moving environment such as popular music and film. Given the enormous successes of the pre-war period, the failure of the German film industry to make an impact internationally is an equally surprising and no doubt related phenomenon. It has recently been argued (Helmes 1996, 71) that the *Schlager* shares its escapist tendencies with the philosophy, literature, film, and radio drama of the period. This is perhaps the most compelling argument for choosing popular music as the basis of an encounter with the cultural diversity of the German nation.

Notes

1. http://www.blitz.de/egm/gabriel.html
2. http://www.geocities.com/Wellesley/2343/musik_luci.html

References

ADORNO, T. 1991: Culture industry reconsidered. In ADORNO, T. *The culture industry: selected essays on mass culture*. London: Routledge, 85–92.

ANON. 1994: *Stars und Schlager*. Bergisch Gladbach: Gerig, vol. I.

BLÜHDORN, A. 1997: Rocking the syllabus: the lyrics of Udo Lindenberg. *German Teaching* 15, 2–5.

BARDONG, M., DEMMLER, H. and PFARR, C. (eds) 1992: *Lexikon des deutschen Schlagers*. Ludwigsburg: Louis.

CHOTJEWITZ, P.O. 1971: Einsamer nie oder Love me do. Zum Sprachgebrauch in Beat- und Schlagertexten. *Akzente* 18, 194–207.

DURRANI, O. 2000: Language and subversion in GDR rock music. In JACKMAN, G. and ROE, I.F. (eds) *Finding a voice. Problems of language in East German society and culture. German Monitor* 47, 145–70.

FESSMANN, M., TOPP, K. and KRIEGS, W. (eds) 1998: *L'Allemagne deux points. Germany two points. Deutschland zwei Punkte*. Frankfurt/M: Ullstein.

FISKE, J. 1989: *Understanding popular culture*. Boston: Unwin Hyman.

FRITH, S. and GOODWIN, A. (eds) 1990: *On record. Rock, pop and the written word*. London: Routledge.

HALL, S. and WHANNEL, P. 1990: The young audience. In FRITH, S. and GOODWIN, A. (eds) *On record. Rock, pop and the written word*. London: Routledge, 27–37.

HARING, H. 1984: *Rock aus Deutschland West*. Reinbek: Rowohlt.

HEBDIGE, D. 1990: Style as homology and signifying practice. In FRITH, S. and GOODWIN, A. (eds) *On record. Rock, pop and the written word*. London: Routledge, 56–65.

HELMES, G. 1996: Popularmusik und Gefühle. Beobachtungen und Überlegungen zum deutschen Schlager. *Der Deutschunterricht* 48, 62–84.

HERRWERTH, T. 1995: *Itsy Bitsy Teenie Weenie. Die deutschen Hits der Sixties*. Marburg: Jonas.

HERRWERTH, T. 1997: *Partys, Pop und Petting. Die Sixties im Spiegel der BRAVO*. Marburg: Jonas.

HERRWERTH, T. 'Platten-Oldies', URL: http://online.prevezanos.com/schlager/
HILBK, M. 2000: Das Ende vom Lied. *Die Zeit* 20, 13–15.
Hit Bilanz 1990: Deutsche Chart Singles 1956–1980. Hamburg: Taurus.
HÜGEL, H. and ZEISLER, G. 1992: *Die süßesten Früchte. Schlager aus den
    Fünfzigern.* Frankfurt/M: Ullstein.
JÜRGENS, C. 1999: We are Mittelstand. Die Fantastischen Vier melden sich mit
    Buch und CD zurück. *Die Zeit* 18, 47.
KATER, M.A. 1992: *Different drummers: Jazz in the culture of the Nazis.* New
    York: Oxford University Press.
KEMPER, P., LANGHOFF, T. and SONNENSCHEIN, U. (eds) 1998: *'but I like it'.
    Jugendkultur und Popmusik.* Stuttgart: Reclam.
KÖSTER, A. 1998: *Udo Lindenberg in eigenen Worten.* Heidelberg: Palmyra.
KRAUSHAAR, E. 1983: *Rote Lippen. Die ganze Welt des deutschen Schlagers.*
    Reinbek: Rowohlt.
LEVI, E. 1994: *Music in the Third Reich.* London: Macmillan.
MÄSKER, M. 1999: *Das schöne Mädchen von Seite eins. Die Frau im Schlager.*
    Rheinfelden: Schäuble.
MÖBUS, F. and MÜNCH, M.B. 1998: 'Weiß nicht, was ich '98 davon halten soll?'
    Über Schwierigkeiten beim musikalischen 'Ghetto'-Diskurs. *Testcard* 6. 52–64.
NIEDECKEN, W. 1999: *Verdamp lang her. Die Stories hinter den BAP-Songs.*
    Cologne: Kiepenheuer & Witsch.
QUINN, F. 1999: 'Mein Leben hört sich an wie eine Erfindung'. Ein Gespräch mit
    Freddy Quinn. *Die Zeit* ('Leben') 37.
ROLAND, P. 1999: *Rock and Pop.* London: Hodder and Stoughton.
THELEN, C. 1993: Schubidu und Geschlecht. *Die Zeit.* 22, 80.
TOOP, D. 1984: *The rap attack.* London: Pluto. Expanded reprints include 1991:
    Rap attack 2: African rap to global hip hop. London: Serpent's Tail.
VERLAN, S. and LOH, H. 2000: *Zwanzig Jahre HipHop in Deutschland.* Höfen:
    Hannibal.

Websites

http://www.blitz.de/egm/gabriel.htm (on Gunter Gabriel)
http://www.spooNo.ecords.com/ (on CAN)
http://www.geocities.com/Wellesley/2343/musik_luci.html (on Lucilectric)
http://www.ichwillspass.de/geier.htm (on Geier Sturzflug)
http://liberty.uc.wlu.edu/~msmitka/102/brutt.htm (on Geier Sturzflug)
http://www.weihenstephan.org/~mayerale/liebe_tod_und_teufel1.htm (on Erste
    Allgemeine Verunsicherung)
http://www.subwayradio.de/magazin/2000/01tachi.shtml (on Tachiles and Fresh
    Familee)
http://online.prevezanos.com/schlager/ (on German popular music)
http://www.hiphop.de/infos/ (on German Hip Hop)

|11|

Encountering stories from contemporary German theatre

BY MEG MUMFORD AND ALISON PHIPPS

Encounters with multiple forms and divisions

Theatre provides us with a public way of coming together to reflect on our everyday lives, at a common time and in a common space. Other forms of cultural activity also provide us with ways of reflecting our experiences and in the individualized cultures of the Western world such as Germany, television, film and other media are perhaps statistically more significant as forms of public performance. Theatre, however, according to the theatre anthropologist Victor Turner, 'is perhaps the most forceful, *active,* if you like, genre of cultural performance' (1982, 104). Theatre can affect attitude with its peculiar power, it can motivate, and within a media-saturated postmodern society, as a marginal form, it often acts as a democratizing counterweight to the hegemonic voice of mass culture. That theatre is a powerful force for change and for collective reflection is well known (see Chapter 13). The history of theatre may be told through the many bans and restrictions that have been placed upon it by those who were afraid of its ability to undermine their power. How the power and interests served by different forms of German theatre may be explored is therefore an important issue.

What exactly a contemporary German theatre event entails is difficult to define. For those engaging with German culture from a position outside of the country various stories are told in the newspapers, journals, books and through the websites devoted to discussion of the contemporary German theatre scene. Many of these stories continue to present a relatively unidimensional phenomenon. For example, those engaging with the curriculum of German literary studies at an advanced level, one where Goethe, Schiller and Brecht are still omnipresent, may expect to find the texts of the 'Great Masters' dominating the German stage in much the same way as Shakespeare dominates at Stratford. The literary and ideational theatre of the German Enlightenment, as promoted by theorists and playwrights like

Gottsched and Lessing, has indeed dominated German theatre and its commentary since the eighteenth century.

However, the dominant rationalist and usually patriarchal view is not the whole story. According to Ulrich and Wöhlert (1994, 357) German language plays now take up less than half the public repertoire. Thanks to the many traditions of theatre performance, production and commentary alive today in German culture and the way – through language and history – that culture could be said to extend to countries such as Austria and Switzerland, the category is multidimensional. Alongside the world of the canonized, German metropolis theatre centres today offer the now ubiquitous western diet of modern Anglo-American musicals, that, when taken out of context would seem to suggest the sidelining of accepted German fare by a culinary internationalized repertoire of blockbuster spectacle. In 1990 three new and unique houses doing large-scale musicals, opened in Hamburg and Bochum performing works by Andrew Lloyd-Webber, among others, to audiences of 1.3 million (ibid., 354). In the subsidized theatres of the regions the repertoire mixes the famous with the contemporary, experimenting with postmodern styles of production that work against the idea of a standard canon of authors, texts, staging methods and norms. Such productions, rather like the blockbuster musicals, are also influenced by Anglo-American forms. Attend an amateur production or a school play and the story will be different again.

Among the various stories from the polyphonous contemporary German theatre scene, recently there has been, however, at least one constant: the leitmotif of crisis. Crisis – a 'turning-point; time of danger or suspense' (OED) – seems to us to be a key term for understanding different aspects of the cultural role played by theatre in contemporary Germany. While in the pages of national newspapers and theatre journals the waning of the importance of the ensemble is mourned and theatre closures or amalgamations are highlighted, in other places the work of internationally celebrated directors is acclaimed, and rules of a new theatre game are heralded, one where symptoms of crisis – uncertainty, fragmentation and a lack of interest in local concerns – are paramount. Be it the body in crisis, the audience in crisis, the author, ensemble or director in crisis the turning points, dangers and suspense that play themselves out in theatre are helpful as a starting point for reflection. Proclaiming crisis is in itself a cultural performance, showing the places where transitions from old cultural forms to new are occurring. The deep structural changes that have followed the appropriately named *Wende* have fostered a sense of threat or of loss for some and of opportunity for others, bringing questions of cultural identity to the fore. Whatever form a performance takes, the simple fact of its representing live the identity myths and stories by which people live, opens spaces and time for reflection, in itself a form of action. Turner thus sees performance as a potent force for establishing, revealing and questioning the stories by which people live:

By means of such genres as theatre ... performances are presented which probe a community's weakness, call its leaders to account, desacrilize its most cherished values and beliefs, portray its character-istic conflicts and suggest remedies for them, and generally take stock of its current situation in the known 'world.' ... Through the perfor-mance process itself, what is normally sealed up, inaccessible to every-day observation and reasoning, in the depth of sociocultural life, is drawn forth.

(1982, 11)

In the context of contemporary German culture, meshed as it is with local and global concerns, the theatre can be expected to provide an important site where identities are remade, conflicts are staged and values are chal-lenged that other cultural forms are unable to expose as live, embodied and material.

The question, then, is how to evaluate the different stories, i.e. the narra-tives and accounts given, and the competing standpoints they embody? How to view the range of work that comes into the fluid and multidimen-sional category of German theatre without rendering some aspects invisible or drawing impossibly trite conclusions? How to understand the cultural impulses towards unity and fragmentation in the theatrical field? Yet it is precisely this fascinating breadth of performance event and style, and more especially the divergent stories productions engender, that enable us to raise specific questions about theatre and performance in contemporary German culture. Breadth, diversity and multidimensionality of theatrical output may appear on the surface to be healthy signs of a functioning liberal society and make it tempting to conclude that contemporary German theatre is posi-tively placed. However, diversity also brings division, with different theatri-cal fields defining their activities not so much as what they are, as what they are not. Diversity is also the other face of a quest for unity in all its various guises, as our discussions here shall demonstrate.

Encountering contemporary German theatre, describing and commentat-ing on its stories necessarily leads to the discovery, creation and activation of divisions and categories. Some of the divisions between the multiple forms of German theatre have been part of self-understanding in Western theatre for a considerable time, such as that between populist and *avant garde* art, or they are attributable to trends that have occurred over the past 25 years with the rise of consumer capitalism, such as city-break package tours that take in a musical that point to the local vs global commercial divi-sions. Others are perhaps, as we shall discuss here, peculiar to the German scene, influenced by upheavals since the *Wende,* by certain traditions of the ensemble, by the relation of theatre to Germany as a nation–state. Neither the divisions nor the quests for unity in the contemporary German theatre scene are new phenomena when considered in the overall historical context of Western theatre.

Cultural studies enables us to ask questions of the material and ideological interests served by different forms of theatre, the construction of classificatory divisions and crisis narratives. Crises, and the telling of stories of crises, may bring their own rewards in certain quarters. Within Cultural Studies, French sociologist Pierre Bourdieu is very clear on the subject of the rewards of public artistic work and rather than subscribing to romantic notions of the embattled genius artist or actor he returns repeatedly to questions of the comparative material contexts out of which forms of art are produced. Bourdieu explores this idea in depth in his work *The Field of Cultural Production* (1993) where he defines a 'field' as the microcosms with their own structures and laws, inhabited by specific groups – artists, intellectuals, poets, directors whose 'strategies owe their form and content to the interests associated with the positions which they occupy in the structure of a very specific game.' (ibid., 13). In other words, works of art of any kind may *appear* to be free from social and cultural context, to be produced autonomously by independent and objective artists, but in actual fact they need to be understood in terms of their relations to other works of arts, other artists and cultural producers and most especially in terms of their relations with the social world. In order to understand the sense of upheaval, crisis and resistance at work in German theatre it is important to consider what the stakes are that are being struggled over that could lead theatre makers in general to identify so strongly with such different cultural forms. Bourdieu is certainly illuminating on the cause of the chasms between so-called 'high art' and 'commercial art':

> During this period [the nineteenth century], the opposition between art and money, which structures the field of power, is reproduced in the literary field in the form of the opposition between 'pure' art, symbolically dominant but economically dominated ... and commercial art, in its two forms, boulevard theatre, which brings in high profits and bourgeois consecration, and industrial art: vaudeville, ... cabaret. ... The intellectuals, rich in cultural capital and (relatively) poor in economic capital, and the owners of industry and business, rich in economic capital and (relatively) poor in cultural capital are in opposition.
>
> (1993, 13)

Here Bourdieu accounts for division not through a reference to quality but to the different rules of the respective games as established during struggles for financial and social power in the latter part of the nineteenth century.

In what follows we seek to examine aspects of contemporary German theatre in order to explore the crises, fears, cherished values and beliefs that compete for attention on and around the German 'stage'. Our aim is to explore some of the ideological and material interests underpinning the definition and subdivision of German theatre as carried out by second-hand modes of encounter. For the purpose of exemplification, we will focus on the debated characterization of German theatre as theatre in crisis. We have three different, but related aims; first, to look at some of the varied ways second-hand encounters with different forms of German theatre may be made and to survey the present scene; second, to look at whether contemporary German theatre is indeed a theatre in crisis; and third, to examine the legitimacy of the contested views and descriptions of the state of theatre as crisis-ridden using tools from Cultural Studies to understand the interests German theatre serves in different material and cultural contexts. As such, our aims suggest that the issue is not only *where to stand* in discussions of forms of German theatre, but *how to understand and evaluate the competing stances*. In order to give the discussion manageable parameters we have chosen to deal mainly with actor-based theatre – as distinct from opera, musical, dance or puppet theatre – originating in the German nation since the *Wende*. In addition, our focus will be limited to those divisions – namely, amateur/professional, East/West, and local/global – which have attracted the attention of theatre commentators across the world in recent years. Aware that we belong to and are writing predominantly for an Anglo-American audience, and that this situation is often neglected in scholarship, we have also decided to focus on the material modes of encounter which 'outsiders' have with this field. That is, rather than performance itself, our object is the narratives from and about German theatre and the interests they represent.

Materials for encounter

Understanding live theatre events from a position outside of the immediate performance and cultural context presents certain difficulties, not least of which is the dependency on second-hand textual accounts. Due to this situation, together with factors such as the important role played by the play-text in the formation of a national theatre tradition, German theatre has been presented in literary and drama departments often as part of a literary canon, regarded as text and analysed for its aesthetic, historical and narrative interest, but rarely viewed as performance bedded into a live cultural context. British theatre scholar Alan Read problematizes this way of engaging with theatre:

> Put bluntly, the idea that theatre, along with dramatic literature, can be subsumed within a department of literature is nonsense. These are not ... the only stories of theatre. Such narratives provide the canon of one theatre tradition, a theatre governed by the script, and lack the perspectives derived from discursive practices endemic to everyday life.

> (Read 1993, 11)

In addition to the stories to be gleaned from analysis of published (and translated) repertoire, other places in which 'stories of theatre' are available for the observer at a distance include: production reviews, anecdotes from spectators, interviews with practitioners, activity and funding statistics, critical literature and histories of theatre. Providing ways of analysing how these second-hand materials of encounter speak of contemporary German theatre and the material and ideological interests their accounts serve is our concern here.

In order to illuminate such methods of analysis we have selected a representative example from each of the materials which provide common and useful sources of encounter. Typical sites for production and performance accounts include the *Feuilleton* (cultural feature article) section of the weekly national broadsheet newspaper, *Die Zeit*, and the monthly journal, *Theater heute*. The newspaper is renown for its in-depth reporting and its staff invariably has training in relevant academic fields as well as in journalism. The *Feuilleton* section includes alphabetical listings of productions and festivals taking place in German-language cities and regions as well as reviews, interviews and commentary debates. A flagship for serious German culture and the liberal democratic tradition, its subject matter is predominantly mainstream theatre events and institutions, although noteworthy marginal productions are sometimes addressed. *Theater heute* shares many of the aspirations and some of the writing staff in common with *Die Zeit*. West German in origin, it is Germany's leading theatre journal, although since the *Wende* the former East German *Theater der Zeit* has become increasingly prominent. By and large the journal's focus has long been state- and metropolitan-subsidized theatre, although occasionally articles are devoted to alternative performance, such as Henning Rischbieter's recent account of the festival 'Impulse', a showcase of fringe theatre events organiszd by the cultural ministry of Nordrhein-Westfalen (Rischbieter 2001, 16–21). A promoter of heritage, contemporary German-language writing and the theatre scene beyond the nation–state's boundaries, *Theater Heute* currently is concerned with the fostering of both tradition and new beginnings, and the meeting of the local with the international.

An important source of statistical information is the *Deutscher Bühnenverein* (the German Theatre Association), whose website contains facts and figures about, for example, institutions, playing spaces, festivals and audience figures. Formerly a West German national association, the DBV continues to represent the interests of theatre managers, producers and authorities (Ulrich and Wöhlert 1994, 353) and as such has an agenda to foster performance within the nation. Its recent statistics suggest a thriving, variegated contemporary theatre scene: 140 state theatres, around 280 private theatres, 150 playable spaces, 160 music auditoria, around 60 festivals, over 200 touring companies with their own permanent ensemble and innumerable independent groups perform annually to audiences of over

35 million, in all age groups through 120,000 productions representing 2,500 different works:

> Dies belegt das nach wie vor ungebrochene Interesse an Theater ... und macht deutlich, dass die Bürger ihr Theater als öffentlichen Denk- und Erlebnisraum, als Ort direkter Kommunikation, als Teil des öffentlichen Diskurses und somit als unverzichtbaren Bestandteil urbaner Lebensqualität begreifen.

> (This testifies to the unbroken interest in theatre ... and makes clear that German citizens understand their theatre as a space for public thought and experience, as a place of direct communication, as part of public discourse and consequently as an irreplaceable component of a good quality of life.)

(www.Deutscher-bühnenverein.de)

However, statistics do not have the final story and umbrella organizations, formed to serve, in this case, the interests especially of those organizing and leading German theatre are likely to paint a rosy picture as a way of maintaining support for their activities and, especially in times of crisis, for their continued existence and funding. Other narratives suggest that contemporary German theatre is actually in crisis and has suffered a decline, especially since the *Wende*.

In contrast to the DBV materials, the writings of theatre academics, both within and without Germany, represent mainly the concerns of spectators and pedagogues and are broad-ranging in their attitude towards contemporary national culture, sometimes serving a preservative function in a manner similar to the DBV but also critically interrogative and informed by comparative studies and international aspirations. We have selected two examples of encounter which exemplify different aspects of the academic spectrum. The first is an article from the mid-1990s by the British academic Michael Patterson, a key figure in English-language scholarship on twentieth-century German theatre, which deals with cultural challenges since unification from the vantage point of an outsider sympathetic to a threatened socialist heritage. The other text is an editorial introduction by the internationally renowned German theatre academic Erika Fischer-Lichte to a volume based on a conference held in Berlin 1999, one concerned with the theme of transformation in theatre of the past decade. Rather than preservation, this piece promotes change via engagement with the international scene.

Theatre in crisis: East turns West

Public culture in Germany has gone through many upheavals and crises in the last century. Most recently the events of 1989 and the *Wende* ('change', 'turning point') have led to a considerable restructuring of public cultural life. What may be described, in cultural terms, as the 'body theatrical' is a part of the 'body politic' and the body politic, as Foucault reminds us should be understood as 'a set of material elements and techniques that serve as weapons, relays, communication routes and supports for the power and knowledge relations' (1991, 28). Changes in material elements, especially funding, but also the closure of buildings, job losses etc., in Germany post-*Wende* and their effects on the theatres of the former GDR are helpfully described by Patterson. The GDR used to have more subsidized theatres than any other nation relative to its size and population and the state paid for nine out of ten of all theatre tickets. The theatres and cabarets were important to the socialist vision because they were places where officially sanctioned collective reflection occurred. As live performances, however, the cabarets also became places where resistance to state ideologies could be expressed. Despite the fact that financial support for the theatre in West Germany was around seven times that of all the funding for the arts in the United States, after unification the relatively generous funding did not stretch to all 65 public theatres in the former GDR (Ulrich and Wöhlert 1994, 351). In the consumer society that is now being established in the former East it is clear, according to Patterson, that theatre is having to compete with a much wider choice of leisure activities for its audiences and it is having to be more economically viable. Patterson's analysis displays an interesting bias. He takes a socialist stance, concerned for the loss of the GDR theatre and is positive towards the decisions taken by actors left in the theatre. His analysis does not, however, offer an explanation as to why certain sacrifices, job losses and theatre closures have been possible, other than attributing this to the heroism of the theatre practitioners:

> It is a huge compliment to the seriousness and commitment of those making theatre in the east that they have so willingly abandoned the projected status of their profession and that the expected pain and sacrifice in terms of losing jobs and audience have not been as extreme as at first predicated.

(Patterson, 1995, 274)

The compliment paid here by Patterson demonstrates the way that theatre activities attract economic and also so-called cultural capital. As the rules of the game and stakes involved in the western professional theatres owe much to continuing to at least appear to exist with little need for economic capital, then sacrifice and commitment and seriousness bring their own rewards in the form of 'cultural capital' – the capital of prestige, status, public acclaim – which also has value in other professional theatre systems. The story of a GDR theatre in crisis is a story that helps mobilize support in political, material and financial terms, as well as bring 'cultural capital' to those whose struggles begin to be seen as succeeding against the odds. Other crisis narratives take less materialist views and focus on the ensemble and the audiences.

Theatre in dangerous crisis

A reading of *Die Zeit* and *Theater heute* since the millennium provides an insight into the current critical commentary of crisis with regard to German audiences and ensembles. A series of articles in *Die Zeit* during Spring 2001 points to a crisis in the contemporary mainstream theatres:

> Publikumsverweigerung: Die Theaterbesucher spielen nicht mehr mit. Empört, gelangweilt oder resigniert ziehen sie sich aus vielen Häusern zurück. (Gerhard Jörder, 15 March 2001)

> (Audience refusal: theatregoers refuse to play the game. Disgusted, bored or resigned they are retreating from many theatres.)

> Wird die Theaterkrise im Theatermuseum enden? (Jens Jessen, 23 March 2001)

> (Will the theatre crisis end up in a museum of theatre?)

> Ehret die Dichter! Was schert uns denn das Publikum? Das Theater inszeniert sich lieber selbst. Der jüngste Akt: Kampf der Generationen. (Ute Nyssen, 23 March 2001)

> (Celebrate the Poets! What does the audience care about? Theatre prefers to put itself on stage. The latest act: Battle of the generations.)

> Theater ist Gegenwart, nicht Gegenwelt. (director Michael Schindhelm, 5 April 2001)

> (Theatre is for the present day, not against the world.)

What concerns the commentators in these articles in *Die Zeit*, is the downturn in audiences in the state-subsidized theatres in Germany, Austria and Switzerland and reasons for this particular trend. Audience crisis is not a new phenomenon for post-war Germany, at least in the West. Attendance and related financial problems have dogged theatre history there and in other post-industrial countries since the mid-1960s due to factors such as a proliferation of leisure time and activities and the increasing prominence of mass media entertainment. In Germany, as elsewhere, new forms of audience development, improved public relations and local connections have been pursued in a bid to remedy the situation. However, *Die Zeit* commentator Gerhard Jörder argues that the recent crisis has a more threatening dimension as the problems seem deeper rooted and less likely to be resolved by local action or the isolated successes of individual newcomers, particularly given a context where the safety net provided by communitarian politics has been replaced with an emphasis on economic rationalization (15 March 2001).

Journalists repeatedly present the German audience in a homogenizing manner as bored of constant provocation from director's theatre and disgruntled with the fragmented navel-gazing nature of post-structuralist productions. Theatre, as described in these articles, is thought to be obsessively self-reflexive and hermetically sealed, constantly referencing and citing itself and dominated by a few powerful (invariably male and intellectually oriented) directors and dramaturgs who apparently presided over the 'death of the author' in the 1960s and 1970s only to install themselves as 'authors' instead. Director's theatre, and the elevation of the dramaturg and the scenographer as collaborators in the director's vision are a particularly strong tradition in Germany. It is attributable both to the legacy of innovators in the field such as Brecht and Piscator, and more recently to the reworking of both their adaptive approach and the Reinhardt tradition of spectacular experimentation by director's such as Zadek and Stein who emerged in the politicized and liberal atmosphere of the 1960s.

Ironically, those who sought to engage and activate the audience through interrogative provocations are now brought into association with the disconnection of a large section of the audience. Rather than a deconstruction of the classics – and some *Feuilleton* writers like Jörder point to their own complicity in fostering this trendy marketable intellectual game – commentators claim that the spectators who have turned away apparently crave a theatre which offers the comforting certainty of 'untouched' classical narrative forms and/or which engages with familiar and recognizable social life. The popularity of Stein's 23-hr *Faust* production staged in 2000, presented by Jessen as a text-oriented scenic reading and an instance of museum theatre, is arguably one manifestation of the former desire for a return to a unified author's canon or tradition. The recurrence of a concern among both journalists and theatre practitioners with resistant content and the concept, history and practice of realism testifies to a related desire for an inclusive theatre community genuinely concerned both with its spectators and their current socio-political context. These different manifestations of the search for a theatre of certainty, rootedness and connection may in part explain a wide-ranging interest on the part of critics and practitioners alike in the pragmatic or aggressively confrontational neorealist stagings and new writing of contemporary British theatre.

However, practitioners such as Basler Theater director Michael Schindhelm claim that the type of reactionary patterns outlined by Jörder cannot be said to be typical of the audience at large. He and others, like Stephanie Carp in a *Theater heute* millennium interview with the Hamburger Schauspielhaus dramaturgy team (*Theater heute, Das Jahrbuch* 2000, 23), refer to the need to address the new and future generation of theatregoers. This sector is presented as rejecting the example of the *moralische Anstalt* and the familiarity of the classics and some are characterized as belonging to Generation Golf, a phrase coined by Florian Illies to describe a 'cool' petit-bourgeoisie for whom external style and an ever-changing aesthetics of appearance are of more importance than position, values and political attitudes. These theatregoers are described by Schindhelm as trademark-conscious supermarket shoppers: 'Ist das Theater gerade mal hip, so liegt es im Korb, wenn nicht, bleibt es im Regal.' (If theatre is currently 'in' it sells like hot cakes, if not it is left on the shelf) (5 April 2001). But, as Schindhelm concludes, the rejection of rootedness by these shoppers of the *Spaßgesellschaft* (fun society) is symptomatic of their own need for a centre, one he believes the theatre needs to address by rediscovering reality and meanings, and reasserting humour and pathos against postmodern irony. In a similar vein, Thomas Ostermeier of the new directorial team at the Berlin Schaubühne am Lehniner Platz, calls for a realism which is not simply the depiction of the world as it looks but

> ein Blick auf die Welt mit einer Haltung, die nach Änderung verlangt, geboren aus einem Schmerz und einer Verletzung, die zum Anlaß des Schreibens wird und Rache nehmen will an der Blindheit und Dummheit der Welt ... Der Einzelne leidet, auch wenn das Subjekt nur konstruiert und ohne Kern sein soll.

> (a view of the world characterized by a demand for change, born of pain and woundedness which becomes a reason for writing and wants to take revenge on the blindness and stupidity of the world ... The individual suffers even when the subject is supposedly only a construct without a core.)

> (Franz Wille, *Theater heute*, January 2000: 2)

In *Theater heute* the celebration of international and globalized theatres of the post-industrial world co-exists alongside discussions similar to those in *Die Zeit* about decline on the national stage and threat to its community. One area of concern given somewhat greater emphasis in the journal is the crisis of German ensemble theatre, an emphasis perhaps attributable to the journal's concern with issues of direct relevance to practitioners. The nostalgically tinged references to ensemble theatre, which reverberate throughout articles such as Michael Merschmeier's January 2000 reflection on the death of actor Ulrich Wildgruber and Ensemble theatre of the past 30 years, carry the traces of a long-standing national concern with connection and unity. In German theatre history that concern has been expressed in the numerous attempts to create a national theatre, each frustrated by a history of territorial division and decentralized power and resources – be it monarchical principalities or the East–West divide – which has militated against the creation of national cultural centres. The nineteenth-century preoccupation with the concept of a *Gesamtkunstwerk* ('synthesis of the art forms') is another expression of that concern and one connected with the rise of ensemble theatre as founded by the Duke of Saxe-Meiningen's company and then developed in divergent ways by the left- and right-wing politicized theatres of the twentieth century. Ensemble theatre involves at the very least the close collaboration of cast members in the service of a text or interpretative vision and usually also the careful co-ordination of all artistic practitioners and their different media (sound, light, set design and so on) involved in the production, often by a director figure or directorial team.

The forces peculiar to the German context which are described as contributing to the crisis in this field include the end of the 'great' ensembles, such as the old Schaubühne under Stein, Jürgen Flimm's Thalia company in Hamburg, Dieter Dorn's Kammerspielern and the 'Zadek family' among whom Wildgruber was a key player. The manner in which reunification unfolded is also given as a factor, particularly the manner in which the communitarianism of the East was usurped by the capitalist individualism of the West and a decade of cuts to public funding. In contrast to the celebration of international and global forces elsewhere in *Theater heute*, when the ensemble is mourned, an accusatory finger is pointed at the mass media's fostering of star systems and a general culture of narcissism.

Outside the picture of decline painted in the pages of *Die Zeit* and *Theater heute* there is evidence that the audience has not entirely left the theatre, just specific forms, and that the ensemble spirit lives on in other realms. The debates in the newspaper and journal could lead us to believe that the mainstream theatre is the only stream. Statistically the numbers are down for those attending the theatre at the centre, that of the metropolis, heavily state-subsidized and sporting big name directors. However, a closer look at, for instance, the reviews section of the local press of small town Germany will reveal a different story. True, the criticism is perhaps less astute, given at times to the hackneyed prose of provincial journalism, but it does show that the theatre in the schools, the amateur halls, the old beer cellars, barns and factories, on the market places and in the open-air is watched enthusiastically by those who feel this form of theatre has what the 'theatre in crisis' does not have – *Verbindlichkeit* – connection. Schmidt-Mühlisch (1992:12–13), in his assessment of the figures produced by the *Deutscher Bühnenverein*, shows how the popularity of alternative, non-mainstream theatre has risen in the past 25 years:

> 4,2 Millionen Besucher (auf Jahresgesamtzahl gerechnet) sind den Stadt- und Staatstheatern im letzten Vierteljahrhundert davongelaufen ... Vor 25 Jahren waren die Stadt- und Staatstheatern unangefochtene Favoriten in der Publikumsgunst; heute werden sie von den besagten 4,2 Millionen jährlich in der Tat gemieden- die gehen nämlich in zwischen lieber in die Privattheater oder sind zu den Festspielen abgewandert.

> (4.2 million spectators (calculated per annum) have walked out and left the municipal and state theatres in the last 25 years ... Twenty-five

years ago the municipal and state theatres were the undisputed favourites with the public; today they are avoided by the above mentioned 4.2 million every year – they prefer to go to private theatres or to the festivals.)

In contemporary Germany the theatre form that is flourishing and producing the most significant output in terms of quantity of productions – and some would argue in terms of quality also – is that of the amateur theatre, private theatres and festivals.

Such information raises the issue of which audience is being referred to in the crisis narratives. The simple notion of the audience as fee-paying strangers, long the definition of the modern theatre audience, becomes problematic in the amateur context. Instead it comprises friends and family or at least an acquaintance. It is an audience that has roots and a connection to the actors on stage. In addition, the audience member is often also elsewhere, an actor. According to the statistics produced by the *Bund Deutscher Amateur Theater* (BDAT: 2001) there are over 1800 groups registered as members of this umbrella organization spread across all 16 German states. Members of these amateur theatre groups are often dedicated hobbyists and will give up many hours of evenings and weekends and their holidays to pursue their passion for the theatre. Attendance at training courses in all aspects of theatre is always impressive on any course offered by the BDAT, as are attendance and participation at national conferences and at the amateur theatre festivals at regional and state level. These amateur theatre activists, working in their 'free' time, produce alternative theatres and agendas for repertoire than those pursued under different funding regimes and with different symbolic and cultural aspirations. The educational and moral aims of theatre as an institution may not be claimed as the work of the state theatre as enthusiastically as they have been in the past, but they are very much owned by many of the amateur groups and also by their audiences. In the *Naturtheater*, a form of summer open-air community theatre in southern Germany, audiences feel they have a certain intimacy and shared ownership with the theatre, even if they come as tourists. For amateur productions in Germany the ensemble is still of prime importance and psychological realism, even socialist realism are to be found in the repertoires. The success of the amateur plays revolves largely around time and energy expended on the production 'for the love of it', and press criticism is usually warm and appreciative, if not of the quality of the production, then of the community spirit it has engendered.

To imply, therefore, as is the case in some of the writing in *Die Zeit* and *Theater heute*, that theatre has cut free from its community roots, that it is in crisis, that it has a postmodern commitment to uncertainty and fragility and is insufficiently concerned with ensemble work is to present a unidimensional view of the subject of German theatre and to ignore the way that some popular forms have been developed into a democratic and participatory past-time, with significant resources also being deployed, privately and through small grants to amateur groups. What the theatre crisis narrative in the press and journal demonstrates is not that there is one single crisis in theatre-going in Germany, but that there are different crises arising as threats to different interests, power structures and traditions are played out. These include: the financial and ideological crisis manifest in theatre closures and job losses (especially in the East); community crisis as the professional ensemble is perceived as increasingly under threat both by director's theatre of the 1970s and media stars; ethical and political crisis as the old moral institution changes to embrace new moral orders, reactivating nostalgia for the securities of socialist theatre and various forms of realism.

Some care is needed, however, for the focus on crisis in the press and journals also points to the interests served by these media. To a certain extent crisis occurs when the press decides to report it as such. The crisis, is, partly a cultural construction. Just as facts and statistics tell certain stories, so too do the press. Threat to the forms of theatre that are the staple of the reviewers' diet is also a threat to the work of review. If certain theatre productions no longer attract, or no longer appear to be rooted in everyday concerns, then audiences and material is also lost to the reviewers. The debate in *Die Zeit* is significant because it reveals some of the places where power and money are located in the theatre system. It helps establish a picture of state theatre as out of touch, self-referential and ethically disconnected from everyday life. Such views tend to present a single homogeneous view that suggests a majority is dissatisfied with the majority of German theatre. There is little evidence that any other perspective could be valid for readers of *Die Zeit* as there is minimal coverage of alternative theatres. If the work of literary critics is consulted, work that is supposed to be characterized by careful research and preparation and which is published under very different material conditions to that of journalism, a happier picture of the work of the theatre emerges – one where there is indeed connection – just not to German culture and the *Heimat* but to the global stage.

Healthy crisis: opportunities for regeneration

In some of the academic literature discussing contemporary German theatre, crisis is defined in more positive terms as regenerative rather than as a moment of threat and loss. There is a strong sense of a theatre that thrives on transformations and that looks beyond the borders of Germany for inspiration. Indeed, the mainstream theatre that is apparently in crisis is precisely the theatre that is celebrated and forms the dominant focus of academics working in theatre studies. Following a conference in Berlin focusing on the theme of transformation and looking retrospectively at the theatre of the 1990s, Erika Fisher-Lichte, a prominent scholar on the subject of German theatre wrote:

Die Transformationen, welche das Theater vollzieht, verstärken so noch die Krisenerfahrung, welche die gesellschaftlichen Transformationsprozesse ausgelöst haben. Im Unterschied zu diesen jedoch eröffnet das Theater dem Zuschauer die Möglichkeit sich mit Unsicherheit und Destabilisierung, mit Entgrenzung und Grenzüberschreitung, mit Irritation und Verstörung spielerisch auseinanderzusetzen.

(The transformations the theatre has undergone strengthen the sense of a crisis, which has its roots in social transformation processes. In contrast to this, however, the theatre is opening up opportunities for its audiences to engage playfully with uncertainty and destabilizing experiences, with exclusion and with border crossings and with irritation and confusion.)

(Fischer-Lichte *et al.* 1999: 11)

This particular academic conference, together with other recent writing by journalist reviewers on the subject of contemporary German theatre, focuses on the influence of experimental theatre practitioners of Britain and North America such as British playwrights Sarah Kane and Mark Ravenhill, Canadian director Robert Lepage, or American director Robert Wilson. The theatre that some academics and broadsheet reviewers follow closely is a theatre that uses different performative media, that delights in overturning supposed norms and in examining voyeurisms, obscenities, monstrosities and the end of community. In this theatre it seems, the *moralische Anstalt* has had its day. The classics of Goethe and Shakespeare are no more and *Pipi Langstrumpf* – the most popular of all children's plays – is dead. It is a theatre which, according to Lehmann 'puts the human body in the front line, makes it a battle field and turns it into destructive energy' (ibid., 17).

In a slightly earlier publication Fischer-Lichte (1993) celebrates the influence on contemporary German theatre of French-based Adriane Mnouchkine, New York's Richard Schechner, Poland's Jerzy Grotowski, the British director Peter Brook, together with the Odin Teatret, a Danish-based international performance company that explores links between anthropology, performance and theatre forms with the Italian director Eugenio Barba.

Interestingly, the theatre that these international practitioners are creating is not a theatre 'of the theatre' in the traditional sense of buildings, but rather a one that colonizes other, post-industrial spaces such as warehouses, disused factories, old tram depots, etc. Border crossing in the theatre is therefore not just occurring with interest in plays from outside of the German context, but is equally occurring in material terms, as the theatre abandons buildings dedicated to its purpose and uses the symbolisms of other spaces that have themselves been through crisis and are enlivened again by theatre.

To encounter German theatre through this academic criticism, then, is to encounter the theatre of the world stage, of significant and famous world

directors and performance artists and to discover German-based practitioners whose work lends itself to poststructuralist commentary, such as the
Tanztheater (dance theatre) exponent Pina Bausch, or the Austrian feminist
dramatist Elfriede Jelinek, or the Berlin-based writer Heiner Müller who
died in 1995. These German or Austrian theatre and performance makers
are examined and celebrated in the academic literature for their fluidity,
their challenge to dominant norms, their deconstruction of fundamental
ways of understanding the world, their ability constantly to defer meaning
and to represent the world in fragments and through discomfort. They are
practitioners and dramatists who do not fit into Germany's Enlightenment
tradition of reason, clarity and unity aimed at creating a theatre with a
moral purpose and Fischer-Lichte is disparaging of those who attempt to
recreate this kind of theatre:

> Wer Theater als moralische Ansalt betrachtet oder als Institution zur
> Pflege des kulturellen Erbes, wird in ihr in jedem Fall den Ausdruck
> einer Krise des Theaters erkennen.
>
> (Whoever regards theatre as a moral institution or as an institution
> whose purpose is to preserve the cultural heritage will most certainly
> recognize the expression of a theatre in crisis.)
>
> (Fischer-Lichte *et al.* 1999: 11)

The theatre that appears happily at home in the global, postmodern world
is not at all comfortable with its moralizing, classical, canonical traditions.
This is not particularly surprising given that theatre, as Alan Read puts it, is
'worthwhile because it is antagonistic to official views of reality' (Read
1993, 1). In a Germany obsessed at the official level with questions of its
own post-unification identity, and with the apparent difficulties of its own
language and spelling reform (see Chapter 2) the dominant theatre has,
according to Fischer-Lichte (Fischer-Lichte *et al.* 1999, 7) steadfastly refused
to engage with any questions of national identity through, for example, endlessly producing conventional classics, preferring instead to engage with its
own transformation and look outside of its own borders. In celebrating anything other than homespun German-language productions it has contributed considerably to the climate of uncertainty and irritation.

The suggestion that the mainstream theatre has not dealt with questions
of cultural identity, is, however, debatable for engagement with theatre
outside of one's own national or local context is not a random, or even
deliberately resistant act – instead it can point to a need to reinvigorate the
local by selecting certain global forms. The forms that are chosen and translated, according to Aaltonen (2000, 47), have a significant contribution to
make:

> The relationship among the source text, its translation and the type of
> intertextuality in the time-sharing of theatre texts does not result from

independent choice; the choice is always tied to the time and place of the occupancy, and based on the contribution the translation is expected to make to cultural and social discourse in the target society.

It is therefore possible to interpret the focus of one strand of contemporary German theatre, the strand that has considerable resources to deploy, as being deeply concerned about its own traditions and as expressing this concern by drawing inspiration from other traditions in order to associate itself with the status or, the cultural capital, of celebrated productions, as a way of coping with its own crises, uncertainties and fragmentations. Equally, it is possible to interpret the stance taken by the German academic writing considered here, as playing for the now global stakes that require an internationalized and intercultural perspective on questions of national identity in critical work.

As perspectives from cultural studies allow us to understand, crisis occurs where vested interests and power are under pressure. In addition, the act of distancing oneself from crisis or from a negative interpretation of change can in certain contexts be interpreted as a move to protect one's own powers from the dangers of crisis. Distancing manoeuvres such as a shift away from questions of national identity and from the classics raise a series of interesting questions. What does the academic and mainstream fascination with contemporary North American and, especially British theatre, tell us about theatre in Germany? Why might a German theatre wish to look beyond its borders for inspiration? And at what cost? Who benefits from celebrating fragmentation and the body in extremis? In the 'crisis' of the 1960s and the student revolts theatre turned to local concerns and to popular, realist forms. After the *Wende* and the millennium arguably there is a greater tendency in the mainstream sector to turn from the local to the global, and help for regeneration is being sought from outside.

Conclusion

Encountering German theatre, second-hand, through different examples of its narratives, especially the crisis narratives, raises questions of power, rewards and interests served. This chapter has aimed to demonstrate, using the tools of Cultural Studies, that these narratives are not simply given and cannot simply be read as fact. In this we, as the authors, are aware that we have our own biases and interests in favour of Cultural Studies readings of academic texts and reviews of theatre, and that our presentation here is contingent. This said, we feel that some conclusions may be reached.

German theatre has played a particular role in the past in providing a vehicle for the hopes and aspiration of those wishing to see the united

German cultural nation grow from the disunities of past political organization. In the nineteenth century intellectuals sought theatrical forms that they felt quintessentially expressed the German nation. The success of Wagnerian opera in Bayreuth and the ensemble work of the Meininger theatre together with the discovery by intellectuals in the late nineteenth century of the Oberammergau passion plays, first established in 1637 as an act of thanksgiving following the end of the plague in a small village in Bavaria, all became a focus for national aspirations. Although consisting of different aesthetics, the desire to see German unity and community expressed in performance is not structurally dissimilar to the contemporary interest in creating a German theatre that engages with and invites global players and directors, especially from the symbolic Anglo-American scene.

In the case of the nineteenth century, German theatre presented a nationalistic display of its 'togetherness', its ensemble work, its *Gesamtkunstwerk*. In the contemporary epoch it appears that certain categories of German theatre are inviting other forms to colonize them, in order to address their own insecurities and problems of identity. Whereas in the nineteenth century, nationalisms of all kinds were on the rise in Europe, so today the dominant discourse is that of globalization. However, as Sharon MacDonald is quick to point out:

> Questions of identity come to the fore at times of social and political change. While on the one hand it might seem that as borders become weaker – as people and goods traverse them more easily – there will be a consequent relaxing of the sense of allegiance to place and people, very often the reverse is actually the case.

> (Macdonald 1997, 1)

The claim made by Fischer-Lichte, that the German theatre has resolutely avoided the question of cultural or national identity is flawed when examined more critically. The opening up of theatrical fields may, as we have seen, be a move to invite other forms to colonize and regenerate at times of change. Equally, the desire for unity and for the safety of classical form is a response to change from other standpoints. What those working in and with theatre are all engaged in, in different ways, is establishing and renewing their theatres in ways that serve their different interests and which respond to cultural change.

Those in the amateur scene, for all their pronounced love of their art, survive because they can pack their theatres with paying customers, who are happy to watch plays and musicals that do not fit into the current struggles and rules of the professional game. The BDAT does not exist to support amateurs in their desire to become more concerned with the intellectual rules of the game, but instead offers essentially artisan support in the form of courses on all technical aspects of perfecting the craft of acting and of production. In the field of southern German open-air theatre, for instance, there is intense rivalry between different theatre groups, each seeking their own form of distinction by mimicking the craft and techniques of the professionals, but rarely their conceptual interests. The question to be answered at the end of the season is not so much whether the play had aesthetic coherence, or addressed the questions of uncertainty and fragility through representations of actors' bodies *in extremis*, but whether tickets sold, applause was hearty, friends and family had a good night out and the coffers are full enough to allow another season. Nor do those working professionally in the theatres of Bonn, Wuppertal or Berlin, pushing the human body to its limits and presenting brokenness and uncertainty in discomforting ways to their perhaps small, but resolute intellectual audiences feel in anyway professionally concerned with the Lloyd-Webber musical that has been playing continuously down the road for the last five years, or with the group of senior citizens who perform plays each Christmas for their local community. German theatre is not a continuous field but is intersected by differing cultural understandings of the rewards and the crises associated with the work of theatre.

Crisis in public culture works itself out in different ways on the theatrical body. The 'theatre in crisis' relates to upheavals in companies and employment, ensemble work, in audience attendance patterns, in understandings of morality and realism and their place on the stage, in the centrality of the author, director or actor to the creative process, in the ways of renewing performance. The complexity and vibrancy of the values and beliefs that different theatres and different German traditions bring to light point not to a struggle between east and west, amateur and professional, avant garde and populist, musicals and state theatres, whatever the different literatures may suggest. Encountering theatre and performance in Germany means encountering stories of theatres and performances that have different relationships with different everyday lives. It is ultimately futile and impossible to make grand statements such as 'German theatre is in crisis' because German theatre does not actually exist as a finite fixed entity. Popularity is part of crisis, quests for unity are part of fragmentation and diversity and those forms that fill the theatres or that excite the theatre makers have their own stories to tell of the decline of national identities or of financial malaise. In this way the fact that three of the most popular plays in the overall repertoire of the German theatre are all by Shakespeare could suggest a crisis in the German theatre, but not in box office terms and ultimately looking beyond cultural boundaries for stimulation and renewal has always been the way of the theatre.

What is interesting in all this, and in the context of this book, is that crises and threat in contemporary German culture are felt and expressed where the body is in the front line, in the context of food (Chapter 9) in the threat to the environment (Chapter 3), as it passes across borders (Chapter 1), and, importantly, in the theatre. At times of crisis, when rewards are redistributed the effects will be felt materially. In some contexts the new rules of the game will serve to provide a sense of ease, in others they will be felt and experienced as threat. The stories told of these experiences of life, in the theatre, in the border-crossing body, in the channels of digestion, relate to these material pressures.

Note

1. All translations are by Alison Phipps unless otherwise stated.

Resources

Magazines

Vogue; Der Spiegel; Focus; Stern

Newspapers

Die Zeit; Die Welt; Frankfurter Rundschau; Süddeutsche Zeitung (Munich*); Frankfurter Allgemeine Zeitung; Tageszeitung* (Berlin)

City culture magazines

Taz (Berlin); *Zitty; Tip* (bi-weekly)

Journals

Theater heute; Deutsche Bühne, Spiel und Bühne, Theater der Zeit

Websites

ww.bdat-online.de/
www.Deutscher-bühnenverein.de

References

AALTONEN, S. 2000: *Time-sharing on stage: drama translation in theatre and society*. Clevedon: Multilingual Matters.
BALITZKI, J. 1995: *Castorf, der Eisenhändler: Theater zwischen Kartoffelsalat und Stahlgewitter*. Berlin: Ch. Links.
BASSNETT, S. and LEFEVRE, A. 1998: *Constructing cultures: essays on literary translation*. Clevedon: Multilingual Matters.

BOURDIEU, P. 1993: *The field of cultural production*. Cambridge: Polity.

FISCHER-LICHTE, E. 1993: *Kurze Geschichte des deutschen Theaters*. Tübingen and Basle: Francke.

FISCHER-LICHTE, E., KOLESCH, D. and WEILER, C. (eds) 1999: *Transformationen: Theater der neunziger Jahre*. Berlin: Theater der Zeit.

FOUCAULT, M. 1991: *Discipline and punish: the birth of the prison*. London: Penguin

Freie Volksbühne Berlin: nichts muß bleiben wie es ist 1890–1980. Bremen: Hamburg, 1980.

KIRSCHNER, J. 1997: *Fischer Handbuch: Theater, Film, Funk und Fernsehen*. Frankfurt am Main: Fischer.

KLOTZ, V. 1987: *Bürgerliches Lachtheater*. Reinbek bei Hamburg: Rowohlt Taschenbuch.

KÜHN, V. (ed.), 1994: *Hierzulande: Kabarett in dieser Zeit ab 1970*. vol. 5 Weinheim and Berlin: Quadriga.

LENNARTZ, K. 1992: *Vom Aufbruch zur Wende: Theater in der DDR*. Seelze, Velber: Erhard Friedrich.

LEWIS, D. and MCKENZIE, J.R.P. (eds) 1995: *The new Germany: social, political and cultural challenges of unification*. Exeter: University of Exeter Press.

MACDONALD, S. 1997: *Reimagining culture: histories, identities and the Gaelic renaissance*. Oxford: Berg.

MÖHRMANN, R. (ed.) 1990: *Theaterwissenschaft heute*. Berlin: Dietrich Reimer.

PATTERSON, M. 1976: *German theatre today: post-war theatre in West and East Germany, Austria and Northern Switzerland*. London: Pitman.

PATTERSON, M. 1995: The German theatre. In LEWIS, D. and McKENZIE, J.R.P. (eds) *The new Germany: social, political and cultural challenges of unification*. Exeter: Exeter University Press, 259–75.

PHIPPS, A. 2000: *Acting identities: an investigation into South West German Naturtheater*. Frankfurt am Main: Peter Lang.

READ, A. 1993: *Theatre and everyday life: an ethics of performance*. London: Routledge.

ROBER, D. 1981: *Theater muß wie Fußball sein: Freie Theatergruppen – eine Reise über Land*. Berlin: Rotbuch.

RÜHLE, G. 1982: *Anarchie in der Regie?, Theater in unserer Zeit*. vol. 2 Frankfurt am Main: Suhrkamp.

SCHMIDT-MÜHLISCH, L. 1992: *Affentheater: Bühnenkrise ohne Ende?* Erlangen: Verlag Straube.

STUBER, P. 1998: *Spielräume und Grenzen: Studien zum DDR-Theater*. Berlin: Ch.Links.

Theatre in the Federal Republic of Germany. Trans. Patricia Crampton Bonn: Inter Nationes, 1993.

TURNER, V. 1982: *From ritual to theatre: the human seriousness of play*. New York: Performing Arts Journal Publications.

ULRICH, P. and WÖHLERT, W. in RUBIN, D. (eds) 1994: *World encyclopedia of contemporary theatre*. vol. 1, *Europe*. London and New York: Routledge.

WEIHS, A. 1981: *Freies Theater*. Reinbek bei Hamburg: Rowohlt.

References to theatre journals and reviews

CARP, S., RAABKE, T. and SCHULZ, W. 2000: in discussion with *Theater heute*, Die geheimen Verführer: Die erfolgreichste Dramaturgie der 90er Jahre feiert Abschied im Gespräch. *Theater heute*, Das Jahrbuch, 16–31.

Jürgen Flimm in discussion with *Die Zeit* 2001: Populismus? Dass ich nicht lache! 'Das Publikum ist nicht doof': Ein ZEIT-Gespräch mit Jürgen Flimm über die Zuschauerverluste am Theater. *Die Zeit*, no. 14 (29 March 2001).

GREFFRATH, M. 2000: Gedanken eines bekennenden 68er über das Leben zwischen den Zeiten und ein nicht mehr neues Stück. *Theater heute*, Das Jahrbuch, 62–78.

JESSEN, J. 2001: Abschied der Kannibalen. Wird die Theaterkrise im Theatermuseum enden? *Die Zeit*, no. 22 (23 May 2001).

JÖRDER, G. 2001: Publikumsverweigerung: Die Theaterbesucher spielen nicht mehr mit. Empört, gelangweilt oder resigniert ziehen sie sich aus vielen Häusern zurück. Was sind die Ursachen der dramatischen Zuschauerverluste – in Basel und anderswo? *Die Zeit*, no. 12 (15 March 2001).

MERSCHMEIER, M. 2000: Ein Zeitalter wird besichtigt: Über Ulrich Wildgruber, das Ensemble-Theater der vergangenen drei Jahrzehnte – und seine Zukunft. *Theater heute*, no. 1 (January 2000), 18–29.

NYSSEN, U. 2001: Ehret die Dichter! *Die Zeit*, no. 22–23 (May 2001), 41.

RISCHBIETR, H. 2001: Sie sind so frei: Bilanz eines Jurors – über das Festival 'Impulse' und viele Themen der Freien Szene: ... *Theater heute*, no. 11 (November 2001), 16–21.

SCHINDHELM, M. 2001: Theater ist Gegenwart, nicht Gegenwelt. 'Die öffentliche Kunst lebt in bleierner Zeit': Auf der Suche nach dem unbekannten Publikum der Zukunft. *Die Zeit*, no. 15 (5 April 2001).

WILLE, F. 2000: Startdeutsch: Über die abgründige Lust zu programmatischen Texten und Äußerungen unter jüngeren Theaterleitern. *Theater heute*, no. 1 (January 2000), 1–2.

|12|

Scene change: pluralized identities in contemporary German cinema

BY DICKON COPSEY

Throughout its semantic evolution the notion of the 'encounter' has retained a connotation of the adversial or conflictual. A particularly pertinent noun, then, when applied to the study of German film. Whatever our exposure to this national cinema – be it through the bizarre and sinister horror of Robert Wiene's *Das Cabinet des Dr Caligari* or F.W. Murnau's *Nosferatu*, the ideologically tainted anti-Semitic propaganda of Veit Harlan's *Jud Süß*, or the heavily politicized and often slow-paced *Kopfkino* of Rainer Werner Fassbinder's *Die Ehe der Maria Braun* or the collaborative *Deutschland im Herbst* – it is unlikely that our initial encounters with German film have ever extended beyond the occasional foray or chance meeting. Unless, that is of course, our interests were channelled by an academic course of study. In this case, the selection of films studied is quite likely to have been mediated by an overtly 'high culture' emphasis on the canonic moments of German film history and their politicized critical reception. In both case scenarios German cinema runs the risk of marginalization, either as an overly-serious or overtly dead cinematic phenomena. However, for anyone who has seen Caroline Link's detailed and thematically innovative *Jenseits der Stille* (1997), Fatih Akin's pacey and violent *MultiKulti* gangster movie *Kurz und schmerzlos* (1998), or even the frenetic MTV montage of Tom Tykwer's multi-media extravaganza *Lola rennt* (1998), it will be clear that there is another, and very different side to German cinema. My aim in this chapter is, therefore, to redress the historic imbalance within German Film Studies towards the historical and critically acclaimed, by conducting an elliptical but hopefully illuminating survey of some of the most characteristic and illustrative moments of 1990s' German cinema.

From aesthetics to commercialism

Ende gut, alles gut. Das deutsche Kino ist dahin. Tot, verabschiedet.
(All's well, that ends well. German cinema is finished, dead,
dismissed.)

(Laurens Straub)[1]

Both media (*Der Spiegel* 1996) and academic (Lischke-McNab and Hanson
1997) film discourses in Germany in the 1990s have been dominated by
speculation as to the extent and meaning of a paradigmatic shift from art
house *Kunst* to mainstream *Kommerz*. Despite debate as to the actual final-
ity of the decline of the *Autorenfilm* and the New German Cinema product,
1982 has generally been accepted as a turning point in the fortunes of the
post-1968 generation of film-maker and the social and artistic imperatives
they broadly adhered to. This revision is articulated most clearly by the new
fraternity of young directors who would appear to reject as indulgent their
forbears 'langatmige Egotrips auf der Leinwand' (long-winded ego-trips on
the cinema screen, *Der Spiegel* 1996, 215) in favour of a populist manifesto
which embraces the potential of cinema as a mass medium.

Whatever the merits of this new stable of directors, their narrative-driven
films have become symptomatic of a wider trend towards the 'rehabilitation
of the story in German cinema' (Coury 1997, 285). Typically defined in
opposition to the non-narrative and anti-commerce film theory of the New
German Cinema, Thomas Elsaesser (1999) sees this redefinition of the thematic and aesthetic concerns of a previous generation of film-maker as concomitant to a reassessment of the public role of the director. Mirroring the
theoretical collapse of all essentializing notions of identity formation[2] – be
they sexual, racial, or national – the construction of cultural identity, in the
newly defined physical space of post-unification Germany, has become radically pluralized. As a result, the status and high cultural capital previously
enjoyed by the New German Cinema directors is being hotly contested.
Often unashamedly commercial in their intentions, and in direct contrast to
their predecessors, the aim of the new directors is invariably to make films
which are popular and entertaining, thus recognizing the status of film not
merely as post-1968 *Kulturgut* but also as commercial product. Whatever
the reasons for this shift in cinematic practices, the political, economic and
cultural imperatives responsible for the critically acclaimed moments of
German film history – from the Expressionism and *Neue Sachlichkeit* of
Weimar to the New German Cinema's revival of the nationally significant
Autorenfilm – have undoubtedly changed.

However, in parallel to this revitalization of a popular commercial mainstream, pressure has been mounting to reassess the critical reception of
German cinema, and in so doing, challenge the continued dominance of the
high–low cultural paradigms of Frankfurt School discourse at work in the
writing of German film histories. Undoubtedly, the literary cultural para-

digm, which has dominated German studies, has been equally significant in the writing of German film history. Drawing upon the idealist philosophical tradition and based upon 'objective' qualitative judgements which assess film in terms of its intellectual and artistic merits the canon of German film theory has constructed itself around a body of work which eulogizes the creative genius of the director, while seeking relationships to literary, artistic and theatrical sources.

According to Jan-Christopher Horak, the exclusions and omissions of official German film histories demonstrate clearly the political nature of the canonization process:

> Diese Beispiele stellen anschaulich dar, wie wenig sich die Filmgeschichtschreibung in Deutschland mit der Realität des deutschen Kinos auseinandergesetzt hat. Die für das Bildungsbürgertum verfaßte Filmhistorie fällt stets normative Werturteile, die den Film als 'siebente Kunst' in den Vordergrund stellen und Künstler entdecken sollte.

> (These examples show clearly how little the writing of German film history has actually had to do with the reality of German cinema. This film history, constructed for the educated, middle classes, embodies normative value judgements which promote film as 'high art', and its creators as 'artists'.

> (1997, 13)

As Raymond Williams explains the processes through which texts are lifted high, and canonised, are equally effective at bringing low and excluding.[3] In this case the films which are excluded are clearly implicated within a popular, commercial, and thus 'tainted' and 'low', mainstream.

Drawing on this reassessment of the cultural significance of the popular – a reassessment at the heart of the Cultural Studies project to politicize the cultural text, and thus resist all narrow definitions of culture as objects of supposed aesthetic excellence[4] – I wish, in this chapter, to reference a broad cross-section of German films, including both popular and critical successes. While recognizing the innate weaknesses in any attempt to ascribe boundaries to a national cinema – boundaries which have up until recently remained at the forefront of the project of German cinema studies – and also the fallibility of any attempt to extrapolate oversimplified generalizations from my brief survey of 1990s' German cinema, my intention in this chapter is to highlight some key cultural sites of identity contestation within the realm of contemporary German film and investigate the ideological imperatives behind their representation of gendered, national and racial identities.

As the thematic focus of this chapter shifts from issues of sexuality and gender, to national and social identity, and finally to racial and cultural identity, its fundamental concern remains with the cultural processes of othering, that are central to capacities for social change. Just as the identification and exclusion of 'others' has historically been the fundamental project of nationalism, the co-option and expropriation of identity and difference can be equally instrumental – and equally exploitative – in the construction of neo-nationalist identities. It is in the context of this recognition of the inherently political nature of identity formation that I engage with Ginsberg and Thompsons' German cinema studies project to articulate a transformational understanding and theorization of national, social and sexual subjectivities, one which recognizes and resists 'the complete collapse of difference endemic to much post-modern film theory' (Ginsberg and Thompson 1996, 9) but also refrains from regression into the normative labelling of what Edward Said terms 'muscular reassertions of traditional values, as characterised by the global neo-conservative movement' (1994, 67).

At the start of the twenty-first century, identity, as a site of cultural contestation, has rarely been more animated. Feminist theory's critique of the co-option and expropriation of gendered difference within mass culture, and its positing of critical ways of seeing and alternative models of representation, is as relevant to the post-emancipation, mainstream, woman-centred relationship comedies of my first section, as it was to the evolution of the *Frauenfilm* of the 1960s and 1970s. Equally, as the task of rebuilding an economically devastated East and reuniting it to an ideologically diametrically opposed system continues, the ideological battle for ownership of its past and present through cultural representation takes on a central significance, both to the future of the country and perhaps, more generally, to the tenability of the ideal of western, capitalist democracy.

The filmic portrayal of GDR past and eastern Germany's present, constitutes the focus of my second section.

In the wake of recent racist attacks in the *neue Bundesländer*, and in the context of an increasingly tense and fractious social climate, the flux of new immigrants from the East has reopened the *Ausländerpolitik* debate and raised some uncomfortable parallels with an apparently *bewältigt* past. The discourse of stigmatization and othering of ethnic minorities upon which the increasingly visible, pan-European neo-nationalist stronghold depends, holds particular relevance for the largely naturalized Turkish population, whose second and third generations are entering a significant sphere of cultural influence with their inroads into the German film industry. This shall be explored in my final section.

Das Lachen macht's: gender and the new German comedy

Drawing on such earlier successes as Dorris Dörrie's *Männer* (1985), Sönke Wortmann's *Allein unter Frauen* (1991) and Peter Timm's *Ein Mann für jede Tonart* (1993), Katja von Garnier's 1992 film *Abgeschminkt* set a trend for a revival of the romantic comedy genre within the German film industry. Widely cited as the turning point in the commercial fortunes of the German film industry[5] and responsible for the relocation of the German film within the national popular imagination, these early films gave birth to a stream of comic features ranging from slapstick *Prolkomödien*[6] to male and female buddy movies but dominated by star lead middle-class relationship comedies obsessively reworking the themes of gender and sexuality.

More recently this trend has been responsible for such box office hits as Wortmann's *Der bewegte Mann* (1994) and *Das Superweib* (1996), Rainer Kaufmann's *Stadtgespräch* (1995), Dörrie's *Keiner liebt mich* (1996) and more recent *Bin ich schön* (1998), Sharon von Westerheim's *Workaholic* (1996), and Sherry Horman's *Irren ist männlich* (1996). Representing a significant sub-genre of the critically dubbed *Neue deutsche Komödie* (Kilb 1996), these gender comedies have foregrounded women, both as subject of representation and consumption.[7] In their centring of female protagonists – such as the precedent-setting 'strong, blond' role model and star vehicle, Katja Riemann – and their conscious targeting of women, these texts have invited a degree of feminist interest (Caprio 1997), which has attempted to explore and account for the films' relationships with their predominantly female audiences. This in turn has lead to a revaluation of the role of the psychological, political and aesthetic importance of such post-modern concepts as 'pleasure' and 'play' in the female-centred[8] text.

As Cultural Studies has always insisted, the ideological unravelling of representations of identity can never be divorced from the cultural context in which a text is produced. In other words, it must acknowledge the complex web of economic and political interests at work in its production and distribution. In the case of this specific generic articulation of contemporary gender relations, the woman-centred, German relationship comedies of the mid-1990s are firmly embedded within the system of economic imperatives and normative aesthetic practices of a commercial mainstream. In this respect, these films could be seen as representing a significant departure from the highly politicized, low-budget and critically acclaimed *Frauenfilme* of the early to late 1970s and the feminist political project they grew out of. However, in line with contemporary cultural study's challenge to an overly deterministic ideological reading of cultural consumption, a theoretical position can be opened up which allows for a politically progressive reading of these texts. As John Fiske points out:

> If the cultural commodities or texts do not contain resources out of which the people can make their own meanings of their social relations and identities, they will be rejected and will fail in the marketplace. They will not be made popular.
>
> (1989, 2)

Three films at the heart of what quickly came to be seen as the revival of the commercial fortunes of the German film industry, were Katja von

Garnier's *Abgeschminkt*, Rainer Kaufmann's *Stadtgespräch* and Sönke
Wortmann's *Das Superweib*. To pursue our exploration of identity representation in the contemporary German film let us now take a closer look at
these three mainstream cinematic texts, and their particular articulation of
the relationship between gender construction and sexuality.

Failed romances?

Auf   flachem   Unterhaltungsniveau   werden   in   vielen   der
Junggesellinnen-Farcen – auch hier gilt das Vorbild 'Abgeschminkt' –
die Nachwirkungen der Frauenbewegung verhandelt.

(In many of the 'lone female' farces – and here too is the prototype
'Abgeschminkt' valid – the after-effects of the feminist movement are
dealt with and disposed of on the superficial level of mainstream entertainment.)

(*Der Spiegel* 1996, 222)

According to Caprio the 1990s' shift of emphasis from socially critical
Frauenfilm to politically correct *Frauenkomödie* should be viewed with a
substantial degree of caution. Norman Denzin defines post-modern culture
as a 'masculinised culture of Eros, love, desire, femininity, youth, and
beauty' (1991, 149). The patriarchal imbalance of this culture ensures that,
for women at least, the 'path to happiness and fulfilment is sexual and lies
in the marital, family bond' (ibid.). To what extent then, can these woman-
centred romantic comedies of the mid-1990s be seen as substantiating this
belief in the promotion of sexualized and domesticized female identities,
and should the films' positioning of a new brand of anti-patriarchal
Powerfrau – as epitomized by the strong, blond role models, Katja Riemann
and Veronica Ferres – within a genre of (heterosexual) *relationship* comedies, be treated with a certain amount of scepticism?

   Firstly, it could be argued that female characters, such as Riemann's
Frenzy (*Abgeschminkt*) or Monika (*Stadtgespräch*), and Veronica Ferres'
Franziska (*Das Superweib*), do more to reinforce patriarchal conceptions of
feminine identity than to challenge them. In *Abgeschminkt* the identity crisis
which faces the central female protagonist Frenzy (Katja Riemann), and
which articulates itself in her artistic block, is ultimately resolved through
her relationship with the German-American soldier, Mark (Max Tidof). In
Stadtgespräch, radio presenter Monika, as Frenzy, is thirty and partnerless.
A 'biologische Zeitbombe' (biological time-bomb) just waiting to explode,
she is constantly reminded of her 'inadequacy' by her mother, Frau Krauss
(Karin Rasenack). As with all 'ideal' (Radway 1987) romantic heroines, the
greater her initial resistance to this realization – 'Ein Mann ist wirklich das
letzte, was ich brauche' (A man is really the last thing that I need) – the
greater the significance of her ultimate transformation. Enter the positively

charming Erik (August Zirner), whose attributes include good looks, a large car, a good job, a flair for Slavic languages and incredibly slanting eyebrows. For Monika, a veritable 'Mr Perfect'. Her subsequent overnight transformation from apparently strong, independent, career-minded woman to gooey-eyed, lovesick teenager mirrors the 'feminization' process that Frenzy undergoes in *Abgeschminkt*.

On attainment of their male love interests, both Frenzy and Monika undergo immediate transformations from rebel to reactionary constructions of femininity – a narrative model central to the construction of the traditional romantic heroine in the reactionary 'ideal' romances of romantic fiction (Radway 1987). Interestingly, in Sönke Wortmann's 1996 hit comedy *Das Superweib*, this model of female transformation from rebellion to conformity would appear to be inverted. As its title would suggest this film engages arguably most directly of all with the question of women's rights and position in a male-dominated society. Veronica Ferres plays Franziska, mother of two and wife of successful young film director and archetypal 'mieses patriarchalisches Arschloch' (disgusting chauvinist pig), Will Groß (Thomas Heinze). Despite this rather inauspicious opening Franziska quickly divorces her exploitative and unfaithful husband – albeit unintentionally – and embarks upon her transformation from 'plain Jane', everywoman housewife and mother, to glamorous, best-selling authoress. On the surface at least, a truly progressive female heroine. However, both the accidental nature of her divorce and the representation of male/female relationships as existing purely on a sexual level – an aspect of relevance to all three of the case study films here under examination – undercut this initial 'Girl Power' stance. Arguably, this purely sexual reading of the male/female relationship can only work in favour of a patriarchal ideology, which seeks to place women in the role of wife and mother, and prevent any meeting of the sexes on equal terms.

Significantly, at the same time as these three female protagonists are being feminized, sexualized and positioned within heterosexual relationships, they are also required to compromise their professional and artistic integrity to satisfy patriarchal bosses. Frenzy's feisty *Mosquitofrau* is transformed into a 'fast pornographisch' male sexual fantasy, Monika's advice to her listeners changes from incitement to feminist revolution to loved-up peace and reconciliation *Schwärmerei*, and Franziska consents to her husband's sensationalized reworking of her autobiography for the cinema. In this respect, the apparent threat, which these 'strong', 'autonomous' women initially pose to their patriarchal counterparts, is never as serious as it may at first seem. Apart from a certain 'superficial bolshiness' (*Living Marxism* 1996) all of these women ultimately conform to specifically patriarchally defined concepts of feminine beauty and sex appeal, bearing out Denzin's critique of the post-modern society as obsessed with 'a pornography of the visible' and the concomitant 'commodification of sexuality and desire' (1991, p.vii) In other words, the reactionary traditionalism of their presentation as glamorous sex objects, negates the radicalism of any potential feminist stance, and the sexual division of gender stereotypes is reproduced. In this respect, their 'Girl Power' would appear to rely quite heavily on their appearance. In other words, the 'rebelliousness' that our heroines initially display is at once ratified and delegitimized by their unquestionable 'femininity'. This reactionary representation of femininity brings into question the progressive nature of this new brand of feminism, as the following quote taken from an article on that peculiarly British phenomenon, the 'Spice Girls', suggests:

> This brand of 'Girl Power' really is a kind of ad-agency version of what 1990s feminism has become: a safe form of self-expression that has more to do with changing your hairstyle than changing the world. It is a strange combination of superficial bolshiness and girlier-than-girliness, of shocking appearance and utter conservatism ... it is no real threat to anybody.

> (*Living Marxism* n.p.)

However, this reading does not take into account the relationship of these stars to their audiences. Richard Dyers, in his work on stars, argued that the appeal of stars lay not in the charisma of the particular individual but in the meanings which that star signified, and in particular, in the ideological contradictions which their image could resolve for the audience (1979). In the case of Riemann and Ferres the 'contradictory' notions of femininity and female sexuality offered to their female audiences operate around such false dichotomies as 'strength' and 'sexiness', 'innocence' and 'aggressive sexuality', 'success in love' and 'success in career'. Understanding these female stars as objects of desire for their female audiences, we can begin to explore the possibilities of a signifier, which could represent the ideal of a 'complete' female self.

The exploration of female camaraderie is undoubtedly central to any politically progressive reading of the texts and their relationship to their audiences. The suggestion of a sensual, almost sexual dimension to Frenzy and Maischa's (Nina Kronjäger) relationship is repeatedly toyed with in *Abgeschminkt* – from Frenzy's hovering over the 'sleeping beauty' form of Maischa, tempting her lips with various delicacies designed to 'arouse' her from her slumbers, to their sharing of the 'marital' bed, and the inversion of the traditional cinematic male-gaze, as Frenzy observes Maischa dressing and undressing. Echoes of this playful exploration of a woman-to-woman sensuality can also be seen in the romantic imagery of the first-date scenario which frames the meeting of Monika and Sabine (Martina Gedeck) in *Stadtgespräch*. On a more practical level, it is the relationship between Franziska and her surrogate mother, Frau Winkel (Liselotte Pulver) which allows her to pursue her professional career in *Das Superweib*.

While representing a significant departure from the positioning of subsidiary female characters as hostile 'others' – a construction common to the ideal romances of romantic fiction (Radway 1987) – this portrayal of women who appear to both 'love women' and 'promote the interests of women' (Sedgwick 1985, 3) defines itself initially around a challenge to the 'utopian' promise of successfully managed heterosexual relations. This exclusively female homosociality[9] relativizes the importance of the heterosexual relationship and marriage as the source of 'or path to' female individuation and fulfilment, and in the process questions '[t]he rules that govern intelligible [female] identity, ... rules that are partially structured along matrices of gender hierarchy and compulsory heterosexuality' (Butler 1990, 145). As the narratives of all three films ultimately bear out, it is the best (girl)friend, the non-patriarchal male and the sympathetic mother- in other words, the bonds of 'homosociality' and 'homosexuality' – which prove to be the most reliable support systems. In this respect, as in the narrative quest for romance is ultimately subordinated to the more important concern of the emotional and intellectual flow between the two female protagonists.

Unsurprisingly, in the course of this challenge to traditional constructions of female identity, the general inadequacies of the traditional, heterosexual patriarchal male to provide the emotional care and support that the career woman of the 1990s both requires and demands, are clearly exposed. The 'demise of the affirmative culture' which Thomas Elsaesser saw as such an integral part of the 1950s' melodramas is equally apparent here, as the ironic treatment of marriage and men disturbs 'an unproblematic transmission of affirmative ideology' (Klinger 1995, 81). The ideal romance's utopia of patriarchal promise is exposed for the fantasy it is. As Monika puts it in *Stadtgespräch*: 'Romantische Bootstour, Liebe, Mondschein ist einfach gelaufen' ('Romantic boating trips, love and moonlight are a thing of the past').

This by no means implies, however, that the new woman-centred German comedies do not deal in fantasy. In all three films the strength of the central female protagonists is supported largely by virtue of their professional and creative aptitude, as well as the associated financial independence. Radio presenters, graphic designers, novelists and scriptwriters, the creative professions which the female protagonists of *Abgeschminkt*, *Stadtgespräch* and *Das Superweib* occupy, act both as markers of middle-class status and character individuation. Integral to the themes of identification and reassurance which the films offer the 'wirtschaftlich abgesicherten Elite' ('financially secure elite', *Der Spiegel* 1996, 223) at which they are aimed, career concerns also represent an ever-increasing reality for a large proportion of the middle-class women.

The films' explorations of non-patriarchally defined notions of female sexuality reflects a wider contemporary obsession with the promotion of strong and sexy cultural icons for female identification – icons which positively extol the merits of a new aggressive and promiscuous female sexuality. As in Monika Treut's more radical investigation of female sexuality *Die Jungfrauenmaschine* (1988), female promiscuity is cited as an antidote to the myth of romantic love, which is viewed as a mechanism designed to prevent women from pursuing their own sexual pleasure. This 'unleashed female sexuality', which is 'capable of satisfying itself outside the structures of patriarchal dominance that are still perpetuated most effectively through marriage' (Radway 1987, 74), is representative of a new morality of female promiscuity directly threatening to the utopian promise of traditional bourgois romantic ideology. In the new woman-centred German comedies, sex is never taken to represent a point of romantic climax or mystical, magical union. Instead, it is marginalized to merely another site of traditional male control and one that requires aggressive occupation by the 'new', self-determining woman of 1990s.

In this respect, these films can be seen as consciously contributing to a reclamation of an active heterosexual desire for women. This would seem at odds with Steve Neale and Frank Krutnik's interpretation of the revival of the 'comedy of sexes' as symptomatic of a need to re-invoke the concept of 'the couple' 'as a safeguard not merely against the divisions of modern life but also against the post-AIDS danger of 'illicit' sexuality (that which is outside the 'norm' of heterosexual monogamy)' and as representative of a 'desire to return, nostalgically to pre-1950's conceptions of romance' (1990, 172). Indeed, romantic closure, in the woman-centred new German comedies, is invariably resisted. Consequently, the endings are never sufficient to contain the 'excess of meaning produced in the course of the film' (Klinger 1995, 83). They unambiguously reject the vicarious nurture of the ideal romance while at the same time offering a tantalising glimpse of a future alternative object of desire. Merchants in the brokering of women's pleasure themselves, they yet make explicit the 'temporality of satisfaction' (Shumway 1995, 393) the romantic consummation of the traditional romantic comedy is at such pains to conceal. Perhaps, it is in the avoidance of this 'death of desire' that these new German comedies are ultimately brokering pleasure to their female audiences. 'Failed' romances, which re-animate the female homosocial bond while questioning the 'post-modern cult of Eros' (Denzin 1991, viii) and its idealized conceptions of love and intimacy, these films resist the fixing of desire, thus resisting the consummation of the narrative for their female audiences. Perhaps, in so doing, they leave it open for a future re-negotiation of the romantic fantasy.

Vergangenheit bewältigt?: The treatment of the *Wende* in contemporary German film

Despite the commercial dominance of the relationship comedies in the mid-1990's and the portrayal therein of an affluent, problem-free, West Germany, considerable effort has also being expended in the German public sphere to investigate and position East German history within a reanimated and widened national context. Significantly, of the few non-documentary films which initially took as their thematic focus the events of the immediate post-Wall period the majority were comedies.[10] Immersed as they were in the euphoria of the times, and popularly acclaimed for their portrayal of positive East German identities within the context of a national cultural mainstream, the progressive symbolism of these early comedies was drastically circumscribed by their predominantly clichéd protagonists. Confined within the limits of the mainstream comedy genre, the stereotypical labelling of East and West German identities, in films such as Peter Timm's *Go Trabi Go* (1991) and Manfred Stelzer's *Gruß Gott, Genosse* (1991), relied upon simplistic binaries, which posited provincially backward or weak-willed, conformist 'Ossis' against self-satisfied and affluent *Lederhosen*-wearing *Wessis*. While significant as a rather elementary lesson in identity as constructed through difference, the risk of the comedies is that through their superficial exploration and comic exploitation of the 'othering' process, they are in danger of trivialising the true problems of unification.

Despite the contemporary focus of these few comic *alles wird gut* (all's well that ends well) *Wende* films, the majority of feature films produced in the 1990s have been preoccupied with reconstructions of the German Democratic Republic's past. Margarethe von Trotta's 1994 film *Das Versprechen* posits the wall as a barrier to romantic consummation, and in its rigid adherence to the narrative conventions of mainstream genre cinema is perhaps more typical of the West German *Wende* films. Recognized as one of the first serious films to combine treatment of both the partition and ultimate reunification of Germany, and amidst great media interest, it was selected to open the Berlinale Film Festival in 1995.

In spite of a symbolically ambiguous conclusion, in which the two former lovers – Sophie (Meret Becker and Corinna Harfouch) and Konrad (Anian Zollner and August Zirner) – and the two halves of Germany, are reunited on Berlin's *Glienicker Brücke* on the night of 9th November 1989, its focus is primarily on the past. Significantly, this is a past which not only excludes any reference to contemporary problems and difficulties of post-unification Germany but also romanticizes both East German and West German life through its narrow social focus. For example, any discomfort for Sophie as she arrives illegally in the West, is immediately cushioned by her wealthy aunt who takes her in and offers the beautiful niece a job in her fashion house, while Konrad's lightning rise to status and respect as prodigious apprentice to a famous astrophysicist marks him out as an equally privileged individual, with freedom to travel and relative affluence. 'Wir sind noch im Osten', the young refugees exclaim with surprise on arrival in the West, 'hier sieht es genauso aus wie bei uns', and according to the film it would appear there really was little difference. Dieter Mann's comment as the central protagonist's father, that as a working-class youth his son may well enjoy more opportunities in the East than in the West does little to dispel the exclusivity of the film's limited social tableaux.

In addition to this superficial treatment of the realities of everyday life under a communist regime, actual political events – such as the Prague Spring and subsequent reassertion of repressive Stalinist policies – are viewed only in relation to the extent they impinge upon the microcosmic worlds of our fictional characters. The arrival of the Soviet tanks on the streets of Prague is exploited merely as a narrative device to heighten the dramatic tension of the reunited lovers' frantic lovemaking. Although this elevation of the personal over and above the political does not necessarily diminish the text's social and political message, its mainstream billing as 'Eine Liebe, eine Hoffnung, eine Mauer' ('One Love, One Hope, One Wall'), is perhaps most symptomatic of the problematics of the balance that von Trotta and her co-script writer Peter Schneider have attempted to strike between entertainment and romance, on the one hand, and historical verité, and political engagement, on the other (Kilb 1995, n.p).

Seen in the context of a wider cinematic landscape of the mid-1990s of depoliticized gender comedies this apparent lack of true critical engagement has been argued to represent a post-New German Cinema transition to a period of increasingly conservative cultural legitimisation (Davidson 1997, 307). Accurate as this may be as an indication as to the extent of the revival of a domestic commercial mainstream, eclectic and uninhibited in its search for themes of identification for its reanimated German audiences, it does not, however, reflect the true cross-section of contemporary German film production. In addition to the plethora of documentaries investigating the roles of prominent East German politicians, the *inoffizielle Mitarbeiter* (unofficial employees) and the Stasi in the running of the communist regime, both western and eastern feature film-maker have produced works which critically engage with the legacy of the GDR state.

Of the East German feature film-makers to approach the subject most have focused their energies on an exploration of the power structures of the former communist republic, rather than direct engagement with the social problems of post-*Wende* eastern Germany. Frank Beyer's *Der Verdacht* (1991) goes back into GDR past to examine the complex web of torn loyalties, tensions and betrayals invoked by the official and unofficial organs of the East German 'surveillance state', while Herwig Kipping's *Das Land hinter dem Regenbogen* (1991) explores the brutal and repressive reality behind the utopian imagery and language officially subscribed to the 'golden years' of the republic's origins. Interestingly, in his more recent work, *Nikolaikirche* (1995), which examines the 1980s' resistance movement centred around the Nikolaikirche in Leipzig, Beyer is clear in his intention not to attempt a documentary account of the last days of the Republic. Instead, he wishes to construct a fictional biography – 'Familiengeschichte als Zeitgeschichte' (Family stories as national histories, Schenk 1996, 17) – the central family and its variant members functioning as a microcosm of the wider socialist state. Through its portrayal of key individuals within the political resistance movement, the film succeeds not only in its reinscription of a politically activist and pro-democratic East German self, but also in mapping out an alternative national psychology, which resists exclusive association with and definition by the apparatus of the state.

Of the small percentage of feature film productions to critically engage with the social reality of the post-*Wende Ostprobleme* (the problems of the East) Andreas Kleinert's *Verlorene Landschaft* (1992) and *Neben der Zeit* (1995) develop a critical counter-balance to the popular *Ostalgie* renderings of GDR life by tracing the transition from the ideological prescriptiveness of the communist state to the equally confining economic strictures of the new post-Wall world of global capitalism. Kleinert's most recent exploration of the darker social consequences of unification, *Wege in die Nacht* (1999) follows a quest to impose meaning and structure by force in a society in which loss of power and position is accompanied by an apparent loss of morality and justice. Centring its narrative on the easily identifiable and stereotypically authoritarian personality of Walther – ex-'Genosse Direktor' of a now 'rationalized' East German factory, who finds himself unemployed and unable to adjust to the new democratic 'freedoms' of western society – the film is concerned with a critique of the communist political system which formed such characters but also the inherent inequalities of the new capitalist Germany and the apparent ideological and moral redundancy of its culture (Knoben 1999, 51). In this respect the film offers a treatment of post-*Wende* social reality which resists simplistic 'othering' of either political systems or their inhabitants. In addition, as one of five German films released in 1999 to treat the GDR past and post-*Wende* present, it represents a renewed interest, at the end of the millennium, in all things East German, reflected both in film production and audience popularity (Knoben 2000, 10).

From post-Kohl era urban deprivation to pre-unification *Spaßrepublik* ('Fun-Republic'), Leander Hausmann's film version of Thomas Brussig's novel *Sonnenallee* was one of the most successful German films of 1999, with audiences of over 1.8 million. Set on the eastern end of the wall-divided *Sonnenallee* this playful, theatrical romp through the annals of 1970s' East German pop history situates a coming of age narrative in the actually 'not so gloomy after all' shadow of the Berlin Wall, citing in the process the universalizing and extra-political themes of teenage angst, romance and rebellion. Despite being cited as contributing significantly to the cinematic treatment of the 'unspektakulaere Normalität des Alltags' (unspectacular normality of the everyday, Knoben 2000, 10) in the former GDR, this film has, along with the film version of Brussig's second novel *Helden wie wir* (Sebastian Peterson, 1999), been primarily credited with the repositioning of a positive East German imaginary in the national conscious. In tone this film undoubtedly continues the work started by the comedies, but at a time when the *Vereinigungs-Euphorie* (unification euphoria) of the pre-currency unification period has faded in both East and West, and the harsh reality of life in the *neue Bundesländer* is becoming increasingly apparent. In the context of an increasingly prevalent portrayal of GDR past as exclusive site of oppression and social injustice – as exemplified by the work of Kleinert and Beyer – which would appear to seek to remind people just how badly off they were then (Davidson 1997, 318), Hausmann's film takes on an even deeper significance.

While its reinvestment of the minutiae of East German life with a nostalgic sentimentality and humour positions the film firmly within the context of the *Ostalgie* debate, and the narration of a past many people would *like* to remember (Heimbach 1999. n.p), it also offers a radical revision of the cultural presentation of the East and a critical counterpoint to the devaluation of East German experiences after the fall of the Wall (Rall 1999, n.p). Its popularity, especially in the new federal regions, may truly attest to a contemporary readiness to reposition the East as cult (Peitz 1999, n.p), and a concomitant falsification of GDR past, but perhaps the very artifice of this self-consciously ironic trip down socialist memory lane filmed entirely on set at Berlin's Babelsberg studios, could be taken as wider metaphor for the surreal atmosphere of a claustrophobically oppressive and restrictive society, in which social reality was never anything but a politically mediated contingency (Peitz 1999, n.p). 'Guck mal! Ein Zoni!' (Look over there! A zoni!), remarks the stereotypically voyeuristic West German, as he trains his binoculars on the inhabitants of that 'other' world East Berlin, from his vantage point on the viewing platform of the Wall, and, as if unwilling to disappoint, both the GDR and its inhabitants put in a truly entertaining performance in this film. However, the elevated position occupied by the West Germans on *Mauerschau* is subsequently humorously debunked by the cinematic gaze reversal to the viewpoint of the East German protagonist watching the West German watching him. Not only does this force us to reflect upon our increasingly common positioning of the East as museum piece and its people as zoo animals, but also the ideological implications of western expectations of a filmically 'objective' portrayal of a 'liberated' people's political past.

Undoubtedly, the production of films dealing with the GDR past and the East German present has become increasingly common in the 1990s. From apparently harmless comic portrayals of national stereotypes, whose formulaic reliance on happy endings ensures that 'nach der Wende pflichtgemäß alles gut ausgeht' (after the 'change' everything must all go well, Knoben 2000, 10), to epic wall romances, which rearticulate the personal as political; from the dark *Totenreich* (kingdom of the dead) symbolism of critical biographies- such as Kleinert's *Wege in die Nacht* – to theatrical *Ostalgiefilme*, which prove that in the realm of cultural production nothing, including history, is safe from the forces of commodification. As Stuart Hall puts it: '[t]his year's radical symbol or slogan will be neutralised into next year's fashion; the year after, it will be the object of a profound cultural nostalgia' (1981, 235). However, alongside this normalization of the filmic depiction of the East exemplified by Volker Schlöndorff's *Die Stille nach dem Schuss* (2000), Andreas Dresen's *Die Polizisistin* (2000), and Vanessa

Jopp's *Vergiß Amerika* (2000), in which the eastern problematic has been relegated from narrative subject to filmic background, a shift of focus has taken place with regards to the notion of *Vergangenheitsbewältigung*. While the treatment of the Nazi past still remains of paramount interest in international reception of the German film treatments of history (Davidson 1997), and indeed, of German cinema in general (Ginsberg and Thompson 1996), there appears to be a contemporary willingness within Germany – as demonstrated by film-makers, critics and audiences alike – to transpose the problematics of national history eastwards. This is perhaps of particular relevance when viewed in the context of the racist attacks in Solingen, Mölln, Rostock and Hoyerswerda. In an increasingly tense and fractious social climate, the flux of new immigrants from the East has re-opened the immigration debate in Germany and raised some uncomfortable parallels with an apparently *bewältigt* (overcome) past. In this respect, any exploration of the reinscription of an East German imaginary within the national consciousness – which the post-*Wende* films could be seen as representing – must take into account the potential assimilation of social concerns regarding *Vergangenheitsbewältigung* with the *Aufarbeitung* (working through) of East German history. The dominance of filmic treatments of GDR past within the *Wende* film genre is undoubtedly deeply implicated in the process of reintegration of the two Germanies into a single and ideologically unified state. However, as Davidson points out, the therapeutic potential of this 'working through of the past' is not without ideological implications:

> The annexation and obliteration of the GDR brings with it a need for an 'overcoming of the past' ('Vergangenheitsbewältigung') in its own right, which, while absolutely necessary in some respects, also acts as a *de facto* legitimisation of West Germany's development.
>
> (1997, 318)

Academic and journalistic debates surrounding these films have tended to revolve around notions of narrative verisimilitude, the *Ostalgie* debate and the ideological imperatives behind the varying representations of the 'other' Germany. As a key cultural site of national identity representation and construction, it is imperative to investigate the extent of and willingness for a critical use of cinema to explore the relationship between East and West, past and present, and the forces of cultural legitimization which can be seen at work within those texts which do so.

'*Currywurst und Döner*'[11]: race relations and the 'Kanaksta'

As Ginsberg and Thompson point out in their discussion of the place of German Film Studies within the wider postmodern debate, 'German cinema' as subject of critical cinematic inquiry has always been a highly politicized field of study. Indeed, unlike other areas of cinematic enquiry concerned with the investigation of aspects of global social reality, German Cinema Studies has long since remained a discipline 'obsessed with the logic's of its own conceptual identity- the 'German' (Ginsberg and Thompson 1996, 5). As we have seen, German reunification has brought with it its own problems with regards to the cultural representation of national identity. Another contemporary cinematic film phenomenon, problematic to German film study's historical propensity towards the promotion of an ideal, normative concept of 'Germanness', and with its roots in the political cinema of the 1970s, is that of the *Immigrantenkino* (immigrant cinema). Situated around the success of Fatih Akin's 1997 internationally acclaimed 'Multikulti-Gangsterballade' (multicultural gangster-ballad, Suchsland 2001, n.p.) *Kurz und schmerzlos*, films such as Christian Baudisins' *Tadesse: Warum?* (1993), Roland Suso Richter's *Eine Hand voll Gras* (2000), Yüksel Yavuz's *Aprilkinder* (1998), Horst Sczerba's *Eine unmögliche Hochzeit* (1996) and Tevfik Baser's *40QM Deutschland* (1986) have reanimated the debate surrounding the portrayal of ethnic minorities within film and the possibility of a new wave of post-New German Cinema, third- and fourth-generation immigrant films, which extend beyond traditional formulations of *Kino der Fremdheit*, or socially oppositional *Problemfilm*, to allow for the exploration of the actual day to day reality of life between two cultures – a *cinéma du métissage*.

This theorization of the to and fro of cross-cultural exchange, which explores the ability of minority cultures to adapt, assimilate and resist dominant cultural discourses, is as relevant to the reunification of Germany and the summary 'integration' of the *neue Bundesländer* into the national (western) whole, as it is to the fate of the Germany's ethnic minorities. Essentially, both 'minority cultures' represent ideologically, socially and culturally devalued peoples who have fallen victim to the normalizing and othering forces of western, capitalist society. In a recent article in the German film magazine *EPD Film*, Georg Seeßeln investigates the history of the representation of immigrant voices in German and European film, focusing in particular on the recent rise in popularity and acclaim of the Turkish-German cinema. In films such as *Aprilkinder*, *Geschwister* (Thomas Arslan, 1996), *Hochzeit* (Antonia Lerch, 1996), the dramatic tension of the immigrant dilemma – caught as they are between the desire to maintain their own culture and the need to assimilate the new – is located in the family. Through the portrayal of family life, and more particularly, the conflicts that are fought out between the older immigrant generation and the younger naturalized Turkish-Germans, such films attempt to shed light on the codes and double meanings which constitute the means of communication between fellow inhabitants of this mixed, *métissage*-culture.

In Thomas Arslan's first film of a trilogy aimed at exploring the plight of second-and third-generation Turkish immigrants in Germany, *Geschwister*

(1996), the focus is almost exclusively on this younger generation and their struggle to find purpose and construct identities within the web of the often conflictual multicultural discourses to which they are exposed. Born of a German mother and Turkish father, 17-year old Leyla (Serpil Turhan) and her two older brothers, Ahmed (Savas Yurderi) and Erol (Tmer Yigit) have a particularly intimate experience of life between two cultures. Sevim (Mariam El Awat), Leyla's best friend, represents her only salvation from the deeply ambivalent relationship she has with her parents and brothers, and the tedious apprenticeship which she is serving out in a local textile factory. However, despite the shortcomings of their familial and social environment both Leyla and her brother Ahmed have, with the retraction of their dual nationality entitlement, opted for German citizenship. Erol's experience of life in the adopted culture is, however, even less positive. With no qualifications and an overwhelming compulsion to play the macho gangster, his ever-increasing debts and, resulting illegal activities, ultimately persuade him to opt for Turkish nationality. The film concludes, four weeks later, with Erol's departure for Turkey to complete his military service. The extent to which the problems of all three children in their attempts to assimilate the native culture, are cultural and not social is, however, extremely debatable. As Seeßeln points out, in the *Immigrantenkino* of the 1990s, '[d]ie kulturelle vermischt sich mit einer sozialen Marginalisierung' (the cultural merges with a social marginalization, 2000, 22), and both in *Geschwister* and Arslan's third feature film *Dealer* (1999), it is the deprivation of the social environments in which these Turkish protagonists live which ultimately represents the biggest hindrance to social and material betterment.

While occupying an alternative cinematic stratum which has up until now attracted much critical but little popular acclaim, films such as Arslan's have been essential in securing a visibility for themes hitherto excluded from the cultural sphere. Primarily concerned with the problematization of the social reality of immigrant populations, and the poverty which remains an integral part of this reality – as Seeßeln puts it, the 'Terra Inkognita der postindustriellen Gesellschaften' (terra icognita of the post-industrial societies, 2000, 27) – these films also constitute a critical counterbalance to an increasingly popular, mainstream Turkish-German cinema.

The international and domestic success of films such as Akin's *Kurz und schmerzlos* and Lars Becker's *Kanak Attack* (1999) testify to the increasingly fashionable status of Turkish-German culture (*Jung, deutsch …:* 2000). Akin's film opens with his main protagonist, Gabriel (Mehmet Kurtulus), the son of a Turkish immigrant, being released from jail. Following on from the opening credits – a montage of shadowy, anonymous street fighting and harsh technofied Turkish-German folk music – the machismic performance of Gabriel's reunion with his hood buddies, 'Costa the Greek' (Adam Bousdoukos) and 'Bobby the Serb' (Aleksandar Jovanovic), sets the scene for a film about multicultural male bonding, violence and crime, all set against the backdrop of urban ghetto life. In line with the consciously evoked filmic markers of the gangster genre – from the elaborate and performative male greeting rituals, the repeated fetishized preoccupation with the gun, the positioning of protagonists within a seedy underworld, and the constant reassertion of their willing and effective recourse to violence – the film is clearly more concerned with the delivery of an exciting, punchy narrative and the sympathetic poratrayal of its three macho, heroic social misfits, than it is with any social study of the environmental, cultural and economic realties responsible for the narrative's final downward spiral into crime and violence. While succeeding in a powerful evocation of personal tragedy – through its exploration of the bonds of male friendship which ultimately seal Gabriel's re-entry into the criminal underworld – any social message the film may attempt is obscured by its phallocentric love affair with the trappings and narrative progressions of the gangster film. In the social environment inhabited by the three friends, the pressure to constantly perform and reassert their masculinity is apparently unrelenting. As such 'Bobby the Serb's' ultimate defection to the perceived glamour of the Albanian(!) mafia is merely a question of time. However, the fundamental question of the origin of this pressure to revert to overtly reactionary formulations of masculine identity – whether cultural, social, or merely a matter of personal choice – is lost in the film's more pressing agenda to celebrate macho posturing and male camaraderie. Not even the film's tragic and bloody conclusion – equally, a generic norm of the gangster movie – can efface the primacy of this narrative focus.

In this respect, while films such as *Kurz und schmerzlos* and *Kanak Attack* have been responsible for the introduction of the new immigrant cinema to a much larger mainstream audience, they often flirt dangerously with a semiotic unity of representation which casts Turk as gangster and environment as ghetto, while resisting any true critical engagement with the socio-political realities which give rise to this social marginalization. In this respect, German cinema's revived *Immigrantenkino*, and in particular, the *Kanak-Spraak* of new Turkish-German film, highlights popular culture's fundamental dialectic as site of both resistance and consent. To quote John Storey, 'culture is a terrain on which there takes place a continual struggle over meaning(s), in which subordinate groups attempt to resist the imposition of meanings which bear the interests of dominant groups' (1998, xii). However, whether integrated into the dominant discourse – or rather, the commercial mainstream as exemplified by Fatih Akin's most recent feature, *Im Juli* (2000), starring Moritz Bleibtreu and Christiane Paul, and replacing the problematic theme of immigrant cultures with the generic conventions of mainstream romance – or left on the alternative fringes of the cultural mainstream, the plight of film-maker attempting a broadening of the public sphere through their representation of otherwise excluded voices, is highly problematic. This represents the fundamental dilemma of the new, critically dubbed 'Kanak-Bewegung' (Kanak movement). By remaining on the fringes, these films allow themselves to be marginalized as dissident voices whose reality and concerns need have no impact on the problem-free collective 'we' of mainstream cinematic representation, while, if commercially successful, they risk incorporation into the cinematic mainstream where they invariably fall prey to the economic and ideological imperatives of dominant interest groups. Even if they do succeed in retaining their focus on the socially marginalized there is also the additional danger that they will contribute to a 'hardening of existing boundaries, as the "Problemfilm" becomes increasingly associated with "others"' (Davidson 1997, 319) and the traditional positioning of immigrant as victim.

The future of German film studies

> The aim is to come to a balanced assessment of recent German film, and to gain a better understanding of opposition in cultural production as a process in late capitalism that is marked by progressive and conservative, challenging and legitimating elements.
>
> (Davidson 1997, 309)

Situated within a cinematic age, a critical cultural study must orient itself to the cinematic narratives and images which define the times, whether apparently implicated in the ideological imperatives and film critical discourses of a commercial mainstream or an oppositional alternative. It is in this context that my investigation into the ideological implications of the representation of gendered, national and racial identities, in 1990s' German cinema, seeks to reanimate the debate surrounding the significance of this latest reincarnation of the 'young German film' and open it up to new and critically attentive practices of reading. Only when we transcend simplistic demarcations of aesthetic boundaries can we begin to move toward an understanding of cinematic image and narration as central to the construction of cultural identity.

Notes

1. Laurens Straub quoted by Eric Rentschler (Jacobsen, *et al.* 1993, 285)
2. The deconstruction of essentializing theories of idenitity formation has been conducted in a variety of disciplinary areas, all of which are critical of the notion of an integral or unified identity (Hall, 1996, 1).
3. This corresponds to Raymond Williams' theorization of the canonization process. In his essay, 'Analysis of Culture' (1961, 55–70), he attempts to denaturalize and demystify the apparently objective process of canonization. Williams saw this process as traditionally founded upon an 'ideal' definition of culture. In other words, a view of culture as the peak of human perfection. The 'selective tradition' describes the ideologically implicated process through which cultural

texts, be they literary or artistic, are chosen to represent the dominant cultural content of a particular historical period.

4. John Fiske makes clear the basic assumption of British Cultural Studies in his definition of 'culture' as 'neither aesthetic nor humanist in emphasis, but political' (1996, 115).

5. In 1996 the German film industry was celebrating a 16 per cent market share of domestic film production. This represented a significant turnaround turnaround from the steady decline which saw the German film drop from a 48 per cent share of the domestic market in 1927, to 25 per cent in 1956, and then into the post-1971 period of unchallenged American dominance with a 1993 low of 8.4 per cent.

6. This term, originally cited by Georg Seesseln in an article for *Die Zeit* (1997, p.56), has come to represent a body of films which centre their slapstick narrative trajectories around the misadventures of uncouth, lower-class males, as typified by Tom Gerhard's popular successes *Voll Normaal* (1994) and sequel *Ballerman 6* (1997).

7. Gerhard Neckermann, author of market studies for Germany's Federal Film Board, points out the revision of film production and marketing strategies that this change in audience demographics has prompted. 'Women and children have become central target groups' (20). 'All our marketing campaigns for films that could appeal to women are directed at them first' (Hagen 1996, 20).

8. This term, often used in opposition to the representation of women and women's issues in a more traditional avant-garde, explicitly feminist context, has gained increasing parlance in the contemporary debate surrounding the representation of women within mainstream cinema, and indeed, within mainstream popular culture in general (Moi 1989). I have taken it to imply a meta-genre of mainstream cultural texts, which centre women as subjects of representation and consumption, and thus connect with the feminist project of making women and women's issues visible. In this instance I read the term as carrying with it no preconceptions as to the relative progressive or regressive nature of this representation.

9. Eve Sedgwick (1985) develops the notion of 'homosociality' to account for the nature and significance of male/male relationships as represented in the mid-eighteenth- to mid-nineteenth-century novel. Sedgwick explores the power structures which this system of relations has historically held in place, and the implication of this for women.

10. Films such as Peter Timm's *Go Trabi Go* (1991), Manfred Stelzer's *Gruß Gott, Genosse* (1991), Heiko Schier's *Alles Luege* (1991), Manfred Stelzer's *Superstau* (1991), Vadim Glowna's *Der Brocken* and Peter Kahane's *Cosimas Lexikon* (1991). For a fuller list see: Knoben (2000, 10–13).

11. This title is a direct reference to Cem Özdemir's 1999 book *Currywurst und Döner. Integration in Deutschland.*

References

Der Spiegel 1993: Tempo, Tempo, Tempo: Die Regisseurin Katja von Garnier über ihren Überaschungserfolg *Abgeschminkt*. (6 September), 375.
Der Spiegel 1996: Das Lachen macht's. (16 June), 214–25.
Living Marxism 1996: Girl Power: Safe Spice. (November).
2000: Jung, deutsch und türkisch (18 September), (3sat.de), Available: http://www.3sat.de/specials/09883/index.html (Accessed: 2001, April 1)
BAUDRILLARD, J. 1990: *Cool memories.* London: Verso.

BHABHA, HOMI. K. 1996: Cultures-in-between. In HALL, S. and DU GAY, P. (eds), *Questions of identity*. London: Sage, 53–60.
BUTLER, J. 1990: *Gender trouble*. New York: Routledge.
BUTLER, J. 1993: *Bodies that matter: on the discursive limits of 'sex'*. New York: Routledge.
CAPRIO, T. 1997: Women's cinema in the 1990s: 'Abgeschminkt' and happy ends? *Seminar* 33, 4, 374–87.
COURY, D.N. 1997: From aesthetics to commercialism – narration and the new German comedy. *Seminar*, 33,4, 356–73.
DAVIDSON, J. 1997: Overcoming Germany's past(s) in film since the 'Wende'. *Seminar*, v 33, 4, 307–21.
DENZIN, N. 1991: *Images of postmodern society*. London: Sage.
DYERS, R. 1979: *Stars*. London: British Film Institute.
ELSAESSER, T. with WEDEL, M. 1999: *The BFI companion to German cinema*. London: British Film Institute.
FISKE, J. 1996: *Cultural studies and the study of popular culture*. Edinburgh: Edinburgh University Press.
FISKE, J. 1989: *Reading the popular*. Boston: Unwin Hyman.
FISKE, J. 1996: British cultural studies and television. In STOREY, J. (ed), *What is cultural studies?: a reader*. London: Edward Arnold, 115–146.
GAINES, J. 1995: Feminist heterosexuality and its politically incorrect pleasures. *Critical Inquiry* 21, 382–410.
GINSBERG, T. and THOMPSON, M. 1996: New perspectives on German cinema. *Perspectives on German cinema*. New York: G. K. Hall.
HAGEN, B. 1996: Women control Pic picks. *Variety*, 1 (August 19–25), 20.
HALL, S. 1981: Notes on deconstructing the popular. In SAMUEL, R. (ed.) *People's history and socialist theory*. London: Routledge and Kegan Paul, 227–40.
HALL, S. 1996: Introduction: who needs identity? In HALL, S. and DU GAY, P. (eds), *Questions of identity*. London: Sage, 1–17.
HEIMBACH, A. 1999: Die Republik der Spaßvögel. *Deutsches Allgemeines Sonntagsblatt* (8 October).
HORAK, J-C. 1997: Die Tradition des deutschen Films. In AMEND, H. and BUTOW, M. (eds) *Der bewegte Film*. Berlin: Vistas, 13–24.
JACOBSEN, W. 1993: Filme der achtziger Jahre. In JACOBSEN, W., KAES, A. and PRINZLER, H.H. (eds), *Geschichte des deutschen Films*. Stuttgart: Metzler.
KILB, A. 1996: Ein allerletzter Versuch, die neue deutsche Filmkomödie zu Verstehen. *Die Zeit* (26 April).
KILB, A. 1995: Zahme Herzen. *Die Zeit* (17 February).
KLINGER, B. 1995: Cinema/ideology/criticism revisited: the progressive genre. In GRANT, B.K. (ed), *Film genre reader II*. Austin: University of Texas Press, 74–90.
KNOBEN, M. 2000: Sie kamen als Freunde und wurden zu Wurst. *EPD Film*. 8, 10–13.
KNOBEN, M. 1999: Wege in die Nacht. *EPD Film*, 12, 50–1.
LITSCHKE-MCNAB, U. and HANSON, K. 1997: Introduction. *Seminar*, 33, 4, 283–9.
MOI, T. 1989: Feminist, female, feminine. In BELSEY and MOORE, J. (eds) *The feminist reader*. London: Macmillan Education, 117–32.
NEALE, S. and KRUTNIK, F. 1990: *Popular film and television comedy*. London: Routledge.
PEITZ, C. 1999: Alles so schön grau hier. *Die Zeit* (4 November).
RADWAY, J. 1987: *Reading the romance*. London: Verso.
RALL, V. 1999: Der surreal existierende Sozialismus. *Frankfurter Rundschau* (October 7).

SAID, E. 1994: *Representations of the intellectual*. London: Vintage.

SCHENK, R. 1996: Neu im Kino: Nikolaikirche. *Filmdienst*, 4, 16–17.

SEDGWICK, E. 1985: *Between men: English literature and male homosocial desire*, New York: Columbia University Press.

SEEßELN, G. 2000: Das Kino der doppelten Kulturen. *EPD Film*, 12, 22–8.

SHUMWAY, D.R. 1995: Screwball comedies. In GRANT, B.K. (ed), *Film genre reader II*. Austin: University of Texas Press.

STACEY, J. 1994: *Star gazing: Hollywood cinema and female spectatorship*. London: Routledge.

WILLIAMS, R. 1961: The analysis of culture. In WILLIAMS. R. *The long revolution*. London: Chatto and Windus, 55–70.

|13|

Mediascapes

BY HOLGER BRIEL

Media have become an intrinsic part of the world humans inhabit. In fact, so much so that it would seem unthinkable to a large part of the world population to live without them. While there are still broad swathes of the earth whose inhabitants do not have access to media, many of whom having never seen, let alone used, a telephone, read a newspaper or used the Internet, this is obviously not the case for North America, Europe and other economically more developed countries[1]. Germany is by far the largest media market in Europe. An encounter with German media is vital if one wants to get a better understanding of Germany, its (media) cultures and its relationships to its European neighbours. Furthermore, in an age of decreasing national and increasing transnational foci, global and local forces encounter each other in these mediascapes. The question of exactly how this scenario is played out within German media will be the subject of this chapter.

Media, and this is the definition which will be used for the remainder of this text, will mean the channels for printed and electronic mass distributed information, especially newspapers, magazines, films, television, radio and the Internet. While there are other media to consider, such as theatres (which actually were the beginning of mass disseminations of ideas in ancient Greece), arguably it is the aforementioned that most strongly shape modern-day German society in a technically mediated manner[2] (see Chapter 11).

The rise of the mass media can be traced to the European invention/usage of the printing press in the fifteenth century,[3] enabling the dissemination of information to large parts of the population for the first time. Since media then were by and large graphocentric media, written discourse, this was of course only the case for those who had acquired the skill of reading and writing, something which for the most part would take some time, centuries actually (see Chapter 2). Already in its inception, therefore, mass media were co-dependant on technology, technology here understood not only as mechanical devices, but also as the skills needed to decode that which was disseminated.[4]

Today, Germany, like most other European states, has a large number of media available, as shown in Table 13.1.

Table 13.1   General media available in Germany in 1998[1]

	Number	Users in millions
TV programmes[2]	ca. 94	33.5*
Radio programmes[3]	227	37.5
Daily newspapers	402	30.1
Weekly newspapers	25	2.2
General magazines/journals	778	142.1
Trade/Professional journals	1,029	25.4
Advertising flyers/leaflets	1,316	84.0

Notes: [1] In Werbung in Deutschland, ZAW, 1998
[2] Federal and regional TV programmes
[3] Federal, regional and local
* 14 years of age or older
Source: Adapted from www.br-online.de/br-intern/medienforschung

Even more striking, Germany has the largest free TV market in the world, with over 40 TV programmes and hundreds of radio programmes available free of charge via satellite and terrestrial broadcasting. Satellite broadcasting in particular has increased German television and radio's catchment area to many more areas than only those in the centre of Europe and inhabited by 120 million-plus German speakers. Walking into a conveyor-belt sushi bar in Leicester Square, London, it is not unusual to catch the German version of MTV, English language interviews and lyrics subtitled in German. Already this small example shows the convergence of media markets worldwide, a fact which has a strong impact on the notion of the local and the global when and where media are concerned.

In the following sections, these media will be discussed in detail. Often, quantitative methods will be used to make a point. While this is not the only way to discuss present-day media (more qualitative, individualized methods spring to mind), the strong mass-media component in the media discussed strongly suggests such an analysis in the first instance.

Print media

Turning to individual media, historically the earliest one is of course the book. To state it quite emphatically, books must be assigned a prominent place in the dissemination of information, and for the longest period, they were considered to be the *Leitmedium* (leading/main medium) *par excel-*

lence, the storage medium for cultural information. While this monopoly has been put under strong pressure from newer, more adaptable storage spaces for written information, their position is so entrenched that it seems safe for now. Table 13.2 verifies this by highlighting the sheer number of books produced in Germany over the last quarter of a century or so.

Table 13.2   Book production in Germany, 1970–98

Year	Total	First Imprint	Reprint	Ratio First Imprint: Reprint	Soft Cover Percentage
1970	47,096	8,703	8,393	82:18	8.4
1975	43,649	35,486	8,163	81:19	11.4
1980	67,176	54,572	12,604	81:19	11.6
1985	57,623	45,000	12,623	78:22	14.2
1990	61,015	44,779	16,236	73:27	16.9
1991	67,908	48,897	19,011	72:28	17.4
1992	67,277	48,836	18,441	73:27	17.2
1993	67,206	49,096	18,110	73:27	16.5
1994	70,643	52,767	17,876	75:25	15.8
1995	74,174	53,359	20,815	72:28	16.4
1996	71,515	53,793	17,722	75:25	14.6
1997	77,889	57,680	20,209	74:26	9.1[1]
1998	78,042	57,678	20,364	75:26	9.5[1]

Notes: [1]Basis: First imprint
From 1991 onward, the new *Länder* are included
Source: Börsenverein des Deutschen Buchhandels e. V.: Buch und Buchhandel in Zahlen
1999; in: *Media Perspektiven*, Basisdaten, 1999, adapted from
www.br-online.de/br-intern/medienforschung

As can be seen from Table 13.2, book production has increased by approximately one-third in 28 years. German speakers have always been avid readers and the amount of books produced does speak for this fact. While in West Germany, to be well read always carried a strong cachet; in the East the reasons for this were more complex. For one, there were not as many other media vying for attention as there were in the West. And it was also felt that the reading of literature in particular was a way of both resistance to and escapism from a politically over-bearing system. What has changed, however, and this a global trend, is the ratio of new books to reprints. If in 1975 it was 5:1, it had dwindled to 4:1 in 1998, highlighting the increasing re-usage of older texts and the economic need of publishing houses to reproduce best-sellers which after all are their all important day-to-day money-makers.

At the end of the eighteenth century, media played a decisive role in the shaping of society, namely by creating a *public sphere* to begin with, a social process well described for Germany by the philosopher Jürgen Habermas (1990).[5] At this time, resistance to media by the authorities was a common thing and media have continued to be in contention. This, of course, was to do with their ability to shape, move and change 'public' opinion. But it was only in the nineteenth century that mass media became part of daily life, mostly due to the invention of faster printing presses churning out more copies and the increasing ability of people to read and write. The same century also saw the major inventions that would shape media in the twentieth century – photography, radio, cinema, gramophone.

Turning to the more immediate present, the structure of German mediascapes[6] has undergone at least two major changes over the past 50 years or so. First, after the end of the Second World War in 1945, when German media were thoroughly restructured by the Allies, and then once again in 1989, when the two Germanies united.

In 1945, the Allies introduced media systems into the occupied zones that were already present in their home countries. For example, the American sector received press and broadcasting in line with American private broadcasting and press standards, in the British sector the BBC broadcasting system was introduced, and the French adopted a more centralized system. As a common basis, all three western Allies shared the sentiment that the one thing to be avoided at all cost was a completely centralised press and broadcasting system as had existed in Joseph Goebbels' *Reichspropagandaministerium* (see Chapter 2). Today media theorists stress the need for decentralized systems. Appadurai stresses that globalizing and localizing processes, or 'global homogenization' and 'heterogenization' feed and reinforce each other rather than being mutually exclusive, and calls for more anthropological studies on the 'production of locality' (1996).

It had been largely due to the iron grip on media that Hitler had been able to exert control over most of the German people. And this was not to be repeated. A similar centralization, however, was the lynchpin of the Soviet occupied zone mediascape, a fact which would not change until German unification in 1989. West German legislation mirrored the feelings of the Western Allies: regional newspapers were introduced, such as the *Süddeutsche Zeitung*, the *Frankfurter Allgemeine Zeitung* and a host of local newspapers; in broadcasting, the authority for radio and television stations lay with the *Länder* and not with the federal government. By and large, these regionalized standards have survived quite well and are still in place today, as witnessed by the sheer number of newspapers and journals (see Table 13.3).

Despite electronic media muscling in on print media, the former nevertheless seem to be holding their own; while the number of newspapers has decreased slightly, the number of magazines has almost quadrupled over the past 25 years. Several contributory factors can be cited in this development: a broadening of the market and an ever-increasing wish of the public to receive more specialized information; the rise of new subjects, such as computers and health awareness; and, finally, a new interest in magazines due to new layout techniques, e.g. postmodern moves such as firstly inaugurated in

Table 13.3 Newspapers and journals' circulation, 1980–99*

	1975	1980	1985	1990	1991	1992	1996	1997	1998	1999
Newspapers										
Daily Newspapers										
Number	410	407	395	394	419	426	408	402	398	394
Copies sold in millions	21.5	24.1	25.1	24.7	28.8	30.9	29.9	29.4	29.0	29.0
Weekly newspapers										
Number	56	48	47	29	29	31	27	25	27	23
Copies sold in millions	1.8	1.8	1.8	1.8	1.9	2.2	2.1	2.0	2.1	2.0
Journals/Magazines										
General										
Number	223	271	369	565	596	619	758	778	809	835
Copies sold in millions	69.7	84.6	96.1	109.7	121.7	121.0	127.6	127.2	126.5	127.0
Trade/professional journals										
Number	658	745	779	903	921	951	983	1,029	1,080	1,083
Copies sold in millions	19.5	15.0	13.0	16.0	16.1	16.7	16.7	17.1	17.1	17.3

Note: *From 1991, the new Länder are included
Source: IVW-Auflagenlisten; in Media Perspektiven Basisdaten, 1999, quoted at www.br-online.de/br-intern/medienforschung

the 1980s in the British magazine *The Face*, and then retooled for the German speaking market in *Wiener* and *Tempo* (now defunct, yet hugely influential in their time).

The second upheaval of the German print mediascapes was ushered in by unification in 1989. All of a sudden, a new market of 16 million people opened up for West German media conglomerates, which were, of course, eager to exploit it. While most Easterners had had some (by GDR laws illegal) exposure to West German television, West German print media, with their heavy dependence on glossy glitz and advertising, were a novelty for the East. Very quickly, East German newspapers were bought up by and/or consolidated into the holdings of West German media companies, with only few independents remaining. Even a wave of *Ostalgie* (Eastern nostalgia) was not able to turn the tide, leading to a contracted East German print media market. Despite the fact that ca. 90 per cent of the German population state that they read a newspaper at least once a week, the number of copies sold has decreased since 1993 by 11.7 per cent (Schütz 2000).

Electronic media and broadcasting[7]

Turning to electronic media, by now cinema and film have had over a hundred years to establish themselves as cultural mainstays. In the beginning of its meteoric rise, cinema was violently opposed by representatives of the print media, who feared losing their clientele. In the 1970s, fostered by the cultural changes of the 1960s, this resistance crumbled and film was able to claim a stake in the cultural high ground, returning to a point which it had already occupied once before, namely during the Weimar Republic. With the establishment of the *Neuer Deutscher Film* and the *Autorenkino*, with directors such as Werner Herzog, Wim Wenders and Alexander Kluge leading the way, film was recognized as an important cultural ideological battlefield and given its theoretical due. As had been the case with books, within a German context the medium of film was charged with a definite pedagogical mission, similar to that prescribed for the theatre ever since Lessing and Schiller's days. While the theoreticians of high culture did finally admit film into the pantheon of high art, the price that film had to pay was also high: The only film 'texts' scrutinized were avant-garde films. Not surprisingly, audiences remained unconvinced, a fact, which was actually seen as a badge of honour, handed out by the cultural avant-garde. However, by the 1980s things had changed, with theory also looking at the still tellingly named '*Trivivalkultur*' (trivial or low culture), including its books, television programmes and films. Theoretical underpinnings were such that the purely pedagogical factor of high culture (to better its consumers) was weighed against the entertainment value of more popular texts. An important instance in this regard was the arrival of Doris Dörrie's

Männer (1985), a seminal film dubbed 'the first German comedy', which was a success with both national and international critics and audiences alike. Audiences began to return to German cinemas, and German film production picked up[8] (see Chapter 12). After unification in 1989, a whole barrage of comedies of varying quality was produced, often thematizing unification or post-unification social phenomena. If cinemas seemed to be destined for a slow death from the late 1950s onward, largely due to the arrival of televisions, the cinema market recuperated nicely, a trend which is continuing today (Table 13.4).

Table 13.4 Numbers of German cinemas and seats, 1996–98

	1996	1997	1998
Cinema screens	4,035	4,128	4,244
Seats total	760,282	772,515	801,314
Per screen	188	187	189
Tickets sold	143,121,670	132,885,491	148,875,873

Source: www.statistik-bund.de

Despite the slump in 1997, the upward trend continues. Yet, in spite of the increased production of German films, and here we enter one of the more contentious issues surrounding modern media, the number of German films screened once again began to decline. It seems that the Hollywood studio system was and remains just too powerful to resist. Despite efforts by the European Union and the German Federal Government to freely subsidize European productions, audiences continue to prefer American films.[9] The case of Germany is not an exception here; rather, it is the norm. The internationalization (or, to be more precise, the Americanization of international culture) continues unabated on a global level.[10]

Germans spend a large chunk of their time engrossed in both print and electronic media. In 2000, the average media usage in Germany was as follows: newspapers 30 minutes, magazines 10 minutes, books 18 minutes, TV 198 minutes, radio 209 minutes, video 2 minutes, CDs/audio tape 22 minutes, computer 12 minutes. Audio-visual media therefore account for an average of 443 minutes a day, over 7 hours. This figure is up from 296 minutes in 1987, which means that on the average, Germans spent an extra two hours with the media today compared to the figure from 13 years ago (adapted from www.ard.de/ard_intern/ mediendaten).

Germans, just like other nationalities, have taken to television in a major way and made it their number one mass medium. There exist ca. 41 TV channels in German, of which almost all are Free-TV; during prime time (in Germany roughly from 8–10 o'clock in the evening), an average of 6.5 million television sets are switched on. Table 13.5 shows just how prevalent television has become.

Table 13.5   Radio and television sets in Germany, 1998–2000

Beginning of	Radios 1998	1999	2000	Televisions 1998	1999	2000
Millions of sets	37.52	38.23	39.16	33.52	34.05	34.72
Growth from previous year in	1.4	1.9	2.4	1.4	1.6	2.0
Sets per 1000 inhabitants	457	466	477	408	415	423

Source: www.ard.de/ard_intern/mediendaten

Over the past 30 years or so, there were several major changes affecting German broadcasting. The first one was the re-introduction[11] of television in Germany in the early 1950s, when the Football World Cup Final of 1954 proved to be a nationally galvanizing event. It was screened live and Germany won, a fact which allowed for collective national pride for the first time since 1945. Moreover, this victory was also the victory of televisual technology, associating the transmission technology with the actual event screened. While those national media events became a firm feature of the 1950s, 1960s and 1970s, due to the proliferation of programmes, such events have become increasingly rare, a phenomenon which has splintered the whole of the broadcasting market.

Another turning point one can distinguish was the beginning of colour broadcasts in the late 1960s, providing a clear watershed for television production and consumption. It cannot be stressed enough how this new colourful 'presence' relegated everything before 1967 into a black and white past, in effect de-colorizing the world's visual archives. The fierce debate over the colorization of black and white films with the arrival of new technology in the 1980s only stresses this fact. After all, what was at stake here was the colour of our past.

A further huge battle loomed in the 1980s when private television stations entered the market. Unforgotten was the statement of then chancellor Helmut Schmidt that private television was 'more dangerous than atom bomb'. And so it also seemed to the German monopolist public broadcasters. Private television providers seemed to threaten the hard-won victories over the more liberal and privately financed American broadcasting system during the creation of the German broadcasting system. This system of *öffentlich-rechtlicher Rundfunk* (public broadcasting) had been modelled on the BBC, having at its heart a decentralized system, with each German *Land* granted content sovereignty over its broadcasting stations. These stations in turn were governed by a representative sample of their listeners/viewers, with churches, political parties, citizens and politicians all having a say.[12] This finely balanced system was now under threat from private stations. Nevertheless, private radio and television stations finally did receive their licence, but with heavy restrictions placed upon them.

What became very clear right from the onset of private broadcasting was the immediate trend of consumers moving away from the public broadcasting station toward private stations, a trend which is continuing today, as Table 13.6 indicates.

Once again, politics had struggled to keep up with technology and had lost. Satellite distribution systems had not been part of the original blueprint for broadcasting media. For one, their reach and distribution area was much harder to control. True, broadcasting had always had this trans-national propensity. One only has to look at border regions where bordering national broadcasters were able to broadcast their programmes, Radio Luxemburg for instance, or even foreign stations broadcasting from within Germany, such as the American Forces Network (AFN), whose influence in the willing Americanization of German culture cannot be underestimated. One can even think about short-wave and long-wave radio in general. But Europe under *Astra* and *Eutelsat* satellites meant that anybody with a satellite receiver and dish could receive the same TV programme with impeccable quality, from the Canaries to Russia, from Iceland to Turkey.[13] Furthermore, these programmes often included subjects deemed politically incorrect in their various home countries. It was feared that they would be built on the most common denominator, screening sex, violence and other unsavoury topics which would undermine the pedagogically lofty goals set by German public broadcasting programmers. Leaving aside whether these goals were ever reached, even under the public broadcasting monopoly, early satellite TV appeared to prove its detractors right. As a precautionary measure, the German legislature had required satellite operators to include all German stations on their satellites for free, which meant that there are still over 40 German television stations which can be received for free via satellite. While there still are many programmes or channels which might be considered 'problematic', competition forced the erstwhile monopolist public broadcasters to improve their own programmes, in the final analysis, benefiting the consumers of their products. In this regard, the perceived gap in the screening of films (which especially in early TV days was already viewed with suspicion, since films possibly subtracted from the pedagogical aims of television, yet conversely had the highest audience numbers) between the more entertainment-oriented private channels and the public channels proves to be unjustified; in 1998 the private stations screened 5697 films, compared with 5167 films screened by public stations. The gap is certainly not as significant as is usually imagined.

Furthermore, cultural initiatives led to the conception of such stations as the Franco-German *ARTE* station, based in Strasbourg and broadcasting in German and French, and the German-Austrian-Swiss station *3Sat*. Even collaborations on a pan-European scale were attempted, however, with varying results.[14] Today these efforts continue in the guise of the relatively successful *Euronews* and *Eurosport*.

Another important change brought about by the advent of private television was that the German regulatory broadcasting authorities strengthened the regional television structures through the introduction of cable projects,

Table 13.6   Percentage of German TV viewers, 1990–2001

14–49 years	1990	1991	1992	1993	1994	1995	1996	1997	1998	1999	2000	2001
ARD	28.7	24.5	19.6	14.7	13.6	11.1	10.9	10.7	11.2	9.8	9.6	9.0
ZDF	24.9	21.2	17.1	12.9	11.9	9.6	9.5	8.5	9.0	8.2	8.2	8.0
RTL	14.6	16.6	19.2	21.1	19.7	20.1	19.3	18.5	17.8	17.8	17.2	16.8
SAT.1	10.1	11.8	13.6	15.2	14.8	14.9	13.8	13.4	12.9	12.8	12.0	11.9
PRO 7	1.8	5.5	9.0	12.8	13.8	14.6	14.3	14.7	13.9	13.5	13.4	14.4
Kabel 1	–	–	–	–	2.1	3.5	4.1	4.4	4.7	5.3	5.4	5.9
RTL 2	–	–	–	–	4.7	5.7	5.7	5.3	5.0	5.7	7.2	5.8
Super RTL	–	–	–	–	–	–	1.7	2.1	2.6	2.3	2.2	2.5
VOX	–	–	–	–	2.4	2.9	3.6	3.9	3.7	3.9	3.9	4.0
TELE 5	7.6	8.4	7.9	–	–	–	–	–	–	–	–	–
tm 3	–	–	–	–	–	–	0.6	0.5	0.7	1.2	1.1	0.9
Dritte	4.4	4.9	6.0	6.2	6.7	7.6	8.4	8.3	8.3	8.1	7.9	8.5
DSF	–	–	–	0.9	0.8	1.1	1.0	0.9	1.2	1.1	1.3	1.1
Eurosport	1.9	1.6	2.1	1.8	1.3	1.4	1.4	1.1	1.3	1.2	0.9	0.8
arte	–	–	–	0.2	0.2	0.3	0.4	0.3	0.3	0.4	0.3	0.3
KI.KA	–	–	–	–	–	–	–	0.5	0.7	0.6	0.6	0.5
3 sat	1.3	1.5	1.4	1.4	1.1	0.9	0.8	0.9	0.8	0.7	0.7	0.7
n-tv	–	–	–	–	0.4	0.4	0.5	0.6	0.7	0.8	0.8	0.6
Nickelodeon	–	–	–	–	–	–	0.3	0.4	–	–	–	–

Source: www.tv-quoten.de

the so-called *Offene Kanäle* or *Bürgerfernsehen* (open or public access channels), of which there are currently 62 in existence all over Germany. These
channels, funded by a percentage of the TV licence fee, provide an opportunity for everybody to create their own TV programmes, giving instructions
on how to shoot a film, selecting topics and general technical support. In
this way, many people have been able to participate in the public TV
domain. In the process, they learned more about television making and how
it is able to exert influence, thereby blurring the line between producer and
consumer and heightening the ability of viewers/producers to understand
what it is exactly that they are viewing.

Young people in particular seem to be interested in these projects. Being
the avid media consumers they are, they also drift towards the variety particularly offered by private stations. Daily soaps and sitcoms are the preferred programmes of German-speaking 12–19 year olds, with private
stations *Pro7* (29 per cent) and *RTL* (22) occupying positions one and two
in their preference scale, followed by the German music station *Viva* (16
per cent). Public stations do not play a large role in their visual menu.
Least-liked programmes are political, scientific and cultural programmes
(MeFo-Info 1/97 und 2/97, quoted at http://www.br-online.de/br-
intern/medienforschung/md_allgemein/jugend_medien.html). The average
number of viewers between 14–49 years of age watching the two flagships
of German television news, *Tagesthemen* (ARD) and *Heute Journal* (ZDF)
declined from 1.6 million for *Heute Journal* and 1.25 for *Tagesthemen* in
1992 to 0.7 and less than 0.2 respectively in January 2001 (Heiter bis
wolkig . . ., *TVSpielfilm*, 23 August 2001).

While these figures seem to paint a 'gloomy' picture of young Germans'
viewing preferences, what needs to be stressed here is that this hierarchy of
viewing preferences (news > factual subjects > literary films > 'bad' films,
etc.) no longer applies. In particular, the younger generation has had the
chance to become media savvy in a way older generations did not and it is
therefore generally more able to differentiate between realities and fantasies,
certainly much more readily than their less-mediated elders. What was
lacking until very recently in German media research were discussions about
this canon and hierarchy – why does a soap opera have less intrinsic value
than a news programme?, how is violence perceived?, etc. Fortunately, with
the proliferation of programmes, these discussions have by now begun to do
away with the prescriptive media views exerted by researchers who still
mostly trained as graphocentrists, i.e. researchers who were used to dealing
with the written word as prime cultural artefact and then had to slowly and
grudgingly concede the increasing importance of (moving) pictures for
German cultural spheres. Recently, German media studies have come into
their own, beginning to decode the system of electronic broadcasting, along
with most of its sub-sets, such as advertising, market research, conglomera-
tion of media houses, audience research, etc. Furthermore, the lack of interest in politics that many young people seemingly display does not

necessarily reflect badly upon their own choices; rather, it questions the biases of present-day politics. If the term 'Big Brother' is removed from its political Orwellian terminology and becomes a the synonym for Reality-TV, then this raises serious questions for our society, but perhaps not quite in the way the Orwellian fraction would have us believe.[15]

There do exist significant changes, however, in viewing habits not only between different age groups, but also between genders. Gender studies has become a rapidly expanding field in media studies.[16] One such area of inquiry has for instance been the problematization of the traditional gender divide between magazine readers (women) and newspaper readers (men). While there is still a certain valence in this gender divide (often fostered by publishers and advertising companies who appreciate a stable grouping of addressees), the postmodern proliferation of magazines has contributed to a more permeable media relationship between the sexes. Such is also the case for TV and Cinema. The new frontier of Internet communication has also contributed to new phenomena in this regard, prompting such practices as on-line gender switching and he-mail and she-mail, which seem to elicit distinct and different linguistic markers along gender lines.

Furthermore, there exist pronounced differences in media consumption between various geographic regions in Germany. Most pronounced is the East – West difference, with East Germans watching up to 41 minutes longer television per day than their western counterparts (in 2000, age group 50–64) (www.ard.de/ard_intern/mediendaten). As was the case already with newspapers, it seems that people in the new *Länder* are less interested in general social goings-on than the inhabitants in West Germany. East Germans of lower income brackets also spent more money on electronic media equipment than their counterparts in the West. While even people who do not normally watch it generally acknowledge the necessity of the universal news coverage provided by the public service broadcasting system, its viewers are ageing fast, raising serious questions about the public sphere as a whole. Moreover, this fact also questions the notion of 'prime time', which in Germany traditionally started with *Tagesthemen* at eight o'clock in the evening and continued until ten. It seems that the ubiquity of 24–hour news programmes on stations such as *N24* or *N-TV* have eroded these structures, and while prime time still exists (viewer numbers peak at about 9 o'clock in the evening) and *Tagesthemen* continues to be the flagship of German news programmes, more and more viewers switch to private stations with less news coverage for their evening entertainment, or make the jump to the Internet altogether.[17]

The Internet

In recent years, by far largest growth area in media has been the Internet. It has already become *the* new hypermedium of the developed world.

Germany is no exception. With the Internet and its digitalization of information, new cultural processes have begun to take hold.

In 2000, 50 per cent of German youths aged between 12–19 had a computer available, with 15 per cent even owning their own. The latest GfK Online-Monitor study conducted by telephone during the period November 2000 to January 2001 found that of the 8,021 persons questioned, 3,697 had Internet access. Within the six months prior to the study, the number of Internet users had shot up by 34 per cent to 24.2 million, a far cry from the 5.6 million online in 1998.

In terms of gender, in the spring of 1998 the ratio male–female users was 70 per cent to 30 per cent; however, by January 2001, the ratio had changed to 58 per cent to 42 per cent. For young people in particular being online has become the norm. In the age bracket of 14–19 year olds, 76 per cent were online. Usage intensity is also on the rise, 27 per cent of users were online on every single day of the week, with the average time period spent online clocking in at 69 minutes (www.tomorrow-ag.de). With always-on technology and flat-rate accounts, these online-times will increase in the future. And to show why big business is so interested in web technology, as if it really needs proof, in the period from January 2000 to January 2001, 13.5 million Germans purchased products on the Internet.

But what is this Internet exactly, why has it become so successful and why should we care? The Internet appeared on the media scene in 1989, with Tim Berners-Lee at CERN, Switzerland, expanding on an earlier US-computer network (ARPA-net) and giving his project the name *World Wide Web* *(www)*, now commonly known as Internet. With the arrival of Internet browsers, such as *MOSAIC, Internet Explorer, Netscape* and others, navigation and the search for terms on the Internet took off with amazing speed. In 2000, there were over 7 million websites in existence (wcp.oclc.org/stats).

It is helpful to remember once again that the contentiousness of mediascapes had been in existence from the onset of communication – going back to the Egyptian myth of the creation of writing which would undermine people's memorial abilities, the biblical reference (Genesis 11) to the multiplication of languages to undermine people's wills to create for themselves, the Church objecting to the availability of Bibles for their parishioners to read for themselves, etc. In more recent times, the various media have fought it out amongst themselves, with the chronologically older medium trying to keep out competition from the newer one, be that books vs cinema, newspapers vs radio, radio vs television or *Napster* (an online music file-swapping programme) vs. CDs. These fights over communication channels, over access to people's minds will probably continue, given what is at stake – influence, power and money. Media theoreticians like Jean Baudrillard have coined the term 'hegemony' for such an overarching paradigm which refuses to allow other interpretations or practices to enter the equation. Especially in our Internet times, highly mediated humans are always in danger of incarceration within such a hegemonic structure and many

Internet users have therefore begun to fight back against entities perceived of harbouring hegemonic tendencies, be they Microsoft, government or big business. This struggle is also going on at German language websites (e.g. http://www.quintessenz.org/gilc-coe-de-1200.html).

Unlike these earlier media scuffles between emerging and established media, the broadcasting and print media did not see the Internet as an immediate competitor; however, recently it has become such, due to increasing speed of Internet connections and the increase in computer memory.[18] These improvements now allow computers to act as multimedia machines through the Internet, incorporating music, pictures and texts. In addition, the Internet is accessible from anywhere where there is telephony, including mobile telephones. If broadcasting had already internationalized things to such an extent that traditional nation states had problems keeping tabs on the information processes instigated by their subjects within the more confined realm of satellite dissemination, now this information dissemination has gone global. And while there are still serious technical and social problems to be worked out – the retardation due to slow information assembly, gender issues, questions of access, content control and privacy[19] – the Internet has already revolutionized the world. Although it sounds perhaps too bold a statement to make, the Internet has at least the propensity to sublimate all other media and redefine the relationship between humans and their technologically mediated realities. Nevertheless, this statement begs some clarification.

Beginning with the arrival of broadcasting, global influence via moving pictures was exerted. This phenomenon has been called the end of the Gutenberg galaxy (Bolz 1993). Pictures began to challenge writing as the primary means of gathering, disseminating and storing information.[20] Already in 1931 Otto Neurath spoke of the 'opticalization' of all experience (quoted in Hartmann 2000, 151). Given the ever increasing amount of time we spend immersed/cocooned in media, philosophers and educators have highlighted the need for a new 'school of seeing' (Schnell 2000), incorporating such erstwhile diverse fields as optics, sociology, epistemology, psychology, etc. Relying heavily on Walter Benjamin's seminal essay *Das Kunstwerk im Zeitalter seiner technischen Reproduzierbarkeit* (1936), Schnell (2000, 19) for instance demands a *visuelle Geistesgegenwart* (visual presence of mind) which would incorporate interdisciplinary efforts leading to visual creation of new and diverse 'sense'. These interdisciplinary efforts are only apt, as the media themselves continue to grow together, with the Internet only the most recent point on this trajectory. It is therefore not in one universe that we find ourselves in any more, if we really ever did, but rather in *docuverses* of varying shape and form. And this process that has been going on for all of mediated-time already; it is only that it took the Internet for humans to realize it.

One of the first to point to the far-reaching consequences networked computers would have on humans was Vilém Flusser. In a well-known passage, he sketches the history of humanity and its relationship to media when he writes:

> Zuerst trat man von der Lebenswelt zurück, um sie sich einzubilden. Dann trat man von der Einbildung zurück, um sie zu beschreiben. Dann trat man von der linearen Schriftkritik zurück, um sie zu analysieren. Und schliesslich projiziert man aus der Analyse dank neuer Einbildungskraft synthetische Bilder.

> (At first, people stepped back from the actual life-world in order to imagine it. Then they stepped back from this imagination in order to describe it. Then they stepped back from the linear critique of writing in order to analyse it. And finally, new synthetic pictures were projected from within this analysis thanks to new powers of imagination)

> (Flusser 1995, 149, my translation)

With this elegant description, Flusser makes sense of the various steps media undertook throughout history. Starting with cave paintings which were supposed to depict and *fix*, in one way or another, realities outside these caves, humans then invented the alphabet in order to interpret these images further. In a next step, sometime at the end of the nineteenth century, philosophy came to terms with the fact that our knowledge of the world had become merely 'literal'. Humans recognized and described the world through language and rather than looking for a removed, unknowable Kantian 'Ding an sich' (thing in itself) in vain, it was the study of language which would help them further in dealing with reality. Already here, reality was no longer a given, as the scientific worldview of the Enlightenment had believed, but, rather, was actively produced by the observer.[21] Language itself, however, could not be trusted either. It was plastered with Freudian slips which had to be analysed in order to gain more knowledge about the world and our description of it; for Freud, one way of doing this, was through visual codes produced by dreams. In yet a further step, the dream factories of UfA-Studios, Hollywood, Pinewood Studios, Cinecitta and Bollywood increasingly supplied these images. It is these images that shape our world today, pixels received by our eyes in a rather jerking motion which are then processed to and as realities by the receptors and neural networks of our brains. Reality is no longer to be discovered, but to be constructed or processed (cf Hartmann 2000, 295ff.) The Internet would take these optical impulses yet another step further, not broadcasting them to a general and at worst disinterested public, but making them available to new virtual networked communities.[22]

Flusser's history of media begins with a simple, yet very important point, that is, the stepping back from life in order to simulate it. This was the beginning of *mediality*, of the process of mediation between humans and realities. As this process continued, more and more machines were interspersed between the senses and the phenomena they seemed to perceive.[23]

This is a process which, while superficially made in the name of the quest for knowledge, nevertheless subtracts so much from this knowledge that it becomes an unknowable; furthermore, it elicits the danger of always advantaging those who inhabit and rule the *code du jour*. However, it is a moot point to fight this process, since this battle was lost millennia ago. What can be done is to try and make these processes as transparent as possible and thereby allow as many people as possible to create their own best of all possible worlds. And this has become a global endeavour, reaching far beyond the borders of any nation–state.

German media, then, provide a rich and varied area of inquiry. As has become apparent, media cannot be judged according to an essentialist vein, trying to ascribe subjectivity to them.[24] Rather, these media cultures allow one to seek out and point to differences between cultural practices. This is the case when one adopts a *diachronic* point of departure, comparing different time periods within German media histories, but also when adopting a *synchronic* viewpoint, comparing media phenomena of a single time period. Distinct Germanness in media practices has never existed and if such claims are made, they should be viewed with utmost incredulity. However, distinct local and regional media practices, both on structural and content levels, can be detected and allow themselves to be set into fruitful relation with media practices of an Other or Others.

Notes

1. While this aspect of inclusion/exclusion of large parts of the populace in relation to media is a very important one, it cannot be done justice in this chapter. Suffice it to say that most democratic countries attempt to tackle issues of inclusion; for example, such an attempt would be the legally binding principle of *universal* access when it comes to German telephone service. In relation to the Internet, the Electronic Frontier Foundation has been in the forefront of providing information and discussions regarding privacy, access and censorship on the Internet.
2. Theatres, of course, cannot be completely dismissed in this regard. As an example, it must be noted that the theatre system played an important role in resisting the regime of the GDR, as in fact it did throughout the eastern bloc; especially discussions after performances were often used to voice dissent. In West Germany, the role of the theatre as a means of social change was also publicly acknowledged, with state subsidies making the West German theatre system the best funded in the world. With the demise of East Germany, it was especially Berlin that had to contend with theatre closings, the most notorious having been that of the Schiller Theater in 1993. Nevertheless, theatres in general are still flourishing in Germany, with 731 theatres in existence during the 2000 season, which had revenues of DM 698,031,000.00 and public subsidies guarantees of DM 4,019,028,000.00, with more than 20 million tickets sold (www.br-online.de/br-intern/medienforschung/md_allgemein/theaterstat.html).
3. In actuality, China had preceded the West by centuries in inventing the printing press. This, however, did not have any impact on the European mediascape of the Renaissance.

4. For extensive coverage of the history of media, see Faulstich (1997, 2000); for Germany in particular, see Humphreys (1994).
5. A less social and more postmodern assessment, focusing more on the subversity of technology than on its effects on society, can be found in Kittler (1992).
6. A thinker who makes the notion of 'mediascapes' part of the focus of his research, is Arjun Appadurai (1996). He differentiates between five different global 'scapes': 1 ethnoscapes, people moving across boundaries; 2 technoscapes, the global configuration of technologies; 3 financescapes; 4 mediascapes, which he defines as the distribution of the capabilities to produce and disseminate information and the large complex repertoire of images and narratives generated by these capabilities; and 5 ideoscapes, ideologies of states and counter-ideologies of movements, around which nation–states have organized their political cultures. While I am making use of his notion of mediascapes, it seems to me that, as communication networks begin to affect all of the above-named 'scapes,' the differentiation between these 'scapes' is becoming more and more problematic and would need further clarification.
7. In this section, I will focus on mass media proper once again, and not on other, more peripheral media, such as the remote control or the telephone. For the remote control, see Seiter *et al.* (1989), for the telephone, Ronell (1989) and Flusser, Kleine Philosophie der Telefonie in: Flusser (1995).
8. In a similar vein, the production of German pop music had gained much momentum in the early 1980s. If before only *Schlager* (literally, musical 'hits', a derogatory term for 'homegrown' music) made use of the German language, and subsequently were belittled by German youths strongly positioning themselves on the side of the Anglo-American rock scene, it now became *de rigueur* (and also financially interesting) for musicians and bands to sing in German. Case in point was the hugely successful band *Ideal*, who had a string of hits in the 1980s (see Chapter 10).
9. This is not only the case with films in cinemas, but also with screenings on cinema's erstwhile rival, television. The ratio of American films to German films screened on German TV stations is about 3:1, and much higher in the cinemas themselves. Furthermore, not only do American productions dominate the film/TV world; this is also true for English as a media language in general. As Grosser and Hubmayer (1998) have shown, the usage of English is also up in advertising, denoting a trend that has accelerated even more during the 1990s.
10. With regard to foreign films, however, German audiences prefer to have them dubbed into German, whereas other European nations, such as the Benelux countries and Scandinavia, prefer subtitles. One could speculate that this process of dubbing does de-exoticize these films more than subtitles; as one hears one's own language spoken by the characters in the film, these characters 'become' German, or French, etc.
11. There had been experiments undertaken with television already in the 1920s and 1930s in Germany, but the outbreak of the Second World War put an end to them.
12. For comprehensive accounts of this system, see Humphreys (1994); Bleicher (1993) and Briel (1999).
13. Germany is certainly not a homogeneous mediascape. As was the case with American, British and French radio and then TV stations broadcasting to the respective troops in Germany, the increasing number of foreign workers in Germany demanded their own media. Already in the early 1970s, the ARD and ZDF television stations began broadcasting foreign language segments, mostly on Saturday afternoons. Today, there exist a plethora of Turkish, Italian and Spanish newspapers and magazines in Germany, with Turkish television also having come into its own. With the Internet, this trend has accelerated once

again. Yet, despite all these intellectual and technical strides, racism and xenophobia still exist, even in liberal media, as Koch (1996) demonstrated.

14. An exhaustive account of the chances and problems of these attempts, most notably the satellite broadcasts of EUREKA and EUROPA, is given by Collins (1998).

15. A good example of the culture change happening in media today is found when looking at books published in German in 2000 with the term 'Big Brother' in their title. In December 2001, according to www.amazon.de, there were four titles, two dealing with the Orwellian Big Brother, the other two with the Reality TV show. Opinions, it seems, are divided right down the middle.

16. Cf. the texts by Andres-Müller *et al.* (2000), Angerer and Dorer (1994) and Fröhlich *et al.* (1995), all of which give very good introductions to German media and gender studies.

17. While the amount of time televisions are switched on is on the increase, media research since the 1980s has begun to differentiate between a set being switched on and a person actually watching a programme. While in the early days of television, in the 1940s and 1950s, audiences generally focused on the programmes, more recent users have begun to have sets running and only occasionally tune in to the programmes, skimming scenes of interest. Television has become more of a background medium, such as the radio has been for much longer already. One could speculate that the 'shock' associated with paying attention to a new medium has decreased as the number of programmes have increased and as the years of television programming have made it a common, well known occurrence. Another factor might have been the introduction of the remote control in the mid-1970s, which allowed for a much more relaxed, yet speedier interaction with the set.

18. Older media have learnt their lessons, however, and have attempted to create a symbiosis with the Internet. Most newspapers and journals have Internet pages; even TV guides such as *TVSpielfilm* provide a sizable area for Internet information. TV stations have also acted; the German version of the American NBC station has been broadcasting a successful programme called *Giga*, which is for hours on end engrossed in web culture. In addition, there are thousands of Internet TV and radio stations. In the commercial world, the recent merger between AOL and TimeWarner shows how important Internet technology has become.

19. It seems that by far the greatest problem at the moment is web page volatility, i.e. the speed with which web pages disappear and render even the best bookmarks list out of date within weeks or months. Web page volatility continues to increase, such that of websites in existence in 1998, by 2000 only 35 per cent remained in place (wcp.oclc.org/stats.htm).

20. However, not all media theoreticians view the Internet as such a universal threat. While acknowledging the influence of the Internet, Ralf Schnell for example believes that book culture is here to stay, albeit in a modified form: 'One of the stereotypes of a graphocentric culture criticism is that the cosmos of moving pictures threatens the world of literature' (Schnell 2000, 5, my translation). He, among many others, sees books, due to their specificity regarding portability, readability and ruggedness as continuing to lead the way culturally.

21. This production of reality is necessarily also involved when speaking about culture; for a good discussion on this subject, see Wentworth (1999).

22. In 1977, Deleuze and Guattari described this phenomenon with the metaphor of the *Rhizome*, a term borrowed from biology where it denotes the spreading network of roots of trees and bushes.

23. It is true that there are many inherent and manifold problems with these machines. For one, they become obsolete faster than one can buy them. Platform

decisions are generally made as business decisions and to empower consumers (remember the Betamax video recorder, or perhaps in the near future, Digital Audio Broadcasting (cf. Ins Leere gesendet. *Der Spiegel* 15, 2001, 94–6). Furthermore, the dependence on machines can create serious health risks for humans, the history of the industrial revolution and its victims bearing witness to this premise. Finaly, and a favourite topic of science fiction, there is a danger (or hope, depending on one's view of the human race) that these machines may take over from humans, obliterating them in the process of creating a race of post-human cyborgs.

24. Cf. Appadurai (1996, 12–13): '[C]ulture is not usefully regarded as a substance but is better regarded as a dimension of phenomena, a dimension that attends to situated and embodied difference. Stressing the dimensionality of culture rather than its substantiality permits our thinking of culture less as a property of individuals and groups and more as a heuristic device that we can use to talk about difference.'

References

ANDRES-MÜLLER, H., HEIPCKE, C. and WAGNER, L. (eds). 2000: *Interaktionen. Formen und Mittel der Verständigung*. Königstein: Helmer.

ANGERER, M. and DORER, J. (eds). 1994: *Gender und Medien*. Vienna: Braumüller.

APPADURAI, A. 1996: *Modernity at large: cultural dimensions of globalization*. Minneapolis: University of Minnesota Press, 1996.

BENJAMIN, W. 1974: Das Kunstwerk im Zeitalter seiner technischen Reproduzierbarkeit (1936). In *Gesammelte Schriften* I.2. Frankfurt/M: Suhrkamp.

BLEICHER, J. 1993: *Chronik zur Programmgeschichte des deutschen Fernsehens*. Berlin: Ed. Sigma.

BOLZ, N. 1993: *Am Ende der Gutenberg Galaxis*. Munich: Fink.

BRIEL, H. 1999: Media of mass communication: the press, radio and television. In VAN DER WILL, W. and KOLINSKY E. (eds) *The Cambridge companion to modern German culture*. Cambridge: Cambridge University Press, 322–37.

COLLINS, R. 1998: *From satellite to single market: new communication technology and European public service television*. London: Routledge.

DELEUZE, G. and GUATTARI, F. 1977: *Rhizom*. Berlin: Merve.

FAULSTICH, W. (ed.). 2000: *Grundwissen Medien*. Munich: Fink.

FAULSTICH, W. 1997: *Die Geschichte der Medien*, 2 vols. Göttingen: Vandenhoeck & Ruprecht.

FLUSSER, V. 1995: *Die Revolution der Bilder. Der Flusser-Reader zu Kommunikation, Medien und Design*. Mannheim: Bollmann.

FRÖHLICH, R. et al. 1995: *Frauen und Medien. Eine Synopse der deutschen Forschung*. Wiesbaden: Westdeutscher Verlag.

GROSSER, W. and HUBMAYER K. 1998: Wieso Sabine? – Time to think. Auswirkungen von 'global advertising' auf den deutschen Werbediskurs. In KETTERMANN, B. (ed.) *Mediendiskurse. Verbal Workshop Graz 1996*. Frankfurt: Lang, 29–43.

HABERMAS, J. 1990: *Strukturwandel der Öffentlichkeit* (1962). Frankfurt: Luchterhand.

HARTMANN, F. 2000: *Medienphilosophie*. Wien: WUV.

HEITER BIS WOLKIG UND NACKIG. 2001: Strip-News, Boulevard, Politikerblabla: Sind die Nachrichten noch seriös? Sechs Fragen an Ulrich Wickert und Wolf von Lojewski. *TVSpielfilm* (2001.8), 23–4.

HUMPHREYS, P. J. 1994: *Media and media policy in Germany. the press and broadcasting since 1945*. Oxford: Berg.
INS LEERE GESENDET. 2001: *Spiegel*.15, 94–6.
KITTLER, F. 1992: *Discourse networks 1800/1900*. Stanford: Stanford University Press.
KOCH, R. 1996: *Medien mögen's weiss: Rassismus im Nachrichtengeschäft*. Munich: DTV.
MILOS, L. *et al.* 2000: *Im Auge der Kamera*. Berlin: Vistas.
RONELL, A. 1989: *The telephone book: telephony, schizophrenia and electric speech*. Lincoln, NB: University of Nebraska Press.
SCHNELL, R. 2000: *Medienästhetik. Zur Geschichte und Theorie audiovisueller Wahrnehmungsformen*. Stuttgart: Metzler.
SCHÜTZ, W. J. 2000: *Deutsche Tagespresse 1999*. *Media Perspektiven*.1: 8–29.
SEITER, E. *et al.* (eds) 1989: *Remote control: television, audiences and cultural power*. London: Routledge.
STÅHELI, U. and SCHWERING G. 2000: *Big brother. Beobachtungen*. Bielefeld: Transcript.
WEBER, F. *Big Brother. Inszenierte Banalität zur Prime Time*. Münster: Hopf.
WENTWORTH, W. M. 1999: *Media and society. the production of culture in the mass media*. London: Allyn & Bacon.

Teletext

ARD page 444: recent audience numbers

Websites

www.ard.de/ard_intern/mediendaten Media data provided by ARD TV channel
www.br-online.de/br-intern/medienforschung/md_allgemein/jugend_medien.html)
www.eff.org Electronic Frontier Foundation
wcp.oclc.org/stats.htm Statistics of the Internet
http://www.quintessenz.org/gilc-coe-de-1200.html
www.statistik-bund.de Federal German Statistics Office
www.tv-quoten.de Audience numbers for television programmes/stations
www.tomorrow-ag.de Internet user research

Conclusion

BY ALISON PHIPPS

Intercultural returns

All journeys must come to an end. This journey into and through contemporary German Cultural Studies is no exception. The pilgrimages of the past, were, according to Turner (Turner *et al.* 1978) not linear but elliptical, with travellers returning home transformed. The road is not one road, but two. To engage in contemporary German cultural studies, as with any critical and disciplined learning enterprise, is to change, to grow, to broaden the mind. Spending any significant length of time in and with German culture is to make aspects of that culture one's own, to develop relationships through encounter, in other words, to develop intercultural sensibilities and to become translators of culture, language and experience. This is, I hope, also true for the experience of reading and reflecting on this book. Reading this book is, in itself, an intercultural experience. There is no single framework, no one picture of German culture that emerges, nor is there any stable model of Cultural Studies. This is not a comprehensive book with an agreed line of argument. This has not been the aim of the book. Each scholar who has contributed their insight, learning and critical perspective has done so in a different style, with a different view of cultural study and has therefore opened different but complementary worlds. Surveys, descriptions, facts and examples all serve to illuminate. Critical frameworks, deconstruction, examinations of issues of exclusion, power and interests then trouble our sense of grasping what is ultimately illusory. The overlapping, intersecting layers of perspectives that fill the pages of this book point to the fluidity and multiplicity of frameworks that are now available to us for the purpose of making sense of what Barnett (2000) sees as an age of supercomplexity. Supercomplexity may be understood as an emergent quality of postmodernity, requiring not just cultural understanding but new ways of being in the world, ways which Byram (1997) associates with what he terms the 'intercultural speaker':

> Relationships between different cultural and linguistic groups are at
> the heart of diplomacy and the need to choose appropriate ambas-

sadors of one group to another is as old as civilised societies. What is
new, however, is the condition of the world which allows and encourages all the people in a cultural and linguistic group, not just diplomats
and professional travellers, to take up contact with other groups.

These motifs of travel and dwelling, key theoretical frames in the development of intercultural studies, are not new to Cultural Studies or to
Anthropology. They may be found in the work of the modernist German
culture critics such as Georg Simmel and Walter Benjamin and also in the
work of James Clifford, Tim Ingold, Zygmunt Bauman, John Urry, Clifford
Geertz, etc. They allow a structuring of experience which breaks with con-
structivist notions and focuses on lived events and concrete practices.
Byram's preferred term for the 'travellers' reaches back to the old idea of the
'sojourner' – someone who 'makes a temporary stay', not just lightly
passing through but able to speak interculturally, engaging in the messy
business of a deeper critical engagement:

> The experience of the sojourner is one of comparisons, of what is the
> same or different but compatible, but also of conflicts and incompati-
> ble contrasts ... Where the tourist remains essentially unchanged the
> sojourner has the opportunity to learn and be educated acquiring the
> capacity to critique and improve their own and others' conditions.[1]

This is true for those learning to be 'intercultural speakers', but it is also true
for German Cultural Studies. As perspectives on questions of materials,
identities and power are raised German Cultural Studies transforms itself
into an intercultural practice – working with thoughts and theories from different disciplines, no longer the work of white British males – but of trained
scholars – male and female – with origins in cultures all around the world,
but with common concerns that unite them in their interest. It is worth
musing on the idea that contemporary German cultural studies comes home
transformed into an Intercultural German Studies after its journey and its
encounters. With its borders leaky and its stance one of openness to other
approaches – it becomes a discipline committed to growth and transformation, aware of its heritage and important intellectual history and not stag-
nating or with the seeming death wish that falling roles and the functional
marketing of reified languages and cultures could suggest.

German Cultural Studies is committed to a political project of engagement with questions of power, and of engagement with different German
experiences of race, gender, class, ethnicity. Intercultural German Studies
embraces all these perspectives but adds to them a question of difference
and distance. What difference does it make that these experiences, practices
and patterns of German life are examined here from an anglo-phone perspective? Just as Cultural Studies has asked questions of the particular experiences of race, gender, class and ethnicity so intercultural studies asks
questions of geographical detachment, language gap and the difference

made when the distances are closed through learning and critical engagement. It is currently rare to find work on German culture, written in English, which reflects upon such intercultural questions. As interest in the intercultural paradigm grows, it is important to find ways of exploring intercultural aspects to German cultural studies. The tensions between the different varieties of cultural and intercultural interpretation are not resolved by this volume but it is hoped that its potential for creative practice may be part of the journey, and tempt to new horizons.

Note

1. See Michael Byram (1997, 1–2).

References

BARNETT, R. 2000: *Realizing the university in an age of supercomplexity.* Buckingham: Open University Press.

BYRAM, M. 1997: *Teaching and assessing intercultural communicative competence.* Clevedon: Multilingual Matters.

TURNER, V. and TURNER, E. 1978: *Image and pilgrimage in christian culture; anthropological perspectives.* New York: Columbia University Press.

Glossary

die Aufklärung The Enlightenment. A philosophical movement of the eighteenth century that valued reason and the rights of the individual.

Aussengrenze Outer border – often used in association with the outer-border of the European Union, which separates member states from non-member states (*EU-Aussengrenze*). Germany's outer-borders are its state borders which separate Germany from neighbouring states.

Binnengrenzen Borders within Germany, e.g. the borders between the different German regions, or 'Länder', and the borders between towns.

bürgerliche Küche The closest one comes to a national German cuisine, essentially German home-cooking of the sort prepared by one's grandmother.

Codes Systems of signs governed by a set of social and cultural rules.

Codification The placement of empirical observations into categories and classification for purposes of subsequent knowledge construction.

Difference Difference is an antonym for identity, yet the two terms are inextricably related. Borders 'mark difference' between the peoples and cultures on either side of the border, they thus separate and differentiate between people with different identities (see also **identity**).

Fernweh Opposite of ***Heimweh***, a desire for travel and exotic experiences.

Functionalist A term used to describe a theory which views society as a complex system whose parts works together to promote stability.

Gassenhauer An aria from Viennese light opera that caught the imagination of the masses and became a popular 'hit'.

Gastarbeiter Foreigners (typically Greeks, Italians, Yugoslavs, and Turks) officially admitted to Germany during the 1950s and 1960s in order to make up for deficits in the labour pool.

Hanseatic League A trading confederation of city ports in the Baltic and North Sea which was founded in 1161 and included the German cities of Lübeck, Hamburg, Bremen and Rostock. It began to decline in the fifteenth century and disbanded in 1669. The only relic today is the letter H in the car registrations of these cities, e.g. HH for Hansestadt Hamburg.

Hegemony Disproportionate prestige and influence. Domination, usually to the exclusion of others.

Heimweh Literally: 'homesickness', 'nostalgia', often associated with absence from Germany ('*Heimat*') or things German.

Identity A person's social identity is his/her sense of allegiance or belonging to a certain social group. German national identity is the sense of belonging to Germany and of sharing common characteristics with others who define themselves as German. It suggests similarity to others in the social group, but is also expressed in terms of difference from other social groups (see also **difference**).

Kommunikationsgemeinschaft Speech or communication community.

Kultursprache The language of (high) culture.

Liminal Betwixt and between. Taken from the Latin term 'limen', which means 'threshold'. Liminal is a term used by van Gennep and Turner in their studies of rituals to mark the 'in between' phase in three-stage rites of passage. Border-crossing is the liminal phase of a journey between countries. A border is a 'liminal' space because it is the space between two territories or two cultures.

Magenfreundlich A distinctly German term designating easy digestibility.

Marshall Plan Named after its champion, General George Marshall, this European Recovery Program was planned to finance Europe's recovery from the ravages of the Second World War. The Plan ran from 1948 to 1951 and amounted to $12,500 million, the bulk of which went to Britain and France, but in keeping with the generous spirit of the plan, a large amount was also allocated to Germany and other former enemies as well as neutral countries.

Material culture The amalgam of the cultural meanings and physical manifestations of objects created by members of a society.

Metonomy A linguistic term for an object or attribute associated with something which is used to refer to that thing. For example, using Berlin to refer to the German government. Here the term refers to the way in which attributes and perceived characteristics of people and national groups come to be a shorthand for them.

Reductionism The act of reducing diverse and complex social and cultural phenomena to basic principles of explanation.

Reformation A religious movement in sixteenth-century Europe that challenged the lax morals and practices of the Catholic Church of the time (the only Christian religion). This ultimately resulted in a split, with the founding of the Protestant religion.

Reification The process through which an abstraction or a model e.g. the idea of society comes to be seen as if it were a real, material thing and assigning it causal powers.

SPD: Sozialdemokratische Partei Deutschlands (**German Social Democratic Party**) Centre-left party currently governing Germany in coalition with the Green Party.

Social actors A conceptual label given to human beings to signify that they creatively shape reality.

Social constructionism A generic label applied to theories which suggest that people actively create reality through social interaction.

Staatsangehörigkeit German citizenship – the right to vote and to carry a German passport, the right to call oneself 'German'.

Stunde Null Literally year zero. The period in the immediate aftermath of the German capitulation in 1945 when public life came to a standstill (e.g. newspapers ceased to be printed) and the Allies began their period of occupation. The term also encapsulates the new beginning this period of denazification was intended to be.

Swabians From the south-west of Germany, Swabians are noted in the popular imagination for tight-fistedness.

Volkslied 'Folk-song', cherished examples of German popular culture, much collected and anthologized during the Romantic period (1790–1840).

Weimar Republic First German Republic (1919–33), whose constitution was drawn up in the small town of Weimar.

Wessis The name given to West Germans living in the Federal Republic of Germany during the years of a divided Germany. East Germans living in the German Democratic Republic were similarly called Ossis.

Wirtschaftswunder Economic miracle. The period of unprecedented economic growth in the post-war period, roughly from the founding of the Federal Republic to the first oil crisis of the 1970s.

Index